The
Triumphant
Return of
Christ

The Triumphant Return of Christ

Dave Breese • Ray Brubaker
John Barela • David A. Lewis
J.R. Church • Joseph J. Carr
Phil Arms • John Wesley White
with William T. James

New Leaf Press

First printing, March 1994
Second printing, October 1994
Third printing, March 1995
Fourth printing, April 1998

Library of Congress Catalog Number: 93-87260
ISBN: 0-89221-250-0

Cover photo: Barry Blackman Studio, Inc., New York, NY 10010

Printed in the United States of America.

For
Jesus

Watch the raging tempest build,
See this sphere with violence filled.
Occupy while storm clouds roll,
Proclaim Jesus, who's in control.
Pray, study, work with great concern,
Look up! Look up, for Christ's return.
                              — Arbra Carman

Acknowledgments

All acknowledgment must, in truth, begin and end with the Eternal God, of whom there is but One. He is the Alpha and the Omega who gives not only the conceptual level of functioning necessary to create the written word, but who infuses the very breath and establishes the heartbeat that sustains life from second to second. More than that, He gave His precious Son so that life, and that abundant, will never cease for the person who accepts Jesus as the Father's matchless grace gift. To be spiritually and intellectually honest, can we do anything less than seek to give Him all glory and honor in everything we do under the sun?

Those who labored to produce this book, each in his or her own way seeking to honor their Lord, are many. Without their gifted contributions, kindnesses, and eager cooperation, the project would have been a cruel taskmaster rather than the uplifting experience it has been.

My heartfelt thanks to these, my Christian family and friends: Phil Arms, John Barela, Dave Breese, Ray Brubaker, Joseph Carr, David Allen Lewis, J.R. Church, and John Wesley White. Also, to each and every person in their respective ministry offices who helped in any way to bring *The Triumphant Return of Christ: Essays In Apocalypse, Series Two,* to publication — my sincere thanks.

My very special gratitude to David Allen Lewis for his wise counsel and to Mary Hitchcock of his office, whose interest and help have been most welcome.

To my good friend and Christian brother Tim Dudley, president of New Leaf Press, and to his talented and dedicated associates who have so expertly brought the book to publication, my warmest appreciation and thanks.

Thanks to Kathy Brown for her insights, enthusiasm, and amazing way with a computer keyboard. As always, her assistance has been invaluable.

To my mother, Kathleen James, whose prayerful support from my earliest remembrance has never ceased — through our Lord's graciousness and her wisdom — to hold my brother, Robin James, and me above the troubling waters of life — our love and our thanks.

To Margaret, whose bright presence at times when the dark moments start to close in never fails to drive them from my world, and to our sons, Terry, Jr. and Nathan who, like their mother, make my life rich beyond my ability to fully express — all my love.

Contents

Introduction

Setting the Stage

William T. James

Earth-convulsing events crash in wave upon wave against a generation torn by wide and, in some cases, catastrophic disparities in circumstance.

The breaking apart of the Soviet Union, which exposed the insanity of communism for the whole world to see, rather than making the planet safer from nuclear conflict, has served only to compound that threat. Much of the former USSR's massive thermonuclear stockpile is now spread among a number of the newly independent republics.

It is feared that Iran and other diabolic customers are buying former Soviet weaponry of the nuclear variety from leaders who are out to make quick, easy, personal fortunes or to prop up their failing regimes.

Meanwhile, woolly-minded people in high places continue blindly — or pre-meditatedly — and certainly foolishly, to tear apart the United States military, which, this side of the staying hand of God, has been the only truly effective deterrent force against nuclear aggression since the atomic age began.

Russia's people, becoming agonizingly impoverished because of their leaders' ineptness with free-enterprise methodologies, grow angrier and more demanding. As a result, hard-line brutes of the former system gleefully anticipate a return to power that promises to guarantee them control even greater than that exercised before the so-called "second revolution."

With the astonishing dismantling of Khrushchev's Berlin Wall came tears of joy to East and West Berliners alike as they celebrated with champagne atop the crumbled concrete and barbed wire that had separated them for three decades. Now, the jubilation has turned to apprehension, even fear.

Neo-Nazism is on the ascent in reunited Germany, spewing once again anti-Semitism and fanatic nationalism that preaches hatred against all but the elite, which they — as did their fallen god, Hitler — claim to be.

When God Is Left Out

From Somalia, Bosnia, Croatia, Bangladesh, and Ethiopia, to South and Central America and a growing number of other regions of the world, dictator and/or terrorist-engendered deprivation creates poverty, famine, and death on a massive scale.

Pestilence, embodied in the AIDS virus, which is wildly mutating into many new strains making finding a cure or immunization unlikely, poises to ravage the planet.

Gestating economic cataclysm threatens to burst forth upon a world whose fabric of civilized behavior is already irreparably torn.

The United States, because of insurmountable indebtedness, would itself be in abject poverty if not for the illusion of wealth created out of economic nothingness by sleight-of-hand computer wizardry. Still, America is expected somehow to be the fiscal lifeboat for the entire world. Man, it seems, does not need God but rather Uncle Sam.

The economy of things — when Almighty God is deliberately left out — drives men to madness and even nature itself to tumultuous upheaval. Jesus said, upon approaching Jerusalem in the so-called "Triumphal Entry" just before the Crucifixion, that if the people did not praise Him, the very stones would cry out in testimony to His Majesty. (See Luke 19:40.)

Recent natural catastrophes readily come to mind. Volcanoes erupting in Japan and the Philippines, actually causing, the scientists say, temporary global cooling; hurricanes wreaking unprecedented devastation, following in rapid succession within days of each other; earthquakes of major magnitudes happening literally around the world, and sometimes simultaneously; record level flooding of the Mississippi River throughout America's heartland — all make it seem as if nature were shouting to be heard.

Increasing Tensions

Jesus said that at the time of the end of the age, nation will rise against nation. The word used for "nation" in the Greek is here given as "ethnos," from which is derived "ethnic." The connotation is one of "race." Jesus was speaking of greatly increased racial conflict.

The tensions in the Middle East (despite the mutual recognition pact signed September 13, 1993, by Israel and the PLO) and the bloody strifes in former Eastern Bloc regions — such as Bosnia and other parts of the now dissevered Yugoslavia — signal the growing trend of ethnic violence.

Within our own nation, we witness with horror the streets of riot-torn Los Angeles, California, and the daily parade of car bombings, civilian bus machine-gun strafings, teen-age gang violence, drive-by shootings, drug-related murders, and deadly inner-city turmoil. All reflect the racial or "ethnic" factors that present major obstacles to law-abiding people's desire to live peaceably.

A Deadly Mixture

Current, unsettling world economic conditions — and, a number of experts say, dire prospects for improvement in the future — should not surprise Christians who have studied their Father's Word. Jesus said the love of money is the root of all evil. The Bible also states that the human heart is deceitful above all things and desperately wicked. Because God's Word does not lie, we can expect materialistic endeavor and wicked human minds to mix with no less volatility than does liquid oxygen with petroleum-based substances.

Despite glowing promises by politicians and would-be world-governing bodies, there smolders at the hearts of even the most optimistic the gnawing feeling of ominous, impending threat that lurks just beyond the ability to fully grasp.

The fear is not without foundation. God is no respecter of persons, and He will not be mocked. We can be sure that just as preceding generations suffered the consequences of rebellion against the Loving Creator of all things, this generation, rapidly becoming perhaps the most perverse of all generations, will reap the deserved, bitter harvest of God's righteous judgment.

Morality and justice now appear to be merely quaint notions

meant for no more than cursory consideration, looked at through mocking, New Age eyes by social engineers. All the while they formulate and adopt methods by which to begin herding all peoples into the one world order soon to come.

America faces, at best, a Third World future primarily because of her citizenry's unwillingness to live within their means and due to politicians' absolute refusal to deal realistically with the nation's fatally flawed debt management structure.

All the while, powerful forces scheme and labor to unravel history's most noble experiment with liberty in law: the concept of God-considered, self-government based upon God-reverencing self-discipline.

Positioning for Power

Europe has been shaken to its already-fractured foundations by the dissolution of the Soviet Empire, monetary crises, fiscal instability, and reunification of an economically powerful Germany bent on dominating matters concerning currency.

Meanwhile, the rapidly emerging, economic entity that is the heart of that reformulating world-power-to-be struggles to find the beat to which, God's Word says, all inhabitants of earth will someday be forced to march.

Increasingly, we watch men power their way to positions of national and international prominence, many whose quality of character and personal comportment should raise serious questions. And their compulsion to govern — or more truthfully, to "rule" — rather than their desire to "serve" is what drives their need to control and reshape in their own images, everything they touch.

"Peace," whether of the world-peace variety, or whether tranquillity that resides within the individual, is the elusive commodity these would-be "leaders" come promising the hurting, confused masses. They offer peace that Americans infer to mean security of life, liberty, and the pursuit of happiness. To most of the rest of the world, however, the cry for "peace and safety" is a desperate plea for an end to war and killing, and enough food to bring relief to the empty stomachs of their starving children.

One geopolitical think-tank group, of which former President Jimmy Carter is a member, reported that as of June 1993 there were 32 wars and 112 conflicts raging throughout the world.

Two Leaders

There are coming, God's prophetic Word tells us emphatically, two leaders who promise to deliver peace.

The first will be a leader the likes of which human history has never produced. His platform of tranquillity and security for everyone, with prosperity for all, will come as close to winning unanimous acclamation as is possible in a multi-cultural world whose diverse and innumerable factions demand placation. But, when he has consolidated his power and takes the reins of the New World Order — which is even now being created for him by the deluded politicians, sociologists, scientists, and religionists of the earth — he will *not* seek approval, unanimous or otherwise. He will demand unquestioning, universal obedience, obeisance, and, ultimately, worship.

This absolute dictator will, in the final analysis, produce not world peace, but the last and most destructive war of the age.

The Triumphant Return of Christ: Essays In Apocalypse, Series Two, however, proposes to turn the reader's attention not to the ferocious one who will bring total war upon the judgment-bound, end-time generation but to the One whom God's Word calls the "Prince of Peace." He is the only One who can bring "the peace that surpasses human understanding" (Phil. 4:7) to each and every person who accepts His offer of redemption from sin. He will put an end to all war and will fulfill every need.

Those same momentous events that are sweeping mankind toward its appointment with history's most frightful tyrant are also focusing a laser-like stream of Divine Light upon the returning King of kings. God's light, shining upon these disconcerting, sometimes terrifying occurrences, is revealing His glorious, unfolding prophetic truth on an almost minute by minute basis. Rather than being seen as a flood of doom and gloom, the future should be viewed as that marvelous, effulgent river of illumination that is lovingly moving all who truly believe and trust in Jesus Christ toward His second advent.

The first phase of His coming again will begin with His calling His own out of this world to be with Him forever. That stunning event will stupefy the peoples of earth and mystify their leaders, all of whom will be left to exist in a world ripe for the full-blown wrath of the apocalypse.

Deciding Your Destiny

The essayists within this volume — widely recognized as

among the most qualified analysts, writers, and reporters of world issues and events as they relate to biblical prophecy — propose not a world condemned to extinction. Instead, they view an earth destined for a future dynamic with light and life and achievement beyond anything imagined by philosophers and Utopian dreamers.

> But as it is written, Eye hath not seen, nor ear heard, neither have entered into the heart of man, the things which God hath prepared for them that love him (1 Cor. 2:9).

Those who love God love Jesus Christ because HE IS GOD! He came to this sin-cursed planet to redeem lost mankind by offering himself as a sacrifice on the cross at Calvary. He arose from death the third day so that all who believe in His name can be perpetually with Him in an eternity of humanly unfathomable heavenly glory.

Accept Jesus today and become "joint heirs with Christ" forever! That discomforting subject called the "Second Coming" will then thrill rather than mystify or frighten you.

Your perspective changed, you will watch with anticipation as even more staggering events bombard planet earth. These will signal the last act as God continues to draw closed the curtains of this greatest of all dramas. Like it or not, it is a drama in which you, in God's omniscient, omnipresent, omnipotent eyes, play a most meaningful part.

Section I

The Cast
of Characters

1

The Founding Fathers:

What Did They Really Believe?

William T. James

Paul Harvey, one of the most listened-to news commentators in the United States, gave a disturbingly poignant soliloquy in an April 1993 nationwide news broadcast. The volume of response "Paul Harvey News" received from listeners was unprecedented, according to the show's host. The piece began:

> If I were the Devil, if I were the prince of darkness, I'd want to engulf the whole world in darkness. And I'd have a third of its real estate and four-fifths of its population. But I wouldn't be happy until I had seized the ripest apple on the tree . . . Thee.
> So I'd set about however necessary to take over the United States . . . .

America — the leader of the free world, the champion of the oppressed.

America, the Republic, achieved even beyond that of which Plato could but dream.

America, upon whom God's grace has indeed been abundantly shed, has observably far exceeded any other nation in technological splendor and in guaranteeing a free people the right to life, liberty, and the pursuit of happiness.

Thinking on her glorious accomplishments and mighty deeds since her birth, her wondrous contributions to most every significant aspect of civilization dazzle the mind. Her brilliance burst upon this previously dim, flame-lit sphere, producing Thomas Edison's light bulb and radiating, for the benefit of the whole world, illumination far more profound — real liberty found only in Jesus Christ.

America. Her freedom-fire — whose glow, John Kennedy proclaimed, could "truly light the world" — has burned brightly for two centuries. What causes that flame to flicker so low today as to be in peril of dying?

Twisted thinking by deluded humanist social architects opposed to the uniquely American concept of liberty in law incessantly chips away at constitutional foundations. Angrily they protest that to be truly liberated we must reinterpret and rewrite the very precepts that made America a bastion of freedom. All this must be changed, they are demanding, in order that the individual's right to choose be made paramount above all other considerations.

In their demands resides the hedonistic lust for rights without responsibility, which is really freedom of action without accountability for actions. The end product of any such undisciplined societal anti-structure is not liberty, but libertinism; not law and order, but anarchy and chaos, leading ultimately, to a brutally policed state.

For evidence of where we stand at present in this regard, we need only see or hear a news report at any given hour.

Liberty, the sort that produces genuine achievement and freedom worth living, requires dedicated adherence to noble conduct based on acknowledgment that the giver of all light is the One who is supremely qualified to rule in the affairs of men. That belief, firmly held by the founding fathers, despite what the revisionists are telling this generation, is being sorely undermined today. When those in power first determined to begin circumventing America's belief in God, her radiant gleam began fading quickly into the twilight of history.

Columbus: Guided by the Holy Spirit

The earliest stirrings of America's coming into being had at their roots recognition that the Lord God of heaven was the one dependable light by which to navigate the course to and through the New World.

Christopher Columbus, writing in his journal, said, "It was the Lord who put into my mind (I could feel His hand upon me) to sail from here to the Indies . . . . There is no question that the inspiration came from the Holy Spirit, because He comforted me with rays of marvelous illumination from the Holy Scriptures . . . encouraging me continually to press forward and without ceasing for a moment they (Holy Scriptures) encourage me to make haste."

In the book entitled *American Prophets and Preachers*, the writer tells more about the man obviously chosen by God himself to establish a beachhead for a most special nation to come.

If we read the history of our country objectively, it will be seen that from the beginning the sovereign God was moving mightily to raise up a people that would accomplish His purposes in this world. The eternal God knew and planned the end from the beginning, but from the human standpoint, we go back in history for 500 years to see Him raise up a Christian Jew to discover the New World — his name was Christopher Columbus.

I find that most of our citizens do not know that Columbus was a Christian. It is not so taught in most history classes, and this gives us a defective view of the founding of our country. I believe that the American public should be taught the history of our country based upon the truth of divine providence that put the pieces of the jigsaw puzzle together, each piece in its place, to form the beautiful picture of what God has accomplished in this nation. First of all then, let us look at the conversion of Columbus.

To find that Christopher Columbus was a genuine and devout Christian, that he experienced a thorough conversion to the saving grace of God adds a new dimension to our understanding of our national history. In his document entitled "Books Of Prophesies," Columbus gives the following testimony: "I am a most unworthy sinner, but I have cried out to the Lord for grace and mercy, and they have covered me completely."

This was no mere "church-joining profession!" Here is a man who, under deep individual exercise, learned his own depravity, and knowing his desperate need, called upon the Lord. The answer is clear — "grace and mercy have covered me completely." Doctrinally stated, he experienced:

1) Holy Spirit conviction,
2) genuine repentance,
3) personal conversion,
4) blessed assurance,
5) the amazing grace of God.

It is characteristic of all who have been truly converted to be found seeking the fellowship of the Lord, and thus we find Columbus enjoying divine communion. "I have found the sweetest consolation since I made my whole purpose to enjoy His marvelous presence."

Columbus' dedication to Bible study is well documented through his writings (an evidence of the fact that) he was not ashamed of being a deep and devoted student of Scripture during the agnostic times in which he lived, and under the conditions of his service to those for whom he undertook the adventures which led to the land that would become America, he wrote: "It is possible that those who see this book will accuse me of being unlearned in literature, of being a layman and a sailor." I reply with the words of Matthew 11:25: "Lord . . . because thou hast hid these things from the wise and prudent and hast revealed them unto babes. . . ."[1]

All those who have accepted Jesus Christ as Saviour — acknowledging that His sacrifice on Calvary's cross and that alone provides redemption from their sins — and who diligently study His Holy Word with the desire to learn His truth and how it relates to His plan for their lives, will be guided by the Holy Spirit to exactly that result. God promises us in Proverbs 3:5-6: "Trust in the Lord with all thine heart, and lean not unto thine own understanding. In all thy ways acknowledge him, and he shall direct thy paths."

Columbus knew this through his own spirit, which was attuned to the Holy Spirit. The result of his reliance upon God's guidance in his life, thankfully, is that we now live in a nation which, although diminished from its glory days as the gospel lighthouse for the world, still guarantees a degree of religious, political, and socioeconomic freedom tolerated by no other governmental system on earth.

The Pilgrims: Led by God

God's plan for the nation through whom the good news of the gospel of Jesus Christ would be "preached throughout the whole world" continued to progress precisely on His unerring time-line. The overriding reason the pilgrims were forced to leave England was the intolerance and persecution they endured. These brave, devout people willingly faced multiple dangers posed by sea voyage rather than live under the heavy, oppressive hand of a governmental system that said worship our way or not at all.

How refreshing and invigorating must have been the feeling of solid earth beneath them and the marvelous smells of the vegetation as those scents replaced the odors of the ship's hull and the fish smells of the Atlantic.

When the Pilgrims landed at Plymouth Rock in 1620, it was after a forced course alteration that many historians — and the Pilgrims themselves — believed to be divinely providential. Unfavorable winds and numerous other circumstances combined to bring about a dangerous crisis. No doubt, they considered that landfall, with the fierce surf and rocky shoreline, could end in the loss of many lives and provisions. They went to their knees in much prayer and thought about where to attempt the landing.

William Bradford said years later of the safe landing at Plymouth Rock, "(They) blessed the God of heaven, Who had brought them over the fast and furious ocean . . . and a sea of troubles before." He continued, "Let them therefore, praise the Lord, because He is good and His mercies endure forever."

America's founding fathers expressed recognition that the Pilgrims' safe landing at Plymouth and all that ensued was not by chance.

John Adams said, "I always consider the settlement of America with reverence and wonder as the opening of a grand scene and design in providence for the illumination of the ignorant and the emancipation of the slavish part of mankind all over the world."

The Puritans: Religious Educators

There is no one "perfect" human doctrinal interpretation of God's inerrant, Holy Word in its entirety. All faiths and denominations within the body of Christ contain misunderstandings and mistaken presentations of God's errorless truth to one degree or another. Some, of course, hold dogmatically that their interpretations and presentations are "perfect" and thus, there can be no room for other views.

This, and more grievous problems confronted the Pilgrims, who fled England under persecution by the Church of England and the monarchy's one-view-will-be-the-same-for-all dictate. The Puritans faced much the same dilemma but chose for a time to try to reform those things they viewed as wrong within the state-church. Finally, many Puritans also fled to the new land and became an important founding element, free to worship and put into practice their convictions about the society in which they lived.

One of the greatest influences the Puritans had on the founding era of American history was that exerted in the realm of education. In the book *American Prophets and Preachers,* the writer tells of that profound influence:

> In Puritan New England, the Bible and education went hand in hand. An unusually high percentage of them were university graduates," says Robert Flood in his book entitled *America, God Shed His Grace On Thee.* "The Ivy League schools of Harvard, Yale, Princeton, and Dartmouth have turned out a great number of illustrious graduates from the start. And to many even today these prestigious schools represent the elite secular universities in the United States. But with the exception of Cornell and the University of Pennsylvania, every Ivy League school was established primarily to train ministers of the gospel and to evangelize the Eastern seaboard. From these schools there went out dedicated and educated gospelers with burning hearts to evangelize both the white man and the red man.[2]

"Blessed is the nation whose God is the Lord . . ." (Ps. 33:12).

George Washington, A Deist?

All Americans think of Washington as the first president of the United States. Many know that one of his unofficial titles is "the father of our country." Not so well known is the fact that this monumental patriot was a vestryman in the Episcopal church, who swore by signed oath that he accepted totally the church doctrine.

John Eidsmoe, reporting his research from the documents of Washington's time, says:

> Washington was a vestryman in the Episcopal Church. To become a vestryman in the Episcopal church, he had to sign a sworn oath that he accepted the doctrine of the Church. That doctrine, at the time, included a belief in the trinity, the divine nature of Jesus Christ, the atonement of Jesus Christ on the cross as a substitute, the sinful nature of man, the justification of man by grace through faith — all these being basic tenets of orthodox Christianity. Washington swore under oath that he accepted these beliefs. That tells us that if Washington was a deist, he had to be a perjurer as well.
>
> As commander-in-chief of the Colonial army, Washington wrote a letter to the 13 governors, in which he referred to Jesus Christ as the divine author of our blessed religion.
>
> Henry Cabot Lodge, writing about that statement, said that "either Washington believed in the Divinity of Christ, or when he wrote those words, he deliberately said something he did not believe."[3]

George Washington, in a letter to the 13 governors while commander in chief of the Colonial army, referred to Jesus Christ as the "Divine Authority of our blessed religion."

Today's revisionists imply that if Washington held religious beliefs at all, they were those of a deist.

How sad and how tragic that the record of this magnificent soldier and patriot is so shamelessly treated by the conspirators and their media lackeys. Their desire seems to be to bring America down so they can, in Lucifer-like fashion, lift themselves up as the governing elite.

In another correspondence of historical record, addressed to his commanders while general of the Colonial army, Washington expressed his indignation at the foul language rampant in the ranks. He ordered his commander to lecture the men on the matter, asking how the Colonial army could hope to solicit God's continued blessings when His holy name was being blasphemed so wantonly. He put teeth in his indignation by issuing an order making cursing punishable with 50 lashes for the first offense and one hundred for the second.

When we consider language we've read about or heard coming from some of our more recent American presidents, we would do well to ask the same question. How, when the leader of our country blasphemes the name of God — despite the fact the media reports the profanity by using a lower case "g" (yet another revision) — can we expect to continue to be blessed by Him?

When George Washington toured the new Republic in the summer of 1790, he was greeted with tremendous enthusiasm at the seacoast town of Newport, Rhode Island, by the town's Hebrew congregation, and especially by Moses Seixas, the warden of the religious body and a personal friend of Washington. The recently-elected president's response to the Hebrew congregation's display of affection reflects our first president's reverence for God, his love for the Jewish people, and his prayerful hope for America's future.

In his address on that occasion, President Washington said in part:

> The reflection on the days of difficulty and danger which are past is rendered the more sweet from a consciousness that they are succeeded by days of common prosperity and security. If we have wisdom to make the best use of the advantages with which we are now favored, we cannot fail, under the just administration of a good government, to become a great and happy people.
>
> The citizens of the United States of America have a right to applaud themselves for having given to mankind examples of an enlarged and liberal policy, a policy worthy of imitation . . . happily the government of the United States gives to bigotry no sanction, to persecution no assistance, requires only that they who live under its protection should demean themselves of good citizens, in giving it on all occasions their effectual support. . . . May the children of the stock of Abraham who dwell in the land, continue to merit and enjoy the goodwill of the other inhabitants, while everyone shall sit in safety under his own vine and fig tree, and there shall be none to make him afraid. May the father of all mercies scatter light and not darkness in our paths, and make us all in our several vocations useful here, and in His own due time and way everlastingly happy.[4]

The evil one, Lucifer, entertains thoughts about the House of Israel, the world, and this nation much different from those of the first president of the United States.

This same George Washington was the man who was chosen by his noble, courageous peers — our nation's founders — to be chairman of the Constitutional Convention, from which the very roots of the United States governing concepts sprang!

James Madison: Bible Scholar

Another patriot, James Madison, a small and frail man physically, was known as the "little giant" because of his great contributions to the early founding efforts. As a matter of fact, so tremendous was his influence in writing the Constitution that he is sometimes referred to as "the father of the Constitution."

His view of what government should be, sometimes termed "Madisonian Democracy," was based on his observations about the fallen nature of man. His was a concept grounded deeply in the Calvinist-Christian belief.

In fact, James Madison would have been a minister of the gospel, having been educated in theology at Princeton, where he stayed after graduation to pursue further study in Hebrew and Old Testament. It is conjectured that his soft speaking voice, among other factors, made him feel unsuited for what he considered the most high calling of the Christian pulpit.

Reverend John Witherspoon, president of Princeton during the time of Madison's matriculation at the school, was one of Madison's mentors and a signer of the Declaration of Independence. The doctrine of separation of powers (executive, legislative, judicial) was heavily influenced by Witherspoon who, according to his writings, taught that the power wielded by government should be separated into branches for the purpose of checking and balancing one another. This should be done, Witherspoon said, because man is basically a sinner who can't be trusted with too much power.

This was also Madison's concept of how to have republican government, and was based on what the Bible had to say about fallen human nature.

Hamilton, Jefferson, and Franklin

Alexander Hamilton, George Washington's closest aide during the Revolutionary War, later became the new president's secretary of the treasury. Hamilton was also the father of the Federalist Party and author of most of the Federalist Papers. Although born an illegitimate child, Hamilton was raised by a loving family.

Brought up on Calvinist teaching, Hamilton believed unswervingly in the depravity of human nature. In fact, he was so certain of the fallen nature of man that he stood up at the Constitutional Convention and made the declaration, "Take mankind in general, they are vicious and their passions may be operated upon. One great error is that we suppose mankind more honest than they are."

Eidsmoe, in reporting his research on Hamilton, said,

> Not long before he died Hamilton made plans for the establishment of an organization that would preserve the two things necessary for the salvation of this country: the Christian religion and the rule of law under the Constitution. He wanted to call this organization the Christian Constitutional Society. His plans were cut short in a duel with Aaron Burr.
>
> As a Christian he determined that he could not return Burr's fire . . . indeed, [Hamilton] did refuse to return fire.[5]

The documents show that Hamilton lingered on for some 31 hours. Eidsmoe said:

> Shortly before he died, he took communion and declared, "I have a tender reliance on the mercy of the Almighty through the merits of the Lord Jesus Christ"
>
> We're talking about the man who was the leader of the Federalist Party, author of most of the Federalist Papers, the secretary of the treasury under Washington, founder of the U.S. currency system, founder of the national mint, founder of the first national bank. In other words, he was one of the really great leaders of the nation, one of the men who shaped this nation, and he was clearly a committed Christian.

Thomas Jefferson is considered by many scholars of American history to be the least inclined of America's founding fathers to hold to religious convictions. In his own words, however, he demonstrated that he viewed God of primary importance in the matter of governing the young nation.

Another founding father thought to be among the least religious was Benjamin Franklin, who nonetheless asked that daily prayer be made a part of the Constitutional Convention.

Of One Mind

Let us ask, and hopefully answer, the questions: Where did the founding fathers get their ideas for establishing this nation? What were their personal views on government, law, and God?

The revisionists, who are bent on changing America to conform to their vision of a one-world utopian tomorrow, continue to indoctrinate us by propagandizing that the founding fathers, almost without exception, held to an existential, or deist view of God. These champions of change take great pride in proclaiming that Benjamin Franklin and Thomas Jefferson were in complete agreement with "legal positivism." What does that mean? That man rules totally in government, apart from any higher authority.

The record left by these two great men, the humanists boast, are proof that the Constitution of the United States has no basis in "divine law." In other words, they want us to believe it is not founded on absolutes, moral or otherwise. Rather, the Constitution, they say, is in a constant state of evolution or — to use the in-vogue word — "change."

John Eidsmoe, in his research, found that "the founding fathers were of one mind in their basic view of the world, but in what to do about it they were different . . . . They held to a Calvinist view of the total depravity of human nature. That's not just a Calvinist view, but a Judeo-Christian view. Jews and Christians have traditionally recognized that man is a sinner. The founding fathers recognized that."

Eidsmoe expanded on his findings. "Patrick Henry, and many others, believing in the (fallen) nature of man, didn't want to trust too much power in the hands of sinful rulers. So what to do about it caused differences of opinion, but their basic view of man was the same."

It is a well-documented fact that the majority of the signers of the Declaration of Independence had strong Christian beliefs. Two notable exceptions were Benjamin Franklin and Thomas Jefferson. It is thus very important that we look at these two monumental American historical figures more closely to see just how much they differed from the other great patriots in the matter of philosophy that framed this nation's principles of liberty in law.

What Is a Deist?

Both Jefferson and Franklin are most often portrayed as deists. Deism is the belief that a Creator-God made the heavens and the earth and established certain absolute laws regarding mathematics, physics, etc., by which the universe operates. This god also established absolute moral laws by which people are to govern their affairs. This higher being then withdrew from having any contact with his creation, choosing merely to observe what goes on throughout the universe. Having set all things in motion, he allows them now to operate under their own power.

The *Encyclopedia of Philosophy* characterizes deism as "a belief in an absentee god."

The deist's view of government, it is vital to note, was very compatible with the Christian view so far as acknowledging a higher authority than man is concerned. Thomas Jefferson wrote in the Declaration of Independence, ". . . the laws of Nature and Nature's God . . . ." In so doing, he was using language that both Christians and deists could agree upon. Both factions agreed on God-given law and God-given rights.

The deist belief, however, like the Christian's belief, is totally incompatible with today's secular humanism, which espouses that there is no law of God. Man is no more or less than an animal in the scheme of things and derives his authority to make, execute, and adjudicate laws purely on the basis that he has arrived on an evolutionary level that makes it possible for him to do so.

The deist's view is also incompatible with the New Age movement's view that man has the potential to be his own god, and, therefore, is free to make and constantly change — in accordance with expediency — the laws that govern.

According to Benjamin Franklin's autobiography he was a deist early in his life. He was under tremendous influence by the Calvinists during the War for Independence and underwent dramatic changes with regard to his perspectives on a higher power. This is seen when at the Constitutional Convention, at the age of 81, he asked that daily prayer be made a part of the proceedings. Franklin said, "I have lived a long time, and the longer I live the more convincing proof I see of this truth, that God governs in the affairs of men."

Jefferson: Child of the Enlightenment

Jefferson stands the farthest apart, ideologically and theologically, from all the other founding fathers. While his fellow founders were mightily influenced by Calvin and reformation thinking, Jefferson was a strong adherent to belief in the power of human reason. He was a child of "the enlightenment." His devotion to rationalism caused him to entirely reject the doctrine of the Trinity. He did believe in a God, but that there was a single God, not three in one.

Eidsmoe said of Jefferson in this regard:

> While he respected Jesus Christ, he didn't consider Him to be divine. So Jefferson could not be called a Christian, but he was far from being a deist. He strongly believed that there was a God who answered prayer and was involved in human affairs. In fact, he made this statement in giving his second inaugural address: "I shall need the favor of that being in whose hands we are, who led our forefathers as Israel of old to the native land and planted them in a country with all the necessities and comforts of life, who has covered our infancy with his providence, our riper years with his wisdom and power, and to whose goodness I ask you to join me in supplications that he will so enlighten the minds of your servants, guide their councils, prosper their measures, that whatsoever they do shall result in your good and shall secure to you the peace, friendship, and approbation of all nations."[6]

It is crystal clear from the true, documented historical record that the two founding fathers the revisionists claim as kindred spirits are not as they portray them. Instead, Franklin and Jefferson held to beliefs about government and law much more in tune with their Christian contemporaries than with the luciferian doctrines of the present day conspirators who seek to exclude God from law and government.

Jefferson, Franklin, nor any of the other courageous forefathers ever intended to separate people from the One who created them and loves them so much He sent His Son to die so they might be redeemed.

Their Collective View of God

What, then, was the founding fathers' overwhelming, collective view of God Almighty in relationship to the government they established at the risk of forfeiting their lives?

"We hold these truths to be self-evident, that all men are created equal, that they are endowed by their Creator with certain inalienable rights . . . ."

These powerful words were penned by Thomas Jefferson, with very minor changes by John Adams of the draft committee and by the body of the Second Continental Congress. This document, declaring independence from the oppressive British crown, must be accepted by thinking people as representing the founding fathers' core-being convictions. Their dedication was demonstrated by putting their necks in danger of the redcoat noose when they boldly scrawled their signatures on that piece of parchment, the Declaration of Independence.

They all agreed, especially the man who formed the document out of his fertile and brilliantly expansive mind, that there is a "Creator" who authored the rights of man. Nay-sayers who claim Jefferson was not talking about a Creator-God, but merely a creating-force of nature, cite the words preceding those given above. They claim Jefferson's words about man's right to be free from ". . . the political bands which have connected them with another, and to assume, among the powers of the earth, the separate and equal station to which the laws of nature and of nature's God entitled them . . . ."

Refuting this argument, historian John Eidsmoe says in *Faith of the Founding Fathers:* "When Jefferson wrote the words in the Declaration of Independence, 'the laws of nature and of nature's God,' he was using language that Christians and deists could agree upon."[7]

Jefferson, in his great intellect, could not find rationale or reason in the biblical concept of the Trinity, apparently revering Jesus Christ as a great and holy man, but not as deity. Thus, although only God himself knows for sure, Jefferson was most likely not a Christian. He also was not a deist as many secular humanist historians would have us believe, but was one who believed that a single "Creator-God" ruled and intervened in the affairs of man.

There were, however, a number of founding fathers who believed in the deist concept of God, that is, a God who indeed created, but then went off somewhere to watch, never to interfere with the thing he had begun. Theirs was basically the existentialist view of deity.

John Eidsmoe said about this: ". . . in their view of law and government, the deists were very compatible with Christians . . . . Since deists believed in God-given laws and God-given rights, they held a belief that was very compatible with Christianity."

So to answer the question posed earlier, "What was the founding fathers' collective view of God in relationship to government?", it should be concluded that they, indeed, held fast to the conviction that their "Creator" — that is God — set the standard by which all earthly governments must abide; their "Creator" authored the rights of man.

God was there in the midst of the councils and committees and battles when the United States was conceived and born. He was there at the very foundation of the world! He was there *before*, in eternity past, because He is the Great I Am.

"And Jesus said unto them, Verily, verily, I say unto you, Before Abraham was, I Am" (John 8:58). We can be sure that God Almighty will ultimately rule over governments of planet earth; He has spoken it and recorded it in His Holy Word.

Keep this thought in mind as we unveil the main characters in the drama unfolding before our very eyes in America and around the world.

Paul Harvey's words of that April, 1993, newscast sets the stage and summarizes the plot that is being carried out even today:

If I Were the Devil

If I were the prince of darkness, I'd want to engulf the whole world in darkness. And I'd have a third of its real estate and four-fifths of its population. But I wouldn't be happy until I had seized the ripest apple on the tree. . . . Thee.

So I'd set about however necessary to take over the United States. I'd subvert the churches first. I'd begin with a campaign of whispers. With the wisdom of a serpent, I would whisper to you as I whispered to Eve. "Do as you please."

To the young I would whisper that the Bible is a myth. I would convince them that man created God, instead of the other way around. I would confide that what's bad is good and that what's good is . . . square. And the old I would teach to pray after me, "Our father which art in Washington."

And then I'd get organized. I'd educate authors in how to make lurid literature exciting so that anything else would appear dull and uninteresting. I'd threaten TV with dirtier movies, and vice-a-versa. I'd peddle narcotics to whom I could. I'd sell alcohol to ladies and gentlemen of distinction, and tranquilize the rest with pills.

If I were the Devil, I'd soon have families at war with

themselves, churches at war with themselves, and nations at war with themselves until each in its turn was consumed. And with promises of higher ratings, I'd have mesmerizing media fanning the flames.

If I were the Devil, I would encourage schools to refine young intellects, but neglect to discipline emotions. Just let those run wild, until before you knew it, you'd have to have drug-sniffing dogs and metal detectors at every schoolhouse door.

Within a decade I'd have prisons overflowing, I'd have judges promoting pornography. Soon I could evict God from the courthouse, then from the schoolhouse, then from the Houses of Congress.

And in His own churches, I would substitute psychology for religion. And deify science. I would lure priests and pastors into misusing boys and girls and church money.

If I were the Devil, I'd make the symbol of Easter an egg, and the symbol of Christmas a bottle.

If I were the Devil, I'd take from those who have, and give to those who want it, until I had killed the incentive of the ambitious. And what'll you bet? I could get whole states to promote gambling as the way to get rich.

I would caution against extremes . . . in hard work, patriotism, in moral conduct. I would convince the young that marriage is old-fashioned. That swinging is more fun. That what you see on TV is the way to be. And thus I could undress you in public, and I could lure you into bed with diseases for which there is no cure.

In other words, if I were the Devil, I'd just keep right on doing what he's doing.

2

The Revisionists:

Changing Truth into Lies

William T. James

"Holocaust? What's that?" vast numbers of Europe's young ask when the "final solution" to the "Jewish problem" is mentioned.

"The Holocaust? It's time to forget the past and to get on with the business of unification," much of adult Europe demands when Nazi atrocities come up in conversation.

"A Holocaust? Never happened! Just Jewish lies!" scream growing numbers within proliferating, anti-Semitic groups bent on cleansing the world on behalf of the new order they intend to create.

Anti-Semitism swirls above reunited Germany in clouds as dark as was the smoke that poured from the stacks above the ovens at the extermination camps. The spirit of revisionism grips not just a Europe anxious to get on with the business of unification but the whole world. Phrases like "the Jewish problem" and "the final solution" dramatically expose the revisionism-eraser that the self-appointed, new-world builders are using in the process of rewriting the historical record to fit their own purposes.

Theirs would be a world as elitist and oppressive as that

envisioned by the fuhrer. To build it they intend to do all within their power to make us forget portions of the past. The ethnic cleansing and hate-filled rhetoric we see and hear in daily accounts from various news sources make George Santayana's words ring true for our time: "Those who cannot remember the past are condemned to repeat it." Such is the primary reason for keeping before us a constant reminder of past horrors committed by previous would-be world-builders against Jews and other "undesirables." Future tyrants who would construct such a society at our expense must be made to realize that we, the people, are aware of why tyranny cannot be forgotten.

Lest We Forget

Although it appears that memories of past atrocities are in the process of being erased, particularly in Europe, fortunately there are still those who refuse to let the excruciating memories pass into history's sea of forgetfulness. Alice Lok Cahana is one such resister. Her story is told in part through the following excerpts from an article by Suzanne Fields in the May 14, 1993, issues of *Insight* magazine. It is the chronicle of one who lived the history of Auschwitz about which some Europeans either know nothing, want to forget about, or claim simply never happened.

> Alice is an artist whose paintings are on exhibit at the Klueznick museum of B'nai B'rith, coinciding with the April dedication of the Holocaust Memorial Museum in Washington. Like the phoenix, she recreates life from fire, art from the ashes of an experience.
>
> Alice was fifteen when the Nazis ordered her mother, her sister Edith, seventeen, and two younger brothers into the marketplace of Sarvar, a small town in Hungary 120 miles from Budapest, where her father had a large weaving factory.
>
> Her paintings are filled with empty windows testifying to the silent observers, friends, and neighbors who watched the Jews march toward the cattle cars and said nothing.
>
> No one came out from the houses, no one demonstrated or screamed or protested, she says. It was just another day.
>
> Her paintings are filled with images of jagged railroad tracks leading to a blackened sky, oppressed with

tattooed numbers rather than shimmering with stars, fusing experience and metaphor, the journey of life and the rigidity of death . . . . (In one of the paintings) a tiny shape intersects one of the railroad tracks. It's a child's shoe. Art imitates brutal reality. Across town in the Holocaust museum an exhibition of four thousand shoes bear witness to those who walked to the gas chambers. James Ingo Freed, architect of the museum, visited Auschwitz and as he tramped through the mud of the concentration camp, the soles of his shoes picked up bits of human bone . . . .

Not everyone believes the Holocaust should be remembered in Washington with a museum on the Mall, feeling it runs the risk of trivializing memory and history. But such criticism overlooks the power and purpose of memory and history — to recall, to teach, to recreate an experience for each generation with hope that the future can be protected from repeating the past and the profane."

And the past is not truly past when those inhumanities still tug powerfully at the emotions affected by loved ones lost in the Holocaust. Charles Fenyvest writes of those emotional ties in the May 3, 1993, issue of *U.S. News & World Report.* The article is entitled "Seeing 6 Million Through the Eyes of One."

Washington, DC — When confronted with film from the Holocaust, I look for relatives. It's futile, but that's what I did in the new Holocaust museum: I searched for features I dimly recalled from childhood and old snapshots. Yet how could I be sure a frightened face of a woman whose hair was shorn was my Aunt Elza, a red-haired beauty, or that a listless girl in a shawl might be a freckle-faced, lively cousin Katy?

My tears welled up at an early exhibit, a wagon owned by a Gypsy family the Nazis liquidated. The wagon had the (same type) trusses and shafts as those my ancestors drove across Hungary's Great Plain, taking their potatoes and fleeces to market . . . . My heart sinks when I see a procession (of the same type of wagons) on the news, carrying Bosnian Muslims, victims of another murderous gang.

I spent half an hour in the dark stock car that took people to Auschwitz. To reach that village in Germany-occupied Poland, it took my Grandma Rosa, 72, nearly two days from Derbecen, Hungary. The same cars still haul cattle and coal. In 1955, I had a summer job shoveling coal. An uncle said to look for words scratched on the wood panels by someone en route to a death camp. I probed countless gashes but found no message.

I was drained by the time I reached a bright spot: the boat Christian Danes used to ferry Jews to safety in Sweden . . . ."

Redefining History

Despite museums to Holocaust victims and the still-standing chambers of horror themselves, the denials and revisions have allowed the resurgence of racial hatreds, rivaling those that brought national socialism and Hitler to power in pre-World War II Germany. *Insight* magazine, January 4, 1993, in an article by Henrik Bering-Jensen entitled "A Flood of Strangers in Estranged Land," regarding growing refugee problems in Europe, says:

In once well-ordered Western Europe, there is a siege mentality developing, a feeling that the elaborate welfare systems created since the war, even the national characters, are under threat.

Asked for his mission, a German guard on the border between Germany and Poland put it bluntly: "We are guarding our wealth."

The backlash is frightening especially in Germany. Firebombings of refugee centers and pitched street battles between police and neo-Nazi youths in leather gear have become nightly TV fare since the August anti-foreigner riots in the eastern port of Rostock spread to thirty other cities. There have been some 2,000 attacks on foreigners. So far, 17 people have been killed, including a Turkish grandmother and two young girls whose house was firebombed.

Concentration camp memorials and Jewish cemeteries are being defaced and sprayed with anti-Semitic slogans. Skinheads wearing hobnailed boots roam the streets carrying imperial flags and shouting "Fremde raus" —

"Foreigners out." There have been countless counter-assaults on neo-Nazis by left wing groups.

The images of left and right brawling in the streets have made some commentators warn about conditions similar to those in the Weimar Republic, the post-World War I democracy that ended in street chaos and the rise of Adolph Hitler . . . .

. . . Just south of Berlin 1,500 police reinforced with military border guards prevented a neo-Nazi march that was timed to November 15, Germany's National Mourning Day for the dead of two world wars. The marchers plan to visit and pay homage to a Waffen SS graveyard where some 20,000 Nazi troops killed at the end of the war by advancing Soviet troops lie buried . . . .

. . . The Federal Censorship Office is also taking action against hate music from groups like Stoer Kraft (Destructive Power) and Boehse Onkelz (Evil Uncles), which in savage, anthem like tunes call for the annihilation of foreigners living in Germany. "Kill their children, rape their women," one line goes. The sale and distribution of the songs have been banned and concerts have been canceled.

Still, despite official crackdowns on emerging neo-Nazi groups, the governments of Europe, particularly that of Germany, seem less interested in putting a stop to racial violence and anti-Semitism than in employing revisionist public relations. Their purpose? To divert attention from themselves regarding responsibility for past sins of ethnic genocide and Holocaust. Instead, these government officials point the finger of accusation at the entire international community in an attempt to dilute their own national guilt.

Certainly, the revisionists are doing their part to encourage the contemporary street-thugs of Germany and Europe to continue their campaigns of violence, which include the vile lie that there was never a Holocaust.

The *Encyclopedia Britannica*, acknowledged by world academia as the foremost repository of knowledge and truth is, it seems, on the leading edge of the wave of revisionism. An article in the May 1993, issue of *The Front Page* contains the following article entitled "Britannica Redefines History."

Jerusalem, Israel — Harmful enough when they pervade the media, historical myths can do inestimable damage in college texts, scholarly publications and encyclopedias.

The authoritative *Encyclopedia Britannica* depicts Israel as a racist, aggressive society that has driven hundreds of thousands of Arabs from their homes and subjected them to a brutal occupation and periodical senseless violence.

When the encyclopedia reported violent acts by Israelis before it became a state, nothing is said about the seven thousand Israeli soldiers and civilians killed in the war, the attacks on nearly all Jewish populated areas, or the numerous massacres perpetrated by the Arab fighters (the slaughter of 41 doctors and nurses in a convoy to Hadassah and Jerusalem, or the bombing that killed 64 passersby on Jerusalem's Ben-Yehuda Street, etc.).

Arab professors from the American University in Beirut contributed to BOTH the "Israel" and "Palestine" articles: but no Israeli scholar contributed to the section on modern "Palestine."

Despite all the talk of peace, the real intention of Israel's enemies is summarized in a story just beneath the one above, "Arafat Still Wanting to Burn all Jews in Israel:"

Monte Carlo Radio — PLO leader Yasir Arafat, broadcasting in Arabia over Monte Carlo Radio, urged Palestinians to escalate violence against Israel "and burn the earth under the feet of the occupiers."

Our nightly network newscasts and major newspapers choose to spare us such statements by Israel's avowed enemies, instead portraying Mr. Arafat as a man who is trying desperately to bring his terrorist friends to the negotiating table in the Mid-East peace-seeking process.

The revisionists are hard at work in America, too.

Revisionism Comes to America

Headlines flash explosively from the pages of our daily newspapers. Most of us seem to be blind to them, yet their combined impact is troubling and unshakable — as if God, himself, is declaring to this generation of Americans:

By deeds or in spirit, you say in your self-sufficiency that there is no proof that My Word is Truth — that my prescription for living peaceably is the only cure for the deadly malignity that infects you.

Your leaders take oaths on Bibles; your governing bodies open and close with prayer; your money says "In God We Trust." You have a form of godliness, but deny the power thereof. You say and do what is right in your own eyes; thereby, you deny that My Word is truth.

Smugly, you twist, pervert, reinvent, revise, rewrite to your own non-disciplining specifications, scripturally-based foundational principles of godly government.

You say in your hearts that My Word is not truth, that, therefore, there is a great need for change, a need to turn from those "intolerant, narrow-minded" foundational precepts if you are to compete and to prevail in the "new world" of change that is upon you. In so doing, you have said, "There is no God."

Behold the inerrancy, the infallibility of My Word. Behold but a foretaste of things to come upon this "New World Order" you deludedly think you can build. Behold the oncoming whirlwind that issues from the winds of change to which you have sown — to which you continue to sow your seeds of lawlessness. Behold the truth found in My proclamation: "The fool hath said in his heart, 'There is no God. Corrupt are they, and have done abominable iniquity; there is none that doeth good' " (Ps. 53:1).

You most probably ask — with good reason — "What's so shocking about the great majority of headlines and the stories they encapsulate?" For the most part they are run-of-the-mill nowadays. Murders, even those involving young children, as well as misdeeds of politicians, simply do not induce shock sufficient to cause one to almost hear the Almighty's voice speaking through the matters reported.

Likewise, learning about the massive, forced reductions of a giant company like Sears, Roebuck and Company — legendary in the annals of American commerce though Sears might be — with the resultant loss of 50,000 or more jobs, is hardly the stuff of which apocalypse is made.

Good appears to these terminal ones to be evil. Evil appears to be good. Wrong becomes right, and right becomes wrong. The Eden serpent's venom first desensitizes then disorients by affecting moral equilibrium — the compass by which man was and is designed to navigate life's course. Perversion becomes accepted as the norm, followed in due course by the latter, withering, emaciating stages of degeneration to incorrigibility and even genetic contamination.

By the question, "What's there to be unduly concerned about in these headlines?" we have proof that we suffer from at least the first stage of the serpent's bite. We are desensitized to the socio-toxic process that is going on around us.

We fail — even as Christians — to comprehend the serpent's part in the monumental story that we call human history. Much more egregious than that failure is the refusal to acknowledge the one, true God and His authority over and involvement with all things He created, which is EVERYTHING — including you and me.

Pulling Rank

"Enlightened, broad-minded, caring, liberated" thinkers, who promise to lead humanity out of this century of "insensitivity and intolerance," disagree totally with this assessment. This brings us again to the headlines, such as that seen on the front page of one of my daily newspapers. It read, "Clinton Pulls Rank on Chiefs; Accept Gays."

God says homosexuality is sin. The practice of homosexuality, the Creator of all things says, is an abomination in His holy eyes. Enlightened man — personified for the moment in the person of the leader of the Western world — was saying that we will accept homosexuality, like it or not. Through this attempted edict, homosexuality gets the official stamp of approval by government. Homosexuality is now to be accepted as normal rather than condemned as deviant.

Enlightened, modern men have renamed homosexuality "gayness." What God calls absolute evil, man now calls beautiful, wonderful, fulfilling — and wants it to be accepted by one and all as no different than the love between a husband and wife.

The "gay" issue seems to me to epitomize and galvanize that great deceiver, Satan's, attempt to totally turn the created universe upside down. Calling such perversity a "gay lifestyle" is, to me, at the sin-diseased heart of the serpent's plan to conduce man to forget the truth of history. Because, to forget truth, you see, is to forget God.

Light at the End of History

This essay's purpose is to likewise lay bedrock, of a sort, upon which to erect a framework that might help us better understand the luciferically-spawned cataclysm termed "the fall of man." Moreover, this essay, like this book in its totality, is intended to point to the glorious light at the end of the long, sin-darkened tunnel we call human history.

That light, toward which all mankind is streaming, is none other than God, who personally came to dwell among fallen man in fleshly form. The God-man, Jesus Christ, died, then arose on the third day, to redeem lost humanity. Be warned! If you do not know Jesus Christ, Satan fully intends to forever do away with you in the devilish process.

Reinventing Godliness

To begin understanding why there is a dark conspiracy to re-write all of human history, it is essential to locate and unveil the foundation that supports the agenda of evil. This foundation, although vast in its implications and ramifications, can be summed up in a single word.

Somewhere in eternity past, Lucifer made the first recorded effort to reinvent all that is godliness: ". . . I will ascend into heaven, I will exalt my throne above the stars of God . . . I will be like the most high . . ." (Isa. 14:13-14).

It was Lucifer's *pride* that brought disobedience and caused his fall from God's heavenly domain. The Scripture tells of the things God hates most. Pride tops the list.

> These six things doth the Lord hate: yea seven are an abomination unto him: A proud look, a lying tongue, and hands that shed innocent blood, An heart that deviseth wicked imaginations, feet that be swift in running to mischief, A false witness that speaketh lies, and he that soweth discord among brethren (Prov. 6:16-19).

Not only does pride top the list of things God hates most, pride is apparently the nucleus around which revolves all other sins within that list. Using this passage as a vantage from which to gain perspective, luciferic influence can certainly be observed within human activity of our time.

Pride, then, is obviously that foundation upon which sin is built. In fact, it is the base upon which Satan's agenda for replacing God's agenda is constructed. Although the foundation that supports the agenda for evil can be summed in that single word, pride, the agenda itself is an intricate, networking, deadly disease. In terms of the history of the human race, pride took root in the Garden of Eden and continues to grow and spread almost unimpeded.

Mankind, through the persons of Adam and Eve, succumbed to the serpent's lie in Eden. As always, it was the same lie with which Lucifer deluded himself in eternity past, believing that he could elevate himself to a position not only equal to, but higher than God. The first man and woman became the willing victims of that iniquitous mystery called pride. It was a willful act of rebellion that put forward the "proud look" that fosters all sin which follows. It is, and was, the thing God most abhors and cannot, in His perfect, holy righteousness, abide.

The human race, today more than ever, marches about with that proud look, carrying on affairs as usual, doing things its own way — to the exclusion of God. Man is fulfilling Satan's evil agenda for "putting his throne above the stars of God." Lost man, who thinks he, too, can "be as god" is willingly ignorant of God's truth — truth which the Creator of all things will impart only to the humble, accepting minds (spirits) of those who believe Him.

In order for man to be a god unto himself — which the serpent, Satan, told Adam and Eve they could become — man must deny God's truth — in reality, the only truth there is. The great deceiver's agenda to usurp God's authority and His throne is predicated upon the abominable lie that God has neither any interest in nor the right to any involvement with the conduct of human affairs.

In order for fallen man to lift himself to the heights of godhood, then, he must deny God's account of what took place before man's creation. In fact, man must deny God's account of creation itself! He must likewise deem as unacceptable God's Word. Why? Because the Bible declares that all disruptive incursion into man's existence on earth streams directly from Eden, through the present time, and will do so with increased intensity as all things gush toward a future of wrath and judgment.

Man, to justify his "proud look," to maintain his illusion and delusion of God-likeness, must deny truth. He must deny God. In so doing, it is necessary that he deny the historical record itself.

Reinventing Truth

God's warning is explicit about these matters. The facts are clear for all but those who willfully refuse to accept them. The Scriptures tell that the closer this earthly age moves toward its climax, the more abundant will be the scoffers toward all that is truth. And, who can refute? Scoffers there are aplenty!

Biblical information about the past, present, and future abounds. God's Word likewise sounds many alarms concerning those who deny the truth He has seen fit, through divinely inspired human writers, to record for all to know and heed. One of the most encompassing texts in this regard is found in 2 Peter:

> This second epistle, beloved, I now write unto you, in both of which I stir up your pure minds by way of remembrance, That ye may be mindful of the words which were spoken before by the holy prophets, and of the commandments of us, the apostles, and of the Lord and Saviour; Knowing this first, that there shall come in the last days scoffers, walking after their own lusts, And saying, Where is the promise of his coming? For since the fathers fell asleep, all things continue as they were from the beginning of the creation. For this they willfully are ignorant of, that by the word of God the heavens were of old, and the earth standing out of the water and in the water, By which the world that then was, being overflowed with water, perished. But the heavens and the earth which are now, by the same word are kept in store, reserved unto fire against the day of judgment and perdition of ungodly men (2 Pet. 3:1-7).

God is, in very specific terms, warning us through the apostle Peter's words that there will, near the close of this present age, be an intensive effort to reinvent truth.

It will begin by questioning God's involvement with man and be steeped in a philosophy — a theology, really — that promotes a willful denial of and antagonism to truth relative to the creation and history of planet earth.

To determine how close we might be to the biblically prophesied end of the age, it is incumbent to ask: Have we, within the recent past, seen evidence that such a quasi-religious revision of God's creation account has begun?

The first thing we must understand — as the apostle Peter, under divine inspiration, says — is that this reinvention, this revision, this rewriting of everything God has said is true will be more pronounced the closer the world moves to the end of this age. We have to understand first that in the "last days" there will come "scoffers."

"Scoffing" is disbelief carried to the point that mockery — a kind of black, vicious humor — is heaped upon the person or idea being scoffed at. It is, in spirit if not in actuality, the type of mocking the Roman soldiers did the day they scourged and beat Jesus to a point His facial features were barely recognizable as human.

The scoffers, Peter is saying, will still be mocking the One who, historically, is singularly the most focal human being ever to walk the earth's surface. The object of their scathing derision will still — and more so than ever — be that same Jesus at the time the age winds up for its devastating climax.

"Where is the promise of His coming?" This prophecy warns what they will be asking through tight, clenched-teeth smiles of hatred while mankind moves through the final stage of sin-corroded history. Their question is directed to all who would disagree with their pride-swollen assertion that ". . . since the fathers fell asleep, all things remain the same as they were from the beginning."

Today, such assertion is firmly ensconced within what is believed by most to be the unimpeachable "scientific" postulate called "uniformitarianism."

In acceptance of that belief resides disbelief that scoffingly asserts: "Christ is not coming again, because, if there is a God, He doesn't care, is not involved, and did not come in a first advent." It implies, "The Bible is fantasy; there has been no intervention in the affairs of men by some supreme being." In reality, it is rebellion that declares, "We don't need a God. We ARE gods!"

Change or Changed?

There is a strange irony in this dawning new age, which perhaps again points to the degree to which God's Creation has been convoluted. "Change" is the watchword for this generation of Americans and for globalist thinkers. Change — to what? We are not told exactly, but, we are assured, it is to be change that will produce unprecedented peace, security, and prosperity.

The ironic illogic lurches from the strange to the absurd. They readily accept that man is but an animal who has made a quantum evolutionary leap from a form of anthropoid and has "changed" through evolution to his present superior status among his fellow animals. They call this "scientific fact" but have utterly failed to produce a shred of credible proof through their feverish efforts.

Going back farther, they willingly, even eagerly, agree with the prevailing pronouncements that everything that exists began with what amounts to a happen-stance of chance: the "big bang." Out of the resultant chaos of that explosion, they propose, came perfect, universal order. This, despite the reality that no random or violent occurrence within the experience of empirical examination has ever been shown to produce orderliness of any kind.

At the same time, they vehemently reject as ludicrous and untenable, any thinking that proposes these "changes" that have influenced the course of human history could have come about by means of the cataclysmic flood recorded in Genesis. The idea that there is a Creator-designer who gave the biblical accounts of earth's and man's tumultuous history receives their greatest scorn.

The Key to the Past?

Having injected modern man with the lie of evolution, Eden's serpent has continued to spread its deadly effects. Now in its late stages, it has succeeded in producing the conscience-searing forgetfulness essential to carrying out the plotters' conspiracy. Throughout every strata of society within America and around the world, we see the disorienting, destabilizing, convoluting work of the God-denying, reality-shunning venom that is evolutionary seduction.

Kenneth A. Ham, founder and director of the Christian Science Foundation Ministry, writes in his book, *The Lie Evolution:*

> Evolutionists, atheistic and theistic, use the phrase "the present is the key to the past." In other words, they say that the way to understand the past is to observe what happens in the present . . . . Evolutionists tell us that since we observe mutations (that is, accidental changes in our genes) occurring today, these must have occurred ever since the dawn of time. Thus, mutations must be one of the mechanisms involved in the postulated evolutionary progression. The Bible, on the other hand, tells us that there was a time when there was no sin, and thus there was neither animal nor human death, nor disease, nor mistakes. Mutations are mistakes that occur in our genes, and they are virtually all harmful . . . .

Ham asserts correctly that to believe in evolution, one must believe that these mutations have been occurring since the very beginning of life on earth. Therefore, a Christian who believes in evolution must, to be consistent in adhering to that postulation, believe that mutations have been taking place since the beginning, because man, according to evolutionists, is still evolving. The writer then destroys the argument that Christianity and evolutionary belief are compatible:

> The Book of Genesis claims to be the record from God telling us of the events of creation and of other events in this world's early history which have great bearing upon our present circumstances. Thus, the present is not the key to the past, rather, revelation is the key to the past.

> The revelation in Genesis tells us about such events as creation, Noah's Flood, the Tower of Babel. These are events that have made the earth's geology, geography, biology, etc., what they are today. Therefore, we must also realize that what happened in the past is the key to the present. The entrance of sin into the world explains why we have death and why we have mistakes occurring in our genes. The global devastation caused by Noah's flood helps to explain the fossil record. The events at the Tower of Babel helps us to come to an understanding of the origin of the different nations and cultures around the world.

> Today evolutionists deny that the biblical record can be taken seriously. They put their faith in the belief that "all things continue as they have done from the beginning."

Ham then summarizes the root cause of the reason people can so easily be made to forget God:

> Romans 1:18 tells us that men "suppress the truth in unrighteousness." It is not a matter of lack of evidence to convince people that the Bible is true; the problem is that they do not want to believe the Bible. The reason for this is obvious. If people believed in the God of the Bible, they would have to acknowledge His authority and obey the rules He has laid down.[1]

In our time, one is considered foolhardy if he unreservedly trusts contemporary sources when gathering facts, whether they be facts about the past, the present, or facts involving prognosis for the future.

It is especially risky to rely on any one source.

There is, however, one — and only one — completely reliable source that can tell us everything that is good and necessary for us to know. Best of all, that source, God's Holy Word, gives us the absolute truth from even before creation — until forever! God's history book gives not just a scant overview of the record. No, it goes as deeply into what it means to be a part of the record called human history as one is capable of delving.

Facts or Speculation?

My memory is vivid of my first few days in biology class as a college freshman. The professor, a balding, middle-age man with a pleasant face and calm, southern-accented voice outlined the curriculum we would be following that semester. His easy manner and unthreatening style caused even the most homesick among us to feel that here was a man who, not unlike our own dads, understood somewhat our misery at being away for the first extended time from friends and family.

The instructor, in giving the course's introduction, said something to the effect that the class was expected to pay particular attention to the facts he would be giving in profusion about the subject of evolution. This was "all-important." We were to learn these facts, as they would be a foundation for all other learning we would undertake. Everything was in a constant process of evolution.

A student raised his hand and said something along the lines of, "I thought evolution was just a theory. What if you don't believe evolution is true?"

The memory is even more vivid of the Dr. Jekyll to Mr. Hyde metamorphosis that took place. I remember the shade of crimson on the now-contorted face, the one big vein that bulged bluely from the center of his forehead, the almost literal froth that exuded from between the taut-white lips. In a voice that was now transformed into a low, guttural growl, the professor said something like, "Anyone who chooses to remain ignorant, and in the dark ages, by accepting some silly notion you were taught in some Sunday school, might just as well drop my class now. There's no place for you here. I have neither the time nor the desire to deal with fairy tales."

That's pretty close to the exact admonishment he gave to our freshman biology class that fall day in 1961. His caustic assessment of the biblical creation account is more than ever reflected with even greater vitriol throughout academia today. The Christian belief that evolution is totally untrue was then and is much more so now regarded as "ignorant" and "intolerant" — or worse — by the majority of high school and college educational systems. At the same time, the teachers and professors will not abide any view that does not include strong elements of the evolutional model when dealing with origins. This is not considered by their systems to be "intolerance" but simply as necessary to the unimpeded, empirical pursuit of knowledge.

Larry McClean and Roger Oakland, who wrote *The Bible, Key to the Early Earth*, and have conducted seminars under the title, "The Bible, Key to Understanding History and the Future," give enlightened perspectives in the matter of creationism versus evolution. During interviews on Southwest Radio Church broadcasts, McClean and Oakland told how evolution is presented today and reported some of the devastating impact it has made on society.

Oakland, in giving an overall scope of evolution, said:

> It is presented as absolute fact, and anyone who challenges these ideas in most cases is classified as nothing more than a religious kook.
>
> We've gone to numerous museums as we've traveled in filming *The Evolution Conspiracy,* and in every case we see things like murals and charts and models which are attempting to promote the view of evolution. But in no place have we ever seen any actual fossil evidence which shows that one kind of life is changing and evolving into another. And, many of the ideas that are put forward are entirely speculative.
>
> In fact, at the Smithsonian Institute, when we were there, the curator of the portion of the museum which deals with the non-life to life museum was interviewed, and off camera he said, "You know, a lot of the things I've been telling you are purely speculative. They can't be supported by any kind of evidence."
>
> But each day literally thousands of children are bused to this particular location. No one ever tells them that what's being presented is speculative. It's presented as absolute fact.

Oakland says it is the same on similar trips to places such as the Grand Canyon, the Petrified Forest, and others. Evolution is always presented as absolute fact. Further, he said that as a teacher at a university during his career, he can testify that one of the major objectives of public schools and universities was and is to present the evolutionary view.

He said, "In fact, in an interview we made with a prominent professor at Berkeley, who was an evolutionist, he stated that 'It's the job of a teacher or a professor to change the views of the students.'

"Most students, when they come to an institution, are creationists. In fact, 80 percent or more of the general public are creationists . . . . It's the objective of the university or the secular school system to reprogram them with evolutionary thinking."

Larry McClean added to the overview. "Well, certainly we see that there is all sorts of evidence in the world that supports the biblical view of the origin and history of life. In fact, in all the years of research we've put into this topic, never yet have we found one fact that contradicts the Bible. Oh, there's a lot of theories; there's a lot of speculation that's being presented, but never have we found one fact."

He concluded that evolutionists should not be allowed to prohibit the facts from coming to light just because those facts agree with the biblical account. He said, quite rightly, "Some people talk about whether creation should be taught in the schools, or whether Genesis should be taught in the schools. Really, the bottom line in this whole issue is that people should be able to hear the truth."

Back to the Dark Ages?

Oakland went on to say in that interview that much of the hostility to the Bible's account of creation can be traced to several sources, a chief one being the "Humanist Manifesto."

That luciferian document on the "religion" of humanism — for it is certainly that — was published in 1933. The first tenet of this anti-God declaration is that humanists regard the universe as self-existent and not created. They begin with the proclamation that there is no God.

The second tenet is that man is a part of nature and has emerged as the result of an ongoing process. Humanists say that man exists as a result of millions of years of random, chance events, and not because man was created. What can faith in such a delusional, order-existing-out-of-chaos religion be called, but luciferian?

Bringing the battle of creationism versus evolution into more recent times, the modern version of the "Humanist Manifesto" was updated in 1973. McClean said, "It's interesting that one of the signers of that updated version of the 'Humanist Manifesto' . . . was Isaac

Asimov, the popular science fiction writer [who has since died]. Isaac Asimov . . . March of 1982, was sending out letters promoting people to send in funds to support the ACLU in their attempt to attack the creation movement." McClean makes the point that there has obviously been an organized strategy to repress creationism.

Many things point to the fact that the evolutionist agenda is hostile to anything tending toward creation science. Oakland pointed out, for example, an article entitled "The Response to Creationism Evolves,"[2] which tells of a number of the evolutionists' attempts to attack the creation movement.

The article reports of meetings held by the National Academy of Sciences and The National Association of Biology Teachers, whose membership was upset about the trend toward the creationism view. A number of ways in which to attack the movement were explored in the article.

Later, according to Mr. Oakland, a booklet entitled *Science and Creationism,* put out by the National Academy of Sciences is "entirely directed at attacking the creation movement." In the publication, they say that creationism is putting science back into the Dark Ages because creationism puts forward a religious view.

A Matter of Faith

Although the delusion is widespread, thankfully there are a growing number of scientists who have examined all pertinent aspects of the evolution/creationism matter and have come to the conclusion that it takes greater faith to accept the former than to accept the latter. Again, the theory of evolution — though touted for decades as tantamount to fact beyond question — has never had produced by its proponents anything to prove its validity or even to convincingly substantiate its most basic postulates.

Creationism is also scientifically unproven (or even provable) by presentable evidence. If studied in-depth, however, with an open mind relative to the fossil record and all other data, it still fits much more rationally within its postulations than does evolution within its theories. At the same time, creationists admit fully to the truth that, in the final analysis, the quest to understand origins boils down to a matter of "faith."

Evolutionists hold with iron-willed declaration to the dogma that claims theirs is pure science based upon a model, which no one must be allowed to contest, else civilization will collapse. It is a spiritual, not an intellectual issue. One must either accept or reject

God, the Creator. It involves faith one way or the other.

The rejection of God was the motive behind the founding fathers of the evolutional concept. Erasmus Darwin, Charles Darwin's grandfather, was one of the key individuals who promoted the evolutionary view. Charles Darwin himself is widely presumed to have been educated as a scientist. In fact, the pseudo-science of evolution was popularized by a theologian. Charles Darwin did not have a degree in science but rather a degree in theology from Cambridge.

Darwin's grandfather was a member of an occultic group in England called The Lunar Society, which met when the moon was full. The elder Darwin built his theory of the biological evolution of life upon Lyell's uniformitarianism timetable. Looking for an alternative explanation to the creation concept, he was determined to explain away what that Creator-designer has said was the origin of the universe and of planet earth.

Darwin's *Origin of the Species* and other writings so enthused Karl Marx that Marx, one of the chief architects of communism, wanted to dedicate his own satanic work, *Das Kapital*, to Darwin. Marx was elated that the evolutionist had found a way to eliminate God.

Discredit the Bible through undermining its Genesis account of the creation; promote the theory of evolution, and Christianity will die. Atheism and evolution will take Christianity's place — will replace Jesus Christ the Redeemer. That revision will allow man to usurp the throne of God.

Look at your own newspaper's headlines, and listen to and watch the televised reports for yourself. Witness THE PLAN in action. Revisit your own view of origins, of evolution, of creation. Does the conspiracy as put forward here begin to seem less the fearmongering of an intolerant, narrow-minded world view, and more like your day to day life experience?

Perhaps putting America under the microscope for a much closer look at the conspirators' plan can further expose what the plot's godless cornerstone religion called evolution has wrought. *(Also, see Chapter 8, "America: Liberty At Twilight," for an analysis of why America is on the brink of disaster.)*

The Cry for Change

Revisionism is the luciferic strategy that flows from Eden and through the present world system. Evolution is revisionism, pure and simple. This seductive philosophy that began long ago has now succeeded to a large degree in turning the God-given process of rational thought upside-down.

We will look at some of the specific ways this convolution manifests itself today. But first, we should dwell upon the insidious ways the floodgate was opened, allowing that contamination-filled Eden stream to swamp our once God-reverencing nation.

Humanism's world view predominates. Evolution is humanism's religious cornerstone — the pillar of dogma upon which all social, economic, political, and technological secular doctrines lean for support. Standing on the platform of uniformitarianism — which says there is no God who has ever intervened in the affairs of man and that all things continue as they have since the beginning — humanism declares that all life is in the ongoing evolutionary process.

Human government must, therefore, be based upon the evolutionary model. In order for man to evolve and progress socially, economically, politically, and technologically, adjustments must be made. There must be revision because there is no one, absolute, unchanging reference point to which human government can anchor itself. Change is essential in order to accommodate the prevailing winds of human conduct and all it entails.

The cry for change is upon us now.

Changes involving the so-called separation of church and state issue have been the most disastrous revisions to contribute to America's decline. That issue is the gathering place of and the headquarters for the secular-humanist agenda in this nation. Satan's all-consuming drive to remove God from the thought processes of America's men, women, and children assaults in all directions from this central stronghold.

Like communism, secular humanism lives by the philosophy that the desired ends justifies the means utilized. However, while communist philosophy makes neither excuses nor apologies for that dehumanizing way of dealing with its victims, humanists deny that such a belief is a basic tenet of their way of doing business.

Humanism's view of separation of church and state — now America's law, thanks to the Supreme Court which today legislates more than it adjudicates — is built upon lies. But, remember, the end justifies the means. And what is their ultimate goal? A utopian world built in their own image. And how will they achieve it? By stacking one revisionist lie upon another.

So, everything in the human experience — in the American

experiment with liberty in law — must change as times and attitudes change in conformance with the Darwinian evolutionary model. All is relative, and the "survival of the fittest/natural selection" principles are applicable here. Based on this, atheists and secular humanists can proclaim with a clear conscience that separation of church and state means in fact that God is unmentionable in public schools — even public places in some instances. They have declared Him a non-entity. Why? Because He would represent changelessness that is incompatible with the on-going process of change that is the heart of evolution.

Planned Character Assassination

Through their revisionist lies in today's textbooks, the reformers say that their interpretation of separation of church and state is not a modern concept at all, but one that goes back to the very beginning of the nation — even to the Constitution. Having cast out divine law and even God himself from public school curricula and having substituted a system of continually "changing" laws, these deluders are systematically reinventing American history.

"Multi-Culturalism" and the Politically Correct

Christopher Caldwell, in a book review for *Insight* magazine, scrutinized a work about George Washington (March 8, 1993) and wrote:

> The petty iconoclasts of today's history departments have had an easy time belittling, ironically unaware that a central element of his greatness lay in forging a nation that did not trample on the petty — even those in history departments.

That is a biting commentary on the revisionism that has tilted the world of sensibility to the point of standing moral common-sense on its head. Perhaps trite, but true, is the adage "they cut off their noses to spite their faces." Like harmful bacteria attacking a once healthy organism, they eat away at this most blessed nation's foundations, despite the fact it is those very foundations that give them the freedoms to do so.

"Multi-culturalism" is phraseology of very recent vintage, familiar to all of us. "Colored people" became "blacks," then "Negroes," then "blacks" again — and now, "African-Americans." The jury is apparently still out on those of Spanish/Indian descent. They are now "Hispanic" or "Mexican-Americans," seemingly awaiting the terminology that will be acceptable in the new world to come. The revisionists seem to have trouble with this one.

Indians are "Native Americans," and revisionist brows now narrow with displeasure over such team mascot names as "Redskins," "Braves," "Warriors," and even simply "Indians." There are "Anglo-Americans," "Asian-Americans," "Chicanos," "Euro-Asian Americans," "Latinos," and a vast and growing array of other types of racially classified American citizens.

The reinventor-elitists are quick to point out that they are striving toward making this nation the most unbiased on earth. They are going to see to it that all peoples are treated as equal.

Those who conspire to do such things — and those who are drawn into the conspiracy through willing ignorance — are, however, not cleansing this nation of ethnic bigotry; instead, they are helping further racially divide it.

No matter the supposed pureness of motive that drives these revisionists to attempt to change the face of America, the luciferian conspirators' motive is the same as that which drove the Tower of Babel builders to try to circumvent the purposes of God himself. The ultimate outcome will be to do away with *all* forms of nationalism.

To that purpose, the United States must be weakened and divided in order to become enslaved to the new Roman empire into which Europe is now unifying. The scheme of the ethnic word game is not to make people proud of their racial heritage and to break down bias, bigotry, and hatreds; the conspirators' plot is to tear down national boundaries and make people accept one-world government.

Promoting the General Welfare?

Every suspect of life today is now affected by Satan's Edenic venom. In no other sector of contemporary America is the revisionist spirit more at work than in the area of disease control and the way health authorities deal with Acquired Immune Deficiency Syndrome (AIDS). Here, the public welfare is directly threatened with what is almost certainly history's most dangerous disease. AIDS always ends in death, and there is no hope for cure in the foreseeable future.

Every other communicable disease threatening Americans has been fought with quarantine and by imposing stringent restrictions upon those infected. Those with TB, for example, can't work in jobs involving the handling of foods, medicine, etc. HIV, on the other hand, is actually protected because the revisionists have managed to create a separate category for AIDS, making it a political disease. In most cases, job applicants must not even be questioned about "sexual preference" — now including those applying for military service.

The perverse behavior most responsible for perpetuating and spreading the AIDS plague is fiercely protected by a number of those politicians and judges, who, under oath, are sworn to uphold the United States Constitution. This document states in its preamble that one of the peoples' principal desires and intentions for the U.S. Constitution is that it "promote the general welfare."

The revisionism that has made AIDS a politically untouchable disease is as reprehensible as the behavior that is exponentially spreading it. The insanity of such thinking can be seen in the attempted indoctrination that would have us accept the "gay lifestyle" as a normal, "alternate lifestyle." The ministers of this propaganda insist that the way to deal with the epidemic is to throw more and more tax dollars into research to find a cure and a vaccine for immunization. At the same time, they promote legislation that prevents taking the only truly effective action possible against the disease.

Those who practice the unnatural, unhealthy, perverted, Sodomite activity — which God calls an abomination — must not be "discriminated" against. Their "freedom of choice" in the matter of sexuality must be honored. And while they claim the right to "choose," they at the same time hold to the luciferic lie that they really have no choice because they were "born gay."

To be so concerned as to make the disease-proliferating "lifestyle" a crime — as some states have done — against society is nothing less than barbarous in the enlightened view of the revisionists. To even contemplate such a thing is to be "homophobic." The agents of change want the sodomy laws relegated to the dust bins of the history they are in the process of rewriting.

As stated before, the perverse acts involved in homosex must now be understood and accepted as but slightly different pleasures enjoyed within the "alternate lifestyle." Those who engage in the activity are not practicing sinful abomination but are simply doing what comes naturally to "gay" people.

Our society has been changed in a major way within the last decade and a half by this most wicked revisionism. Without repentance, the sin will be judged by God. Every civilization that has incorrigibly degenerated to the depths of making homosexuality a welcomed cultural activity has been given up by the Creator who made Adam and Eve, not Adam and Ernest or Eve and Abigail.

Nonetheless, God, while hating the sin of homosexuality, loves the sinner who is trapped in that tragic, destructive activity. Jesus Christ, God's own Son, died and arose from the grave so that the homosexual, the same as all other sinners, can be brought into a truly loving, eternal relationship with God the Father. Likewise, Christians are to love the person who is caught up in homosexuality, even while upholding the truth that, in God's eyes, the lifestyle is not "gay" but abominable. If the Holy Spirit-enlightened child of God will not love these people with pure motive and a compassion that desires to bring them into God's eternal kingdom through Jesus Christ, who will? Certainly not the revisionist liars who tell them they were "born gay."

No Rights

Pre-born babies, whose bringing into the world is inconvenient, are not murdered; inconsequential tissue is merely aborted through simple medical procedure. It is not a matter of fetuscide, but, like with the homosexual lifestyle, it is a matter of "freedom of choice."

A great many of the revisionist mindset say unborn human children have no rights. At the same time they fanatically monitor every other form of life in order to defend against its abuse; thus to assure "Mother Nature" is not hurt by man's excesses and intrusions.

We need not concern ourselves with pre-born children, however, because the revisionists have determined they are not people, nor even a life-form for that matter. Therefore, they have no rights. That is why the revisionists promote the use of "fetal tissue" to treat Alzheimer's disease or to simply make facial cream for aging women. All done in the name of "science" and "medical breakthroughs," of course. What they don't tell the American public is that this "tissue" is taken from living, late-term, pre-born babies in painful procedures that defy the most horrific tortures mankind can think to inflict upon another living creature. At the same time they crucify in the media companies who would use animals for testing, whether it be for medical or cosmetic research.

The evolutionist changemakers demand we save the whales, the fur bearing animals, and the dolphins from the tuna nets. While abortionists are heralded as heroes, they seek to punish anyone who dares shoot an eagle and publicly ridicule governments who kill wolves from helicopters. They seek — at government expense, of course — to preserve inch-long fish and aquatic life such as the snail darter; to be kind to the trees and swamp moss of the world; and to protect even the ozone that at one time lovingly, protectively encircled "Mother Earth." We must get in tune with and stay attuned to our fragile ecosystem.

The revisionists write and stridently enforce laws concerning protection of the environment while they interpret the Constitution to mean that it's okay to kill babies still in the womb.

Surely, it is the responsibility of every person of every generation to exercise good sense in caring for the beautiful world in which the Creator placed us. This especially should be the attitude of the Christian, who knows that Creator as his or her Heavenly Father. It is also our responsibility to protect human life, even its tiniest form, and respect the pre-born as a baby created in the image of God.

Who's Rejecting Whom?

They forbid that a Bible be read, or even brought into public schools, while in the former Soviet Union, children are encouraged to read the Scriptures in their classrooms.

While mention of Christ, the Bible, and prayer is in many instances denied our children, we are expected to console ourselves with the fact that growing numbers of our school systems are instructing how to have "safe-sex," issuing condoms and teaching even our preteen daughters the mechanics of putting them on a potential sex partner. These formerly unheard of educational practices are done for the sake of preventing unwanted pregnancy and AIDS, of course.

America herself is now the evil empire in the mindset of the revisionists. Third world nations — and especially those with left-leaning dictatorships — are the true hero nations of our time.

No doubt, the reader can conjure from his or her own mind dozens of revisionisms thrust at us by those who want us to forget truth. Even the devoted humanists among us are on occasion caught wondering what is happening to this nation and to the world.

A wire service report in the February 18, 1993, edition of the *Arkansas Democrat-Gazette* sums up where the raging luciferian tide of revisionism has brought us — and the end toward which it is sweeping us in its wake: "Cornelio Sommaruga, head of the International Red Cross, in Geneva criticized governments for doing too little to prevent atrocities, saying, 'When hatred and cruelty are not the result of war but the aim of it, we can no longer talk of war. We are witnessing a rejection of all humanity.' "

Although they wonder, the humanist revisionists just don't get it. We are not witnessing a rejection of all humanity because the Creator still loves us and tenderly calls us to repentance and redemption. Rather, we are witnessing the end-product of humanity's rejection of God.

3

The Humanists:

Gods of the Mind

Dave Breese

There is a way that seemeth right unto a man, but the end thereof are the ways of death (Prov. 16:25).

This verse simply summarizes mankind's self-determined pathway and ultimate destination in their headlong drive to become self-appointed "little gods." The philosophy behind man's never-ending quest to build a world of his own choosing, in his own image, and for his own pleasure is encysted within the term "humanism."

The notion that man can construct such a world apart from the help or influence of the Deity is self-delusion encouraged by the greatest of all deceivers, Satan himself. Man, in his pride and ignorance decides he must make his own world because, as he has determined, God is either non-existent or existential — that is, He does not intervene in the affairs of man. That very same Lucifer who first told human beings they could, and even had the right to, become "as God" is actively pursuing his agenda to bring God's human creation to destruction during this present age.

Let us examine some of the major movements in this deceiver's plan to use human pride to bring all peoples to the devastating end he wants for them. To do that, we will look at some of the primary figures he has used to foment world chaos. It might be appropriate to call these men who, either unintentionally or purposefully, fostered the deception, which seems to be increasing in scope in our time, the "gods of humanism."

We must all agree that our generation lives in the midst of a swirling tide of events, dreams, promises, threats, and changing ideas of the present and the future.

Certainly our century has been the most politically interesting, the bloodiest, the most revolutionary, and the most unpredictable of any century in history. This confluence of strange conditions presses this generation to ask and answer anew such questions as, "Why am I here? What is the purpose of life?" and especially, "Why is life and reality the way it is?"

The question, "Why are things the way they are?" has been asked by successive generations of curious men from the dawn of history until this very moment. The question is not a superficial, intellectual exercise. No, indeed, for what we view as determining the nature of life in this world and what our response is to that nature is the cornerstone of our living. It is a truism that a person can be expected to put into practice tomorrow what he believes today. That is true of individuals, groups, nations, and entire cultures. Again and again it must be asserted that to believe in the wrong engine of history or the wrong purpose of living can lead to grievous errors, great tragedies, and devastating consequences. Conversely, to have a correct view of God, man, and history is the key to sanity and survival for individual man and for the entire culture.

A Dark Century

In this century, our culture has experienced many dark and fateful events. The leaders of our time are bewildered when they are called upon to explain the reason our world is the way it is or to suggest a direction for the future. Many in positions of public trust confess that they are just trying to keep the lid on, and others have abandoned even that hope.

The contradictions of the present and of what we can see of the future are overwhelming to many. That is so because few persons today have taken the time to evaluate the issues and agree with the true and resist the false. Many believe that they are borne along by extremes of intellectual and philosophical influence that are of their own choosing.

But, alas, they have not chosen at all; rather a high percentage of men and nations today are ruled by a few, select seminal thinkers who, though they are now in their graves, still have influence through their ideas, convictions, and obsessions. Much of modern education, commercial interaction, social planning, intellectual conviction, and even religion is still guided by the constructs formulated by those thinkers of an earlier generation.

My prayerful hope is that even at this late hour we may yet open the windows of our minds in a clear, stronger voice — a voice emanating from a higher provenance than the graves of those who are now gone but whose influence still remains. We may well profit by hearing from a few of these men who rule the world from their graves. If we do not heed what we learn from their messages, we may find ourselves occupying a mass-grave, that at Esdraelon, the grave of humanity itself.

I believe that the few men briefly discussed in this essay are key figures among the progenitors of the most influential movements of this century. Each man was himself influenced by others, but each forged some new concept that became tidal and global. Each man presented his views in so piercing, strident, fanatical, and forceful a way as to introduce a social penetration. For each of them, believing a view was not enough. You had to act on it. And thus these "gods of humanism" did, driving their ideas like spears into the social structure of their time. Those spears have not been removed to this day.

Gods of the Mind

These ruled the world more permanently because they and their ideas became gods of the mind rather than masters of real estate. For them, the battle for the minds of men was their ultimate goal.

It is impossible to say within limited space all that could be said about such thinkers, men of whom whole books have been the subject. I have instead dealt with the particular aspects of humanistic thinking that penetrated the culture, while focusing primarily on the way in which these men have contended and even now from their graves continue to contend for our minds.

The truly powerful leader must influence the minds of men. To do this, he must produce in the minds of others something more, something stronger, something more compelling than what we normally call an idea. This "thing" he must produce within the minds of others actually exists, but in the form of a mental construct. It is an image the influencer sets up in the minds of others, an image that can become an object of occupation, then of concentration, and then — dare we say it — of veneration. The influencer must produce in the minds of those he influences a kind of "little god."

This god of the mind is a "real thing" he plants in the mentality of unsuspecting people. This "real thing" may externally resemble Marx, Lenin, or Freud, but in reality it is a thing unto itself. It goes beyond the limitations of ordinary personality and takes on dimensions of near deity.

Possibly that is why one of the strongest prohibitions in Scripture is the statement *"Thou shalt have no other gods before me."* When the God of the universe uttered those words, He was giving an absolute command that applied to all things and all places for all time, until the end of time and beyond. Obedience to that command is the key to everything. No benefit in this or any possible world is derived apart from the diligent conformity to that eternal and changeless rule.

Conversely, disobedience to the inflexible order results in the irretrievable loss of everything — sanity, security, rationality, health, happiness, civility, civilization. Why? Because the rule God uttered has to do with ultimate good and the final basis of all things — with the foundation for all foundations, the measure of all measures.

Every adverse fortune of life and history for men and nations has come from ignoring that great command. The degree of ill present in that adverse fortune is in direct proportion to the degree an action has deviated from that command.

In fact, there is a sense in which the command, "Thou shalt have no other gods before me," is not finally a command but it is a total absolute, nonnegotiable in the slightest aspect. It is not altered by rhetoric, softened by fears, weakened by reflection, eroded by time, cowed by resentment, or defeated by successive waves of frantic assaults by froth-mouthed enemies. That command is so obviously the essence of existence that one marvels it should ever be questioned by a mind that claims rationality or by a soul that quests for life. So essential is that command to rational life that even the thought of action that directs itself otherwise should be seen by all for what it is: a perverse dementia, a strange insanity.

The Insanity of Religion

Alas, strange insanities exist, present in our time as in virtually all times. History is filled with accounts of other gods. Individuals, then whole families, then entire nations, then teeming civilizations allowed, esteemed, and finally worshipped pagan deities. We read the record, which has always astonished us, of men and women by the millions who have worshipped someone or something else besides the true and living God.

Adding to our wonder, we learn that this worship has not been mere obeisance. No, indeed, it has taken the form of expensive poverty-producing offerings placed upon the stone knees of dumb idols. Worse, this worship has required human sacrifice, infanticide, emulation, and suicide — all for gods of wood or stone that cannot speak. Worshippers have led their tiny children, their trembling wives, even their nations into the cauldrons of sacrifice for other gods.

But not so today, you say.

I disagree. Humanism is the accepted secular world-religion of our day. Devised from the ideas and doctrines conjured up in the sin-polluted minds of human beings who seek to exclude the true God from human affairs, humanism drives the world with the determination to do "what is right in their own eyes." Mankind now puts anything and everything before consideration of the one, true, God of heaven. To acknowledge Him is to bow in worship before Him and to accept His rules for living. This they will not do.

So diverse have become the humanists' basic ideas about life that the notion has emerged that there is no final idea, no absolute truth. Our generation is obsessed with this notion of the absence of finality. "Who is to say who is right?" is the question of dismissal in many a conversation. What's more, many can point to the fallen gods of our time as proof of the instability and non-finality of the best ideas of this world.

Indeed, many an ideology important yesterday seems idiotic in the present — to the point people are embarrassed to have believed in them. The statue of Lenin hanging by the neck as in execution before it finally fell into a Budapest square expresses the spirit of the age: "There are no absolutes."

But, alas, to say there are no absolutes is to say that there is no God. And if there are no absolutes, how can one confess an absolute in the negative? The mind cannot do so, for the statement is a self-contradiction. The mind reacts, stretches out tendrils like a vine in a crannied wall, seeking the next solidity to which it may attach itself. Those questing tendrils are reaching in many different directions today. Some even professed to have found that set of principles upon which they ultimately can rely.

Ruling from the Grave

To aid in our thinking about first and second principles we must emphasize again the divine prohibition: "Thou shalt have no other gods before me." That is the rule. There must be no other first principle than God and His law.

By the same standard, there must also be no other central motivation, no other final goal, no other pursuit or prize, no multiple destinations. We must be ruled by no other human or subhuman creature, alive or dead. But despite many protestations, the world of our time is put upon, influenced — yes, ruled — by the philosophies of others. I suggest, in fact, that our generation is so conformed to the ideas that have come down to us largely from preceding decades — and even from the previous century and the formative years of this century — that the modern mind is ruled by men who are now in the grave.

Men who rule the world from their graves still press their philosophies upon us. We cannot help noting that the degree of reverence bestowed upon them is more than natural men deserve. They are called "world-changers," "seminal thinkers," "sublime conceptualists," "god-intoxicated," "creators," "custodians of the future," and the like. Some, indeed, have gone so far as to repudiate every predecessor, begetting a "new school of thought" — yes, even "a new humanity."

These dead priests of the luciferically-spawned secular religion called humanism have been elevated to almost deity status by the deceived and deluded whose minds these "gods of humanism" have, even in death, been able to enslave.

Their ideas, and successive corruptions of those ideas, have been taught in our schools, promoted in the media, and preached from our pulpits to the point that they are now largely unquestioned and unrefuted, having become the conventional wisdom. Having endured this far, their ideas may even be carried as foundational elements into the next millennium.

Should that be the case, the next millennium may also, as has this one, refuse to bring forth the utopia most of the "seminal thinkers" have implied and some have promised. Concerning the future, time will tell. But time is already telling this generation that it must look higher than a row of tombstones for its inspiration, its knowledge, and its direction from here on out.

Remembering the deadly persistence of the gods of the mind to work upon us, we may well note the call — yes, the command, which God gives to the world. The Scripture says, "He commands all men everywhere to repent." The unfortunate English translation of "Metanoia" serves to obscure its real meaning. Metanoia means "a change of mind." Before a person can step into true reality, he must change his mind. This is commanded to all men everywhere.

We do not do violence to truth when we suggest that God is requiring the world to depose the gods of the mind and receive within us that cleansed mind of the true God, the Lord of glory.

The god of this world has blinded the minds of them who believe not, lest the light of the glorious gospel of Christ who is the image of God should shine unto them. That scriptural truth highlights the importance of the mind to God — and to the devil. Satan works daily to prevent in any person an enlightened mind. By contrast, God promises that we are transformed by the renewing of our minds. Within the mind of man is resident his great capability, which is to give assent to the truth of God and to depose and send into exile the false gods that persistently work to confuse the mind.

The Diary that Changed the World

Charles Darwin, through making daily entries in a diary, began what became one of the most important writings in history. It was a diary that would chronicle a set of experiences that led to a decisive shift in thinking about the natural sciences — a change that would, in turn, influence the world of thought outside the natural sciences, leading ultimately to changes in the entire culture of many a nation.

So it was that, in the introduction to a 1972 reprinting of the diary, Walter Sullivan said:

> This book was prelude to what probably became the most revolutionary change that has ever occurred in man's view of himself. The change, in fact, has still not fully run its course. It demands that we regard ourselves as insepa-rably a part of nature and accept the fact that our descent was from more primitive creatures and, ultimately, from the common origin of all life on earth. It is the view that we will never fully understand ourselves until we understand our origins and the traits — chemical, biological, and behavioral — that we share with other species.[1]

Those are large, ambitious words, but Sullivan is accurate in saying that the diary led to "the most revolutionary change that has ever occurred in man's view of himself." The adventure out of which the diary expanded was so significant and informative for the writer that it grew into a set of concepts, then a book, and then an approach to life. The end result was to change fundamentally man's very understanding of himself.

Darwin's diary, *The Voyage of the Beagle,* chronicled his account of the expedition that embraced the five most exciting years of his life. In fact, most of what occurred in his life before his voyage, Darwin held to be but the prelude to the expedition to the shores of South America. His life afterwards was meditative and sedentary, characterized by illness and reclusion but mostly by the recounting of the observations of the Beagle voyage. It was as if Darwin lived on those memories.

What Darwin formulated came to be seen as a plausible, new understanding of man and nature important enough to be thought the work of a genius and the beginning of a new epoch in world history. During the years following the publication of the diary (1836), other books grew out of the experiences described in the diary, most notably the landmark *Origin of the Species by Means of Natural Selection* (1859).

From that point on, the academic world has attempted to repudiate its pre-Darwinist past and to think of mankind as part of a common continuum with nature and the universe. This intellectual revolution has caused man to reinterpret his past, rethink his present, and revise his anticipations for the future. Darwin is seen as giving mankind a comprehension of the world so unlike the view held in the past that, in a sense, he restarted history. Darwin's influence continues to be pervasive today, and he holds a leading rank among those men who rule the world from the grave.

Let it first be noted that Darwin had a touch of humility about his conclusions. He said, "I am well aware that scarcely a single point is discussed in this volume in which facts cannot be deduced, often apparently leading to conclusions directly opposite to those at which I have arrived."

The overreaching conclusion, and what may well be called the index of Darwinism, is the concept he called, and we continue to call, "natural selection." Darwin himself attempted to explain the concept:

As many more individuals of each species are born

than can possibly survive; and as, consequently, there is a frequently recurring struggle for existence, it follows that any being, if it vary however slightly in any manner profitable to itself, under the complex and sometimes varying conditions of life, it will have a better chance of surviving, and thus be "naturally selected." From the strong principle of inheritance, any selected variety will tend to propagate its new and modified form.[2]

Thus, we have Darwin's definition of the core of his evolutionary faith — the natural selection of individuals who have won the competition for scarce resources. Those individuals whose instinctive capacities gave them a better chance of survival in the surrounding environment lived — and lived long enough to pass on their particular genetic makeup to the next generation. Over time these slight differences accumulated with the result that eventually organisms emerged that no one would claim were the same species.

The Law of the Jungle

Herbert Spencer was later to coin the phrase "survival of the fittest" to describe the effects of the action of natural selection. Darwin argued that if the breeder of a certain species could bring into being changes he preferred (color, size, and so on), then nature could do far better. So numerous were Darwin's observations and so voluminous was the data he accumulated throughout his life that the sheer weight of his writings tended to be a part of the proof of his contentions for the survival of the fittest.

The world of the natural sciences was impressed. It was almost as if the scientists were waiting for such a view. However, the scientists so impressed with Darwin's theory seemed to forget or ignore the fact that no way presently exists whereby data from the present can prove, of itself, anything about ultimate origins. Proof, to live up to its name, must mean demonstrating that something we do not know conforms exactly to something we do know. Consequently, there is simply nothing we know either by observation or through logical proof concerning the origin of individual species or the origin of life itself. Our observations in the present are exactly that — present data. What we think they tell us about the past are subjective considerations. They cannot be held to be science at all.

Again, space limitations prohibit an in-depth debunking of what the "evolutional scientists" say comprises what they term "species."

Appropriate comment could be made to their methodology, but suffice it to say that the naturalist's idea of species and their origins is built on troubled logic, inexact science, and the absence of clear definitions.

Really, then, is the doctrine of the survival of the fittest true? This amounts to what is well-called "the law of the jungle." But when we think about it, there is no law of the jungle. The rule, it is said, that operates in the jungle is that the strong overcome the weak. The strong, therefore, survive, and the weak become fodder for the strong. With the help of Darwin, this rule was dignified by being called "natural selection." Mind you, Darwin called this a "law."

Darwin professed to have "seen," indeed discovered, this "law" when he proceeded to elevate it to an axiom of life. Because biology is destiny for many, this "principle" has become for them the law of life. Whatever we may say, this is the way most people think.

No wonder, we often hear it said in media reports of those who have overcome overwhelming odds, "He (or she) is a true survivor."

But is this the way it really is? We submit to each thinking person that this is not the way it is. The argument against it is painfully simple; if the law of the jungle were indeed a law, if the survival of the fittest were the way it is, there then would be only one being on earth — the strongest — and that not for long.

In truth, so many conditioning factors make for survival that we must see that it is not possible to name a constant, a law concerning the matter of survival. Accident, sickness, surprise, falling trees, lightning strikes, stray bullets, and a thousand other variables impinge upon the life of any animate thing. In fact, a near infinity of conditioning factors is present. So many are there that the argument dissolves into absurdity.

Because the arguments for the false "law" of the survival of the fittest put forward by the Darwinian sycophants are so full of holes, to make "natural selection" the determining factor in history is to make a false assumption. And even if the assumption were true, it could not be proved to be true.

This observably makes no difference to those who hold on blindly to their faith in the secular religion of humanism. The elitist-humanist derives all the proof he needs from his belief that he is the one most fit to construct the world in which he cannot only survive but, indeed, will have a significant part in governing.

Social Darwinism

How, then, does Darwin rule from his grave? The answer has to do with the questions everyone at sometime or another asks: "What makes the world continue? Where did I come from? Why are things as they are?" These are important, perennial questions. Not to ask them is to give evidence of having a mind narrower than the one needed to survive in the world of men and nations. But what is particularly significant in our day is the way in which these questions have been answered by the intellectually elite.

As is so often the case with an intellectual construct, Darwinism has moved out from its original platform to operate in a wider world. The ideas of evolution have left the confines of biology, botany, and paleontology and are now thought to apply to the social structure at large. This application of Darwinism to social structures is called "social Darwinism" and is foundational for our culture. It represents the way Darwin rules our society from the grave.

A major assumption that helps to make up this social Darwinism is the idea that the social structure is engineered and controlled by impersonal forces rather than by God. Until the emergence of social Darwinism, it was generally held in the West that the process of history constantly revealed that the Judeo-Christian God was behind it. The founders of America rested in the confidence that "there is a just God who presides above the destinies of nations." That statement revealed the mind-set of Western culture present at the time. It was a largely undisputed first principle in the light of which other realities were examined.

Darwin changed all of this. His idea of natural selection is meaningless gibberish unless he is in fact referring to an impersonal force, a power that propels history and establishes its direction. As a young man Darwin had Christian associations, but, as his life progressed, he became less and less willing to ascribe the control and direction of history to God. Rather, he came to think of the progress of history as being determined by the impersonal engine of natural selection. God was exchanged for a force, and history dropped into a depersonalized mode.

The Social Darwinists of our time have continued along this line. Our society, once rightly called a Christian civilization, has become secular to a greater degree than the solons of Western civilization would have thought possible. Education, government, business, the media, and, in many cases, religion, have moved through progressive stages of secularization from Christianity to atheism. As a result, God is not merely ignored but is opposed and vilified at every opportunity.

Marx: The Greatest of All Thinkers?

Just as Darwin discovered the law of evolution in organic nature, so Marx discovered the law of evolution in human history. Some have called Karl Marx the greatest thinker in all history. Accolades considering his life and thought border on idolatry, and his promises have been believed by many to offer a future only slightly less than heaven on earth. These delusional expectations, engendered by Marx within the minds of his worshipping disciples, make him certainly one of the core "gods of humanism."

His doctrines, however, with the collapse of a whole empire based on his philosophies have, for the moment, fallen into disfavor and disrepute in the regions that were once the Soviet Union. Still, for some reason, Western humanistic elitist "leaders" seem to be tripping over each other in a headlong rush to incorporate Marxist principles into the equation for bringing under control the peoples over whom they are determined to rule.

Marx observed the simple fact, hitherto concealed by an overgrowth of ideology, that mankind must first of all eat and drink and have shelter and clothing before he can pursue politics, science, religion, art, etc. Therefore, he concluded, the production of the immediate material means of life and consequently the degree of economic development attained by a given people or during a given epoch determines their quality of life. These necessities of life build the foundation upon which the forms of government, the legal conceptions, the art, and even the religious ideas of the people concerned have been evolved. As a result, these ideas must therefore be explained, instead of vice versa as had hitherto been the case.

Marx also discovered the special law of motion governing the present-day capitalist method of production and the bourgeois society that this method of production has created. The discovery of surplus value suddenly threw light on the problem, which all previous investigators — both bourgeois economists and socialist critics — had been trying to solve while groping in the dark.

Philip Foner, in the preface to an elaborate collection in response to the death of Karl Marx called *Karl Marx Remembered,* wrote:

> Marxism is today the most influential body of thought

in the world. Hundreds of millions live in societies whose fundamental principles — socialism — were laid down over a century ago by Karl Marx and his collaborator and friend Friedrich Engles...they propounded principles that were and remain universal and international.[3]

Foner also asserts: "I am confident that when the two-hundredth anniversary of Karl Marx will be observed, the entire world will be socialist."

For most of the era following World War II, communism — Darwinian socialism boiled down to a degree most concentrated and toxic — has been the form of political ideology and consequent government in iron control over the lives and fortunes of one and one-half billion people. From 1918 onward — and it holds true today despite the dissolution of the USSR — no major international political decision has been made by any power in the world apart from the question, What will Russia and the Communists think of this?

Karl Marx has in effect been influencing not only the former Soviet Union but that vast portion of earth we call the Third World. Belief structures sired by his seminal thoughts have held billions of precious souls in their tyrannical grasp.

What then is the result, the end-product of the thoughts of this "greatest of all thinkers" so revered by even the elevated minds within American academia and virtually worshipped by the liberal, intelligentsia? There is now documented what the record of Marx has produced in flesh and in fact. That record is a terrible one indeed.

Aleksandr Solzhenitsyn had this to say of it, in part:

> I am very much aware that eastern Slavic orthodoxy, which, during the sixty-five years of communist rule has been subjected to persecution even fiercer and more extensive than that of early Christian times.
>
> In this persecution-filled age, it is appropriate that my own very first memory should be of Chekists in pointed caps entering St. Panteleimon's Church in Kislovodsk, interrupting the service and crashing their way into the sanctuary to loot. And later, when I started going to school in Rostov-on-don — passing on my way a kilometer-long compound of the Checka-GPU and a glittering sign of the League of Militant Atheists — school children egged on by Komsomol members taunted me for accompanying my

mother to the last remaining church in town and tore the cross from around my neck.

. . . Orthodox churches were stripped of their valuables . . . . Tens of thousands of churches were torn down or desecrated, leaving behind a disfigured wasteland that bore no resemblance to Russia as such . . . . People were condemned to live in this dark and mute wilderness for decades, groping their way to God . . . . Fifteen thousand peasants were brought to death for the purpose of destroying our national way of life and of extirpating religion from the countryside . . . . Hatred of religion is rooted in communism . . . . Khrushchev simultaneously rekindled the frenzied Leninist obsession with destroying religion . . . . The ruinous revolution has swallowed up some 60 million of our people.[4]

Sixty million people dead. What a story of hell on earth! The story of the ultimate outcome for a culture that has made its all-consuming focus that of ridding itself of anything and everything to do with God is the story of humanism come to fruition.

Creating an Enemy

Albert Einstein was born in 1879 to Jewish parents in the city of Ulm, Germany. The definition of his profession is that he was "an American theoretical physicist," although his origins were from the continent of Europe. Surely, the world ought daily to thank God that the word "American" was attached to the name of Albert Einstein. Had his nationality remained "German," how different the world would be today!

Pursuing his studies with his penetrating mind, he obtained his doctorate in 1905 at the University of Zurich. In that year he presented to the world a scientific point of view that captured the minds of the physicists of the world and redirected the course of history. That point of view was called "the special theory of relativity."

While his reputation grew as one of the world's greatest physicists, so, too, did the ominous political problems in Europe, particularly the rise of Adolph Hitler and the establishment of the Nazi government.

One of the early programs of Hitler and the Nazis was the creation of an enemy in the minds of the German people. That indignation, thought the Nazis, would be the instrument to unite the

German people around the Nazi promise for the future. Creating an enemy, whether false or true, is a well-known political device of every incipient dictator.

For the Nazis, that enemy was the Jewish race. There followed the Jewish pogroms, the widest persecution and largest attempt at genocide that man has known in all of history. One of the Jewish persons upon whom that persecution had a profound effect was Albert Einstein. His property was confiscated in 1934 by the Nazi government, and he himself was deprived of his German citizenship. Little did Hitler know that this single act of deprivation was to put into the hands of his future enemies the scientific know-how and the military device which would ultimately extinguish his Nazi promises and halt the war which he was to initiate.

Einstein: Influencing an Entire Culture

It is still the case that most people of the world do not understand the theory of relativity and how it was that the gigantic forces were unleashed in the nuclear bomb. Despite the inadequate knowledge of the details by the average man, however, each of us will at least note that Einstein's incursion into the world of subatomic particles has released a massive amount of energy that has already staggered the imagination. The physicist sees no reason for not believing that there is enough force in a relatively small mass to blow up the entire world.

Lack of understanding about the concepts put forward by the great scientist, in his tremendous celebrity, thrust upon him expectations by his fellow humans that puzzled and frustrated him. In Einstein we see again how a dominant, world-changing set of ideas is soon called upon to put his imprimatur on other things. Einstein, with his obviously confirmed and life-changing views called relativity, was soon to be thought the father of a set of views that were to influence the entire culture.

In the minds of many, "relativity" became "relativism." There is no doubt that "relativism" is one of the prevailing thought modes of our society. Paul Johnson, the historian, comments on this:

> At the beginning of the 1920s the belief began to circulate, for the first time at a popular level, that there were no longer any absolutes: of time and space, of good and evil, of knowledge, above all of value. Mistakenly, but perhaps inevitably, relativity became confused with relativism.[5]

Einstein was chagrined at the way his presentation of physics became twisted in the public mind.

"No one was more distressed than Einstein by his public misapprehension. He was bewildered by the relentless publicity and error which his work seemed to promote."[6]

Expanding on this, Johnson said:

> The emergence of Einstein as a world figure in 1919 is a striking illustration of the dual impact of great scientific innovators on mankind. They change our perception of the physical world and increase our mastery of it. But, they also change our ideas. The second effect is often more radical than the first. The scientific genius impinges on humanity, for good or ill, far more than any statesman or warlord. Galileo's empiricism created the ferment of natural philosophy in the 17th century which adumbrated the scientific and industrial revolutions. Newtonian physics formed the framework of the 18th century-enlightenment, and so helped to bring modern nationalism and revolutionary politics to birth. Darwin's notion of the survival of the fittest was a key element both in the Marxist concept of class warfare and of the radical philosophies which shaped Hitlerism. Indeed, the political and social consequences of Darwinian ideas have yet to work themselves out, as we shall see. So, too, the public response to relativity was one of the primitive, formative influences on the course of 10th-century history. It formed a knife, inadvertently wielded by its author, to help cut society adrift from its traditional moorings in the faith and morals of Judeo-Christian culture.[7]

Changed into Himself

Let us look into the world, the voice, the writings, and the mysterious perceptions of a man who seemed to have discovered how to define the nuances of the psyche. Furthermore, his answers appeared to be not only scientific and scholarly, but interesting, provocative, and even titillating.

Yes, a man from the world of science touched and titillated an age such as none had done before or has done since. Sigmund Freud was his name. Psychoanalysis was his profession, and the world, before it was done, submitted itself to his therapy.

In his lifetime, he had an influence both superficial and profound upon the lives of millions and upon the spirit of his age. Few people who live in Western nations have been able to escape his influence. Few, in fact, have been able to avoid the accusation of at least once thinking along the lines of this man's theory of human personality.

Freud carried with him a complicated set of memories he believed was decisive in determining many of his later decisions. Memories meant more to him than to most people. Freud's biographers note that his school years brought to him a degree of self-confidence that was to be one of his characteristics for all of life. That self-confidence explains in part why, throughout his life, Freud seemed relatively uninterested in conforming, pleasing others, or fitting in. In fact, he was relatively unperturbed by being thought odd or iconoclastic, which indeed was his reputation with many people.

Freud, though part of a Jewish family, never formally adopted the Jewish religion. In 1926, he wrote, "The Jews treat me as a national hero, although my contribution to the Jewish cause consists solely of the fact I have never denied my Jewishness." Nevertheless, the idea of a personal God who intimately interacts with man was not part of Freud's thinking.

A pointed summation of the life of Freud is given to us by Gerard Lauzun in his biography:

> Freud's achievement was that he restored human nature to its original wholeness and unity. He reestablished the connections between the visible behavior and hidden components of character and attitudes. He revealed the importance and extent of impulses whose origin is sexual; he deciphered dreams, and rediscovered in humanity's stock of symbols and legends the conflicts which subtend the life of a collectivity for an individual. With unshakable daring and determination, working completely alone at first and later surrounded by a circle of disciples, he stood firm in the face of attacks, polemics and rebuttals. In a few years, this seeker whom we have watched anxiously groping for the right path to follow, passing from physiology to neuropathology and from thence to psychopathology, acquiring at every turn a mastery that was inadequate to his needs, eager to find masters to respect, was himself to become the master, the father, and at a stroke to take on a new stature. Sigmund Freud was to disappear, and the

father of psychoanalysis to take his place — vituperated, mocked, admired, and gradually becoming "tel que'en lui-meme l'eternite le change" — "changed into himself by eternity."[8]

A Miracle Worker?

Ever questing to penetrate deeper into inner self, Freud resolutely determined to press strongly for the medical use of hypnosis and indeed became its champion. He, himself, testified on behalf of hypnosis, saying "In the years of my activities as a physician, my principle instrument of my work, apart from haphazard and unsystematic psychotherapeutic methods, was hypnotic suggestion."

About the use of hypnosis, he said further: "There was something positively seductive about working with hypnotism. For the first time there was a sense of overcoming one's helplessness; and it was highly flattering to enjoy the reputation of being a miracle worker."[9]

Freud's own conclusions concerning the validity and value of hypnosis, particularly as it involved testimonies of patients about early childhood sexual abuses and involvements, later changed when serious doubts were raised as to whether the seductions the patients reported had ever taken place. Still, his tenets and theories on psychoanalysis evolved to form a most significant portion of the basis for modern psychology.

That inward-looking humanistic attempt to dissect the very soul, the thought to somehow discover and understand its core-problem, to solve, heal, "redeem" the inner-person, presumes a god-likeness. Thousands of Americans pay enormous amounts of money to have their "psyches" probed, analyzed and massaged by Sigmund Freud's disciples. How sad, when in a majority of cases, they need, instead, the Great Physician to come into their lives and clean up their sin-racked souls. Only Jesus Christ, not humanistic psychology, can purify the inner-man.

Lest one is deceived into believing that Freud's thinking on psychology is in any way compatible with true Christianity, consider Freud's own words in voicing his attitude about religion, which we can safely assume meant the Christian religion.

Individuals, Freud said, tend to become psychotic when they are frustrated and despair of the possibilities of civil revolt with society:

Religion circumscribes these measures of choice and adaptation by urging upon everyone alike its single way of achieving happiness and guarding against pain. Its method consists of decrying the value of life and promulgating a view of the real world that is distorted like an illusion, and both of these imply preliminary intimidating influence upon intelligence. At such a cost — by the forceful imposition of mental infantilism and inducing mass delusion — religion succeeds in saving many people from individual neurosis. But, little more. There are, as we have said, many paths by which the happiness attainable for man can be reached, but none which is certain to take him to it. Nor can religion keep her promises either. When the faithful find themselves reduced in the end to speaking of God's inscrutable decree, they thereby arrive at all that is left to them and their sufferings is unconditional submission as a last-remaining consolation and source of happiness. And if a man is willing to come to this, he could probably have arrived there by a shorter road.[10]

Religion — of all kinds — Freud considered as "mental infantilism" and "mass delusion."

Reading Freud on religion, one hears in his words the source of many a modern conversation about the nature of the Christian religion and the coming of Jesus Christ into the world. Freud, an atheist, gave every successive detractor of the value of religion a set of clever psychological remarks through which to express contempt for God and His work. After all, psychoanalysis was the new revelation and psychotherapy the new salvation.

The pervasive influence of Freud's views on religion continues to be a significant factor in the thought life of our present society.

Humanism's Bitter Harvest

There is an inflexible, non-negotiable principle that works in the universe at all times and in all places. It applies to people and nations and to any entity that thinks of itself as being constituted.

That principle is stated by the apostle Paul when he says, "Be not deceived, God is not mocked, for whatsoever a man soweth, that shall he also reap" (Gal. 6:7).

This is called by many "The Law of Sowing and Reaping," and it is inescapable. There is no circumstance of life where it does not work inexorably and inevitably. Many an early grave has been filled by a young person who forgot this principle.

The apostle Paul even expands on this by saying, "For he that soweth to his flesh shall of the flesh reap corruption; but he that soweth to the Spirit shall of the Spirit reap life everlasting" (Gal. 6: 8).

There is no more classic illustration of this truth than a history of our twentieth century. Although heralded by a series of books called *This Fabulous Century,* the twentieth century will instead be noted by murder, rape, pillage, drive-by shootings, an AIDS epidemic, child abuse, abortion, and a thousand other insults to God and civil humanity. The vaunted promise of the past has turned into a bitter harvest indeed. The promises of the past and the present reality are so contradictory that one wonders if those very promises were not a part of the deteriorating situation which we face today.

Why is this the case?

In pursuit of the answer we do well to consider the philosophic (and therefore moral and spiritual) influences which have come upon our world in this century. We have noted in *Seven Men Who Rule the World from the Grave* how the beliefs of one generation become the inescapable reality of another.[11] What has this nation come to believe that is producing that bitter harvest, the ruin of all things decent in our present culture?

Questions with No Answers

Something of the pervasive nature of Darwinism can be seen in the ever more frequent articles in the public press making assertions about evolution. *Time Magazine* (October 11, 1993) said under a paragraph title "Once upon a Time" the following:

> Some 4.5 billion years ago, the solar system took shape inside a chrysalis of gas and dust. Small objects formed first, then slammed into one another to create the planets. Early on, the energy unleashed by these violent collisions turned the embryonic earth into a molten ball. For a billion years thereafter, the young planet's gravitational field attracted all sorts of celestial garbage. Icy comets screamed in from the outermost reaches of the solar system, while asteroids and meteorites spiraled down like megaton bombs.
>
> Yet after a billion years, when the solar system was swept nearly clean and the primordial bombardment ended, life was already flourishing. UCLA's Professor Schopf has identified the imprints of 11 different types of micro-

organisms in the 3.5 billion-year-old rocks of western Australia. Many of the foils closely resemble species of blue-green algae found all over the world today. Still older rocks in Greenland hint of cellular life that may have come into existence a few hundred million years earlier — perhaps 3.8 billion years ago.

As I read this bewildering nonsense presented to us by a respected magazine — along with impressive photography — I found myself asking a number of questions, such as:

1) From whence came matter in the first place?

Those who write pushing the evolutionary point of view in these days simply skip over the origins of anything. There is no scientific principle or theorem which can explain creation "ex-nihlio." The evolutionary point of view is very presumptuous because it can't even consider the obvious questions of origins.

2) How do we know the age of anything?

After all of the talk, it's impossible for us to know the age of any entity whatsoever at whose creation we were not present. Even the so-called "fossil record" that presents a ladder of fossils from the more simple to the more complex is fictional. This exists in no place in the world.

3) What change constitutes upward evolution (improvement) and what change is devolution? How do you know?

This seems like a very simple question, but it must be answered. "Change" of itself is without significance, but it must be attached to the word "improvement." No one can know that "improvement" has taken place unless there is a final goal toward which a change is traversing. Just as this is true in the realm of science, it is also — or should be — considered true in the government of the United States.

4) Whence came intelligence?

Understanding must be of a different nature from the thing understood! Within the atomic and molecular structure and the analysis of any of these, there is simply no answer to the question of the origin of intelligence itself. No suggestion can possibly be made as to how molecular matter can produce reasoning powers. Reasoning takes the perception to compare what is and what ought to be. No one knows "what ought to be" apart from some kind of revelation that does not come from nature.

5) Does man have a soul? If so, where did it come from? If not, what is love?, fidelity?, honor?, curiosity?, civility?

The idea that all of these imperative nuances of life could have come from a chemical source is simply absurd. But, of course, we have a perverse generation living in our time that has made of itself "the drug culture." They are even now pursuing the deadly fantasy that love, honor, and life itself can be produced from a fix of heroin.

6) *Whence come the moral values of man? By what standards are things "right" and "wrong?" Who decides?*

The evolutionist has no answer whatsoever — not even a suggestion — in response to these questions. Everyone who is not a fool knows that morals, the laws by which we live in the universe, are not products of a test tube somewhere. Rather, they were given to us by the Eternal God who alone has the right to arbitrate the lives that we live in this world.

Who Decides?

The idea of the existence of God is a constant embarrassment to the evolutionist. In fact, it is to be argued that evolution existed in the first place because man wanted to invent several layers of insulation between himself and the God before whom he stands.

Those layers of insulation will instantly disappear on that great Judgment Day. Would that they could disappear now, so that our generation could face the naked truth that God is and that He is a consuming fire. Judgment Day will dispel the foolish notions of the evolutionary process. That Judgment Day may be soon to come.

Despite the falsity of the notion of natural selection, the world continues to thrive on it in these days. It is the rare public school, and increasingly it is the rare Christian school, that does not preach that man is just a human animal. They assert that man is atoms in motion and has no significance that is not chemical.

When will our society discover that if we give way to the argument of evolution we've lost all other arguments? The statement of the judge to a criminal that says: "You have committed a crime. You are wrong and should be punished for it!" — these statements are simply absurd apart from an external, over-arching moral design in the universe.

This points up the problem of our generation. The people living today have not agreed to the question, "Who decides the nature of reality?" For the world, this question is always up for grabs, and they imagine that it changes with each new generation and sometimes each new day. The fact is, it does not — because Jesus Christ is the Creator of the universe, and He is the same yesterday, today, and forever.

A More Dangerous Enemy

When we talk about the bitter harvest of anything, we cannot avoid listening to the gunfire in the city of Moscow. For 80 years the dead hand of communism lay upon this hapless nation of Russia and the larger Soviet Union. All autonomy was destroyed, individuals became cattle, the Communist party became God, and this brutal system of incredibly stupid concepts obtained to the place where it built a cage for all of the people. Within this cage, communism became the classic example of bad seed bearing bitter fruit.

At the beginning, the Communists preached the humanist's doctrine of atheism, materialism, and economic determinism. They touted this point of view to the place of saturation with the people of Russia.

Not only were the Russians forced to believe it, but muddle-headed academics across the world also became Marxists one after the other. One waits to hear from them an apology, but they carried the ideas of Marxism into the open, trusting, gullible minds of millions of young people. Committing themselves to this cause, these young people began a program of mental depravation and finally, utter disappointment. Today, they are staggering around our culture like desiccated zombies, knowing not what to do or where to go.

This is a most interesting phenomena. The Marxist world once retained a modicum of confidence because it could point to Russia and claim that Marxism was fulfilling "the great dream" there. Now, of course, that dream has vanished into agony and pain; Marxism has disappeared as a viable concept in Russia. The consequence is that the Marxists of the other nations of the world have become wandering and leaderless, being without a true home.

As evidence of the continuing, intractable confusion of Marxism, we listened in recent days to the staccato of gunfire as the Russian army attacked the Parliament Building, killing numbers of people in the name of stabilizing the government. That anyone should still call himself a "Marxist" is an evidence of inflexible insanity on their part.

There is, however, a residual influence of the real cause of Marxism in our world, namely Liberalism. Some have suggested, "We need not worry about communism, but rather liberalism as the enemy."

Spiritual Defection

Of the perhaps one billion people in the world today who claim to be Christians, a very high percentage have been infected by the dread concepts of liberalism. We can thank Julius Wellhausen for this, but, of course, many others follow in his train.

It all began with the expression of the doubt that the Bible is truly the Word of God. Wellhausen suggested that it was a collection of fine, perceptive human documents but certainly not the necessary Word of the living and true God. With this open door to spiritual subversion, one thing led to another.

Finally, the Church came to the place where it denied not only the inspiration of Scripture, but the virgin birth, the deity of Christ, the vicarious atonement, the bodily resurrection, and the second coming of the Lord Jesus. The result was that Christianity became just another humanistic religion with no more power to affect the world or change the lives of people than any other of the passing points of view.

To this day, the landscape of Europe is dotted with old churches, high steeples, and brownstone staircases where once were the laughing voices of earnest and committed Christians. Now, these spectral buildings are the testimony of a faith that was but which has long since disappeared. The ghostly, cemetery-like buildings that formerly were Christian gathering places scattered across the world are a mute testimony to the killing liberal poison.

Are we learning that lesson by observation today? The answer is, we are not! The very same grievous defections which destroyed the Church in other generations are defections which continue to this very hour. We appear to be blind and deaf to the fact that the same speeches and the same programs that destroyed the great denominations at the leadership level in America — these same programs continue even among the Evangelicals of our time.

Liberation theology has affected not simply Latin American Catholicism, but North American Evangelicalism as well. The moment we say that we cannot reach people with a message of a spiritual Saviour unless we improve their economic condition first — at that moment we have begun a program of spiritual defection.

Soon, we will redefine the purpose of the coming of Jesus Christ by saying that He came to deliver the world from economic stringency. Soon, the function of Christ as the spiritual Saviour of the world will be gone. By taking this path, churches and then denominations have moved down the primrose path to oblivion. It is a thing to be wondered at that the very people taking this path today do not sense the spiritual defection which has set in.

The Corruption of Education

In the field of modern education, the bitter harvest is beginning to come in also. The continued influence of the relativism of John Dewey and the existentialism of Soren Kierkegaard is in the teaching of our time. It is a sad situation where schools — once the foundation for the truth of society — are now part of the subversive program.

From whence came the radicals, the "flower children," the hippies of the last generation? They did not come from the back streets somewhere, they came from our schools. They came from Columbia, Yale, Harvard, Princeton, the University of Wisconsin, UCLA, Stanford, and many others. They raged about the streets spreading indignation and telling everyone that it was time for a change. Because "all things were relative," there was no one to resist the call for change. Change was simply the alteration of things that would create new interest, new participation, new money, and the like.

What then do we have today? We have drastically rising costs, drastically lowered standards, and more and more ghoulish young people wandering about looking for a place to stand. The pronouncements made by modern educators who retain some perception tell of the drastic deterioration of the university campus in our time.

Bill Bennett, former secretary of education, is one of these. He also speaks in articulate fashion about what is taking place in the American high schools. He points out that there are entire school systems, like Chicago, where no education at all is taking place. Still, the school system has consumed money to the place where it is perhaps $250 million in the red, and the schools are either closing or most reluctant to open.

One of the strange anomalies of our time has come out of all of this. On the high school level, we have two contrasting developments in the world. One hundred twenty thousand schools of the Soviet Union have requested that Christians from America come and show the "Jesus" film and other Christian productions. These schools represent an average of 600 students per institution.

Russia today is in effect crying like the man from Macedonia saying, "Come over to Russia and help us!" The door to the gospel is open, making Russia one of the greatest opportunities for evangelism the Church has known in all of its history.

The contrast with the United States is very remarkable. If one attempted to show a Christian film in a high school in America, he would be threatened by the ACLU and accused of corrupting the precious minds of our young people. Indeed, we are close to the place in America where Evangelical Christianity is becoming a "religio illiciti," an illegal religion. That this should happen in one short generation is a thing to be wondered at. It cannot be denied that the corruption of education today surely compromises everything and prefigures the corruption of everything tomorrow.

The Sexual Revolution

As if that weren't enough, Freudian concepts continue to influence our nation and the world mindset. Sigmund Freud, as we all know, promoted many things, but the most dangerous of all might well be the sexual revolution. He taught that the expression or repression of libido made or broke the realities of life. Consequently, the door to fantastically open sexual license was yawning before our lecherous world. Early on, this was thought of as being an innocent and perhaps even "cute" development. A suggestive remark was called a "Freudian slip," and that was the end of it.

Now we have the situation where the things that people were once ashamed to do by the darkness of midnight they do boastfully in the light of the noonday sun. Many times they put these prurient activities on television and produce a thing called "a soap opera." The existence of such massive television presentations is the evidence of the last stages of sexual insanity that has come upon a nation.

No wonder we have millions of young lives that are dissipated to the point of weakness or death in our nation today. How hypocritically do we cry against AIDS and venereal disease when our nation produces the very resistless motivations that bring these fearful consequences to pass.

In the prayer that our Lord taught us to pray, He said, "Lead us not into temptation." Probably the most cynical, defiant activity to that prayer is modern television. It is carefully planned to produce as much titillation as possible. Then a further calculation is introduced where the intention of the viewer is turned to buying this car, smoking this cigarette, or committing themselves to some other absurdity. It is a huge joke, but it is taken with deadly, fatal seriousness by many.

The Government as God

Also remember the continued influence of John Maynard Keynes. His doctrine, which amounts to teaching that "the government is god" and responsible for producing prosperity, is coming on stronger today.

We now have a program of socialized medicine coming to pass in the United States, which is the same as socializing the nation itself. The government is arrogating to itself the right to control and be the broker of the health of every person within the nation. The program is certainly a colossal fraud, but nevertheless once again the stupid and the wicked take it seriously. Any fool should know that there is not enough money in the nation to keep the promises made by the pushers of this program.

However, over long years, the electorate has been built up into believing that the government can do anything and pay for it as well. The sophomoric among us have forgotten that the government can only give to us what first it takes from us and, of course, cannot give it all back. But, Keynesian economics, which still prevails in our world, has apparently proved otherwise (which it has not).

Time would fail to speak of the many ways in which we are reaping the bitter harvest from all of these activities in our time. How long can this continue? The answer is, "Not forever!" We must face the fact that we live in a finite universe, which means in plain English that it must come to an end.

Yes, a day of reckoning is coming for our society and that judgment cannot be far off. Be sure that when the Day of the Lord comes to pass, every man, woman, and child will be judged according to the works that they have produced. People will be condemned in their own life for having believed and practiced the corrupt philosophies that saturate the society of our time. What a day that will be!

Frequent Reminders

Let us remind ourselves of the blessed hope that we have lest we despair in the midst of these many concerns. How wonderful that God has spoken to the Church of our time and has said, "Because you have kept the word of my patience, I also will keep you from the hour of temptation, which will come upon the whole world" (Rev. 3:10).

To what is the Lord referring? He is speaking to the believers of our time and reminding them of a tremendous delivering event, which is called "the rapture of the Church."

Of this, the apostle Paul speaks when he says:

> For the Lord himself shall descend from heaven with a shout, with the voice of the archangel, and with the trump of God; and the dead in Christ shall rise first; Then we who are alive and remain shall be caught up together with them

in the clouds, to meet the Lord in the air; and so shall we ever be with the Lord. Wherefore, comfort one another with these words (1 Thess. 4:16-18).

So, we can make to each one of our readers a categorical promise today that the Scripture says,

Behold, I show you a mystery: We shall not all sleep, but we shall all be changed, In a moment, in the twinkling of an eye, at the last trump; for the trumpet shall sound, and the dead shall be raised incorruptible and we shall be changed (1 Cor. 15:51-52).

Let us be sure then that the world is even now treasuring up unto itself "wrath against the day of wrath and revelation of the righteous judgment of God who will render to every man according to his deeds" (Rom. 2:5-6).

While remembering that, we Christians can rejoice in the fact that "God has not appointed us to wrath but to obtain salvation by our Lord Jesus Christ" (1 Thess. 5:9). Therefore, we can observe the deteriorations of our world with concern but also with godly detachment.

In the last analysis, our future is not at stake with the mouthings of Charles Darwin or the absurdities of a Soren Kirkegaard. No indeed, our trust is safely placed in Jesus Christ who presides above history and who will not suffer His foot to be moved.

As we think of that, let us labor to touch the world with the gospel of Christ, and let us also look up for our redemption which draws nigh.

4

The Mystics:

Prophets or Psychics?

John Barela

> *Beloved, believe not every spirit, but try the spirits whether they are of God: because many false prophets are gone out into the world* (1 John 4:1;KJV).

"Mysticism." Think it doesn't affect you personally? Think again! This is one of the most relevant and dangerous threats to you and those around you that has ever confronted society — and the Church. Mysticism is operative in so many different areas that it would be impossible to cover even a small portion of the subject in one chapter. Therefore, I will deal with just a few of its many menacing faces — those that I feel are most perilous and threatening to you and to me.

Like an insidious cancer, mysticism has gone virtually undetected, especially in the Church; nevertheless, this silent "killer of the soul" is spreading its poison throughout "the body." It has now metastasized and is spreading so rapidly that it is claiming members of our families and friends at breakneck speed. If you care about your family and others you love, you must read this chapter carefully and prayerfully. The alarming information that I will present is done so in love.

Megatrends, Ten New Directions Transforming Our Lives, by John Naisbitt, was a sensational volume deemed as "a road map to the twenty-first century" by the *American School Board Journal* and called the "field guide of the future" by the *Washington Post.* It remained on the *New York Times* "Best-seller List" for over 60 weeks and became almost a standard textbook for corporate and private business decision making. John Naisbitt bases his predictions for the future on an analysis of what America is today.

One of Naisbitt's predictions is, "Religion: A National Revival." Under this insightful topic, he proposes the following:

> The United States is today undergoing a revival in religious belief . . . . During turbulent times, many people need structure — not ambiguity — in their lives. . . . The demand for structure will increase, supplied not by the old, established denominations . . . . but by . . . the Mormons, the Seventh Day Adventists, and by the great array of the new, native-grown fundamentalist faiths, by the charismatic Christian movement . . . . Since the 1960s, there has also been the widespread interest in Eastern religions, and such groups as the Hare Krishnas are gaining a growing number of followers.[1]

"Mysticism," the foundation of Eastern religion and its many offshoots, has crept into almost every discipline, profession, science, and practice in our modern society. How did this happen? Because mysticism has been grossly overlooked and misunderstood by businessmen and women, by Christians, by the medical profession and nutrition fields as well as by the ordinary "Joe" who is treading merrily on his way through life. It is promoted on radio, television, and in virtually everything we read. Now it is in the Church.

We must "wake up" or face the disastrous consequences. The wonderful truth is that even if we have been deceived and led astray, we have a loving God who is ever eager to forgive and cleanse. He is also depending on those who "see the truth" to warn others.

Reestablishing the "Lost Link"

Obsession with "mystery, mysticism, and the mysterious" has

always been an inherent part of human nature. God created us to function in two worlds: the natural and the spiritual. Since God is a spirit, He built within us special communication capabilities that are able to function in the spiritual realm.

When Adam and God walked together in the Garden, they communed with each other. Although Adam was flesh and God was spirit, a perfect mode of communication existed between them. At the fall, the spiritual link with God was severed, and thus a void or an empty space was left in the spirit of man. But God in His infinite mercy, wisdom, and love, placed a "yearning" within this empty space that seeks to reestablish the "lost link" to God.

Thus far, it would seem simple, then, to restore the God-man communication — except for one factor. Man was not the first to disobey God and sever that perfect relationship that existed "once upon a time, in a perfect universe." Before Adam was gathered out of the dust of the earth, God had already been at work creating other forms of life that He could enjoy and with whom He could also commune.

He had created a masterpiece of wisdom and beauty, whom He named, "Lucifer, son of the morning." God placed him in the highest position of authority next to himself. He gave him insights and keys to wisdom and knowledge beyond our comprehension.

Lucifer was the epitome of created creatures. After a time, however, his superiority of mind and beauty filled him with poisonous pride. He knew that no other creature could compare to himself — except God. He allowed his pride and "lust" to consume him until his sole motivating desire was to advance to the ultimate position in the universe. This insidious goal became the focal point of all his energies and activities.

> For thou hast said in thine heart, I will ascend into heaven, I will exalt my throne above the stars of God: I will sit also upon the mount of the congregation, in the sides of the north (Isa. 14:13;KJV).

In Lucifer's swell of pride, he overlooked the fact that he was a "created creature," and God was divinity. In His divine holiness, God could not allow sin in His heavenly realms. He cast Lucifer to the earth, along with one third of the angelic host that he had seduced into following him. Satan's warfare against God for dominion of the universe continues to this day. We know the final outcome and the victor, but nevertheless, the drama must be played to the full.

Since Lucifer was present at the creation of man, he knew that God had designed man to have a wonderful, spiritual fellowship and a very special relationship with himself. In the evil recesses of his mind, he began plotting a method by which he could destroy the communion between God and man, and replace it with a "counterfeit link" to himself.

You can recognize references to this "link to Lucifer" in New Age terminology as "connectedness." It is usually used in reference to our "connection" to nature, Mother Earth, or the godhead.

Thus began the competitive struggle for the souls of men. Just as Lucifer deceived the third part of the angels, leading them in rebellion against God, so he intends to subvert as many souls as possible, to add to his own dark kingdom.

Because man was created to commune and fellowship with God, Lucifer continues to don varied, and extremely effective, masquerades to convince man that "he" is the "true god." He attempts to convince man that he is the god who controls the universe and that he desires to unite the soul of man with his own to reestablish that "lost connection" with God. In fact, he entices man with the same proposal he made to Eve in the Garden:

> For God doth know that in the day ye eat thereof, then your eyes shall be opened, and *ye shall be as gods,* knowing good and evil. And when the woman saw that the tree was good for food, and that it was pleasant to the eyes, and a tree to be desired to make one wise, she took of the fruit thereof, and did eat, and gave also unto her husband with her; and he did eat (Gen. 3:5-6;KJV).

One popular televangelist said, "Man is the only creation of God that is in God's class . . . . I believe that through these Scriptures we can very clearly see that God made man a god."[2]

Another one from Texas said, "Pray to yourself, because I'm in your self and you're in My self. We are one Spirit, saith the Lord . . . . You need to realize that you are not a spiritual schizophrenic — half-God and half-Satan — you are all-God . . . . Man had total authority to rule as a god over every living creature on earth, and he was to rule by speaking words . . . . You don't have a god *in* you, you *are* one! . . . I say this and repeat it so it don't upset you too bad . . . . When I read in the Bible where He [Jesus] says, 'I Am,' I say, 'Yes, I am, too!' "[3]

A proponent of the "Kingdom Now" teaching said, "Just as dogs have puppies and cats have kittens, so God has little gods. But we have trouble comprehending this truth. Until we comprehend that we are little gods and we begin to act like little gods, we cannot manifest the kingdom of God."[4]

Satan desires what God has — he wants us to enter into an intimate, personal relationship with himself, so he offers a *counterfeit* "born again" experience. In this way, man is deceived into a quest to re-establish the lost connection to the Godhead. Then under Satan's tutoring, he begins his obsession with the mystical, or mysticism.

Counterfeit Mysteries

In order to better understand the scope of our subject, let's examine the definition of "mysticism," then I will give you some specific scenarios of mystical situations that will surprise and shock you.

Mysticism is derived from the word, "mystery." *Webster's New World Dictionary* defines a *mystery* as a "divine secret." *Mysterious* comes from the same root word and "is applied to that which excites curiosity, wonder, etc., but is impossible or difficult to explain or solve . . . that is inscrutable which is completely mysterious and is altogether incapable of being searched out, interpreted, or understood [the inscrutable ways of God]; mystical applies to that which is occult or esoteric in connection with religious rites or spiritual experience."

A *mystic* is defined as "one who professes to undergo mystical experiences by which he unintuitively comprehends truths beyond human understanding." Therefore, mysticism is "the doctrines of beliefs of mystics; specifically, the doctrine it is possible to achieve communion with God through contemplation and love . . . any doctrine that asserts the possibility of attaining knowledge of spiritual truth through intuition acquired by fixed meditation."

The Dictionary of Mysticism and the Occult further defines it as:

> The act of seeking union with the godhead . . . . "the knowledge of God through experience" . . . . Mystics believe that the godhead or supreme being sustains the manifested universe and is responsible for all aspects of existence and consciousness. This supreme being is portrayed in different traditions as an anthropomorphic ["the attributing of human shape or characteristics to a god, animal, or inanimate thing," *Webster's New World Dictio-*

nary] figure, as a spirit, or as light, or an abstract infinite reality. Despite these variations, all mystical techniques have as their final goal communication with, and knowledge of, that transcendental state of being.[5]

Another related term with which we should familiarize ourselves is, "mystic union." It is defined by the same occult dictionary as, "In mysticism, union with the godhead through contemplation and prayer. Mystic union is sometimes regarded as a type of spiritual marriage with the Creator."

The interesting fact is that for every biblical truth, Lucifer, or Satan, poses a counterfeit. Since our union with God is a mystical one that inspires, fulfills, and intrigues man, Satan, as an "angel of light," offers his counterfeit mystical union. He offers a counterfeit "born again" experience, which leads the "initiate" into the mystical union resulting in a "marriage" — not with the Creator — but with the destroyer.

Of course, we know that the word "mystery" is used many times in the Bible, and there are legitimate biblical mysteries — which is the very reason that Satan offers "counterfeit mysteries." Bible mysteries relate to certain biblical doctrines or truths that are vital and relevant to the Christian faith. These mysteries are very clearly outlined and described in the Scriptures, so they are easily checked with the Word and verified.

If a mystery is presented to you which is not included in the text of Scripture, then you can be sure that this mystery is "extra-biblical," and therefore, "occult." We are told in 1 Corinthians 4:1, "Let a man so account of us, as of the ministers of Christ, and stewards of the mysteries of God" (KJV).

We are "stewards (caretakers or trustees) of the mysteries of God." In order to be a steward of these mysteries, we must first study the Bible to find out exactly what God has entrusted to our care.

The Self-Realization Lie

In this chapter, we attempt to examine but a few of Satan's counterfeit mysteries. One common thread that characterizes counterfeits is that most of them require "works" or "formulas" or "steps" in order to be obtainable. The "grace" of Christ is, many times, conspicuously absent. You will find "self," is strongly emphasized, and most "doctrine" centers around self-gratification of various sorts — self-realization, self-image, self-help, self-improvement, self-motivation, self-worth, self attainment, ad infinitum.

John Naisbitt, in *Megatrends,* writes:

> During the 1970s, Americans began to disengage
> from the institutions that had disillusioned them and to
> relearn the ability to take action on their own . . . . As we
> became more disillusioned we asked, "What, or whom, can
> we trust?" The resounding answer was "Ourselves." . . . .
> Self-help . . . . In the 1970s, it again became a movement
> that cut across institutions, disciplines, geographic areas,
> and political ideologies . . . . It is people reclaiming
> personal control over the mysteries of life and death.[6]

Since the 1970s was the generation of the "yuppies" — and we probably have more statistical research compiled on this "consumer group" than on any other group in modern times — it is very easy to see the metamorphosis of thought.

The emphasis of this generation, as Naisbitt so aptly put it, is on "self." If medicine had failed to effect cures, then Holistic Health might hold the answer. The "yuppies" were also characterized by *spend, spend, spend* — better automobiles, larger homes, diamonds, furs, gourmet food, designer clothes.

Is it then strange that the yuppies religion would be a "custom" designed one to appeal to the "senses?" They must have a god who understood their lifestyles and desires — a giant "caterer" whose goal was to satisfy every whim of the "self."

Enter the new doctrines of self-gratification. "What can God 'do' for 'me,' 'give' to me?" Then, it went so far as to take the diabolical turn to "God isn't so big after all, I am just as big as He is — in fact, I *AM* god! Now 'I can *do, get,* and *perform* everything my little heart desires.' "

This philosophy also spilled over into their ideas on medicine and healing. Naisbitt says, " . . . we seriously considered alternatives to the medical establishment's program of annual physical exams, drugs, and surgery. We talked and wrote about a wealth of new-age remedies — acupuncture, acupressure, vitamin therapy, charismatic faith healing . . . . The new holistic health approach has opened up a new area in search for health and wellness: the human mind. At the radical end of the spectrum is the belief that there is no disease that cannot be cured through the powers of the mind and a positive attitude."

The occult dictionary even gives their definition of "self" ... "In mysticism and occult philosophy, the divine essence of one's being .... The self ... contains the spark of godhead and is the source of pure consciousness." Self-realization is defined as "knowledge of one's true inner self: spiritual enlightenment."

If you remember, the very motive that caused Lucifer to rebel against God was his selfish aspiration to ascend above the throne of God. He was not satisfied with being one step lower than God, his obsession was to become a god.

Therefore, Satan's "faith" centers around the very same concept — the lie he told Eve in the Garden. "You shall become as gods." He offers man a "path to godhood," not a "path to God."

One humanly, or fleshly, aspect that makes this alternate path to god so attractive is that it is not necessary for man to admit he is a sinner, nor is he required to repent or give account to God for sin. In Satan's plan, sin does not exist, and man can indulge his own selfish desires to the ultimate degree. One of the areas in which we can recognize his theology, is what we call the New Age movement.

The Hidden History of the New Age

Most of us assume that the New Age is a rather contemporary concept. A little research reveals, however, that New Agers have been busy developing their networks for a long time now.

The first New Age magazine, entitled, *The New Age Magazine,* began mailing via second class mail in 1914. This magazine is the monthly publication of the "Supreme Council 33 Degree, Ancient and Accepted Scottish Rite of Freemasonry of the Southern Jurisdiction." Interestingly enough, the teachings and symbology of the Freemasons closely resemble those of other "secret societies," as well as those of other occultists and esoteric religious movements. Could it be that networking began much earlier than anyone outside the movement has fathomed?

Most occult or mystical groups are tied together through the use of similar symbols. For example, the papal tiara of the Pope of the Roman Catholic Church — also known as the "triple crown of godhood" was actually copied from the tiara of Brahmatma, the Supreme Pontiff of the Initiates of old India. It is also a perfect copy of that worn by the Dalai-Lama of Tibet, and is also shared by Masons, Kabbalists (a Jewish esoteric movement), Syrian sects, and other esoteric groups.

Why is this important? For two reasons. First, their alliances have been kept secret for a purpose. However, the adepts of each group are able to identify "fellow believers" from their own and from the other members of the "network," through their symbology.

This works in the same way as Masonic jewelry. A Mason can identify a fellow Mason without speaking one word — through the symbols of his Masonic ring or other jewelry.

Second, similar symbols naturally signify similar beliefs and practices. All of the groups sharing the Triple Crown of godhead hold to the doctrine that "man can become a god" — thus the "crown of godhood" is used to convey this belief.

We also see linking "terminology" between these groups and an esoteric organization called the Theosophical Society. Most people have never heard of the Theosophical Society, but it has had more influence on today's New Age agenda than any other single society. Jay Kinney writes in *Fringes of Reason:*

> The Theosophical Society was founded in New York in the fall of 1875 by a group of solid middle-class citizens whose mutual interest in the occult had brought them to the evening salons held by the mysterious Russian emigre, Helena Petrovna Blavatsky. Madame Blavatsky claimed to have received the text of her two voluminous works, *Isis Unveiled,* and *The Secret Doctrine* through dictation from Masters (spirit guides). Her successors, Annie Besant and Charles Leadbeater, formerly an Anglican priest, later converted to Buddhism, and later still, he became a leader in Theosophical Catholicism, freemasonry, and messianism. In a manner akin to that of today's most celebrated channelers, Besant and Leadbeater enthralled their public with clairvoyant revelations that have never been beat for colorfulness.
>
> The Theosophical Society was instrumental in introducing many Eastern religious concepts to the West . . . including reincarnation and karma. It also brought to the surface more esoteric metaphysical teachings such as those of the chakra system, the bodily aura, and the division of consciousness into several subtle planes — all concepts that have been embraced by New Age groups.[7]

There are some religious movements today, who like Anne Besant and Charles Leadbeater, claim to have "revelations," from

God, or departed loved ones. There is a form of religious divination that can be masked under the name of "the word of knowledge," or "the word of wisdom," or the "gift of prophecy." The proponents of these gifts classify them under "spiritual gifts." Some uses of these "gifts" are occultic, and some are just merely showmanship to part the unwary and his money.

Christian Divination

Ben Byrd, a former practitioner of these gifts, tells of one of his first experiences with a "Christian minister" who practiced this sort of divination.

> I was in a small meeting of about fifteen men . . . where a . . . prophet from California was speaking. He gave his little message and then began going around the room to each man. He would touch them and then quote several *totally out of context verses* which God was supposed to have given him to tell each man about his future. The combined effect of these verses was quite exhilarating to each man.
>
> Each of us received a congratulatory and exalting "word from the Lord." One man in the room had been involved in crooked financial dealings as a Christian businessman. The prophet predicted great financial respect and success for him as he "continued to serve God as he had in the past."
>
> The "word of knowledge" and the "word of wisdom" and the "gift of prophecy" are the most often abused manifestation. People's lives have been changed and some ruined by so-called inspired utterances of men and women who willingly accept the role of a spiritual prognosticator, a seer, a person supposedly given a peek into the future by God for the direction or edification of a person or group.[8]

Many times we can identify a false prophet if the stipulation on the blessing is that they must "give" or "plant seeds" in order to receive the promised benefit.

Ben Byrd says that he and his fellow pastors regularly used such "hooks" as, "The Holy Spirit is showing me someone out there with a financial need. If you will give your seed offering TODAY, God will miraculously meet your need."

Here is another example, "Yes, Lord, I hear that . . . there is someone in this room with a pain right here. God is healing you right now, in Jesus' name"

An example of the "word of knowledge" "on the wings of prophecy" would be as follows: "Thus saith the Spirit of Grace, 'my child, you have gone through much pain and suffering for my name's sake. You have not compromised nor have you stumbled over the enemy's barriers. Therefore, I shall openly promote you before men . . . .' "

When we examine the "gift of prophecy," we must put it to the biblical "test of a prophet." That is, that 100 percent of their prophecies must be 100 percent true, 100 percent of the time. If we hold this gift to be operational today, then it must be exercised according to biblical standards. The Bible declares that if a prophet does not meet the 100 percent standard of accuracy on all his prophecies, then he must be put to death.

Christians are just as attracted to the mystical as anyone else, and since Christianity does have "mysteries," we may find it very difficult to distinguish the true from the false. It is so easy to be inextricably drawn by the "mysterious" gift that can help us "see" into our futures as we attempt to "seek God's will" in relation to decisions we must make.

Eastern religions have made a tremendous inroad into a great number of religious circles in America. Many of the practices described in this chapter are a direct result of combining Eastern Mysticism with Christian teachings. A Gallup poll released in February 1978 reported that 10 million Americans were engaged in some aspect of Eastern religion and nine million in spiritual healing. Spiritual experience moved beyond the borders of the establishment so quietly that only the poll takers have measured the change.

The Plan

New Age literature is replete with "The Plan," which is to actually fulfill Bible prophecy by uniting the world into a ONE world church, and a ONE world economy. One of the New Age pioneers is Marilyn Ferguson, author of *The Aquarian Conspiracy, Personal and Social Transformation in Our Time*. The foreword was written by John Naisbitt, popular author of *Megatrends* and its sequels. He wrote:

The book is a powerful and wide-ranging view of

human possibility. Marilyn Ferguson addresses each area of daily living — from home to school to health to politics — with and illumination of the possibilities for expansion and renewal. For millions of "underground Aquarian" networkers who have read it, *The Aquarian Conspiracy* remains a source of inspiration and encouragement for continued striving toward renewal of ourselves, our society, and our planet.[9]

Notice their own description of their efforts, "underground Aquarian networkers." Could we be overreacting? I think not. This movement has been growing over a period of years, and it has become very carefully planned, organized, and, as they admit, networked in an underground manner. As they also admit, they have infiltrated virtually every strata of society.

George Trevelyan, author of *A Vision of the Aquarian Age, The Emerging Spiritual View*, says, "We have stressed that we are living in apocalyptic days. We must expect changes — social, psychological, and even in the outer world. Many think that man's treatment of the living earth has been such that this great sentient being will strike back in protest. Whether that be literally true or not, we are in any case in an epoch for which we have no precedent in history."[10]

Their influence in the political realm is vividly illustrated by U.S. Congressman, Charles G. Rose, in his introduction of "His Holiness" Tenzin Gyatso, the Dalai Lama. He had this to say:

> I have read the Buddhist concepts of karma and dharma . . . . I came to the conclusion that what it is all about is self-awareness. Enlightenment starts with the individual. And if America is to cope with its current dilemmas, it must reach a higher level of consciousness than the level at which our problems were created . . . . Political solutions are linked directly with spiritual growth, and that is why this visit is so timely for America. The message of Tibetan Buddhism is entirely consistent with our Jewish and Christian heritage . . . . All the world's religions lead along the same path.

Listed in the *New Age Catalogue* is the John F. Kennedy University in Orinda, California. "JFK University offers graduate and undergraduate education in psychology, holistic health, arts and consciousness, transpersonal psychology, clinical psychology, counseling, and much more. They also have the unique Graduate School for the Study of Human Consciousness."

A book entitled, *Speaking of Silence, Christians and Buddhists on the Contemplative Way,* is advertised, "For several years Christians and Buddhists have been meeting at the Naropa Institute in Boulder, Colorado, to share their understanding of meditations. As such, it has been an ongoing exchange among spiritual teachers. Despite some superficial differences, their experiences of the transcendent were very similar. Includes a complete resource of Christian and Buddhist contemplative centers in North America."

This should come as no surprise as our own President Bill Clinton and Vice-President Al Gore are radical New Agers promoting mysticism of a most dangerous sort. Masquerading as Southern Baptists, they have revealed their true identities in their own works.

The New Age of Clinton and Gore

Bill Clinton's beliefs and goals for America and her future leadership is vividly brought to life in the curriculum of his Arkansas Governor's School. There, the "cream of the crop" of Arkansas' youth are sequestered for six week periods to undergo intensive "brainwashing" and programming courses. The youth are told that they are members of an elite group who will someday shape and rule the world. They are taken on an "ego" trip, then bombarded with every sort of sordid programming technique one can imagine. They are discouraged from having contact with parents or the outside world while in this horrifying program. Parents of these youth report drastic changes in personality, depression, and a withdrawal from church and family.

Al Gore falls right into step with his commander in chief in his book, *Earth in the Balance: Ecology and the Human Spirit.* The work is a tome of New Age, one-world thought, and calls upon the reader to act on these issues. Gore denounces Bible-believing Christians, "For some Christians, the prophetic vision of the apocalypse is used — in my view, unforgivably." He then goes on to quote the deceased, excommunicated Catholic theologian, Teilhard de Chardin: "The fate of mankind, as well as of religion, depends upon the emergence of a new faith . . . . Armed with such a faith, we might find it possible to resanctify the earth."

Gore then describes what sort of faith he has in mind:

The spiritual sense of our place in nature predates

Native American cultures; increasingly it can be traced to the origins of human civilization . . . the prevailing ideology of belief in prehistoric Europe and much of the world was based on the worship of a single earth goddess, who was assumed to be the fount of all life and who radiated harmony among all living things. Much of the evidence for the existence of this primitive religion comes from the many thousands of artifacts uncovered in ceremonial sites. . . they seem to confirm the notion that a goddess religion was ubiquitous. . . until the antecedents of today's religions — most of which still have a distinctly masculine orientation . . . . The last vestige of organized goddess worship was eliminated by Christianity.[11]

Radical environmentalism is one of the strongest tenants of New Age teaching. As Christians we should all be seriously concerned about caring for the earth and protecting our environment. God has graciously made us custodians of this planet, so we must be good stewards of that which is entrusted to our care. However, radical environmentalism, such as that promoted by Al Gore does not even remotely resemble what you and I call "concern for our environment." Gore sees God in everything and every creature, and strongly encourages his readers to re-connect themselves to earth and the goddess.

Gore makes it evident that he is a pantheist, devoutly calling for a return to goddess worship — the worship of Mother Earth. He espouses the ancient Hindu dictum, "The earth is our mother, and we are all her children." He then poses a problem, then offers the solution — we have "lost our connection" to Mother Earth, and we must become "re-connected" in order to save our planet.

According to Gore, one of the evils that has severed our connecting link to Mother Earth is the emergence of a "patriarchal" religious system, i.e., Christianity. He points out that this degenerative patriarchal philosophy has even spilled over into the "family unit," and as a result has caused "dysfunctional families."

Gore says, ". . . The patriarchal figure in the family (almost always the father) effectively became God's viceroy, entitled to exercise God-like authority when enforcing the family's rules. As some fathers inevitably began to insist on being the sole source of authority, their children became confused . . . severely stressed by the demands of the dominant, all-powerful father."

Since he, and obviously Bill Clinton, are in favor of the "matriarchal" system, is it a surprise then, that so many women are now being appointed to positions of authority in government — including Hillary Rodham Clinton?

The Mystical Underground

The mystic world of the New Age movement is so well networked, and operates on so many planes, quietly and subtly, that it is very difficult for even the most devoted Christian to recognize it in all its various forms.

I'm sure you saw the multitude of television commercials on the book by L. Ron Hubbard, entitled *Dianetics*. It was promoted as a scientific work and sounded so factual and interesting that over eight million copies were sold! It literally took our nation by storm.

It is described in the *New Age Catalog:* "This is the very controversial 'science' of Dianetics." The author claims the reader can gain more confidence, relieve stress, better understand and control the mind, and find success and happiness. We find as we read further that it is a publication of the Church of Scientology.

Self-help is a major dimension of the New Age movement because most people are drawn to metaphysics and a New Age consciousness in search of something that will improve their lives.

"While most people are concerned with spiritual needs, self-help can include anything from subliminal aid in dieting to realizing psychic abilities," says Dick Sutphen, a leading New Age seminar speaker. "The key is that . . . you are not a victim, you can exert control over your life, you can shape your future, and you can transform yourself . . . the answers, your answers, lie within you — not in some established code of behavior or belief . . . . But, before we can accomplish a great many positive things, we have to eliminate a lot of negative programming . . . the organized religions are losing ground."

Spiritual Gifts or Psychic Surprises?

One common technique of deception used by these esoteric groups is gnosticism, the blending of true Bible teachings with occult doctrine.

The topic of "Spiritual Gifts" sounds like we are about to begin a Bible study class, doesn't it? As we proceed, what you must remember is that we are looking at a "parallel spirit world." There are certain terms and doctrines that have been traditionally thought of as uniquely "Christian," such as "spiritual gifts."

We automatically assume that these are gifts bestowed upon

Christians by the Holy Spirit. However, many people have been deceived and led into extremely dangerous territory by making such an assumption. Unfortunately, many who read this chapter will dismiss it as an attack on the genuine and neglect to "test the spirits." It is vitally important to make sure that the person is operating in the Holy Spirit and not on the parallel plane of the spirit of Antichrist. There is nothing to lose by testing the spirits, except maybe a little pride, and there could be your soul to gain. If we fail to heed the warning signs outlined here, we could become unwary "victims" of the master deceiver.

As much as I hate to quote an occultist to illustrate a truth, permit me to include excerpts from the writings of Swami Vivekananda:

> We are all like moths, plunging into the flame fired of the senses, though fully knowing that it will burn us. Sense enjoyment only enhances our desire. Desire is never satiated by enjoyment; enjoyment only increases desire, as butter fed into fire increases fire. Desire is increased by desire. Knowing all this, people still plunge into it all the time . . . . Even religion, which should rescue them from this terrible bondage to desire, they have made a means of satisfying desire. Rarely do they ask God to free them from bondage to the body and senses, from slavery to desire. Instead, they pray to Him for health and prosperity, for long life: "O God, cure my headache, give me some money or something!" The circle of vision has become so narrow, so degraded . . . . None is desiring anything beyond this body. Oh, the terrible degradation, the terrible misery of it! Of what little consequence are the flesh, the five senses, the stomach![12]

This man is well aware of the method by which the souls of men can be captured and enslaved. We would do well to reexamine ourselves to make sure we are not, like a moth, being drawn to the flame of destruction.

Zolar's Encyclopedia of Ancient and Forbidden Knowledge, has this to say of "spiritual gifts:"

> It follows that to each is given the spirit he desires: to one the spirit of wisdom, to another the spirit of science, to a third the spirit of faith, to a fourth the spirit of healing, to

a fifth the spirit of power, to a sixth the spirit of prophecy, to a seventh the spirit of tongues.[13]

This portion is from the Kabbalah, an ancient Jewish occult work. It also brings out the point that there are mediators, or points of contact, between the spirit world and the material world. Sometimes, we may recognize a "mediator," but if a person claims to have supernatural powers, please examine his faith by the Word of God.

A Miracle Settles the Issue

"A miracle settles the issue!"

Where have we heard this popular phrase? If we examine it, is it biblical?

"Even him, whose coming is after the working of Satan with all power and signs and lying wonders" (2 Thess. 2:9;KJV).

Here, it is evident that we are being warned that there are two kinds of miracles — those from God and those that are not of God.

If we use the slogan, "A miracle settles the issue!" as one of the biggest Tulsa faith preachers uses it, then we are leaving innocent people open to accept the works of darkness. In our present day and age, we are well aware of Satan's bid for the souls of men since his time is short. We therefore should be on even greater guard against deception than ever before.

Yes, I believe miracles DO happen, and yes, they can be from God, but a miracle doesn't settle anything in and of itself if you believe what God says on the subject.

The National Spiritualist Association of Churches USA, in article number 9 of their "Declaration of Spiritualist Principles" says, "We affirm that the precept of Prophecy and Healing contained in the Bible is a divine attribute proven through Mediumship."

Silver Birch, the spirit guide of England's Hannen Swaffer's home spiritualist development "circle" says, "Spiritual healing, either by *laying on of hands* or by *mental contact* . . . is a valuable part of the Other-Dide plan. Millions of sufferers, dismissed as medically incurable by hospitals and doctors, have found relief or permanent cures through healing mediums who channel divine power, sometimes being entranced, sometimes linking mentally with their spirit guides. These guides are often former surgeons or doctors still desiring to serve ailing humanity. Always the aim is to touch the sick person's soul, awakening it to awareness of spiritual realities."

If You Need Healing, Do These Things

What is *always* the *aim*? What is the most popular and sought after miracle in the world today? Yes, healing. Since money cannot buy health, and without health it is very difficult to enjoy money, health is probably the most valuable "commodity" today. Why do I use the term commodity? Because healing is being used to deceive and fleece the unsuspecting sufferer more than anything else.

TV evangelists use it as a "lead" to secure "your very best gift," or "seed." Revivalists use it to fill their tents and their offering buckets. And the occultists use it in the very same way — except their *aim* has a much higher price tag — *your soul*.

According to New Agers, Patanjali and the yoga sutras, everything is a product of mind and its modifications; there is no energy that is not connected to mind in some way.

The biggest problem is that the occult practitioner does not wear a sign around his neck, saying that he is practicing healing by occult means. Many dress like preachers, preach like preachers, and take up offerings like preachers. Most of them quote the Bible profusely, and ooze love from their very pores.

The practice of "laying on of hands" is biblical; however, we must not assume that everyone who practices prayer and laying-on-of-hands is doing it in a biblical way. As you can see, there is an occult practice of laying-on-of-hands that is very common and used on a regular basis by occult practitioners. There is so much harm being done by false prophets and healers that it makes my heart break. So many of the victims are like innocent "lambs being led to the spiritual slaughter."

Leap of Faith

As a pastor, my greatest desire is to teach the "whole counsel of God." I am charged to "feed the sheep," and "feed the lambs." If I am properly caring for my flock, I will also be watching for "wolves" who might attempt to creep in and harm the flock. I wish I could say that every pastor, preacher, teacher, and evangelist were God-sent — but even the Bible says to beware — that some are not.

Matthew 24:24 tells us, "For there shall arise false Christs, and false prophets, and shall shew great signs and wonders; insomuch that, if it were possible, they shall deceive the very elect" (KJV).

Leap of Faith, a movie starring Steve Martin, chronicles the antics of a counterfeit faith healer and his team of hucksters. Sadly, there are many "preachers," "divine healers," and "teachers" using God's name and profusely quoting Bible verses — many times taken out of context. The situation has become so bad that even Hollywood felt it deserved to become the topic of a hit movie. Fortunately, the movie included scenes showing a "real" healing, without a "healer," which even made the show biz preacher stop and look toward heaven.

The point of this entire chapter is to encourage the reader to test the spirits by the Word of God. Is the message totally, 100 percent, in line with Scripture? If there is the slightest area of doubt — *check it out.* These people may not just be false teachers but could actually be operating under occultic powers — and transferring them to you. That is what the New Age is all about. That is mysticism in its truest form.

Anointing, Psychic Energies, and Auras

Ben Byrd, Ph.D., a former charismatic pastor, gives us some very enlightening information in his book of "confessions," entitled, *One Pastor's Journey.* In his chapter titled, "Anointing, Psychic Energies, and Auras," we read:

> The anointing of God is a real and wonderful thing for which to be thankful. . . . The term "anointing," is much and casually used in the faith circles to mean a state of being and awareness of a power that is either upon or flowing through an individual . . . . I have found much of what is called anointing to actually be *psychic energy* or *psychic aura* which can be energized powerfully by entering an altered state of consciousness through much tongue-speaking . . . . Each time I entered this altered state of consciousness, I had a pure heart . . . thinking what I was doing was right and holy. I *thought* that what I was doing was from God.
>
> . . . there were tangible, physical, visible manifestations and changes when this power came on me . . . . When this energy is flowing, there is a tingling/burning in the hands that appears with white spots in the middle of the redness. As the "power" builds, the white spots merge into the center of the redness. The red is a feeling of exhilaration and excitement that is difficult to explain. It is as if lasers are coming out of the hands into a person's body.
>
> The tingling on the hands and arms is like a power field or force field that makes one feel he has magnificent

power. It is a heady feeling and an experience that can be addicting. I have heard faith teachers say quite often that they would do almost anything to have this power on them all of the time.

This psychic therapy or aura field of one person can be disrupted by areas of pain or discomfort or even disease in the body of another human being. Many, many times I have placed my hands three to six inches from the body of a person, moved my hands around their extremities without touching them and have been able to stop my hands exactly on the spot where pain or discomfort was located.

My highly agitated psychic aura had been disrupted by the person's troubles or pain-ridden psychic aura, and diagnosis of pain was possible. Of course, this was attributed to the gifts of the Holy Spirit.[14]

An excerpt from *Yoga Journal,* July/August, 1993, gives a quote from *Brain/Mind and Common Sense,* February, 1993:

When non-contact (psychic) healers focus their attention on treating an ailment, they emit significant bursts of electromagnetic energy, according to a study conducted by the Menninger Clinic.

The healers were studied in a room lined with copper. Researchers measured electromagnetic charges at the walls of the room as well as on the skin of the subjects. The surges in electromagnetic energy the healers produced were up to a thousand times greater than the normal fluctuations that accompany emotional responses — and greatly surpassed the bursts of energy that most non-healers studied were capable of generating.

The research team, headed by physicist Elmer Green, does not suggest that the electromagnetic energy itself is the healing agent. "If that were the case, a battery could do the trick," Green told *Brain/Mind and Common Sense.* Rather, they theorize that it is a side effect marking the presence of some as-yet-unknown healing factor.

The Metaphysical Handbook by David and Lucy Pond gives us some information on psychic energy and auras:

The different energy fields connected to the body are

much like various frequencies through which human life can be expressed. These energy centers are called chakras, for the Hindu word for wheel. The chakras are thought to be spinning wheels, creating a vortex of energy . . . . The chakras create the energy field that is known as the luminous body or aura, which surrounds all forms of life. There are some sensitive people who perceive the aura as colors or an electrical field . . . . How you physically, emotionally, mentally, and spiritually feel is reflected in the aura.

The chakras are the batteries for the body. They receive and store energy by interacting with universal life force . . . . Any blocks or restrictions that you might have in either reception or expression of this life energy will result in a malfunction of the organism as a whole and will be experienced as disease, discomfort, lack of energy, or an ailment.

The chakras can more simply be viewed as seven pathways to consciousness, which work together to create a sense of joy and holistic love for life.[15]

Faith Healers?

One particular traveling minister from Oklahoma, fast becoming a popular speaker on the "circuit," is building a reputation for extraordinary mysticism and esoteric manifestations of power. One of these particular manifestations is the filling of people's teeth with gold and silver in his healing services through his "special anointing:"

This man came to our church . . . . During the "miracle ministry" part of the service, I and one of our men in the church observed his tactics, and methods up close. We saw limb manipulation, psychic control, hypnosis, and crowd manipulation by voice tone and timbre. These emotional tactics were accompanied by highly skilled body language and gesture, as well as effective theatrics.

The time came in the service for the offering. He said nothing. He preached his sermon. No offering. He began to operate his charismatic witchcraft on the people. No offering. At a very emotional and crucial time in the healing line ministry, he stopped very dramatically and 'revealed God's plan' for the people if they would give in a sacrificial manner . . . . *He milked the people dry.* The offering was overwhelmingly large. His dramatics were peerless. His timing was flawless.

At the conclusion of the service and after he was ushered off to a room away from the adoring hundreds, this minister showed me his quartz digital watch. The face of the watch was blanked out. His explanation was that the anointing was so strong on him that the numbers would blank out on his watch. (Other Texas faith prophets have bragged about their watches blanking out, as well.) He took a great deal of pride in this watch trick . . . . I later learned from an ex-witch that this kind of trick is used often in witchcraft to lure and impress potential "marks." The actual electricity released from the body's excited psychic aura can affect some devices. It often disrupted my wireless microphone.[16]

Dr. Byrd also noted that at the close of this series of meetings, this evangelist took them, in his private plane, to a nearby city for his appointment with a *dentist*. "His teeth-filling ministry was not effective where his own teeth were concerned."

One of the most recognizable televangelists whose face pops onto the screen almost every time you turn your set on — in any city across America, tells the story of a woman named Mary. "After Mary committed her life to Christ, she seeded a vow into the work of God for her family to get saved . . . . To date, twelve of Mary's family members have been saved and are serving Jesus Christ as Lord and Saviour! . . . Furthermore . . . [he] lists 'Seven Steps of Faith.' Here are the first four. Step One: Let God know what you need from Him. New car. New job. Fitness. House. Finances. Salvation. Step Two: Give God your best gift. Step Three: Pray the prayer of agreement. Take the prayer sheet I've enclosed and lay your hand on top of mine [photograph] and pray, 'Oh God, I pray in agreement right now with my brother, Bob. By faith, we decree my miracle into existence in the name of Jesus. Father, I am giving my best gift to You, today; therefore, we ask that You rebuke the devil from my life according to Malachi 3. Amen.' Step Four: Mail your prayer request and your faith gift back to me, today!"[17]

"But Peter said unto him, Thy money perish with thee, because thou hast thought that the gift of God may be purchased with money. Thou hast neither part nor lot in this matter: for thy heart is not right in the sight of God. Repent therefore of this thy wickedness, and pray God, if perhaps the thought of thine heart may be forgiven thee" (Acts 8:20-22;KJV).

As we look at the spiritual gifts, we must recognize that they fall into different categories. Some were for edification, some were for service, and some were "authentication." During the time of the Apostles, they could not pass Bibles to everyone in the church because the canon of Scripture was still not complete. Today, we can check a preacher's or teacher's credentials by the Word, but in the early church there had to be some other distinguishing verification that they were indeed God's messenger. The gifts of healing, miracles, the gift of prophecy and tongues were "authenticating gifts" placing God's stamp of approval on the messenger. They were primarily "sign gifts" for the Jews. Since we have the completed canon of Scripture, we have a checkpoint to verify the messenger — by the message.

Why does the healer always find a deficiency in the sufferer as an excuse for the failure to receive healing? The Bible says:

> Is any sick among you? let him call for the elders of the church; and let them pray over him, anointing him with oil in the name of the Lord: And the prayer of faith shall save the sick, and the Lord shall raise him up; and if he have committed sins, they shall be forgiven him. Confess your faults one to another, and pray one for another that ye may be healed. The effectual fervent prayer of a righteous man availeth much (James 5:14-16;KJV).

In this passage, it is the faith of the person "praying," not the sufferer — yet, I have never heard a faith healer take any responsibility whatsoever for lack of results.

I remember my wife sharing her childhood experience with me regarding faith healers. Her Aunt Loreen had been crippled from birth, due to an accident at the hospital. Sharon's grandmother loved her little crippled daughter so much that she was compelled to attend every healer's tent meeting for miles around. The "carrot" was ever before them, today might be "the" day that they would be able to muster the right amount of faith to open the way to her healing.

One of today's foremost faith healers was just getting started in his healing ministry. Grandma and Loreen never missed a meeting and always worked their way through the long, tiring prayer line. Each time, two tearful ladies returned, and Loreen still had her crutches. Each time, they had been told that their faith was not strong enough to effect a miracle. Maybe they had not "planted enough financial seeds," if they only had more money to give to the healer — maybe — maybe.

Acquiring "enough faith" became an obsession with Grandma and Loreen. Since the deficiency was "always" placed on them, *they carried a tremendous load of guilt — for their lack of faith.* They felt that they had somehow failed God. Loreen went home to be with the Lord at the age of 50 — still a cripple — *until she entered the gates of her Father's House.* The years of agonizing torture endured by Grandma and Loreen still brings tears to Sharon's eyes.

Creating a Spiritual High

One of the popular trends today among divine "healers" is to "teach" others to heal. We hear of healing schools proliferating. Is it a "gift," or can it be "taught"?

One popular text is entitled, *A Course in Miracles.* Interestingly, this course was "channeled" by Helen Schucman. "Christian" in statement, the course opens our awareness to acknowledging Christ in all our brothers, and His presence in ourselves. Forgiveness is encouraged as the path to enlightenment for it reflects the law of heaven where giving and receiving are the same. Acknowledging that there are many versions of the universal curriculum and they all lead to God, the course specifically states "a universal theology is impossible, but a universal experience is not only possible but necessary."

This is almost a "universal truth" among those who concentrate on miracles and wonders — they throw out theology and concentrate on experience. They reason, "theology is divisive, experience is unifying."

This is the reason so many churches teach so little of the Word, like a moth to the flame, the senses crave to be stimulated. The music is usually carefully planned to increase the emotional flow (through the chakras) until everyone is at a crescendo of ecstatic experience.

David and Steve Gordon, wrote a description of New Age music that appears in the *New Age Catalog.* "In New Age music, intent is more important than form . . . . True New Age music is created with the intent of affecting the very consciousness of the listener; inspiring the mind and uplifting the spirit .... The essence of New Age music lies in the power of sound to actually vibrate the body's psychic energy centers [chakras] and transform our awareness. To awaken within us that spark of universal love and oneness."

Sometimes repetitious words and phrases are sung or chanted, much like the "mantra" of Hinduism, to increase the energy flow and awaken the chakras. This occult term is used to describe the energy centers located in the body that readily respond to stimulation of various kinds. Stimulation of the chakras can produce a "spiritual high," as well as sensual sensation.

Of course, most Christians do not know what a chakra is, and are probably not aware of what is actually happening in their own body during what they "think" are soul-stirring meetings. Most think they are being led into a "deeper spiritual experience." Again, test the spirits. We have video tapes of New Age worship services, and they very closely resemble some of the Christian church services we have attended.

Birthing and Rebirthing

Leonard Orr and Sondra Ray wrote in their book entitled, *Rebirthing in the New Age:*

> Rebirthing is about 99 percent pleasurable. Some people call it fun! ... It is impossible to adequately describe rebirthing. People usually tell us that it is far more wonderful than anything you said. Obviously, God's energy can heal all human problems. Rebirthing is the science of letting in God's energy, wisdom, and love .... Rebirthing is a spiritual gift! In itself it is perfect and harmless .... Your human personality can be filled with serenity, joy, health, and spiritual wisdom. Rebirthing actually delivers more of these things than we can possibly promise. The reality of them is far more glorious than words . . . rebirthing, as we experience it, is God's power in your human form. Only your own personal divine goodness can feel it and know it. It has been called a "biological experience of religion." To get the most out of your rebirthing experience, it is valuable to do it with a loving person who has been trained in the wisdom of how these spiritual energies work.[18]

Dr. Ben Byrd describes a practice very similar to this New Age experience, called, in Christian circles, "birthing" or "travailing:"

> The Spirit of Grace is saying that answer to our prayer is caught in the birth canal. We must travail in prayer in order to bring it to birth. Then, they begin to literally moan, groan, and wail very loudly. They will sometimes rock back and forth while holding their bellies. Many will fall on the floor and curl up in a fetal position while groaning and travailing.... They often would get on the floor on all fours and wail and scream until saliva would pour out of their mouths. Some people fainted from the exhaustive straining. Explanation was given . . . that these people were "out in the spirit."
>
> These kinds of manifestations will most often be found in the more zealous and elitist spiritual types who want deeper and more mystical spiritual experiences than previously enjoyed. One particular female travail teacher has an entourage of rather handsome young men who stand very close to her from the rear and hold her up with their arms around her. The purpose of this physical contact is to provide support while she is so far out in the spirit.
>
> She lays hands on people to impart love, healing, gifts, and the anointing to travail. I have actually witnessed her "special" effect on some men to require a cloth covering them as they lay on the floor recovering from her "ministry" of love.[19]

It is not enjoyable to write such sordid reports, but it is necessary to emphasize the extremes to which some religious groups have gone in the name of the Lord.

Miracles for Sale

Dr. Byrd also describes a convention in Charlotte, North Carolina:

> One of the guest ministers from Tennessee had been promising the people that IF they would praise and worship the Lord MORE than they ever had before, that the Lord himself (who supposedly had appeared to him right before the meeting, relaying the promise) would cause His glory to appear in a visible form.

You have never heard such shouting and praising and clapping and whistling and singing in all your life . . . emphasis on *works* and the *de-emphasis on grace* while using grace terminology. The praise and worship leader had led the congregation in approximately 30 minutes of lively songs and choruses. Then, the transition was made to a beautiful chorus, "O Magnify the Lord." For the next 45 minutes, the entire convention congregation sang this chorus over and over and over. The crowd was swaying. There were trance-like expressions on the faces of most of the people I could see. Eyes were closed, hands were raised, and bodies were matching the rhythm of the instruments.

. . . The song leader had encouraged the people to let THIS be the night when the glory of the Lord would visibly manifest, the popular "prophet" made a rather overdone attempt at omitting the offering for the evening . . . . Following the omission of the offering, the prophet began to stagger around on the platform, "drunk in the spirit," prophesying and making big statements that lathered the crowd into a frenzy . . . . The young protégé of the prophet made his way quickly to the platform and whispered something in the prophet's ear. The prophet informed the crowd that God had instructed the young protégé to preach that night's sermon.

The young preacher exclaimed that Jesus . . . had personally visited him in his hotel room in order to give him a message to give to the people that night. He began his message about giving sacrificially in the midst of famine and calamity. . . this young . . . preacher announced that Jesus had promised him that *whoever gave sacrificially that night would get back one-hundredfold return of that money within one year.*

An invitation was given, not to receive Jesus as Saviour, *but to give their money so that they could get their one-hundredfold return.* People ran to the front and placed jewelry, cash, checks, and some apparently placed notes promising stocks and land they owned. Many, many people completely cleaned out their bank accounts. Others liquidated their nest eggs and others their children's college education funds. Pressure . . . pressure . . . pressure . . . to give THAT NIGHT. An experienced salesman, who knows the subtle intricacies of the sales close and the counter-close and the promise of "no more opportunity to get the same deal," would have been very impressed with the polished display of these faith preachers.[20]

"I counsel thee to buy of me gold tried in the fire, that thou mayest be rich; and white raiment, that thou mayest be clothed, and that the shame of thy nakedness do not appear; and anoint thine eyes with eyesalve, that thou mayest see" (Rev. 3:18;KJV).

The Power Brokers

Then there is the promise of the "power to create" just as God did. He "spoke" and brought into existence things that were not. In many of our churches, we are told that we "can become little gods" and speak things into existence.

Shakti Gawain, an avowed New Ager says:

> When we create something, we always create it first in a thought form. The idea is like a blueprint; it creates an image of the form, which then magnetizes and guides the physical energy to flow into that form and eventually manifests it on the physical plane. When we are negative and fearful, insecure or anxious, we will tend to attract the very experiences, situations, or people that we are seeking to avoid. If we are basically positive in attitude, expecting and envisioning pleasure, satisfaction, and happiness, we will attract and create people, situations, and events which conform to our positive expectations.[21]

This doesn't sound like an occultist statement; it sounds like one of my Christian friends talking to me — in fact, it was only last month that I was reminded that "what you say is what you get."

Positive confession, or positive affirmation, has been around a long time — in the world of mysticism. It is only new in religious circles. It is found in Christian Science, Eastern Mysticism and Yoga, the Holistic Health movement, and a myriad of other esoteric organizations.

Marcus Allen, in his book, *Tantra for the West,* writes, "The measure of an affirmation's success is whether or not it soon manifests in your world. You should be able to manifest almost anything you are affirming within twenty-one days."[22]

Shakti Gawain says, "Keeping the image still in your mind, mentally make some positive, affirmative statements to yourself about it, such as: 'I now have a wonderful, happy relationship with _____.' We are really learning to understand each other. I now have a perfect, satisfying, well-paying job. These positive statements, called affirmations, are a very important part of creative visualization."[23]

A popular Texas televangelist gives his side of the positive affirmation theory:

> You can have what you say! In fact, what you are saying is exactly what you are getting now. If you are living in poverty and lack and want, change what you are saying. It will change what you have. . . . Discipline your vocabulary. Discipline everything you do, everything you say, and everything you think to agree with what God does, what God says, and what God thinks. God will be obligated to meet your needs.
>
> This is the law of prosperity: When apparent adversity comes, be not cast down by it, but make the best of it, and always look forward for better things, for conditions more prosperous. To hold yourself in this attitude of mind is to set into operation subtle, silent, and irresistible forces that sooner or later will actualize in material form that which is today merely an idea. But, ideas have occult power, and ideas, when rightly planted and rightly tended, are the seeds that actualize material conditions.

When we examine the origins of positive affirmations and positive confessions, we can only arrive at one conclusion — they are occultic. In the quote above from one of the foremost faith preachers, he even admits to occult power being involved. The term actualization also came from the minds of the mystics. If you examine a preacher's or teacher's statements carefully, you can usually trace the origins of his theology. You need only open your Bible and search the Scripture.

Seeking Pagan Gods

Berit Kjos, author of *Under the Spell of Mother Earth,* just sent me her paper on "Summoning Pagan Gods" which is an appropriate end to our treatise on mysticism:

Floods, droughts, plagues, and wars . . . . These calamities have crushed humanist dreams and shattered lofty illusions ever since people first turned their backs to their maker. With power that explodes our puny self-sufficiency, nature's fury and wildfire diseases prod people back to God — or demons.

Long ago, God promised to be a shield and a Shepherd to all who would trust Him. But, He withdrew His hand of protection when people spurned His love and sought pagan gods. Moses summarized His warnings: "When you have eaten and are satisfied, praise the Lord your God for the good land He has given you. Be careful that you do not forget . . . . Otherwise . . . your heart will become proud . . . . You may say to yourself, 'My power and the strength of my hands have produced this wealth for me' . . . . If you ever forget the Lord your God and follow other gods . . . you will surely be destroyed" (Deut. 8:10-20).

This warning couldn't be for us today, could it? Would "Christian" America — the world's pinnacle of progress and prosperity — be sliding into paganism? Is our nation reviving "other gods?"

It already has — in some unexpected places. Page 9 of the June 21 issue of *Christianity Today* carried a full page ad promoting *ancient amulets, goddess figures,* and other *idols* available from Sadigh Gallery. By calling an 800 number, interested buyers could get a free catalog peddling a wide assortment of "household gods that would have been worshipped by their original owners." Featuring *mother goddess* from ancient Canaan, Carthage, Mesopotamia, and Egypt, it explained that "Baal was the master of the land" and "Astarte was his consort/lover." Their exaggerated sexual characteristics . . . emphasize their fertility."

We are truly moving toward *Christ's triumphant return.* We see every form of occultism and mysticism creeping into once revered and Godly homes, publications, schools, institutions, organizations — and churches. Whether it is too late for our beloved country, I do not know. One thing I do know is that God stands ready and willing to forgive. If his people have been led astray into the mire of the esoteric, He stands, as a loving Heavenly Father — waiting for his child to "come home."

> But this I say, brethren, the time is short: it remaineth, that both they that have wives be as though they had none; And they that weep, as though they wept not; and they that rejoice, as though they rejoiced not; and they that buy, as though they possessed not; And they that use this world, as not abusing it: for the fashion of this world passeth away (1 Cor. 7:29-31;KJV).

5

The Media:

1. Modern Mythmakers

William T. James

Adolph Hitler's Nazi propaganda minister, Joseph Goebbels, is credited with having made a comment to the effect that if you tell a lie, and tell it loudly enough and long enough, it will eventually be accepted as truth. Certainly, Goebbels and his fuhrer proved that disquieting bromide correct in the case of pre-World War II Germany.

Propaganda that spewed from the National Socialist cesspool of hatred is but one twentieth century example of modern media's mythmaking malevolence. Goebbels' hellish lies, proclaimed that depressed Germany's hyperinflation-cursed plight as emanating primarily from unspecifiable Jewish moneybrokers. This successful, even brilliant, tactic galvanized the anti-Semitism that began in earnest to manifest itself on "Crystal Night" and culminated in the extermination camp crematoriums. The simple phrase "the Jewish problem" was a diabolical stroke of luciferic genius that truly validated the power of the written and spoken word.

The "final solution" was the Nazi term that perfectly defined and summarized the plan that would fuel the fires of Hitler's and Goebbels' engine of genocide. Satan used the Nazi media to totally pervert the great gift God gave human beings — a gift unique to man among all earthly creatures He created — the sense of speech.

Long before Hitler, Goebbels and the Nazis, God warned through His written Word:

> . . . The tongue is a little member, and boasteth great things. Behold, how great a matter a little fire kindleth. And the tongue is a fire, a world of iniquity, so is the tongue among our members, that it defileth the whole body, and setteth on fire the course of nature; and it is set on fire of hell . . . the tongue can no man tame; it is an unruly evil, full of deadly poison (James 3:5-8).

Goebbels' powerful media blitz against the Jews — and all others he and the Aryan elitists viewed as racially inferior — stands out as perhaps the most blatant episode of media mythmaking. Still, there are many media examples of more recent vintage that point to the truth in God's Word that prophesied "evil men and seducers shall grow worse and worse, deceiving and being deceived . . . ."

Should the reader infer that all journalists and entertainment media types are full of hatred as were Hitler? Does there presently exist a cabal of media elitists bent on engineering and carrying through a plot so devious as that hatched by Goebbels and his ilk during that earlier, desperate period of this troubled century? No. Not at all. There are many hard working men and women of impeccable integrity in media who day in and day out prove their immense worth to society.

Anyone who seriously examines the record of contemporary media tactics and their political and philosophical efforts, however, must note how they persistently try to funnel their various leanings. The media, particularly in America, almost without exception, now view issues and events of our day through reportorial senses stilted distinctly leftward.

Evidence that such a near-unanimous world view prevails within media — whether of the journalistic or of the entertainment variety — becomes clear when objectively pondering modern media mythmaking. More and more, media are being scrutinized and analyzed, even within their own ranks by their own kind. Why? Precisely because of the troubling dichotomy that exists, i.e., media's claim to independent, objective journalism (or pure entertainment) and the easily observable evidence that while they speak with many voices, their thoughts seem to issue forth from one mind.

Chapter 2 of this volume, entitled "The Revisionists: Changing Truth into Lies," deals in a broad, general sense with the damage that has been done and continues to be done by those who shape opinion through "telling lies long enough and loudly enough that they become accepted as truth." This chapter is an attempt to present and analyze a number of specific, recent, and hopefully familiar instances of media mythmaking.

They will never admit, of course, to being part of a concerted assault that has brought the world to the point that "evil men and seducers are growing worse and worse by deceiving and being deceived." It is because they are blind to their own involvement that these modern spinners of journalistic fables are pawns in the supernaturally manipulative hands of the most masterful of all mythmakers. They unwittingly, but willfully, constitute Satan's end-time propaganda machine — one far more dangerous than was Goebbels' demoniac propaganda ministry during its height of power to deceive.

The Politically Correct Paranoia

Having looked at the media in context of how it fits within the eternal scheme of things and the eons-old struggle between good and evil, let us take a different perspective and think briefly about how all those lofty matters have been and are being played out in everyday life.

To do this, it might be interesting to look at what contemporary journalists themselves have to say about some of the ways in which media detrimentally affects societies in today's world. It is refreshing when working members of the press recognize and try to alert others within their profession to harm being done to their publics, whom they like to think of themselves as nobly serving.

One such journalist begins an interesting piece on the subject with:

> Over casual drinks, a junior editor at one of our prestigious dailies assumed a lofty tone when my wife characterized his newspaper as liberal. "I would prefer to say," he sniffed, "that we conform to community standards."
>
> What standards? Which community? His community and that of many of today's newspeople is the one

Joseph Schumpeter called the New Class people who owe their jobs to the economic surpluses produced by capitalism, but who were taught in schools to dislike and distrust the market. The old hard-drinking front-page types are history, replaced by people with the tendency to think of themselves as a priestly class, elected by no one, believing themselves to be of the elect, and dedicated to making the U.S. more egalitarian, more multi-cultural. Despite some superficial gestures toward balance, politically correct thinking permeates the news and cultural coverage in most of our daily newspapers . . . .

My thesis is this: if newspapers hope to survive they would do well to be less concerned with a liberal social agenda and more with the lives, hopes and fears of their potential readers . . . .[1]

Another prominent writer says:

Proposition: The mighty American media have begun moving down the politically correct [pc] road long trodden by the colleges, they are doing so for many of the same reasons. The tilt to pc in the press is a sickening phenomenon, and it needs to be distinguished from the nearly maddening liberal bias often groaned about by the conservatives. Indications of this bias have been abundant for years. Polling data on reporters, editors, and anchormen have consistently shown such characters to be more liberal than the public as a whole. A carefully crafted survey done by the Center for Media in Public Policy show that 81 percent of high-level media folks had voted for George McGovern in 1972 (when he got only 38 percent of the popular vote).

Content analysis of the big stories over the years also shows persistent liberal biases . . . .

The media's pc problems obviously reflect increased fears in editors' offices that something might be published that would offend the various movements in the newsroom. This does seem odd. One might suppose the movement members would be fearful of jeopardizing the positions they hold, and disinclined to make waves; after all, good jobs in journalism have been scarce for quite a few years. But it doesn't seem to work that way. News stories about rumbles in the newsroom generally leave you with the impression that the disgruntled or furious staff feels it has the moral high ground, while the senior editors nominally in charge look nervous and defensive.[2]

According to this knowledgeable member of their own fraternity, the more mature members in the profession of journalism, who are primarily responsible for the news product that ends up before the public, are observably "nervous" and "defensive" in their own media domain. How much more so should we, who are the victims of journalistic mythmaking (political correctness) be concerned?

Just the Facts?

Surely, we should assume a higher level of alertness when "smooth talk by the media twists truth," which is the title of an article by L. Brent Bozell III. His article begins:

> In the era of instant communication, it is a prerequisite that journalists provide us with facts, nothing but the facts. Sometimes the media present sheer nonsense ("today it was revealed that Ronald Reagan's era of greed...") as truth through the use of politically charged data presented as objective science ("according to a national study by the reputable Public Citizen, the nonpartisan consumer-rights organization . . ."). More often than not, however, they ignore any semblance of scientific research and present as truth their own conventional wisdom.
>
> In this age of media truth squads and "reality checks," it's time for reporters to examine their own performances. It won't be pretty. Some media "truths" are sheer poppycock that drive billion-dollar government programs . . . .[3]

How does mythmaking by media affect everyday life in America? The writer ends his article by analyzing fables created by the dominant media about the years of Ronald Reagan's presidency.

> Take the myth that the rich grew richer while the poor grew poorer in the 1980s. This gem of a class-warfare weapon comes directly from the Democratic National Committee, and the media routinely take the bait. In the April 26 *U.S. News & World Report,* economic writer

David Hage argued: "The richest fifth of American families saw their incomes rise by a solid 13.9 percent, while
the income of all other U.S. families stagnated or de-
clined." On February 7, 1992, "NBC Nightly News"
reporter Keith Morrison went even further, declaring:
"The fact is that almost nine in ten Americans saw their
lifestyle decline." Nine in ten? Why wasn't Michael Dukakis
elected with 90 percent of the vote? Maybe because
Census Bureau data shows that average family income
increased among every fifth of income earners from 1982
to 1989. Median family income increased in every one of
those eight years, rising 13 percent after inflation.

The facts, Ma'am, just the facts.[4]

Media mythmaking influences can be just as influential and just
as damaging to a society when these shapers of opinion remain silent
about issues that impact the public. Cute labels and catchy labels often
serve the liberal media very well in filling what would otherwise be
a thunderous void of silence. They choose to say substantially nothing
about such dynamic issues as, for example, the total turn toward
socialism represented by the initial Clinton-recommended health care
system.

L. Brent Bozell writes of the media's dangerous failings in yet
another of his outstanding articles:

We are about to embark on one of the most important
debates in American history. Should the federal government control a national health care system in America? To
the liberal media, chopping off one-seventh of the country
and handing it over to the government is almost non-
controversial — and even non-ideological.

In this very ideological age, beware the marching
anthem of the left: "Labels really don't mean anything
anymore." The ideology of the ever-growing government
cannot march under its own liberal colors, because Americans regularly reject it. Ideological camouflage has been
honed to an art by President Clinton and journalists are
willing participants in the labels-don't-matter campaign.

This will certainly happen in the upcoming health
care debate, if history is a guide. For years now, 10 of the
large groups favoring government control over the health

care system escaped the "liberal" tag in *The Washington
Post, The New York Times,* and *The Los Angeles Times.*
They are instead "health advocates" or "consumer groups."
Add all those newspaper stories up, from 1986 to 1993, and
you count 49 ideological labels in 2,604 stories. That's a
whopping 1.9 percent.

Compare that with the Heritage Foundation, which
even with its own 'more government' health plan had
'conservative' next to its name in 217 of 370 stories (58.6
percent).

For a closer look, start in the most moderate-to-
liberal range, with the Brookings Institute, whose advocacy of school choice and airline deregulation might
obscure its regular stand in favor of nationalized health
care. In a three-year study, from 1986 to 1988, Brookings
was labeled 'liberal' or 'moderate-to-liberal' only 10 times
in 737 stories (1.4 percent).[5]

Modern media mythmakers are masterfully slick in their use of
labels and redefining, revisionist techniques. Still, it becomes unde-
niably obvious to the keen observer of these sly propagandists, who
serve one liberal cause after another, that a persistent softening-up war
is being waged. Why? To make America's citizenry ready to pour
more easily into the mold meant to reform everyone and everything
so as to fit nicely within the quickly restructuring world order —
perhaps that end-time system prophesied in Revelation 13.

The astute Mr. Bozell asks in this article: "As America tilts
aggressively toward European-style cradle-to-grave socialism, will
America's reporters continue to suggest that socialism's proponents
have no ideological agenda?"[6]

Who can deny that the media unashamedly attempt to indoctrinate their unsuspecting and/or uncaring public and that their fables
pervade every aspect of society? Name any issue of significance and
the modern media mythmakers' handiwork can be seen doing its
inculcating utmost to keep the public-mind headed in the herd-
mentality direction opposite of that in which Almighty God desires
people to go.

Whenever it is suggested that people be encouraged to return to
values consistent with those encompassed by the Creator's instructions (those found in God's Holy Word), the suggestion is caustically
assaulted as from the "religious right" and labeled "narrow-minded,"

"bigoted," "phobic," and in some recent instances, even "cultic." In truth, exhortation to moral sanity is the antithesis of all those mythmaker-ordained labels.

The topic doesn't seem to matter. Issues of minimal importance, such as whether sports teams like the "Redskins" or "Indians" should be renamed to reflect more sensitivity to ethnic groups, become a media "cause." More weighty issues, such as those involving free speech as it relates to prayer in public schools or legal protests near abortion clinics, bring out the media mythmakers in full force. On these topics, they ceaselessly endeavor to exert their minority liberal insanity upon majority common sense.

Their tactics include giving the liberal minority spokespeople the vast majority of air time and print space. At the same time, the media elite accuse those who desire to see society return to a saner, more moral pathway of being tyrants who want to "impose their values and belief system on others."

Remember the media assault on Vice President Dan Quayle when he dared question the image presented to the viewers of "Murphy Brown" when the character of that name chose to be an unmarried mother?

From Ludicrous to Murderous

Perhaps in no other issues of society are the media mythmakers more visibly manifest than in the inseparable matters of homosexuality and AIDS. Liberalism versus conservatism leaps to a new level when considering this two-headed monster.

Media mythmaking abruptly changes from merely ludicrous to murderous when the propagandists deliberately cover up the facts and twist truth about a disease that is potentially the most prolific killer of all time. To do this they must suppress crucial information about a virus that is one hundred percent fatal to those who contract it. Then, they carelessly report, and even deliberately lie, about the types of human behavior that perpetuate the killer disease. At the same time, they remain virtually silent about the only kind of behavior (abstinence or fidelity to one person within the bonds of marriage), which almost totally eliminates danger of contracting it. Such "journalism" is flagrantly irresponsible.

The news and entertainment media, by championing the homosexual lifestyle, while refusing to report and dramatize the true nature of Human Immunodeficiency Virus (HIV), are guilty accomplices of the plague that threatens the human race. Michael Fumento writes the following in his article titled, "Media, AIDS, and Truth:"

> *The Los Angeles Times* media critic, David Shaw, began the second of a recent two part series on public distrust of the media. "By almost any reasonable measure, the mainstream news media in this country are more responsible and more ethical today than at any time in their history." And yet he declared: "The public confidence in the news media is in steady decline."
>
> He just doesn't get it, that the public doesn't share his glowing appraisal of the media's performance. He also didn't get it three years ago when in an otherwise generally favorable review of my book, *The Myth of Heterosexual AIDS,* he noted scornfully that "time and again (Fumento) suggests the press deliberately misled the public about the likelihood of a heterosexual AIDS epidemic."
>
> There is no issue that shows so clearly the depths to which the American media has sunk. At the turn of the century, William Randolph Hearst is said to have boasted, "You supply the pictures, and I'll supply the war." The modern yellow press has in effect told the government and AIDS activists, "You supply the bulk materials, and we'll supply the war on AIDS."
>
> At least since 1986, the government has been misleading the public about the AIDS epidemic. That was when the Federal Center for Disease Control decided to move all AIDS sufferers of African or Haitian origin into the category of heterosexual AIDS cases. A man from Zaire who had sex with a dozen other men, shared needles and had a blood transfusion would, upon diagnosis, automatically be put in the heterosexual category because of his origin. The results of shifting all these cases into the heterosexual category was a doubling of that category from 2 to 4 percent of the total. Rather than cry foul, however, our media watchdogs jumped on the statistical artifact to launch their first wave of AIDS terror.
>
> *Newsweek* proclaimed, "The nation's heterosexual, drug-free majority cannot possibly take reassurance from (the fact that homosexuals and drug-addicts still account for most cases), for AIDS is not 'their' disease, but 'ours'."
> *U.S. News & World Report* declared, "The disease of

'them' is suddenly the disease of 'us'." *Time* warned: "The proportion of heterosexual cases is increasing at a worrisome rate. The numbers as yet are small but AIDS is a growing threat to the heterosexual population." The cover story of *The Atlantic* was, "Heterosexuals And AIDS, The Second Stage of The Epidemic."

Many of these feature covers with white, middle-class-looking men and women. *USA Today* declared: "Cases rising fastest among heterosexuals," with the more stately *Washington Post* asserting, "Data shows AIDS widening. Increase in the cases among heterosexuals is causing concern."

Indeed there is nothing that the media can't turn into a story on how the AIDS epidemic is exploding into the heterosexual ranks at last . . . .[7]

Fomento points out in his very excellent, quite revealing article how statistics have been put together and reported in ways that present a less than truthful story about the percentage of heterosexual AIDS cases within the total AIDS epidemic. The mythmakers were and continue to be at work to protect those who engage in the politically correct lifestyle that is the primary cause of the disease's exponential growth.

Why would they want to create the myth that there is a heterosexual AIDS crisis equal to that being experienced by the "gay" community? It is not farfetched to surmise that a desire to dip into a much-expanded pool of federal dollars and to solicit greater contributions from the general public is a major factor.

The Media's Deadly Silence

Media dwell almost exclusively on so-called human rights aspects of the "gay lifestyle." At the same time, they are silent about the true facts surrounding the unmistakable link between homosexuality and AIDS. Expediently, they skirt the issue by portraying that unnatural sexual activity as no more than a minor factor in the mix of the disease's pathology.

D.A. Miller, a noted author, lecturer, and researcher on the facts about AIDS, sheds fascinating yet disturbing light on the realities of the disease — truth that has for too long been withheld from the peoples of America and the world. Media silence is not only inexcusable, it has proven to be deadly!

Speaking during a presentation on her findings, she said:

> From the very beginning in the United States there were groups formed because the great fear among the homosexual community is that this disease (AIDS) will be perceived as purely a homosexual problem. And since, among homosexuals, (it was) felt that no one cared for them, they would just be left alone to die. There would be no funding, no studies. So, immediately groups like ACTUP were formed, and other organizations, to try to draw attention to the problem — (that) homosexuals were dying of the disease that was then called "GRID." And almost immediately it was renamed, (changed) by lobbying, to "AIDS" (Acquired Immune Deficiency Syndrome) to draw away attention from the fact that it was largely the homosexuals who were dying. As a matter of fact, the statistics have held that around 90 percent of the deaths (from AIDS) have been in the homosexual community in the United States.[8]

Miller continues later in her presentation:

> AIDS, no matter how you discuss it, is a communicable disease. In California, (to give one example), if a doctor encounters someone with a communicable disease he must report it. There are 58 communicable diseases he must report by law. If, (however,) he reports someone who is HIV positive, there is a $10,000 fine (the doctor will face paying).
>
> AIDS is a disease that is protected by the government. How did that happen? Because it was perceived as a civil rights issue . . . for the first time in history we have a disease with civil rights . . . . Remember, according to regulations policed by the Center for Disease Control (CDC) if your child goes to school, and has measles, they're sent home right away. That is the way you take care of communicable diseases — you isolate them. Again, it is very strange, this is the first disease in history that is a civil rights issue rather than a communicable disease.[9]

She tells startling facts about how the CDC has altered the statistics about AIDS and the way in which the numbers are gathered, translated, and disseminated. As a result, the statistics are rendered useless for the purpose of ascertaining truth about the disease and its progression. Of the figures that are thought to be relatively reliable, she reports:

> In Kinshasa, Zaire, for instance, about 70 percent of the people are testing HIV positive. Seventy percent in one country! There are countries in central Africa where the projections are that in two or three more years there will be no people. It's that bad.
>
> In San Francisco, about 90 percent of the homosexuals have AIDS, now. (What about) the statistics that say (the disease) is (rising more quickly) among women than it is (among) men? (That is so) because most of the homosexuals already have it.[10]

Keeping the Plague Alive

Miller, in the presentation of her well-documented research information, analyzed the causes and effects of this terrifying disease after first asking the important question, "Who allowed the growth of the AIDS virus? How did it keep going (from the very small number who first had it?)":

> There are various groups that are responsible for this. These groups, because of greed, apathy, perversion, manipulation, or irresponsibility, have combined to cause wholesale slaughter. This plague, like most plagues of the past, could have been averted. . . . (It has been pointed out that) back in the Old Testament, God gave the people information about what to do with communicable diseases. You isolate. That's how leprosy was handled. More people have died from leprosy than any other plague. Yet, every time isolation was used it worked . . . . (if) combined with hygiene (recommended in the Old Testament), such plagues throughout history (need never have happened.)

Correctly, Miller says:

> But, isn't that true? God could spare us so much heartache, but we keep forging ahead doing our own thing.
>
> Homosexual groups and other proponents of a philosophy that advocates "if it feels good do it," came up with

all these civil rights issues that kept medicine and the CDC from tracking the disease's progression and doing what should have been done . . . . The problem is that both the heterosexuals and the homosexuals have been lied to in many ways. We've been told to call the homosexual lifestyle "gay." We've been told that being gay is just an alternate lifestyle. We are told that "same-sex" partners are just as loving and committed as heterosexual marriage partners. We have been told never to say that being a homosexual is by choice, rather to recognize that people are "born gay." I say homosexual conduct is not "gay," but tragic. This behavior leads to endless searching for love, to disease and to early death.

She then gives some staggering statistics about the "gay lifestyle."

Are homosexuals as loving and committed as we are told? The statistics would not say so. In 1978 a study found that 43 percent of white, male homosexuals had sex with more than 500 different partners in their lifetime. Twenty-eight percent estimated that they had more than a thousand partners. As it could be accurately measured, about 1 percent of homosexuals have 10 partners or less in a lifetime.

The media never mentions these facts or the perversions in which homosexuals routinely engage — including those involving man-boy abominations. D.A. Miller later points to media's complicity in the deadly deception of silence that continues to cover up most all the frightening realities involved with the AIDS terror.

Who else keeps this AIDS plague alive? The media does. Even those who would like to tell the truth, when they start telling the truth, they lose their contacts. Nobody will call them back. It's called "political correctness." They lose their jobs without contacts. We notice that sometimes the liberal media has a slight slant. This slant is because AIDS is (to the politically correct ones) a civil rights issue — the rights of the infected people over the rights of the, as yet, AIDS-free people.

Interestingly, the *Peoples' Daily World*, a Communist newspaper, objected to routine testing because of dangers to constitutional rights in America. At the same time they were objecting, by 1990, the Soviet Union had performed over 50 million blood tests, screening its populations and those of other Soviet bloc nations, including three-quarters of Cuba. As of December 1988 less than 100 people had HIV in Russia, and only three or four had died. Cuba has the same population as New York City. New York City has had 42,737 deaths from AIDS, Cuba has had 159.

This epidemic didn't have to happen. By making it a protected disease, people have been murdered.[11]

"Safe Sex" and Other Fables

Reckless, irresponsible members of media are guilty of endangering the public, whether overtly lying about AIDS and its realities or covertly failing to report facts people need to know in order to remain safe from this wildly-mutating virus. While the media elite are not the only ones guilty in the spread of HIV, their culpability is as great as that of those who continue to engage in sexual activity despite knowing they themselves have HIV.

The media, who pride themselves in their adherence to the highest standards of investigative journalism, more often than not find their backbones dissolving to jelly when confronted with the truth about AIDS versus their obligation to journalistic integrity.

One most dramatic case in point: Media echo the fable that it is possible to have "safe-sex" in the age of AIDS by always using a condom. In addition to disseminating that lie, they, through their deadly silence, fail to tell their publics that the intrinsic voids (that is the porous holes) in a condom are 5 microns in size. The HIV (the virus that causes AIDS) is one-tenth of a micron in size, or four-millionths of one inch. A human sperm is 450 times larger than the HIV virus. Thus, while the condom might in many cases prevent pregnancy, it obviously cannot prevent the contraction of AIDS.

Devoted to Killing

Consider three blazing issues of our everyday society: abortion, homosexuality, and, as of late, euthanasia. All three are devoted to killing.

Abortion claims millions of babies every year. Homosexuality, which by its nature is not a "gay lifestyle" but a tragic death style, is spreading its mode of genocide exponentially. There is a building sentiment for euthanasia, with a doctor being allowed to execute his victims at will while we watch helplessly from our living rooms. In every one of the foregoing issues, news media bring us these stories with a decided sympathetic leaning toward the abortionists, the homosexuals, and "Dr. Death."

These issues encompass death by the actions of man — death that runs counter to God's sole authority to give and take life. To repeat: Killing human beings is high priority on Satan's agenda; the death — body and soul — of men, women, and children everywhere is his main objective.

God's Holy Word tells us, "Be sober, be vigilant, because your adversary, the devil, like a roaring lion, walketh about, seeking whom he may devour . . ." (1 Pet. 5:8).

The Lord told Noah during those antediluvian times, "The earth also was corrupt before God, and the earth was filled with violence. And God looked upon the earth, and, behold, it was corrupt; for all flesh had corrupted his way upon the earth" (Gen. 6:11-12).

Many biblical scholars believe there is significant reason to think the people of that pre-flood day had become genetically as well as sinfully contaminated. That a disease much like AIDS, perhaps AIDS itself, had infected the entire human race, except for Noah and his family. Because they had remained apart from the horrendous activities of that society, they were not infected.

Jesus Christ, while He stood on the Mount of Olives at Jerusalem, spoke of another generation — that of end-time man — which will suffer corruption so complete that if He did not personally return to earth, all mankind would perish. In addition to the slaughter at Armageddon, this massive killing must surely include incurable diseases — particularly those prophesied for the time of Apocalypse — that would infect all flesh on earth if the plague was not supernaturally canceled.

"And except the Lord had shortened those days, no flesh should be saved . . ." (Mark 13:20).

The Media:

2. Propaganda Pushers

Ray Brubaker

An editorial in *Military Review* (May/June, 1993) states, "The media is in trouble with the American people."

The primary attack seems aimed at television, apparently perceived to be the main culprit. "Television network news — wherein news is entertainment — has fallen from the pinnacle it once held!" In fact, the editorial continues, "Several recent opinion polls have ranked television news as last among the media in accuracy and unbiased coverage." In addition, "A near majority of the public now sees the major news weekly magazines as biased in their reporting, and newspapers rank only a bit higher."

Howard Kleinberg, writing for the Cox News Service, asks: "What is the media?"

He quotes *Webster's Third Collegiate Dictionary* as saying "media" is all forms of communication. But he adds that the mammoth *Oxford English Dictionary* says it is nothing more than the plural of "medium," and defines that word nine different ways, none of them specifically justifying the contemporary usage of the word.

He says when he started in the news business, those in print and electronic journalism were called "the press." He points out that the word "media" entered our lives through terms such as "mass media," as in "mass hysteria" and other phraseology.

The incidents of the exploding Chevy trucks in which smoking devices were attached in such a way as to cause the trucks to catch fire when struck by another vehicle comprise but one blatant example of the news media's intrusive attempts to influence the public mind and shape opinion. The network in question reportedly faked the crash results to enhance their contention that the trucks presented safety concerns for the consumer. Such faked footage, laments Marvin Kalb, a former NBC correspondent, "blurs the line between hard news and entertainment. It undercuts the integrity of a program and the news division."

CBS, which carried the story, found Joe Peyronnin, vice president, admitting the incident cast a shadow over the profession as "all broadcast journalists watched it with horror." He added, "We have to redouble our efforts to (present) fairness and accurate reporting."

Nothing But Contempt

When it comes to fairness and accurate reporting, the National Right to Life committee expresses concern, a spokesman saying, "nothing is more frustrating than the shameful and irresponsible manner in which our side of the abortion issue is dealt with by the national news media and the American television industry."

Wanda Franz, president, notes, "In the area of television news reporting, our major networks — ABC, CBS, and NBC — have shown nothing but contempt for the right-to-life movement." She laments, "Pro-life supporters are commonly referred to as 'extremists' or even 'fanatics.' In contrast, the views of anti-life people are described as 'deep commitments.' "

She explains, "When national surveys show that 90 percent of the people who gather, write, and report our news support abortion, no wonder Americans are still in the dark about this life-and-death issue."

Observes Franz, "In 20 years of legal abortion, we've never seen NBC, CBS, or ABC air a major news report focusing on the slaughter of the 4,400 babies who are killed by abortion every day!"

It is inevitably honest to ask whether such obviously slanted coverage is fair.

Dr. James C. Dobson of Focus on the Family relates biased reporting of the media. He notes, "On February 1, 1993, *The Washington Post* wrote a terrible article about Christians who called the Capitol to protest Clinton's lifting of the homosexual ban. It referred to them as "poor, uneducated, and easy to command.""

Writes Dobson, "How about the recent political cartoon drawn by Pat Oliphant, depicting fundamental Christians as rats dragging the Republican elephant into a mission with a "Jesus Saves" sign above the door? Can you think of any other minority group that could be characterized as rats?"

And he refers to Hugh Downs, host of ABC's "20/20," comparing Christians to Hitler.

Not only is news reporting by the media "biased," but it is becoming common practice for reporters to identify the position of Christians who oppose homosexuality, abortion, etc. as guilty of "hate-crimes."

Billy James Hargis writes, "I know positively that the liberal/ leftist news media that owns ABC, CBS, NBC, and CNN, do not want you to know that they fully intend to get the Supreme Court not only to penalize people that commit murder or theft, but they want to also penalize those who express views that are contrary to the atheist/ liberal/Socialist viewpoints."

Rodney King — Media's Darling

The effect the media has on the nation's population is reflected in the Rodney King beating that was shown on television hundreds of times. The sentencing of the two police officers, Sgt. Stacey Koon and Officer Laurence Powell for only two and one-half years and not for more time was evidence "the justice system does *not* always work," stated our local newspaper editorial.

In broadcasts on Trinity Broadcasting Network, we took the position that men in law enforcement must be respected. As we read in Romans 13:4:

> For he is the minister of God to thee for good. But if thou do that which is evil, be afraid; for he beareth not the sword in vain: for he is the minister of God, a revenger to execute wrath upon him that doeth evil.

Without question, the videotape being shown over and over, seemed to stir up hatred and resentment against the police officers who contend they were simply doing their duty. And, they did not use "swords" as mentioned in Scripture, but stun-guns and night-sticks.

Testified one TV viewer, "For 13 months I've seen a 90-second clip of videotape that shows a man face down on the ground and four police officers taking turns hitting him with batons." She continues,

"It wasn't until . . . on CNN, that I was finally given the opportunity to see the tape in its entirety. Here I saw a man who had been hit four times with 50,000 volts of electricity continue to fight and resist police. I saw him lunging at a policeman. I saw him defying all normal reaction to pain, and behaving as if he could feel no pain. I saw a brief moment when he lay still, and at that moment one policeman reached for his handcuffs. Then the man was up on his hands and knees again."

Blaming the media, she writes, "I wonder, who decided to limit the public's access to the entire tape!"

Laurence Powell, one of the policemen, heard us report on the Trinity Broadcasting Network, and wrote as follows: "I watched your show with great interest . . . bracing at first for another attack upon my colleagues and I[sic] from an under-informed source. However, I was gladdened by your truthful and courageous report. Even though your report only touched the surface of the lies, deceit, and treachery involved in this case, it was a brave and true stand to take in a society with sin as its foundation."

Officer Powell wrote, "I am a Christian, and my faith has been tested greatly during the last two and one-half difficult years. I attend Grace Community Church in Sun Valley, California, ministered by John MacArthur. My Christian friends and Christians from all across the nation have offered me support and prayers that has[sic] helped me to endure this trial called the 'Rodney King case.' It has also been helpful as I try to stand up to constant lies and abuse from the media and small-minded political groups seeking, not justice, but ways to further their own worldly positions."

Powell concludes, "Thank you for being a voice crying in the wilderness of today's satanic[sic] ruled media. I pray that your voice will remain strong and faithful, and stand steadfast against Satan's attacks until we are home with Christ."

What a grateful letter, and one which is at the same time a reflection on the media's position against policemen.

Today, Rodney King roams the streets — a local hero — reportedly with a $53 million lawsuit against the city for violation of his civil rights. Actually, he was on parole for an armed robbery in which he allegedly crushed the skull of a Korean grocer after stealing about $200, having served less than a year for that crime. He previously had allegedly shot a woman video store owner with a .22 caliber gun and has tested positive for cocaine and heroin twice since March 3, 1991. He was caught speeding — while driving drunk the night of this encounter, and though his parole was never revoked, King is free, while the officers who sought to arrest him are sentenced to jail for violation of his civil rights. He has been arrested four times since the videotape was made and shown.

U.S. Attorney General Janet Reno, asked about the case, refused to comment on it.

A local citizen has commented, saying: "I am outraged and sick of the media. First of all, the Los Angeles riots may not have ever happened if the media did not thirst on the racial hatred that ignorant people feel." She writes, "Let it be known that Reginald Denny was on the second page of the paper because he is a white victim. Rodney King was on the front page every day because he was a black victim. The media did that because they knew what would grasp our attention." She concludes, "I'm outraged to see the media take control of the American people's thoughts and feelings. I feel like a horse with blinders on, being allowed to see only what others want me to see."

Media — Arm of the Government?

Louis Beam, news correspondent says, "One critical lesson for the future that all thinking citizens must learn from Waco, is that the *news media* must henceforth be considered as the propaganda arm of the government."

T. L. Caldwell writes, "How strange, and contradictory, that Rodney King, not withstanding the excessive force used by the officers, was a convicted felon, on probation, a drunkard, wife beater, wielding a lethal weapon (car) in public at high speed, resisting arrest initially (per the video), a real threat to the public, precipitating a major, virtually nationwide riot, hailed as a hero for being a victim having his civil rights violated."

Be ye therefore ready also; for the Son of man cometh
at an hour when ye think not (Luke 12:40).

6

The Utopians:

Reshaping the Global Monetary System

Phil Arms

"IT'S THE ECONOMY, STUPID!"

The century's most compelling and ingenious political slogan that signified the "spirit of the age" was fomented during this nation's 1992 presidential campaigns. It appeals to one of the ugliest facets of man's fallen nature . . . his greed. And, it was the Democratic National Campaign Committee that birthed the vote-winning slogan that turned the heart and mind of the American electorate away from such gargantuan social issues as abortion, prayer in schools, homosexuality, family values, and a candidate's personal integrity to the issue of . . . "money."

The Democrats ingeniously succeeded with their slogan, "It's the economy, stupid!"

It seems this arrogant, yet immensely successful appeal, aided by media-induced fear of the perceived to be failing economic policies of the Bush administration, was most intimidating to John and

Jane Q. Public voters. No one wants to appear stupid. And surely the media, the polls, and Phil Donahue could not all be wrong . . . could they?

To further fuel the controversy, came Ross Perot with his wit, his charts, and "crazy-aunt-in-the-basement-that-no-one-wants-to-talk-about" stories.

The net result was that much of the American electorate apparently feared an impending economic catastrophe. This fear, it is reasonable to conclude, caused a plurality to vote for "love of money" over morality and quality of character in leadership issues. And thus, Bill Clinton became the forty-second president of the United States of America.

But, is America — and for that matter, the world — really on the precipice of bankruptcy and universal depression? Are we destined for a monetary collapse, social upheaval, anarchy, and massive starvation in America, and if so, why can't somebody do something about it? If it comes, will I have a job? Will my company fold with the rest of society? How will I pay the rent, feed my children, survive such an unimaginable nightmare?

Well, for once, the would-be architects of correct, political thinking have been as the proverbial broken clock that is right twice a day. They are right about the economy being central to our nation's problem (though hardly to be exclusively blamed are the concurrent Republican administrations). Second, they are right in that we, as a nation, have been quite "stupid" for quite a long time, though not in the ways they have assessed.

Perhaps rightly angered over and unresponsive government, a frustrated electorate — though, at the same time, deluded, gullible, and naive — rambled into the polls to vote out a president because he backed out on a pledge of "read my lips, no new taxes." They chose, instead, a man whose first priority (other than to put homosexuals in the military and in administrative posts) was to hand Americans what many are calling the largest tax increase in history.

We are stupid still, it seems.

However, the millions of hopeful, though unengaged Americans, who voted for "the change" are acting as mere pawns in the hands of the real power brokers of this age.

The Elitist Utopians

Conspiracy theory? No. The Scripture does not deal in theory. It deals only in absolute fact, and the Word of God clearly outlines the events currently unfolding in national and global economics.

God's Word needs no confirmation from the present nor the future. The present and the future are validated (as is the past) by the Word of God. He has "announced," therefore, it must be done, and done so according to the "announcement." Man must bring his life into harmony with God's announcements or face the consequences of actions that fly in the face of those announcements.

You and I are witnessing a dramatic, and soon-to-be traumatic, unfolding of prophesied events that will usher in the most diabolical, horrifying moments of history. And none of these events, especially the economic ones, are happenstance.

President Franklin D. Roosevelt, a secularist, once said, "In politics, nothing happens by accident. If it happens, you can bet it was planned that way."

I suggest to you, as have others more wise than I, that there is an elite group of men (plus a few women) who are, this very moment, planning a worldwide, monetary disaster whose ultimate end is to create global panic. This panic will provoke the people of the world not only to accept but literally to beg for the implementation of a system to bring back economic stability and order.

Ultimately, men will trade not only precious liberties, national sovereignties, and personal rights for this "pseudo-monetary security" but even their very souls.

And who are these "elitists" being manipulated by demonic powers, whose plan it is to usher in the New World Order, complete with its cashless society run by the high-tech wizardry of this computer age? Peter Metzger, scientist-journalist, calls them "coercive utopians,"[1] though he stops very short of their true identities, goals, and motivations.

As utopians, they pretend that man can achieve a state of perfection if an "evil-less" society and environment can be accomplished. This philosophy, of course, is humanistic and espouses the idea that man only needs an ideal society to produce a "heaven on earth," or if you would, a "utopia." Mr. Metzger was right to call them coercive because these utopians feel that the "ends justify whatever means are necessary" to move society toward their dream of utopia.

One of the greatest obstacles to their great society, in their minds, is the economic systems in the United States and other Western nations. Their primary desire is to level the economic playing field.

Bear in mind, these are the *idealists* whom the real power

brokers are manipulating to maneuver society toward their greedy and diabolical ends.

Instant Crowds

The utopians are the pawns whose influence and power are used to produce the desired results of an insider group that is smart enough to appeal to our passions and fears as opposed to our intellect. The utopians, for the most part, are unaware of the dark powers that motivate and stimulate them, yet they control virtually every channel, avenue, and outlet of the media and mass communications in the world.

Via satellite and high-tech audio and visual capabilities combined with contemporary special effects and techniques, they capture the heart, mind, and emotions of millions around the world, twenty-four hours a day. These mental and emotional masters of manipulation exhibit almost supernatural talent in the ability to push all the right buttons and pull all the right strings necessary to mold public opinion and control the thinking of the masses.

Economic advisor and commentator, Larry Abraham, recently observed that:

> In our mass communications society, with its instantaneous satellite transmissions and the whole information overload, the news media have become like so many sharks in a feeding frenzy. Each week some new crisis is trotted out, complete with "special reports," "special editors," and "extended coverage." *Any voices of dissent are ignored or drowned out.*[2] [Emphasis, mine.]

Consider also, this observation about the power of the elite to manipulate men's minds by Gustave Lebon in his brilliant work *The Crowd:*

> "When studying the imagination of crowds, we saw it is particularly open to the impressions produced by images . . . . These images do not always lay [sic] ready to hand. But, it is possible to evoke them by judicious employment of words and formulas. As with art, they possess, in sober truth, a mysterious power . . . they cause the birth in the mind of crowds of the most formidable tempests."

And, note this:

Reason and arguments are incapable of combating certain words and formulas. They are uttered with solemnity in the presence of crowds and as soon as they have been pronounced, an expression of respect is visible on every countenance and all heads are bowed . . . . Certain transitory images are attached to certain words. The word is merely, as it were, the button of an electric bell that calls them up.

Incredibly, Lebon penned these observations more than nine decades ago — in 1895. Can you imagine what his comment would be today after watching Koppel, Rather, Brokaw, Jennings, et al? Talk about images, words, and formulas!

Today, the capacity for creating "instant crowds" is almost limitless. We have become members of an unthinking crowd, collectively lying in bed watching "Nightline." And as Lebon goes on to emphasize, "It is not, then, the facts that strike the popular imagination, but the way in which they take place and are brought to notice . . . . To know the art of impressing the imagination of the crowd is to know at the same time the art of governing them."

Abraham is right, but again, he, too, stops short in his profound and unique appraisal of these "coercive utopians" and their manipulators, the smaller "insider group."

A Worldwide Conspiracy?

While Satan and his co-conspirators work to capture the world's monetary system, and ultimately usher in his day of coronation as king of the earth, the unsuspecting masses seemingly grope along in blind cooperation, apparently believing what they are told by the "coercive utopians."

You may ask, "What is wrong with utopianism?" It means, we want a better world, greater human achievement, global peace and prosperity, the abolition of poverty, racism, sexism, and other social injustices. Sounds good, doesn't it?

However, God's Word tells us repeatedly, but specifically, in 2 Timothy 3:1, "This know also, that in the last days perilous times shall come."

The word TIMES in this verse in its Greek origin, according to Dr. Trench, specifically means "a critical, epoch-making period foreordained by God when all that has been slowly and often without observation, ripening through long ages, is mature and comes to birth in grand decisive events which constitute at once the close of one period and the commencement of another."

In short, we are living in a time prophesied, foretold millennia ago, of things that would surely come to pass.

That time is now, and we are witnessing those "grand decisive events" that will close this period. It is not going to be a time frame where man gradually evolves a utopian society. To the contrary, humanity is about to witness the fangs of the serpent in ways not known before.

Tragically, even many Christians are caught up in the great deception. Obviously, many in the Church are living for the moment — and the money — shaped by their world.

In their secular book, *Social Deception by America's Power Players,* Rael Jean Isaac and Erich Isaac clearly stated the problem when they wrote:

> Perhaps most important, the utopians have had an enormous impact on the way we think. They write many of the articles we read . . . . We watch them on the panels that interpret current events for us on television. We hear them from the pulpit and our children listen to them in the college classrooms. To a large extent, they have set the fashions in thought and fashion is every bit as tyrannical in ideas as in clothes. Publishers churn out their books. (To take only one example, let any reader go to a bookstore and compare the number of books attacking nuclear energy with the number supporting it.)[3]

The utopians never could have been so successful in their seduction and brainwashing if the pulpits in America's churches had been awake and if Christians had known Bible prophecy.

The utopians never sleep.

The central forces behind this grab for global wealth and power have a fascinating, ambitious, and very feasible plan. While most of the Church and the nation have ignored the profound ramifications of current events on the monetary front, these power brokers have moved their agenda steadily forward.

The few voices who have been raised in an attempt to expose this conspiracy have been ridiculed, maligned, ignored, and marked off as "extremists with conspiratorial delusions." One such secular prophet has been financial planner, advisor, and author, Larry Abraham. In his best-selling book, *Call It Conspiracy,* which incidentally, the utopians did all within their power to suppress, he writes:

> It is not true, however, that there are no members of the intellectual elite who subscribe to the conspiratorial theory of history. Professor Carroll Quigley of the Foreign Service School at Georgetown University can hardly be accused of being a "right wing extremist." (Those three words have been made inseparable by the mass media.) Dr. Quigley has all the 'liberal' credentials, having taught at the Liberal Establishment's academic meccas of Princeton and Harvard. In his 1300 page, eight-pound tome, *Tragedy and Hope,* Dr. Quigley reveals the existence of the conspiratorial network . . . . The Professor is not merely formulating a theory, but revealing this network's existence from first-hand experience. He also makes it clear it is the network's secrecy and not its goals to which he objects. Professor Quigley discloses: "I know the operations of this network because I have studied it for twenty years and was permitted for two years, in the early 1960s, to examine its papers and secret records. *I have no aversion to it or to most of its aims and have, for much of my life, been close to it and to many of its instruments.* I have objected, both in the past and recently, to a few of its policies . . . but in general, my chief difference of opinion is that *it wishes to remain unknown,* and I believe its role in history is significant enough to be known."[4] [p. 950; emphasis added.]

The book by Abraham outlined only a glimpse of this conspiracy spoken of by Professor Quigley. Though Abraham's theories need to be developed further, and while we may not agree with all he says, when his overall projections are placed in a biblical context, the conclusions are mind-boggling and right on target with God's prophetic countdown.

Abraham continues:

> However, we most emphatically disagree with this network's aim, which the Professor describes as "nothing less than to create a world system of financial control in private hands able to dominate the political system of each

country and the economy of the world as a whole." In other words, this power-seeking clique wants to control and rule the world. Even more frightening, they want total control over all individual actions, as Professor Quigley observes . . . [the individual's] . . . freedom and choice will be controlled within very narrow alternatives by the fact that he will be numbered from birth and followed, as a number, through his educational training, his required military or other public service, his tax contributions, his health and medical requirements, and his final retirement and death benefits.

This group wants control over all natural resources, business, banking, and transportation by controlling the governments of the world. In order to accomplish these aims, the conspirators have had no qualms about fomenting wars, depressions, and hatred. They want a monopoly that would eliminate all competitors and destroy the free enterprise system. And, Professor Quigley of Harvard, Princeton, and Georgetown approves!

Bill Clinton and the Insiders

Professor Quigley, now deceased, was not the only academic aware of the existence of a clique of self-perpetuating conspirators whom we shall call the "insiders." Moreover, today, other scholars, finding the same individuals at the scenes of disastrous political fires over and over again, have concluded that there is obviously an organization of pyromaniacs at work in the world. But, intellectually honest scholars realize that if they challenge the insiders head-on, their careers will be destroyed.

The plot for this ever building conspiracy that is attempting to unify the world's economy and governments, takes on another staggering element when one realizes that President Bill Clinton seems to be a primary player in these events.

Whether one is inclined to concur with his assessment or not, one must agree that best-selling author, Texe Marrs, in his publication, *Flashpoint,* presents thought-provoking facts and fascinating observations with the following:

> The evidence is conclusive that . . . Bill Clinton is owned lock, stock, and barrel by the Secret Brotherhood, the powerful world elite whom I unmask in *Dark Majesty.*

They first recruited and educated young Bill Clinton at Georgetown University, a Catholic Jesuit school where his Illuminati mentor was the late Professor Carroll J. Quigley.

Next, Clinton was off to Oxford University in England as a Rhodes scholar where he was introduced to the finer points of the plan for a world conspiracy. After that, his elitist superiors shuffled their promising new servant-in-training to Yale University, the home of George Bush's Skull & Bones Society.

A law degree from Yale in hand, Clinton returned to Arkansas, a state that has been totally controlled for decades by the Rockefeller banking family. Soon, the Secret Brotherhood would reward their faithful servant with the political post of governor, a position which he would eventually use as a launching pad for the presidency.[5]

We all know the recent history that placed Bill Clinton in the White House against incredible odds. It really makes one wonder how such a man could possibly unseat an incumbent president who had only months before enjoyed a 90 percent national approval rating.

Texe Marrs continues in *Flashpoint* with the following:

In his acceptance speech in New York at the Democratic Party National Convention, Bill Clinton acknowledged his debt to the one man who was chiefly responsible for his initiation into the ranks of the world's secret elite: Professor Carroll J. Quigley.

When Bill Clinton uttered the following words that night in Madison Square Garden, every syllable was addressed to the hidden men who intend to rule over us, the moneyed czars and potentates of the Secret Brotherhood:

"As the Scripture says, our eyes have not yet seen, nor our ears heard, nor our minds imagined what we can build . . . . We can do it.

"As a teenager, I heard John Kennedy's summons to citizenship. And then, as a student at Georgetown, I heard that call clarified by a professor named Carroll Quigley."

There are two esoteric secrets that were hidden in these passages. First, twisting the Scriptures, Clinton affirmed the goal of the Secret Brotherhood to build a New

World Order. In contrast, the Scriptures refer to what God, not man, has *already* built and prepared for those who love Him. The actual working of the Scriptures is found in 1 Corinthians 2:9: "Eye hath not seen, nor ear heard, neither have entered into the heart of man, *the things which God hath prepared* for them that love Him."

Second, Clinton briefly mentioned John Kennedy's "summons to citizenship," and then, quickly followed that up by assuring his secret society listeners that, at Georgetown University, this call was "clarified" for him by Professor Carroll Quigley.

What is the crucial difference between President John F. Kennedy's summons and Professor Carroll J. Quigley's clarification? Simply this: JFK's famed, patriotic speech was addressed to Americans, not world citizens; "Ask not what your country can do for you, but what you can do for your *country.* "

But, the late Carroll Quigley, like all globalist members of the Secret Brotherhood, detested and reviled the very thought of country and nationalism. Quigley actively conspired for world government, and it was he who first brought Bill Clinton in on the Plan for World Government. How Quigley "clarified" Kennedy's words can therefore be stated as follows: "Ask not what your planet and its masters can do for you, but what you can do for your planet and masters."

So, think about it. In this day, in your lifetime, the Word of God is exploding onto the front pages of our newspapers. It's happening.

Who Are These People?

Some of the personalities promoting a utopian order are already "center stage."

Many of these people who desire to reshape the global monetary system are even household names in the world of banking, economics, politics, and international finance.

We have all heard of the infamous Trilateral Commission (TLC) organized in 1973 with the full sponsorship of David Rockefeller. It is a commonly held opinion that the architect of the commission's foreign policy was Zbigniew Brzezinski, and that international monetary issues were assigned to a Richard N. Cooper.

Remember that name.

These people basically have divided the developed world into three specific "spheres of influence." First, the Western Hemisphere; second, Asia; and third, Europe. They believe that the "movers and shakers" of economic matters are 1) the United States, 2) Japan, and 3) Germany.

The supposed purpose of this commission was to globally scrutinize each nation's economic policies and attempt to coordinate each one's direction with the others in areas of mutual concern, whether it be foreign policy, economic matters, or anything considered to be "of mutual interest."

Of course, it gets very interesting as one peruses through the list of names of members on the TLC. They are the most powerful economic and political names on this earth.

In 1983, another powerful think-tank emerged from the membership of the TLC called the Institute of International Economics (IIE). The chairman of IIE's advisory group is the aforementioned Richard N. Cooper. Other board members include such Council of Foreign Relations and TLC members as international banker, David Rockefeller; former Secretary of State, Henry Kissinger; Chairman of the Federal Reserve, Alan Greenspan; and IIE's managing director, C. Fred Bergsten.

In his "Confidential Investor Report," Larry Abraham observes the following concerning these architects of the New Order:

> In my opinion, the two foremost designers of a New World Order monetary system are C. Fred Bergsten and Richard N. Cooper.
>
> C. Fred Bergsten's background is establishment all the way. He is a former Assistant Secretary for International Affairs of the U.S. Treasury (1977-1981); Assistant for International Economic Affairs to the National Security Council (1969-1971); Senior Fellow at the Brookings Institute (1972-1976); and Council on Foreign Relations Fellow (1967-1968). He is the author of thirteen books on international economic issues, including *The United States in the World Economy; Toward A New World Trade Policy;* and *World Politics and International Economics.*
>
> Richard N. Cooper may be even more important. His credentials . . . are . . . impeccable . . . (among them) . . . the

Maurits C. Boas Professor of International Economics at Harvard . . . a provost of Yale from 1972 to 1974, he served as Undersecretary of State for Economic Affairs from 1977 to 1986.[6]

And, according to Abraham, it is Richard Cooper who has a most highly thought out plan for our economic destiny that he calls, "A Monetary System for the Future."

In 1983, he wrote of this "system" in an issue of *Foreign Affairs,* the influential quarterly journal of the Council on Foreign Relations. In the article, he suggests "the creation of a common, monetary policy and a joint Bank of Issue to determine that monetary policy."

He also clearly states . . . "A single currency is possible only if there is a single monetary policy and a single authority issuing the currency and directing the monetary policy." He continues that in order for each nation to accomplish this feat would mean the ". . . need to turn over the determination of monetary policy to a *supra-national* body."

That ought to raise your blood pressure.

For years now, forces within the U.S. Treasury, Congress, and a multitude of our bureaucracies have been seemingly sabotaging the United States monetary system.

I suggest to you that these forces — simultaneously at work in the economies of the Americas, of Asia, and of Europe — are step-by-step dismantling any semblance of stability in their own financial institutions. They wait as vultures for the coming collapse of global economies so they may pounce upon the opportunity to become the new messiahs with a miracle cure. The only catch will be that those who participate in this "worldwide bailout and refinancing scheme" must relinquish their sovereignty and their destinies into the hands of their financial savior(s).

The Coming Contrived Crisis

What happens next is a horrifying series of events that make Hitler's goose-stepping butchery across Europe look like a Sunday school picnic. First, they'll take our money. Next . . . our lives.

Get ready. It's coming.

Doubters may want to take note of what happened one day in July, 1993, to the Russian people. Their government announced that the old ruble was no longer viable. The Russian Central Bank declared all pre-1993 ruble bank notes invalid as of midnight the Sunday before. This decision threw Russians into a panic. Each Russian was allowed to exchange up to 35,000 rubles each of the old notes — only $34.00.

The Central Bank shocked Russians further by announcing that they were "recalling" all bank notes (rubles) printed before 1993. They must now "start over" with the state's "new money." The nation of Russia was devastated.

But, it was all planned, and is but another baby step toward the same scenario that could explode in the United States of America very soon.

A monetary and banking crisis of unparalleled proportions — on a worldwide scale — is in the works. A crisis so mammoth that it would threaten to plunge the world economies into the Dark Ages. Such economic catastrophe would be so devastating in its ramifications that major population centers in and outside the United States would experience a complete breakdown of law and order. Riots, anarchy, and panic would grip the nations.

But, the "insiders" will rush into their emergency sessions behind locked doors and drool that, finally, "their day" has arrived. Then, they will triumphantly emerge with an incredible, supernatural "plan" that will work, but "only if we all, as a world, join hands and drop our petty differences."

Of course, central to their miraculous cure-all for the worldwide crash is an announcement that, from henceforth, we will share a common currency and a common monetary system, monitored by an elite but small group of very wise men. And of course, one particular man, who just happens to be waiting in the wings for his moment, will emerge from the ashes of this disaster. He will be a cut above the rest, and quite frankly, almost supernatural in his profound wisdom. He will be portrayed as the only one capable of bringing calm to an otherwise "berserk" world crisis.

Will people in America accept such a scheme? Would they surrender Constitutional protections afforded to United States citizens and foolishly join a united, international effort masquerading as the only solution that can bring sanity back to their lives?

Of course! And, why not? Don't you understand, "It's the economy, stupid!"

The schemers have laid their snares. The planners have developed their strategies. The ground work for a One World Monetary System already exists.

The World Court, the International Monetary Fund, the Bank for International Settlement, and the World Bank — to say nothing of multitudes of United Nations sanctioned organizations — are all on "standby" to facilitate this worldwide bailout.

We only wait now for the "Coming Contrived Crisis."

7

The Globalists:

New Think, New Era, New Age

David Allen Lewis

When six European nations signed the Treaty of Rome on March 27, 1957, and launched the EEC — the European Common Market — there was a feeling of exaltation throughout the Western World. Jean Gabriel Monnet declared, "Once a common market interest has been created, then political union will come naturally."

A national news magazine in the USA described the final ratification of the Treaty of Rome on December 28, 1958, with these words:

> When the history of the twentieth century is written, last week is likely to prove one of its watersheds. For in the seven days which spanned 1958 and 1959, Western Europe began to flex its economic muscles for the first time in a decade, and took its biggest step toward unity since the death of Charlemagne 1,145 years ago.[1]

We have that copy of *Time Magazine* in our research files.

The following quote is from Dr. Wilmington's book *The King is Coming* (p. 116).

> On Capitoline Hill in Rome, nearly 2,000 years ago Caesar's legions went forth to bring the first unified rule to Europe's warring tribes. Since the Roman Empire's fall the unification of Europe has been a dream which neither the sword of Napoleon nor Hitler could realize. But on Rome's Capitoline Hill last week six statesmen, with the peaceful stroke of a pen, took the biggest step yet made toward this dream of centuries.

Wilmington attributes this quote to *Life Magazine,* January 9, 1959. We found that issue in the public library in the microfilm files but could not locate the quote. Perhaps someone can help us pinpoint the primary source of this colorful quote.

About 20 years ago, I was invited to participate as an observer in a conference on "European Unity and American Destiny," sponsored by the University of Cincinnati. Present at that meeting were such luminaries as Alterio Spinelli of Rome, who headed the committee that drafted the treaty of Rome which in 1957 brought six member nations into a Common Market, now simply known as the European Community (E.C.).

There was David Schoenbrun, political analyst and commentator, and many others. One evening, at dinner, Sir Geoffrey DeFrietas, who was serving at that time as the president of the Council of Europe, and is to this day a member of the British Parliament, graciously answered many of my questions. At one point he looked into my eyes and slowly said, "You know, Lewis, what we are actually trying to do in Europe is to bring the old Roman Empire back to life again."

A Fierce King

Both the prophet Daniel and the apostle John, writer of the Book of Revelation, predict a revival of the Roman Empire in the last days, prior to the establishment of the visible millennial kingdom of Jesus Christ on earth. The kingdom of God is not brought in through human effort. As Dr. Stanley Horton so often says, it comes through a period of judgment and the outpouring of the wrath of God on earth, climaxed by the personal return of Jesus, who comes to save the world from self destruction.

Before every knee bows to the Son of God and recognizes His supremacy, there will be a vile ruler, the Antichrist, who defies the God of heaven and tries to fulfill the ancient vision of Babel/Babylon. That final Antichrist is foreshadowed by Nimrod, Nebuchadnezzar, Antiochus, Hadrian, Hitler, and a host of others (1 John 2:18 — many anti-Christs).

The Antichrist will not look like a monster. No, he will be the most appealing secular man ever to walk on the face of the earth. The Antichrist will look good. The apostate world will see him as a savior, not a monster; but a beast he is, wearing an almost impenetrable disguise. He is for peace, not war. But he wages war to obtain elusive peace.

The final human effort to produce a New World Order is described in Revelation 13 where John on Patmos depicts the Antichrist beast kingdom. His regime is doomed from the start. Proclaiming world peace, the beast brings havoc and ruin. He is called Abbadon, the destroyer. The beast kingdom will never succeed.

Daniel, whom Jesus called a prophet (Matthew 24), spoke of a coming "king of fierce countenance" whom we understand to be the very Antichrist:

> And through his policy also he shall cause craft to prosper in his hand; and he shall magnify himself in his heart, and by peace shall destroy many: he shall also stand up against the Prince of princes; but he shall be broken without hand (Dan. 8:25).

Most scholars agree that the beast kingdom represents a last days emergence of the Roman Empire. European leaders have dreamed of reviving the Old Roman Empire and forging a United Europe for centuries. One reflects for but a moment to recall Charlemagne, Charles V, Louis XIV, Napoleon, Kaiser Wilhelm II, Mussolini, and Hitler. By force or intrigue, these and a score of others have sought to fulfill their dream of the ages.

The Antichrist's humanist New Age religion will exalt man as the divinity. "He opened his mouth in blasphemy against God, to blaspheme his name, and his tabernacle, and them that dwell in heaven" (Rev. 13:6).

The apostle Paul clearly describes "the man of sin . . . the son of perdition; Who opposeth and exalteth himself above all that is called God, or that is worshipped; so that he as God sitteth in the temple of

God, shewing himself that he is God" (2 Thess. 2:3-4).

Like John, Daniel saw visions of far tomorrows. He described how the coming man of evil would "speak great words against the most High, and shall wear out the saints of the most High, and think to change times and laws: and they shall be given into his hand until a time and times and the dividing of time" (Dan. 7:25). The latter phrase refers to three and one-half years, or half of the seven years tribulation.

Daniel's foreview of the beast-king is parallel to that of the apostle Paul:

> And a mighty king shall stand up, that shall rule with great dominion, and do according to his will . . . . The king shall do according to his will; and he shall exalt himself, and magnify himself above every god, and shall speak marvelous things against the God of gods, and shall prosper till the indignation be accomplished: for that that is determined shall be done. Neither shall he regard the God of his fathers, nor the desire of women, nor regard any god: for he shall magnify himself above all (Dan. 11:3,36-37 — compare: 2 Thess. 2:3-4).

His program is peace, but war dogs his footsteps. He fails, how miserably he fails. "He shall magnify himself in his heart, and *by peace shall destroy many:* he shall also stand up against the Prince of princes; but he shall be broken without hand" (Dan. 8:25 — see also 1 Thess. 5:3 — italic marking is mine).

The "European Idea"

Strange that so few knew the name Jean Gabriel Monnet until now. He is truly the father of the "European Idea," and architect of the E.C. He is one of the most important figures in modern history. When the global World Federation finally emerges out of the Union of Europe, Monnet will be a hero known and lauded by every school child.

Paul Henri Spaak, living in exile in London during the second World War, was inspired by Jean Gabriel Monnet, and into his mind came the Benelux idea, which materialized when the war was over. Before there was a six-member Common Market, there was the economic union of Belgium, Netherlands, and Luxembourg, hence "Benelux." The Benelux Union provided a model for the Common

Market, which, when finalized and reduced to a ten member federation, will provide a model for a World Government, probably divided into ten regions or kingdoms.

On January 1, 1981, Greece became the tenth member nation of the EEC. "This is it," exclaimed excited prophecy students. But no, this was not it, for as I had earlier predicted on national television, Spain and Portugal became the eleventh and twelfth member nations and there will be more. There will be adjustments, unions, dropouts, but finally there will be the ten kingdoms prophesied in the Bible.

The now-famed treaty that was brought into being at Maastricht, Netherlands, is now very close to approval by the 12 member nations of the EEC. The Danish government rejected the treaty, refusing to sign. This was followed by a media blitz that many believe brainwashed enough of the Danes that when it was put to a referendum vote, it passed by a slim margin. But surely England would continue to steadfastly reject the treaty. The House of Commons passed it by a healthy majority. Would not the iron lady, Margaret Thatcher, prevail with powerful arguments before the House of Lords? It was not to be. The Springfield, Missouri, *News Leader*, July 15, 1993, carried the following report datelined London:

> From the seclusion of their ancestral estates or tax havens, bluebloods rallied Wednesday behind a newcomer to the House of Lords, Baroness Thatcher, as she vainly sought to derail a bill on closer European Union.
>
> Her successor and fellow Conservative, Prime Minister John Major, averted a government defeat with the support of most opposition peers, loyal Conservatives, and a rival clutch of aristocrats making rare appearances in the chamber.
>
> Supporters of the bill voted overwhelmingly against the Thatcher-led motion late Wednesday. The vote was 445-176. Thatcher's motion demanded that Britain's 43 million voters hold a referendum before the government could ratify the Maastricht treaty on closer union for the twelve nation European Community.

It's a long, long road to Maastricht, mien Herr? How much further to Babylon? And, what groping beast, slavering as he goes, is this that lurches toward Rome and Ur of Chaldee? He lurches through the dimming gloom of earth's twilight, and night cometh.

Thank God that after the darkest night of earth's history there comes the dawning of a new day, the Day of Messiah and the Regnum Millennium (kingdom of 1,000 years).

Before me is a fascinating book by Merry and Serge Bromberger, published in French in 1968, then in English in 1969. It is titled, *Jean Monnet and the United States of Europe*.[2]

The Brombergers wrote of Jean Gabriel Monnet's devout Christian sister who never ceased witnessing to him, trying to convert him to Christ. But, say the Brombergers, "He, too, is a mystic in his own fashion, dedicated to achieving understanding among his fellowmen, to a quest for the mechanisms of international integration."[3]

Globalism: The Hidden Agenda

Will the January 1993 European agreement only work to abolish tariffs and open borders? Will it effect only the economy of Europe?

I put the question to Wolfgang Behrends, the German Ambassador to Canada. The late George Spaetzel and I were having lunch at the Confederation Club in Kitchener, Ontario, where we met with Behrends.

"Mr. Ambassador," I queried, "will the union in Europe remain economic or should we expect a political federation?"

With a look of great satisfaction, The Honorable Mr. Behrends replied, "To be sure, what we are moving toward is a political federation in Europe."

The year 1950 was a year of fervent activity in Europe. Economic treaties were proposed. It was the year of the Schumann Plan, launched at a big press conference engineered by Jean Gabriel Monnet. Later Monnet lamented to Professor Paul Reuter, "Look here. In 1950 we were wrong. We should have organized Europe politically right from the start. We should have taken advantage of Adenauer's suggestion of a joint Franco-German government, a joint parliament . . . . We probably could have initiated a United States of Europe as easily as we launched the Coal and Steel Community."[4]

Toward the end of his life, French General de Gaulle made an unusual comment: "In order to have a European army — in other words, an army of Europe — Europe must first exist as a political, economic, financial, administrative and, *above all, spiritual entity* . . . . millions of men would be willing to die for it."[5] (Emphasis mine.)

Former President George Bush launched in the minds of men the concept of a New World Order. There is no doubt that he meant a world government. His successor, President Bill Clinton, will be no less enthusiastic in promotion of the federation of all mankind. Only his tactics and rhetoric will differ.

Seldom is the agenda of the One Worlders more clearly declared than in the *Time Magazine* article, "The Birth of the Global Nation" by Strobe Talbott.[6] Noting that in the recent past "the advocacy of any kind of world government became highly suspect. By 1950 'one-worlder' was a term of derision for those suspected of being wooly-headed naifs,{sic} if not crypto-communists."

But Talbott points out that times are changing. "The internal affairs of a nation used to be off limits to the world community. Now the principle of 'humanitarian intervention' is gaining acceptance." Talbott cites U.N. authorized action against Saddam Hussein both in the action to help the Kurds in the north, and of course, the Desert Storm in defense of Kuwait (or was it in defense of oil?).

Strobe Talbott notes that the Rio Environmental World Summit held in June 1992 ". . . signified the participants acceptance of what Maurice Strong, the main impresario of the event, called 'the transcending sovereignty of nature.' " In other words, the main agenda of Rio was actually the promotion of globalism.

The environmental issue simply provided a convenient vehicle to ride down the yellow brick road to the land of Super Oz. Dorothy, I don't think we are in Kansas (or Arkansas) any longer.

No doubt the New World Order will be called a democracy — the most abused and misunderstood of terms.

Strobe Talbot sums it up: "The best mechanism for democracy, whether at the level of the multinational state or that of the planet as a whole, is not an all powerful Leviathan or centralized super state, but a federation, a union of separate states that allocate certain powers to a central government while retaining many others for themselves. Federalism has already proved the most successful of all political experiments, and organizations like the World Federalist Association have for decades advocated it as the basis for global government. Federalism is largely an American invention . . . . If that model does indeed work globally . . . [it would be] a special source of pride for a world government's American constituents."[7]

The spirit of this pride can be seen in the remarks of former President George Herbert Walker Bush:

> "Out of these troubled times, our fifth objective — a New World Order — can emerge . . . . We are now in sight of a United Nations that performs as envisioned by its

founders (September 11, 1990, TV address to the people of the USA).

"The United Nations can help bring about a new day .... a New World Order and a long era of peace" (October 1, 1990).

"When we succeed .... we will have invigorated a U.N. that contributes as its founders dreamed. We have established principles for acceptable international conduct and the means to enforce them" (October 26, 1990, regarding the U.N. sanctions).

Two days after the air offensive was launched against Iraq, he spoke to the Arab nations that were not part of the coalition: "Look, you're part of this New World Order .... You can play an important part in seeing that the world can live at peace in the Middle East and elsewhere" (January 18, 1991).

When President George Bush spoke to the U.S. Reserve Officers Association he said, "From the day Saddam's forces first crossed into Kuwait, it was clear that this aggression required a swift response from our nation and the [world community]. What was, and is, at stake is not simply our energy or economic security, and the stability of a vital region, but the prospects for peace in the post-Cold War era — the promise of a New World Order based on the rule of law" (January 23, 1991).

In his address on the State of the Union, January 29, 1991, Bush said, "What is at stake is more than one small country; it is a big idea: a New World Order, where diverse nations are drawn together in security, freedom, and the rule of law."

"There is no room for lawless aggression in the Persian Gulf for this New World Order we are trying to create, and Saddam Hussein will know this" (January 1, 1991).

We heard our president talking about "our friends and fellow members of the coalition." Some of these friends are the most dangerous cutthroats of modern history. They are the creators and supporters of world terrorism. Blood flows from their hands. They rank with Hitler, Antiochus Epiphanies, and Nero.

Allied intelligence reports that our Soviet "allies" continually helped launch the SCUDS, which they had furnished to Saddam in the first place. The Soviets refused to recall their advisors who were doing this. The USSR kept right on shipping materials to Iraq. Up to the time of the actual attack, the USSR was flying twelve AN-124 and AN-22 transports into Baghdad daily. Gorbachev admitted to President Bush that this was happening and said, "The Soviets need cash."

Brainwashing a Generation

The role of public education in promoting the New World Order must not be overlooked.

In 1955, I was preaching in a midwestern church during the first year of my evangelistic, teaching ministry. From the pulpit I boldly proclaimed that, potentially, the public education system was the most dangerous anti-Christ force and could be used to brainwash the generation that would herald and welcome the prophesied world ruler.

With no thought of being unkind, the pastor's wife chided me for making such a rash statement. Being a school teacher herself, it was hard to receive such a concept. It did seem unlikely in 1955. A year ago, I saw that lady again. She brought the subject up saying, "David, you were right about the educational system in this country."

Kenneth DeCourcey's *Intelligence Digest* is a London, England, based research publication dealing with global affairs. In the September 1963 edition there is an article on UNESCO (United Nations Educational, Scientific, and Cultural Organization). The author quotes the words of William Benton, U.S. Assistant Secretary of State. Benton said the following while chairing the charter-forming meeting for UNESCO on September 23, 1946. "We are at the beginning of a long process of breaking down the walls of national sovereignty. UNESCO must be the pioneer. The Department of State has fathered this national commission. Now you give for the first time a collective brain to the whole nervous system of American science, culture, education, and means of communication." This speech was given at the first meeting of the U.S. National Commission for UNESCO.

DeCourcey also cited UNESCO publication number 356.

> As long as the child breathes the poisoned air of nationalism, education in world-mindedness can produce only precarious results. As we have pointed out, it is frequently the family that infects the child with extreme nationalism. The school should therefore use the means

described earlier to combat family attitudes that favor jingoism [those who favor warlike aggressive foreign policy] . . . . We shall presently recognize in nationalism the major obstacle to development of world-mindedness.

(In 1985, the USA withdrew from UNESCO because of its anti-Western bias.)

Parents are hearing that a new thought system of schooling our children, known as "Outcome Based Education" (OBE), is taking over our schools. Every Christian teacher I have talked to about OBE declares that it is a brainwashing system to turn our children into globally-minded candidates for world citizenship.

Sound radical? Look at what Pam Shellenberger, area representative for the Christian Women's Association, wrote about OBE: "The education goals proposed have nothing to do with testing based on self-worth, information and thinking skills, learning independently, adaptability to change and ethical judgment. I'm not quite sure how this program could improve our academic excellence."

A citizens' OBE task force in Wisconsin has declared that Outcome Based Education has identified one of its desired "outcomes" to be "global awareness."

Janet Parshall writes, "In this new age of politically correct thought and speech, it is not too difficult to imagine how the classroom could become the great social factory, churning out boys and girls who all think the same way . . . . Perhaps the most repugnant aspect of OBE is the overriding philosophy that children belong to the state. More and more schools have tried to assume the role of co-parent with all the vestiges of that high calling. The movement toward collaboration of all social service agencies through the public school can be readily fostered through anti-parent and subjective programs like OBE."

No OBE in your local school? Look again, it may be called America 2000, Success Based Education, Criterion Based Education, Mastery Learning, and a host of other names attached to the New Think Education.

A World Army

If George Bush was a prophet of the New World Order, what about Bill Clinton? Is the William Clinton administration any different from that of the preceding presidential regime? Indeed not, in fact the race toward one world speeds up under his leadership.

What really goes on in that murky, almost hidden bureaucracy of underlings in Foggy Bottom? Let me pull back the veil and give you an inside look. Scenes like this unfold each day in the nation's capitol. C-Span 2 Television cable service pulls the curtain for us.

On July 15, 1993, under the banner of U.N. peacekeeping, the Parliamentarians for Global Action held a congressionally-sponsored, and we assume tax-dollar-funded, conference. The moderator of the conference was Kennedy Graham, Secretary General of Parliamentarians for Global Action.

In his rambling preliminary remarks, Graham revealed that, "Global Action is a worldwide network of politicians, that is of congresspersons and parliamentarians . . . . We now have nine hundred members from seventy countries, including forty-five members from the United States Congress, both the Senate and the House."

Graham stated that members of P.F.G.A., which has been in existence for fourteen years, are committed to "approaching global problems as a coordinated network working across national boundaries." They are "politicians who take the interest of the planet into account along with the traditional national interest." He went on:

> We have been working on issues such as sustainable development and democracy, peace and security, focusing especially in the 1980s on nuclear disarmament issues, and of course, more recently on peacekeeping itself.
>
> I think in the post cold war era all of us are now searching for new structures of peace, new structures of security to replace the strategy of nuclear deterrence that underpinned global security for the better part of four decades. Perhaps somewhat paradoxically that new structure of peace and security is, in fact, not especially new. It is the twentieth century concept of peace, namely collective security. Collective security through the United Nations.

Collective security means a world army that would override the authority of national sovereignty or the authority of national armies. In short, we are looking at a United Nations World Police Force, the ultimate Gestapo.

Kennedy Williams charmed the group with, "It was, as you will recall, a Wilsonian idea in the 1920s. It has had a checkered career through the thirties, in the face of blatant aggression . . . . It was revived and strengthened in the 1940s, in the second cut, through the U.N. charter, put into cold storage as a result of the cold war for four decades. Now in the 1990s we have a third opportunity to make collective security through the U.N. work."

Williams continued his rhetoric with these thoughts on "collective security":

> When one looks at the hot crisis spots of Somalia, Bosnia . . . also the more traditional tension areas, of Golan Heights, Cyprus and Kashmir, which have not been resolved politically and which remain potential explosive spots . . . . It is urgent that we succeed . . . in insuring that collective security becomes the reliable replacement to deterrence for securing the peace around the world.
>
> Collective security is fraught with problems, teething problems. We are on the frontier of progress in this respect — in making global cooperation work in terms of self governance . . . problems of political decision making, and the legitimacy of powers of primary principle organs of the UN, [there are] problems of judgments to be made [as to the] degree of intervention in sovereign states, and levels of engagement . . . .
>
> That is the reasoning behind our decision to convene this workshop in the congress; to enable congress-persons and their staff to listen to recognized experts in the field.

The first speaker introduced by Graham was David Scheffer, Senior Advisor and Council to the U.S. Ambassador to the United Nations. Scheffer's topic was peacekeeping. His thinking and expression was not only New Age, it sounded like something straight out of George Orwell's classic 1984. "We are in a new era [new age] . . . of multilateralism . . . now in an era of engagement on global agenda."

Multilateralism simply indicates that our armies must coordinate with U.N. forces and commanders and in fact, be subjected to them. Never again should the USA act as an independent agent. Of course, many alleged benefits from this were described.

We were told that, in this age of complexity, we must come up with a "new agenda," one that would have a "policy of assertive multilateralism." Of course, there has to be a totally new mindset and if "we are going to be engaged in conflicts multilaterally, must have multilateral perspective."

Scheffer assured us that the "Soviet threat has expired," and that a new kind of engaging multilateral diplomacy on an hourly basis is going on in the U.N. These new tactics "focus on preventive diplomacy."

With up-to-date statistics Scheffer let us know that the USA is currently involved in 14 peacekeeping operations in various parts of the world, and our hard working U.N. officials are in continual sessions seven days a week from early in the morning until late each night.

New Think, New Era, New Age

New Think, a la Orwell, is the avenue for progress to world tranquillity. Scheffer said, "We cannot express strongly enough . . . have to get ourselves out of the old think of the cold war and into the new think of the new era [era = age = New Age]."

Scheffer made a point of the fact that Vice President Al Gore and other leading politicians stress the New Think idea. According to Scheffer, the three steps to peace involve peacemaking, peacekeeping, peace enforcement.

Chapter seven of the U.N. charter deals with peace enforcement according to Scheffer. He said, "Peace enforcement is a much tougher sword . . . authorizes the use of military force pursuant to however the Security Council resolution sets forth in the resolution . . . . We must bring political pressure to bear on the belligerents."

But what if, one day, the U.N. decides that because the USA sides with Israel they are the belligerents? Can the United Nations forces be used to straighten us out? Why not?

I will share one more pithy observation from the Parliamentarians for Global Action symposium. James Sutterlin, former political advisor to U.N. Secretary General de Cuellar strengthened the idea of multilateralism: "This is a time of great change in the world . . . if we are to meet the challenges we face in the world it requires . . . changes in national thinking particularly on the allocation of national resources, and I include in that very specifically the allocation of military force."

There will be a world government. We all understand that there can be no peace without it. It is true that the Saddam Husseins and the Slobodan Milosevichs of this world can only understand a superior power with the will to enforce peace in a region. Someone must "rule with a rod of iron."

There are two ways set before the human race. One way leads to the Antichrist and his short-term, weak, shaky world coalition. The other leads to Jesus Christ and His glorious and peaceable kingdom on earth, the Regnum Millennium — the kingdom of a thousand years. It takes a lot of faith to accept either one.

To put it in terms a secular person can understand, I am willing to "bet the farm" on Jesus. We have staked our all on Him and His divine Word. He will return. He will not fail us. The world's politicians have always failed us, but Jesus never fails. He keeps His campaign promises. It's not a bet at all, we have a sure thing.

> There is no peace, saith the Lord, unto the wicked (Isa. 48:22).

> And he shall judge among the nations, and shall rebuke many people: and they shall beat their swords into plowshares, and their spears into pruning hooks: nation shall not lift up sword against nation, neither shall they learn war any more (Isa. 2:4).

> I will both lay me down in peace, and sleep: for thou, Lord, only makest me dwell in safety (Ps. 4:8).

Talk of Peace

A group of scientists in Hamburg informed us that last year was the worst war year since 1945. At the end of 1992, there were 52 wars being waged in the world.

United Nations forces were (in self-defense) killing the people of Somalia, whom they have been sent to aid and defend. Yes, guerrilla soldiers are the target, but civilians are being slaughtered. Sadly, this is the way of the world.

The "former" Soviet Union (long live the new Russian Empire) still has 30,000 nuclear bombs mounted on 12,000 missiles, mostly targeted at the USA. Politicians continue to reassure us that the cold war is over.

We can't help but wonder, however, why Russia has by far the greatest military machine in the world today. McAlvany's *Intelligence Advisor* clues us in to the fact that the KGB is bigger and stronger than ever before.

But in one tiny area of the world the talk is all about PEACE, and the whole world is taking notice. Israel is the focus of attention.

The world media revealed the astounding information that secret negotiations have been conducted in Norway for over a year, led by Johan Joergen Holst, the Norwegian foreign minister. Holst presided over 14 secret meetings involving representatives of the Palestine Liberation Organization (PLO) and of Israel.

Israel and the PLO have been bitter enemies since the founding of the PLO in 1964. The PLO Charter calls for the destruction of Israel, and Israel has refused to recognize the PLO as the legitimate representative of the Arabs, who since 1964 have been called Palestinians. Prior to 1948, about the only people calling themselves Palestinians were the Jews who lived there under the Turkish and later the British Mandate. The Palestinian Arabs are human beings who have rights and needs that must be met. But is the PLO the honest broker for this peace?

We hope that Israel has not made a tragic mistake.

On the other hand, we remember that Jomo Kenyata, head of the 1950s terrorist Mau Mau bands, was responsible for the slaughter of thousands of innocent Christians and others. Kenyatta reformed and became the moderate, responsible president of Kenya. Could he be a role model for Arafat? Let us hope so.

In August of 1993, in an article that referred to secret negotiations, we predicted what would soon transpire. We have prayed for the peace of Jerusalem. We are careful not to be hasty in passing judgment on what is happening there. What is done is done, and even if Israel has made mistakes, we stand by her for our Lord's sake.

We must remember, peace treaties are not made with your friends. Peace treaties are made with your enemies. Without enemies there is no need for peace treaties!

Israel possesses less than 1 percent of the land mass of the Middle East, yet it is the most hotly contested real estate in the world.

In 1969, when Zeev Kaufsman told me that the nations would gradually turn against Israel and put inexorable pressure upon her to give up land for peace, it sounded unreal. Israel was then the darling of the Western World. Zeev prophesied to me that when the West-World Antichrist confirms an agreement with Israel (Dan. 9:27) that it will be by coercion. He predicted that the world leaders will come to Israel saying, "All right, you Jews, we have had it with you. Trouble, trouble, trouble! Here is a treaty for you to sign, and you will sign or be abandoned."

Peace on the White House Lawn

On September 13, 1993, at about 11 a.m. eastern standard time, Israel's Prime Minister, PLO leader Yasir Arafat, Israeli Foreign

Minister Shimon Peres, along with U.S. President Bill Clinton and Secretary of State Warren Christopher, walked onto the White House lawn for the signing of one of the most incredible documents of our time: a peace accord between the PLO and Israel.

Oh brave New World Order, have you brought us hope for mankind's survival, or do even more sinister agendas lurk in the shadows of international politics and pressure?

What manipulative tactics did you use on Mr. Rabin? What threats fell on his ears? What geo-political blackmail and arm twisting was exercised? Look at the distress in Mr. Rabin's face. What anguish has driven him as he comes to meet and shake hands, reluctantly, with his old enemy. But a peace accord is good — if it is real.

What transpired in Washington, DC, on the White House lawn is not that treaty of Daniel's vision, but it is a foreshadowing. This treaty could serve good purposes, but deception lurks in the shadowy future.

Peace is not evil. It is good. Good treaties, honored by the parties thereto are not bad; they are good. It is better to have peace than war. But these are dangerous times for Israel, and for all of us. We walk a tight rope over chasms of unimaginable depth.

We all want peace, but this is a wicked, greedy and deceitful world that has shown negligible success in keeping peace through the long history of humankind. For all the efforts of sane and hopeful leaders, we still live in a world steeped in war and violence.

Jesus did not gloat when He said, "There shall be wars and rumors of wars." Rather He was weeping over the inability of rebellious humanity to solve its deepest problems.

When each of the World Wars ended, it was said by some that this treaty being signed is the beginning of the tribulation of seven years. In fact, one of the signers or sponsors of the treaty must be the Antichrist, some believed. It proved not to be so.

The peace accord of September 13 is not the Antichrist covenant. We are not in the tribulation. What we see evolving is a framework that could develop into that agreement with hell (Isa. 28:18), but it is not in focus yet.

One thing we have learned in recent years is that prophecy and world events can move at lightning speed. See the Berlin wall falling down! Observe the upheaval in the USSR and Eastern Europe. Watch how the European Community advances toward the formation of New Rome.

The Jordanian-Jewish Connection

The beast will rule over all the earth. A shaky world coalition will be under his dominion. All the nations except one. That nation is Jordan, the only Arab nation to declare war on Hitler's Nazi regime during the Second World War.

Of the Antichrist, Daniel predicts: "He shall enter also into the glorious land [Israel], and many countries shall be overthrown: but these shall escape out of his hand, even Edom, and Moab, and the chief of the children of Ammon" (Dan. 11:41). Edom, Moab, and Ammon are regions of the Hashemite kingdom of Jordan.

A Jordanian Moslem asked me if I knew about the Jewish connection to the Rose Red Lost City of Petra. I replied that I was aware of this but expressed surprise that he would know of an obscure realm of biblical prophecy. He told me that some Jordanians speak of a tradition that in the future a man of incredible evil, with great power will oppress Israel. In that day Jordan must assist Jews who come to Jordan for refuge. Petra will be a sheltering place.

In 1933, Om Saleem, an Arab Christian housewife spoke prophecies in a Pentecostal church in Amman, Jordan. It is well documented that one of the prophesies was that the Jews would return to Palestine in 1948 and would establish a new nation.

Ron Banuk is currently examining records of the prophecies of Om Saleem, which we view as significant but less than perfect. Om Saleem means mother of Saleem, this being the name of her eldest son. She also spoke of friendship between Jordan and Israel, and of prophecies relating to Petra.

For over 20 years we have predicted a Jordan-Israel peace treaty. Since the days of Israeli Prime Minister Golda Meir, secret negotiations between Israeli and Jordanian leaders have taken place, with the hope of bringing about a peace treaty.

In an article appearing in our *Jerusalem Courier* for August 1993 I wrote: "I have long taught that there would be a peace treaty between Jordan and Israel. Israel will find a place of shelter in Jordan during the Tribulation, at the lost city of Petra and perhaps elsewhere in the Hashemite kingdom . . . . Our contacts tell us that ongoing secret negotiations between Jordanian and Israeli leaders may bring a peace treaty in the next five years. May God grant it. Beh Ezrat Hashem!"

Since Jordan's population is 70 percent Palestinian, it stands to reason that King Hussein would not dare to make any accord with Israel without including a solution for the Palestinian's plight. Real-

172 • *The Triumphant Return of Christ*

izing this, a number of years ago I became involved in efforts to privately bring Israelis and Palestinians together for dialogue.

One such meeting was conducted in Ramallah, involving an Israeli government official, myself, and several leaders of the Palestinian District Leagues (now defunct). There was anger around the conference table. Accusations were hurled. Finally, a sense of calm and reason prevailed. At the end of the meeting all agreed that, while there were many problems to work out, it is time to stop the killing and violence, and create a framework of communication in which Palestinians and Jews can work out solutions to the problems of the area.

Peace — Better Than War

A great Civil War general declared, "War is hell." We all prefer to live in a tranquil society rather than a state of chaos.

Peace is good. God is the author of peace.

The goal of prophecy and divine history is a state of peace, the Regnum Millennium (kingdom of one thousand years). In general peace treaties are good. One, however, is evil.

The beast will use humanity's weariness with war and longing for peace to weave a subtle deception that culminates in devastation. Daniel writes of the awful purpose of the Antichrist: "He shall magnify himself in his heart, and by peace shall destroy many; he shall also stand up against the Prince of princes; but he shall be broken without hand" (Dan. 8:25).

When Satan is the promoter of peace, watch for deception.

Does the September 13, 1993, signing mark the onset of the Great Tribulation? No, it does not. That day comes, but not now. It may come swiftly and unexpectedly, but it has not started yet.

In 1978, Anwar Sadat, Menachem Begin, and Jimmy Carter met at Camp David for the signing of a similar peace accord for Egypt and Israel. Some cried, "This is it." But it was not.

In 1979, the actual peace treaty was signed in Cairo and in Jerusalem. More cries, "This must be it" arose. But it was not.

Articles and booklets circulated proving that Sadat, or Begin, or Carter was the Antichrist. Watch for a repeat of this genre of error, for some people never learn. Soon you will read that Arafat or Rabin or Clinton is the "son of perdition." Pick the Antichrist of your choice. Play your games if you must, but leave me out.

How could Israel consider making peace with her enemy, the PLO, with terrorist Yasir Arafat? Very simply, there is no need to make a peace treaty with friends. Peace treaties are made with enemies.

We are to "Follow peace with all men" (Heb. 12:14). Jesus advised, "Agree with thine adversary quickly, whiles thou art in the way with him . . ." (Matt. 5:25).

Moses wisely said, "When thou comest nigh unto a city to fight against it, then proclaim peace unto it" (Deut. 20:10).

Making peace is better than going to war. We read, "When a man's ways please the LORD, he maketh even his enemies to be at peace with him" (Prov. 16:7).

Out of his deep pit of anguish, the sufferer Job asked, "Who can bring a clean thing out of an unclean? not one" (Job 14:4). Wrong, Job.

God can bring good out of evil, purity out of impurity. That is the theme of redemption. God can take a broken, ruined life and bring forth a new creation. "Therefore if any man be in Christ, he is a new creature: old things are passed away; behold, all things are become new" (2 Cor. 5:17).

God will take this ruined planet and renew it. The thousand year reign of Messiah is but the inauguration of an eternity of perfection.

God brings good out of evil. Satan brings evil out of good. "By peace shall he destroy . . . ." Therefore it behooves us to "Be sober, be vigilant; because your adversary the devil, as a roaring lion, walketh about, seeking whom he may devour" (1 Pet. 5:8).

Evil is ever alert, unceasingly probing, continually watching, looking for an opening. We are not ignorant of the devil's devices.

We join the search for peace, but remember: "Hate is strong and mocks the song of peace on earth, good will to men."

We are wary.

True Peace in the Land

Wars and violence will not cease until Messiah reigns from Jerusalem. However we can look forward to advancing peace in the Middle East and a time of relative peace in many parts of the earth. But the tide will turn for, "When they shall say, Peace and safety; then sudden destruction cometh upon them, as travail upon a woman with child; and they shall not escape" (1 Thess. 5:3).

"They have seduced my people, saying, Peace; and there was no peace; and one built up a wall, and, lo, others daubed it with untempered mortar" (Ezek. 13:10).

The beast will use peace to destroy: "The words of his mouth were smoother than butter, but war was in his heart: his words were softer than oil, yet were they drawn swords" (Ps. 55:21).

"We looked for peace, but no good came; and for a time of

health, and behold trouble!" (Jer. 8:15). "Behold the ambassadors of peace shall weep bitterly" (Isa. 33:7). Antichrist "shall confirm the covenant with many for one week [week of years = seven years]" (Dan. 9:27).

Only Israel, of all nations, is guaranteed survival. Only Israel resists the Antichrist. While the entire Gentile world bows to the beast, Israel stands alone and bravely counterattacks his awesome forces. Judah takes up arms against the armies of hell. "And Judah also shall fight at Jerusalem" (Zech. 14:14).

Great leadership arises in Judah! Israel declares of the beast: [he] "shall tread in our palaces, then shall we raise against him seven shepherds, and eight principle men" (Mic. 5:5).

Listen devil, look out for the two mighty prophets, the seven shepherds, and the eight principle men. They are on your trail, oh loser of all time and eternity. Your evil intention will not prevail.

The ill-advised seven-year treaty forced on Israel cannot last: "And your covenant with death shall be disannulled, and your agreement with hell shall not stand" (Isa. 28:18). The beast makes his last ditch stand. It is a darkening day for Israel. Satan seems to have the upper hand. "Thy life shall hang in doubt before thee" (Deut. 28:66). But God is about to bare His mighty arm.

Shortly the skies will open, and the Messiah will appear on a white horse with saints of all ages in His entourage. In the face of darkest doom, a light breaks through the eastern sky. What a day that will be. God fights for Israel and Israel alone.

What is it that so provokes the wrath of God that He launches the Armageddon campaign against the armies of all nations? It is not pornography, crime, human abuse, cultism, wars in general, abortion, violence, crooked politics, nor prostitution. These are evil sins that offend the Almighty, sins He will deal with in the final judgment, but they are not what triggers Armageddon.

What brings the Armageddon battle is earth's nations attacking Jerusalem and threatening Israel. God cannot allow Israel to be destroyed. His Holiness and reputation are at stake (Ezek. 36:19). Contemplate the holiness of the aliyah. God cannot break his promise to Abraham.

"And it shall come to pass in that day, that I will seek to destroy all the nations that come against Jerusalem" (Zech. 12:9).

"If I whet my glittering sword, and mine hand take hold on judgment; I will render vengeance to mine enemies . . . . Rejoice, O ye nations, with his people: for he will avenge the blood of his servants, and will render vengeance to his adversaries, and will be merciful unto his land, and to his people" (Deut. 32:41,43).

> Then shall the LORD go forth, and fight against those nations, as when he fought in the day of battle. And his feet shall stand in that day upon the mount of Olives, which is before Jerusalem on the east . . . . And the LORD my God shall come, and all the saints with thee. And the LORD shall be king over all the earth: in that day shall there be one LORD, and his name one. Jerusalem shall be safely inhabited (Zech. 14:3-5, 9-11).

We have arrived at the Regnum Millennium, the kingdom of one thousand years.

"Pray for the peace of Jerusalem: they shall prosper that love thee" (Ps. 122:6). "And I will give peace in the land" (Lev. 26:6).

There will be a peace treaty between Israel, Iraq, and Egypt, but it will be a millennial peace treaty.

> In that day shall there be a highway out of Egypt to Assyria [Iraq], and the Assyrian shall come into Egypt, and the Egyptian into Assyria, and the Egyptians shall serve with the Assyrians. In that day shall Israel be the third [in partnership] with Egypt and with Assyria, even a blessing in the midst of the land: Whom the LORD of hosts shall bless, saying, Blessed be Egypt my people, and Assyria the work of my hands, and Israel mine inheritance (Isa. 19:23-25).

In the meantime, our peace comes not from knowing that the nations have signed their intentions not to make war with one another. No. Ours is a higher peace that transcends the workings of man: "Therefore being justified by faith, we have peace with God through our Lord Jesus Christ" (Rom. 5:1).

So what should we do? "Let us therefore follow after the things which make for peace, and things wherewith one may edify another" (Rom. 14:19).

And what will be the final outcome? "And the God of peace shall bruise Satan under your feet shortly. The grace of our Lord Jesus Christ be with you. Amen" (Rom. 16:20).

Section II

The Drama Unfolds

8

America:

Liberty at Twilight

William T. James

The humanists-elite would be our overseers, our controllers, and enforcers — for our own good, of course, most of them believe. More frequently and with greater volume we are hearing these idealistic social designers' cries for change in America. What are they really saying?

From this writer's vantage, they are swinging abruptly between two strategies. It seems they can't choose the one best able to accomplish their purpose, which is to reshape America into a socialist nation. Still, they dream of a socialist nation unlike any other in history: one uniquely tailored for fitting into the quickly developing New World Order we've heard so much about. They — the agents of this change — would, of course, govern us — the social class they would create to be dependent upon them.

The two strategies for accomplishing this seem to be:

First, they plan to reinterpret the Constitution through the political process. How do they hope to accomplish this feat? By stacking the deck of the U.S. house of cards with House and Senate rules that totally favor the pushing forward of the liberal, socialist agenda. Their majorities in Congress assure that this process slowly but steadily continues. The appointment of Supreme Court members who are kindred spirits in liberal, socialist ideology is also a huge part of this strategy. We have only to consider decisions made by this body over the past several decades to realize how far they have come.

The free-spending, socialist-leaning majority party intends to continue through brute, self-willed legislative force to "stack the deck" in favor of the liberal agenda. Of course, this is the same majority party that accused the Bush administration of having a secret "litmus test" for Supreme Court justice appointees and condemned Mr. Bush, who never claimed any such test. When the Clinton administration, however, said that any appointee to the Supreme Court would have to be in favor of the woman's right to choose abortion on demand at any time during the pregnancy, the liberal majority applauded his narrow-mindedness.

Second, they hope to rewrite the Constitution.

Because the strategy of appointing like-minded justices is so painfully slow to them, they want a constitutional convention in which the broad, sweeping changes they so desperately desire can be accomplished through writing a new Constitution altogether.

As a result, these change-hounds have managed to get all but a few of the number of states necessary to approve such a monstrosity as would be a Constitutional convention. Still, there remains an ultimate line of defense — the people. Getting ratification of a new Constitution would be a monumental undertaking. The citizens of America would have to agree to forfeit their freedoms, many of which would surely be deleted from such a hellish document. The chance it could happen, however, should make all who love America and cherish liberty to come to attention any time we hear the call for a movement toward such "change."

America's Ten Commandments

The liberal, humanistic elitists who crave a "new covenant" — in essence, a completely changed constitutional document — base their claim of the right to pursue their agenda on the "positivism" philosophy of law. In other words, they manipulate the facts to show that the founding fathers had no intention of establishing constitutional principles upon a moral absolute. Because, they say, the Constitution has no central standard or code of conduct given by a higher authority (God), then man himself, they proclaim, is the ultimate law-giver; man is the final authority.

The only criterion the founding fathers used and intended for future Americans to use, the legal positivists say, is the belief that there are no absolutes. The views of the nation's founders, they say, are in agreement with their own position, which holds that all things are in a constant state of evolution, including law. That means American constitutional considerations must therefore also evolve — or "change" — with changing circumstances of the times. In other words, God and His standards had no place in the minds of the founding fathers when they set about designing what was once a magnificent republic.

That, of course, we have proved to be a lie through reviewing the founding fathers' own words. (Refer to Chapter 1 for more on the subject.)

God was foremost on these great patriots' minds while they meditated upon Jefferson's Declaration of Independence and Madison's Constitution. That the Creator of all things endowed them, and all peoples everywhere, with "certain inalienable rights," among them "life, liberty, and the pursuit of happiness," was the soul-felt belief that drove them to risk life and limb to win and secure the cherished freedoms we now enjoy — but are in danger of letting slip from our grasp.

That same Creator of all things gave His created beings, called man, a set of moral absolutes — divine law and not positivist legal lawlessness that ultimately would come from such a pseudo noblesse oblige philosophy by which to govern.

Could the founding fathers, who demonstrably held their Creator in such reverence, do anything other than make His principles for living in liberty and at peace, their principles? The Bill of Rights was beyond any doubt, if one truly analyzes these matters with a mind toward learning the facts, a list of those "certain inalienable rights" based upon God's divine law — The Ten Commandments.

America's founding fathers knew that their Creator did not intend that government "give" rights to people. They understood, rather, that government's chief responsibility is to "secure the blessings of liberty," as they agreed it be phrased in the Preamble to the Constitution. At the same time, those men realized and expressed that God-given rights require self-discipline, acceptance of personal responsibility, and obedience to divine law.

George Washington, in his farewell address as president, said it well: "Reason and experience both forbid us that national morality can prevail in exclusion of religious principle."

John Adams wrote that "the United States Constitution was made only for a moral and religious people. It is wholly inadequate for the government of any other."

What would these men think of this generation of Americans? What would they think about our chances for surviving as a free society much beyond the present hour, given the current moral climate in this nation?

Let us look in-depth at a number of those most precious rights that comprise, for the moment at least, the most liberty-securing government that has existed in the history of man.

Who Is Serving Whom?

"(James) Madison once said that 'every step in writing the Constitution was a contest between power and liberty.' As a proponent of a strong Constitution in 1787, he had helped to establish the government that he felt would best protect the rights of the people."[1]

About the new, fertile ground the young nation was in the process of breaking, Madison wrote an essay entitled "Charters," which was published in the *National Gazette,* January 19, 1792:

> In Europe, charters of liberty have been granted by power. America has set the example and France has followed it, of charters of power granted by liberty. This revolution in the practice of the world may with an honest praise, be pronounced the triumphant epoch of its history and the most consoling presage of its happiness. We look back already with astonishment at the daring outrages committed by despotism on the reason and rights of man; we can look forward to the period when it shall be despoiled of all its usurpations, and bound forever in the chains with which it has loaded its miserable victims.

Government, for most of history, has been of the type that suppressed the rights of their "victims." This truth was uppermost in the minds of the founding fathers, as witnessed in their writings.

Concerning governments and their relationships to the people they govern, Thomas Jefferson — certainly one of the strongest advocates of orderly government — expressed his concern about how government tends to gravitate toward heavy-handedness and ever greater control. Writing to James Madison in a letter dated January 30, 1787, Jefferson said regarding a free people under the developing American constitutional form of government that such a state ". . . has a great deal of good in it." Jefferson went on to say:

> The mass of mankind under that enjoys a precious degree of liberty and happiness. It has its evils, too, the trouble of which is the turbulence to which it is subject. But weigh this against the oppressions of (the) monarchic, and it becomes nothing . . . . Even this evil is productive of good. It prevents the degeneracy of government and nourishes a general attention to public affairs. I hold it that a little rebellion now and again is a good thing, and as necessary in the political world as storms in the physical. Unsuccessful rebellions, indeed, generally establish the encroachments on the rights of the people which have produced them. An observation of this truth should render honest republican governors so mild in their punishments of rebellions as not to discourage them too much. It is a medicine necessary for the sound health of government.

Jefferson was not implying that a people should take to anarchic violence in the streets anytime political or judicial decisions went against their wishes. He was saying, however, that the people had a right to expect government, which they had chosen to be their servant rather than their master, to be sensitive to doing what was in their best interest, i.e., to "promote the general welfare."

In other words, when those who govern begin thinking and acting as if they know what is best for the people and no longer listen to the people, then government is no longer of the people, by the people, and for the people. Instead, the people are being made an under-class to serve that oppressive government.

One of the most relevant contemporary examples of this is how Congress and most administrations have for more than a half-century shown little regard for the people's welfare in the area of handling the national economy. The majority of our governmental leaders have, in collusion, taxed and spent our nation into fiscal oblivion.

Although they knew then and know now this was and is true, they did not then, nor do they now intend to realistically deal with what is currently the $4 trillion plus deficit. Moreover, they will not even level with the people that such a deficit is, in reality, one that will not be erased without generations of Americans having to live under near-depression conditions.

Instead, those in the majority political party continue to propose wringing greater percentages of tax dollars out of the American workers' paychecks, using the lie that sacrificing to them for the short term will not only cure the country's economic sickness, but will, in the long-term, produce utopian-type prosperity. This is not to promote one such party over another — for both major parties have failed in the process of governing — but to expose and accentuate the absolute foolhardiness that will lead to America's impoverishment or even her demise.

Of the People, By the People, For the People

Consider the United States government today with its gargantuan bureaucracy that oversees our every activity and intruding into most every aspect of our lives. That's not to mention its payroll that takes a staggering piece of the nation's annual budgetary pie. These facts make it apparent that we have fallen for the revisionist false concept that government of the people, by the people, and for the people means more and more people should be employed by government.

The founding fathers' concept of "public service" was in stark contrast to what has become America's collective "Big Brother," who demands that we pay greater and greater tribute through our tax dollars and our acquiescence to the avalanche of regulations that spew forth from these agencies.

America has strayed far from the founding fathers' belief that while there should be strong government for the purposes of defense and promotion of the general welfare and that the people and the states themselves should be responsible for taking care of their business. Why? For the very common-sense reason that people know most about issues, problems, necessities, and desires that affect their locale.

Historian John Eidsmoe said in *Faith Of Our Founding Fathers*: "... When George Washington became president back in 1789, he had a total of 300 civilian employees to govern this nation of three million people. How could he do it? The only way he could do it was by virtually staying out of people's lives."[2] This was the prevalent view of the nation's founders.

Today we are being told — indeed, have been told for many years through growing government running roughshod over society

— that big government is better government. They want to believe that expanding government is what has made America the great and prosperous nation it has become.

This, however, is another revisionist lie, as witnessed by the burgeoning, bureaucratic, regulatory nightmare that requires being fed ever-increasing helpings of our tax dollars in order to sustain its existence. It is a mammoth greed machine that has been in the process of enslaving the very people the founding fathers wanted to enjoy the greatest possible degree of liberty under law.

Rights always fall victim to growing government, which is by its very nature pervasive and intrusive. If allowed to ignore strict limitations, in the end government becomes totally subjugating.

John Eidsmoe, regarding limited government — that is, government of, by and for the people — said:

> It's interesting that that's a biblical principle. We think of Israel as a monarchy, but the monarchy got its authority from the people . . . . Judges 8:22 (states) "The men of Israel said to Gideon, Rule thou over us. . . ."
>
> We can also look at Judges 9:6 where the men of Shechem made Abimelech king. Also, 2 Kings 14:21 says that the people took Azariah and made him king. In other words, while Israel didn't practice strict democracy, they did depend upon the consent of the governed for (their legitimacy to govern). So, that is a biblical concept. One thing closely related is this concept that this government is by limited, delegated powers; that is, when we the people consent to establish a government, we do so giving that government only such powers as we have set forth for that government in the Constitution. We hear the idea today that government should be given the power to do anything it wants to do unless the Constitution prohibits it. That is not the biblical principle nor is that the principle held by our founding fathers. They thought the government should have no powers other than those given it in the Constitution, expressly or implied. That basic concept is the cornerstone of free, limited government. Without that concept, government is free to do anything it wants to do, and that includes becoming absolute and trampling upon our rights.[3]

The Rights of Every American

What are those rights our founding fathers unanimously viewed as "inalienable?" Which they deemed so precious to liberty that they carefully framed them within one of America's most cherished documents, and gave them a special title, "The Bill Of Rights."

If we are to determine whether we have lost freedoms, or to what degree liberty might have slid down the mountainous slope of invasive, big government, it is necessary to look at that document the nation's founders put in the Constitution. Why? Because its purpose was to "secure the blessings of liberty" to themselves and their posterity — you and me.

Of the many suggested changes to the new Constitution, proposed by James Madison and others, 12 emerged for final consideration, and10 were accepted to present to the ratification process:

> On December 15, 1791, when Virginia became the eleventh state to ratify (the ten amendments), they became part of the supreme law of the land. The so-called Bill of Rights as finally ratified, was generally modeled after the Virginia Declaration of Rights of 1776. Its significant contribution was to put into writing as part of the Constitution those protections against government encroachment that had often been assumed, but not before so explicitly defined.[4]
>
> ARTICLE I Freedom of religious choice; freedom of speech; freedom of press; freedom of assembly; freedom of petition.
>
> ARTICLE II Right to keep and bear arms.
>
> ARTICLE III Freedom from military occupation.
>
> ARTICLE IV Freedom from unreasonable search and seizure.
>
> ARTICLE V Right to grand jury process; freedom from double jeopardy; freedom from self-incrimination; right of due process of law in private ownership.
>
> ARTICLE VI Right to speedy, public trial; right to trial by impartial jury; right to trial in district where crime determined by law to have occurred.
>
> ARTICLE VII Right to jury trial in common law matters involving $20 or more.
>
> ARTICLE VIII Freedom from excessive bail; free-

dom from excessive fines; freedom from cruel and unusual punishment.

ARTICLE IX The enumeration in the Constitutions of certain rights shall not be construed to deny or disparage others retained by the people.

ARTICLE X The powers not delegated to the United States by the Constitution, nor prohibited to it by the states, are reserved to the states respectively, or to the people.

Space limitation makes it necessary to examine only briefly the most obvious areas of erosion to our God-given, constitutionally-guaranteed rights. Is our liberty really on the skids?

The first series of rights to be addressed by The Bill of Rights is also the most dramatic gauge by which to measure how much our liberty has been eroded. The very first safeguard Madison and those helping him frame these amendments addressed, must have been — it logically follows — the matter they gave the highest priority.

1. Freedom of religious choice.

Other portions of this book point out, with more in-depth documentation, the thoughts of the founding fathers relative to God and government. Suffice it to repeat here only the historical truth — that their view was based on freedom "of" religion, not freedom "from" religion, as the majority opinions of recent Supreme Court justices have foolishly ruled.

Under this neo-paganistic interpretation, God has been replaced or is in the process of being replaced by gods of other sorts, whose creator is Satan and satanically-driven man. Bibles are out, condoms are in for our school children. Prayer to the one, true God is, despite the 1993 ruling on prayer, still a thing to be shunned; meditation, to who knows what, is the rage of the age for many "enlightened" educators of our precious young people.

2. Freedom of speech.

What a mockery of this God-given right has been made by godless entertainment industry types, and by people who have lost all fear of Almighty God who gave them tongues designed to give Him praise. Instead, they curse Him at every opportunity, on screen and off, making profane light of His Son Jesus Christ, at whose feet God's Word promises every knee will bow and every tongue will confess that He is Lord.

Teenagers wear t-shirts emblazoned with obscenities, which in an earlier time would have brought the wrath of even the liberal free-speech advocates down upon the wearers. Now, most ignore such lasciviousness of language or find it amusing.

3. Freedom of assembly.

Did the founding fathers have in mind 300,000 homosexuals parading boldly around the nation's capital, openly defying the former code of decent conduct we as a people have ignored to the point of losing it, along with our ability to blush either in embarrassment or with anger? The founding fathers certainly must have based the freedom of assembly clause upon their confidence that the people's moral common sense would be the guiding force to govern such displays, private or public.

The Responsibilities of Every American

Every American, as does every human everywhere, has God-given rights. God alone can give them; government can secure them or take them away. We, the people, are either servants or masters of government. Which are we in America today?

If we are to continue to have rights, freedom, and liberty that only God himself has the ability to give, we must accept His rules and abide by them. There is no other way. Every civilization that has ever existed has died to become the dust upon which successor civilizations now walk — that is irrefutable fact.

Hal Lindsey, on the May 1, 1993, broadcast of "Week In Review," gave some emotion-wrenching facts we nonetheless need to heed:

> The Department of Justice says that sixteen thousand crimes occur on or around our school campuses each day, totaling three million each year. Rape in America rose fifty-nine percent in 1991 versus 1990, with one out of every 1,000 women raped in 1991 . . . . These are hair-raising! The per capita teen-age suicide increased more than 300 percent during the 1960-1990 period, while the per capita divorce rate doubled. There is a link between that, because the breaking up of the family has definitely had a great impact on children.
>
> America has the highest prison incarceration rate of any industrial nation in the world, with 1.1 million inmates. America is number one in the industrial world with teen-age pregnancies and in voluntary abortions, and in

illegal drug use, and in per capita illiteracy.

(This is) staggering! With 5 percent of the world's population, Americans consume 55 percent of all illegal drugs consumed in the world.

A million AIDS victims, a number which can quadruple within five years, a direct result of rampant promiscuity in recent years, will cost 1.4 trillion dollars in medical treatment over the next seven to ten years. A staggering sum which may bankrupt the U.S. insurance companies and the health care systems.

Lindsey then asked, "What has caused all this? ... Number one, America has forgotten God as a people and has chased after gods of materialism, entertainment, and sensual pleasure .... I'm going to do it my way. I'm going to look out for number one .... And in the places where you should find God — in the churches — there's been substituted a social gospel by the secular humanists."

So, it is indeed we, the people, who must come to account for allowing our sins to quench freedom's light. Self-government must be tempered by self-discipline. Man, by his fallen nature — the "depravity of man" as termed by a majority of the founding fathers — must have principles instituted from above.

Repeating some of the most notable founding fathers' remarks about the nature of man and moral principles, George Washington said, "Reason and experience both forbid us to conclude that national morality can prevail in exclusion of religious principles."

Alexander Hamilton said, "Mankind in general, they are vicious .... One great error is that we suppose mankind more honest than they are."

James Madison's basic view of democracy had at its center the understanding that man's nature is depraved. Madisonian Democracy, as it is sometimes called, sprang from his view of human nature.

Words of the great champion of the rights of man, Thomas Jefferson, based upon a realistic and biblical view of the nature of man adds the asterisk of reason to Adam's observation. Jefferson warned that to assure that government produce the sort of society America should be, it would be prudent to "... bind (the people) down with the chains of the Constitution."

Not only is man incapable of granting "certain inalienable rights" to his fellows — rather can only secure them — man is incapable, as well, of authoring principles of morality by which to behave. This is because all such principles man might issue would themselves be faulty. Because of his imperfect nature, man is likewise incapable of submitting to principles of any sort, apart from governmental enforcement. Self-discipline, then, is really discipline that people either have forced upon them, or agree to by consent. Any other "society" is anarchic and chaotic.

Every American's Moral Guidelines

Clearly, Judeo-Christian precepts were foremost among priorities considered when the nation's founders set about to "ordain and establish" a document that would "secure the blessings of liberty," thereby creating a government of laws under which the people would happily consent to live. Volumes of the documents from that era testify to the fact that the Ten Commandments of Exodus 20 were the life-source of those guiding moral principles.

It is clear; God gave inalienable rights to man. He also outlined man's responsibilities for the privilege of living in that liberty. It is His law. The founding fathers recognized that their duty was to secure the liberty by incorporating God's law. Their accomplishment of this was more than patriotic, more, even, than brilliant; surely, it was inspired!

Benjamin Franklin was said to have uttered while walking with a friend after the task was completed that now the people had their Republic — if they could keep it. As one who loves this, the crown jewel among all the nations, I must warn that the evidence is overwhelming that we are far into the process of letting America, and our liberty, slip away.

Is it merely irony that the Articles within the American Bill of Rights number 10? This is the same as the number of responsibilities to God outlined in His commandments to not only Israel, but to all humanity. Coincidence? Unlikely.

Is violation of His law — which so obviously permeates our Constitution — the thing bringing this once great republic down? Let us examine Lady Liberty through the stethoscope of the Ten Commandments for a diagnosis.

First Commandment: No Other Gods

"Thou shalt have no other gods before me."
The Creator of all things, engraving with His own finger the law for Moses to give to the children of Israel, and subsequently to the whole world, first made clear that HE IS GOD. In His jealousy, He will not take lightly His creation, man, making their own gods.

Unlike our own conception of jealousy, which is that of hatefulness, spitefulness, pettiness — the green-eyed monster — God's is a righteous jealousy. It is righteous because it is God demonstrating His absolute love for mankind through His omniscience. God and God alone knows what is best for that which He alone created.

For man to choose to make gods in their own image, rather than to accept the true God who made them in His image, is more than simply an embarrassment to Him or an angering slap to His face; it is an act that separates people from their Creator, which always takes the rebellious, unrepentant ones down the broad way to destruction.

In our examination, it is appropriate to ask: Do Americans have gods other than the God of heaven?

Again, it seems more than coincidence or irony that the first right listed in the Bill of Rights deals with religion and the first of the commandments deals with there being only one God. There should be no doubt that the following is neither irony nor coincidence but God speaking directly to us.

The first commandment is that man is to have no other god but the true God. Jesus, while discoursing about things to come, told His followers, ". . . Take heed that no man deceive you. For many shall come in my name, saying, I am Christ and shall deceive many" (Matt. 24:4-5).

Jesus, who is God incarnate, was saying the same thing in the New Testament that He said in the Old. The very first thing He told them in the discourse was, in effect, "Have no other god before me." He was saying, "There is but one God, and one mediator between God and men, the man Christ Jesus" (1 Tim. 2:5).

Lucifer's whole plot to destroy mankind is based on the deception that people don't need God. The devil tells us to go after other gods — to become "as God" ourselves. Should it be surprising that as the end of the age approaches, as Christ's second advent nears, people are choosing to have gods of their own creation?

Sadly, tragically, no nation of people is so programmed by Satan, and by the fallen, depraved nature of man, to succumb to being deceived into accepting "other gods" as is America.

A news press service story on May 6, 1993, reported: "John Lemke, of Denver, whose company is licensing souvenirs for Pope John Paul II's World Wide Youth Day, to be August 12-15, said the company turned down an offer from someone who wanted to walk behind the holy father and scoop up the dirt he'd walked on and sell it as 'ground the pope walked on.' "

The intent here is not to critique or disparage the Catholic faith. Nor is it to make light of the head of the Catholic Church. The story does, however, draw a darkly-humorous picture of how love of money, which Jesus called the root of all evil, is a prime factor in the process of people making their own gods in America today. People whose idea it was to make merchandise of the pope's visit obviously were not primarily concerned with worshipping God to a greater degree through the papal visit. They wished to enhance the god of their true affection, mammon.

Money — loved and worshipped by this materialistic generation — gives Americans power to obtain, attain, acquire, and manufacture the many glittering things representative of this, the most leisurely, recreation-oriented, pleasure-seeking culture in earth's long history of decadent societies.

Second Commandment: No Graven Images

"Thou shalt not make unto thee any graven image . . . . "

Egypt was full of the gods they had carved out of ivory, stone, exotic woods and molded from shimmering metals. The children of Israel, who had to a large degree adopted many of the pagan religious practices involving these idols, were told through the law given to them by God through Moses that this was forbidden.

Why was it forbidden? Because these things directed the attention of the people away from the true, living God, which meant they, in their disbelief, could never come to full knowledge of Him in order to be redeemed from their fallen state and thus reconciled to the Creator.

Anything man shapes with his own hands or creates with his own intellect that preoccupies his heart and mind to the extent that God is pushed out of his thoughts was, and is, a graven idol, no matter the image in which it is cast.

In an article in the May 3, 1993, issue of *U.S. News & World Report* titled, "Technology Titans Sound Off on the Digital Future," a number of top executives for some of America's corporate giants in technology talked about their visions for the future.

William Gates, chairman of Microsoft Corporation, said in part, "Today, a lot of electronic devices perform a few specialized functions. But imagine a single wallet-size device from which you could activate all of your other devices — your tablet-size or desk top personal computer, appliances in your house, whatever large- screen display you have in your home. I envision a wallet PC that can allow interchange and communications between all these other devices."

Barry Diller, chairman of QVC Network, Inc., stated, "... In the next couple of years we can lay out as many home shopping forms as the imagination is capable of .... Digital technology is rapidly merging the telephone, television and stereo with the computer .... We'll communicate more productively, conduct business more efficiently, educate our children more efficiently and entertain ourselves more pleasurably."

Craig McCaw, chairman of McCaw Cellular Communications, Inc., said, "... a wireless environment will allow people personal freedom .... While the telephone was a tremendous advancement, now those telephone wires is [sic] the leash that chokes us ....

"There are now 11 million cellular customers in the United States, and we are adding them at the rate of about 9,700 a day .... We have not even begun to see the future of data over the cellular network."

George Fisher, chairman of Motorola, Inc., stated, "With the convergence of wireless communications and digital computing, it won't be long until you can sit at the beach with your personal communicator and take part in a video conference anywhere in the world .... Today there are about 200,000 wireless data users .... We estimate that by the year 2000, the market will explode to more than 26 million users ...."

There is not necessarily any nobleness of purpose in doing backbreaking work; neither is there necessarily any evil inherent within using labor-saving and time-efficient machinery.

Idolatry is born when man, who is created in the image of God and therefore is himself capable of a limited degree of creativity, first determines to pursue through his own imaginings the shaping of things in such a way as to draw attention to himself and to fulfill his self-centered gratifications. Thus, through his own graven images, he makes himself his own god, and ultimately becomes so hardened in his willfulness that he will acknowledge no other.

"Thou shalt not bow down thyself to them, nor serve them ...."

Jesus put it this way: "... Where your treasure is, there will your heart be also" (Matt. 6:21).

God the Holy Spirit said through the apostle James, addressing end-time man as well as James' contemporaries: "... ye have heaped together treasures for the last days. ..." In the first part of the condemnation, the Scripture says "Your gold and silver are rusted, and the rust of them shall be a witness against you, and shall eat your flesh, as it were fire . . ." (James 5:3).

Can there be much doubt that ours in America today is the most money-oriented society ever to exist? The very term, "The American Dream," immediately elicits fantasies of success, manifested by great accumulation of wealth. Comedy writers have for years put in the mouths of the characters who say them, the expressions "Only in America!" or "I love this country!" in reference to the material gratification available in the United States.

Popular game shows are entitled "Wheel of Fortune," "Let's Make A Deal," "Treasure Hunt," and others in tribute to America's real god — money. Late night television is replete with many gurus of how to make fantastic amounts of money with minimum effort. Entire states hold out the promise of instant wealth with their "gods" of lottery.

Americans spend hours upon hours in front of their television screens. We desire the newest cars, homes, clothing for ourselves and our children. We think of our movie or soap opera stars and our star athletes and their teams far more often than we do of the Saviour who bled and died that we might live forever.

Those screens are filled daily and nightly with the priests and priestesses of fortune. Like those of the ancient pagans, the proliferating hordes of psychic advisers promise to plot the mammon-worshipers' paths to riches and success in all areas of life.

The most tragic of all money-god worship is thriving in America today more than in any other nation on earth. Those false prophets and false teachers come as wolves in sheep's clothing to fleece the flock and bring "damnable heresies." Of them, God warned in 2 Peter 2:3: "And through covetousness shall they with feigned words make merchandise of you . . . ."

These who make merchandise of the saints, and whom God will surely judge in His good time (2 Pet. 2:4), and those who fall for their false "name it and claim it" doctrine, hurt the cause of Christ and give Satan ammunition in three most obvious ways:

1. By diverting emphasis from the gospel message of salvation through grace by faith alone.

2. By directing less biblically well-grounded Christians (babes in Christ) away from God's true Christian growth principles (strong scriptural meat).

3. By providing America's secular media — already antagonistic to the gospel message of Christ — with fodder to heap upon the heads of an unbelieving world.

More and more, all of Christianity is being lumped by media into the same category with the Jim Joneses, the David Khoreshes, and the "wolves in sheep's clothing" of 2 Peter 2:3.

Third Commandment: Don't Profane God's Name

"Thou shalt not take the name of the LORD thy God in vain."

This generation of Americans, if not *the* most profane in use of language ever to inhabit our planet, must certainly closely rival that people who hold the ignoble championship title in that classification.

Much is made today over freedom of speech, the right that is guaranteed within the First Amendment. Those who cry loudest that they have the right to express themselves, free from censorship, under the free speech clause in the Bill of Rights, are some of the ones who curse most vilely the One who gave them the inalienable right to speak. No, it is not one of the founding fathers; it is God whose name they use, profanely — the Creator who gave them not only the right to express themselves but the physical sense of speech with which to do so.

America's entertainment industry, particularly the majority of filmmakers, take God's name in vain and blaspheme the name of Jesus in every movie above the rating of "G."

Profanity in the United States is not limited to the lowbrow elements of our culture. It seems that in a growing number of more affluent and more educated segments of society, use of profane language has become as entrenched as it has always been within the so-called lower strata of society. This verbal perversity is taking its toll on our young.

An article entitled "Teachers Say More Kids Using Profanity" in the January/February 1993 issue of *The Christian World Report* presented the following:

> According to an article in the *New England Baptist,* (October, 1992) kids are (cursing) more today.
>
> Elementary teacher Peggy George notes that she returned to the teaching profession after an 18-year absence and said she has seen a vast difference in the amount of profanity children use. The article points out that she has also noted a difference in the types of children using

profanity these days.

When she left the teaching profession, she was at a school in a low income area of Nashville, where the students often struggled to survive.

Now, she is "more shocked" that her students (curse) because she estimates that "two-thirds of my students are from homes in which both parents have a college education."

Lawlessness — doing that which is right in our own eyes — is not simply violence perpetrated in a physical manner, that is, robbery, rape, murder. Violence in our society and culture is done in and through language with which we communicate as well. How is that true? Because profanity slices, rips, and bludgeons with our most powerful and dangerous physical weapon — the tongue.

Through our sense of speech, a unique gift among all of God's earthly creations, man, by his cursings defies the Creator who made him in His own image. Americans are more and more taking the Lord's name in vain. This sin goes much deeper than just blaspheming God with our mouths. We were created for the purpose of giving pleasure to God through our fellowship with Him. Our tongues were given us to issue forth praise to Almighty God, the Creator of all things.

We use the name of God in vain when we speak His name in frustration or anger or casual context. In addition, when we use our tongues to curse through foul language, we are using them for purposes diametrically contrary to those purposes for which God gave us the ability to speak.

God's Word has much to say about the matter of the gift of speech and its attendant responsibility:

> . . . The tongue is a little member and boasteth great things. Behold how great a matter a little fire kindleth!
>
> The tongue is a fire, a world of iniquity: so is the tongue among our members, that it defileth the whole body, and setteth on fire the course of nature; and it is set on fire of hell.
>
> For every kind of beast, and of birds and of serpents, and of things in the sea, is tamed, and have been tamed of mankind: but the tongue can no man tame; it is an unruly evil, full of deadly poison. Therewith bless we God, even

the Father; and therewith curse we men, which are made after the similitude of God. Out of the same mouth proceedeth blessing and cursing. My brethren, these things ought not so to be (James 3).

America, such things ought not to be! For God also pronounces a frightening prospect of judgment: "Thou shalt not take the name of the LORD thy God in vain; for the LORD will not hold him guiltless that taketh his name in vain" (Exod. 20:7).

Fourth Commandment: Keep the Sabbath Holy

"Remember the Sabbath day and keep it holy."

The American people have, until most recent times, set aside one day a week mostly free from commerce and work — a day of rest. Although a large number of people viewed it as just that — a day of rest — a significant percentage of the American population treated it as a day for turning one's thoughts more specifically to God. This concept grew up with our nation and was based on the Old Testament law: "Remember the Sabbath and keep it holy."

Commerce and business, buying and selling in all forms, today proceeds at half-speed on Sunday in many regions of the country, while for others it's full steam ahead. The only gods reserved for honor on Sunday in the minds of many are the idols earlier analyzed in light of the first three commandments.

The freedom to worship, which our forefathers struggled so long and painfully to secure, is becoming observably less and less important than our own self-proclaimed, self-granted right to do as we please. This is the case despite that the founding fathers included the moral precepts found in the Ten Commandments — one of which is the setting aside of one day devoted to thoughts of worship of the Creator — in their formulation of our Constitution.

The late Dr. J. Vernon McGee, in his commentary, *Thru the Bible with J. Vernon McGee,* said, "The exact day [the Sabbath principle is observed] is not important. After all, the calendar changes that have been made make it impossible for us to know whether our seventh day is our Saturday or not . . . . We recognize the first day of our week because our Lord came back from the dead on that day."

And that is exactly why He deserves our honor, our praise, our worship. He died and was raised again the third day so that lost man can be redeemed. He is God! Those who claim to be His followers, the professing Christians in our land, are far from immune to this nationwide epidemic — the overt national indifference toward God. *The New England Baptist,* October 10, 1992, reported:

> "Churches must make a more basic approach to evangelizing America as the country becomes increasingly secular and more people grow up without a church," a Kentucky seminary professor said.
>
> "It has become possible to say that the United States of America is the largest mission field in the western hemisphere," said George Hunter, professor of evangelism at Asbury Theological Seminary. Hunter was speaking at "Toward the Year 2000," a conference of about 50 denominations, to discuss evangelism goals.
>
> "The whole map of the Christian mission world has essentially changed," he said, adding that Uganda has a larger percentage of professing Christians than America.

Fifth Commandment: Honor Your Parents

"Honor thy father and thy mother."

The apostle Paul's letter to Timothy puts the finger of Almighty God upon what will be one of the key characteristics of mankind as the time of the end of the age nears.

"This know, also, that in the last days perilous times shall come. For men shall be . . . disobedient to parents . . . . Without natural affection . . ." (2 Tim. 3:1-3).

And is there any wonder that this symptom is widespread in every strata of society? From the street gangs comprised of inner-city youth who torch neighborhoods to the children of privilege and affluence who date rape and are exonerated through influence of wealth-secured power, Americans have ignored their children. And now the children, whose gods — like those of their parents — are the gods of pleasure-seeking, are turning their anger and frustration upon their fathers and mothers.

The latent confusion, disorientation, and rage in America's child-parent relationships have surfaced during this generation to dramatically expose themselves through a peculiar manifestation. An article in the May 24, 1993, issue of *Insight* magazine entitled "Total Recall Versus Tricks of the Mind," by Gayle Hanson, reports on the phenomenon. The summary reads:

> Families are being torn apart as adult children sud-

denly appear to recall childhood sexual abuse. Yet there is an eerie similarity among cases. Nearly all the accusers are white, college-educated women in their thirties and forties, and in virtually every case the memory of alleged sexual abuse occurs only after psychotherapy. Are the shrinks to blame?

The writer then introduces the person who is the subject of the article, frequently using her own words. "It started for me in 1986," she says in a voice honeyed by a sweetly resonant Texas twang. "I was seeking help for bulimia at the time, and I heard about a group meeting and I thought I'd go. . . ."

In the language of the group she's addressing, (the woman subject) is what is known as a recanter. What she's recanting are her own accusations, made in the mid-1980s against her family, that she was abused as a child. . . .

As (the woman) tells it, she is a victim — not of abuse but of therapy which sent her into a two-year tailspin of multiple hospitalizations, familial confrontations, suicide attempts, and daily doses of mood-altering drugs.

(The woman) believes that she is a victim of an overzealous therapist who used techniques including trance writing and dream guidance to manipulate her into believing that she had repressed the memories of sexual abuse at the hands of her mother, father, and grandmother.

. . . If (the woman's) audience resembles that of a retirement planning meeting and any well-heeled suburban enclave, it is not. Instead, most of the participants have been drawn together by a commonalty that runs much deeper and darker. To describe them bluntly, they are accused child molesters. But just like (the woman subject), they claim it never occurred.

The one weekend in April they have gathered in Philadelphia from as far away as New Zealand for a landmark conference of a fledgling organization called the False Memory Syndrome Foundation, an advocacy group composed of more than 3,700 families accused by adult offspring of childhood sexual abuse.

According to Executive Director Pamela Freyd, the year-old foundation has been inundated by inquiries from families who have been accused. "When we started we thought we might have 500 families involved after a year," she says. "We had no idea of the scope of the problem. But our phones haven't stopped ringing since we opened our office."

To be intellectually honest, one must conclude that the lack of honor shown fathers and mothers by children, young and older, reflects to a large degree the sins of the parents who have ducked the God-taught responsibility that goes with the God-given blessing children are meant to be.

Regarding the strange, destructive path parent-child relations has been traveling through American society in recent times, author Arnold Beichman writes in an article titled, "Child Abuse Witch-Hunt Threatens Family Unit," for *Insight*, May 31, 1993: "I am not suggesting that Marxists, radical feminists, or radical egalitarians have engineered a diabolical plot against the family by fomenting panic about sexual abuse. But we are awash in surveys of dubious provenance that are interpreted to mean that parents can't be trusted near children."

Perhaps Mr. Beichman can't say so, but, certainly, someone is directing the "diabolical plot against the family." As he points out, we are "awash" in the evidence.

Second Timothy, chapter 3, tells that in the last days a characteristic that will mark end-time man is that he will be "without natural affection" and "disobedient to parents." Disobedience to parents manifests itself in a major way today in the United States. Government, public education, and the media have gotten in on the act, the "diabolical plot" hatched and nurtured by Satan himself. Along with the radical feminists, the radical egalitarians, and the Marxists, the courts now intrude more and more into the "natural affection" that God created to exist between children and parents. The American court system, it is tragic but true, no longer has at its foundation God-given law, as was intended by the founding fathers.

Sixth Commandment: Don't Murder

"Thou shalt not kill."

Some rationalize that capital punishment is wrong because the Bible says "Thou shalt not kill." But they are either employing fallacious reasoning or else are woefully ignorant of truth found in God's Word. The Bible says that he who sheds *innocent* blood shall forfeit his own life (see Gen. 9:6).

It is appropriate to point out that the liberal mind-set, which speciously argues that capital punishment is morally wrong, is more often than not the flip side of the mindset which proposes that there is nothing morally wrong with killing a baby still in the womb through abortion. This commandment is saying to man, however, "You are not to shed the blood of the *innocent,* therefore, thou shalt not murder."

The sixth commandment is an element of God-pronounced law central to the formula our founding fathers used to create the document by which the nation is governed. Is there any evidence that America has violated this statute?

Accounts of murderous acts by adults invade our eyes and ears anytime, day or night, that we come across news reports. The depravity of man, however, becomes most evident when those murders are reported to have been committed by the youngest among our numbers. Tragically, the statistics show that America is in the process of becoming the leader among nations in youth-committed crimes, including those crimes involving murder.

The commandment "Thou shalt not kill" falls upon deaf ears that have become desensitized by entertainment, violent cultural lifestyle, adult example, and even by the public education system itself.

An Associated Press story dated June 11, 1992, reported a disturbing occurrence that requires our heeding:

> Parents in Billerica, Massachusetts, are up in arms over a grade school newspaper article describing "15 Ways to Kill Your Sister," but a teacher considered it "fourth- and fifth-grade humor."
>
> "There's enough violence in kids' lives without the school condoning this as literature," said Essey Foley, mother of a first-grader at the Parker School where the paper was distributed.
>
> The article, written by a fourth-grade boy, included such methods as setting a sister on fire, hacking her with an ax, and dropping her off the top of a building.
>
> "This exhibited poor judgment, and while I don't think there was malice aforethought, it should not have been put in the paper," said School Superintendent Robert J. Calabrese.
>
> Gladys Cerrato, a teacher for more than 20 years, supervises the newspaper. Calabrese sent her a "mild letter

of reprimand," but she will be allowed to supervise when she returns from an unrelated leave of absence.

Based on the unbridled, dynamic imagination within the child's eager mind, and the stimulation children receive in daily megadoses through TV, movies, and video games, it is wise to ponder if the preceding "how to kill one's sister" story — and the educator's philosophy that allowed it — is but a step leading to the sort of activity described in the following accounts.

An article in the *Union Leader,* September 4, 1992, tells the story of a frightening trend.

> Vivian was among 12 people who survived, some-how, a shooting spree of such ferocity and randomness that the case-hardened cops of the 41st precinct were amazed.
>
> The attack reflects a relatively new and terrifying fact of life on New York's mean streets: spray shootings, in which bystanders are killed or injured.
>
> "It's a trend," said Assistant Police Chief Thomas Gallagher, the Bronx's top cop. "One thing is that there are a lot of younger people involved, and when you're young, you think you're immortal, and you have little regard for people other than yourself."
>
> Slightly more than 4,000 people in the city have been killed in gunfire this year, compared with about 3,900 for the same period of 1991, police said. Although no break-down was available, many were bystanders.

The *Los Angeles Times* reported in the September 20, 1992, edition:

> Ronald Ray Howard, a 19-year old Texan, has been charged with the murder of Texas Highway Trooper Bill Davidson. According to accounts, Howard was driving a stolen car and listening to a tape of rapper Tupac Amuru Shakur's violent "2APACALYPSENOW." The album includes six songs that portray the killing of police officers.
>
> In addition to the murder charge, the officer's widow has filed a separate civil suit against the San Francisco area-based Shakur and his Interscope Records label, owned by Time Warner.
>
> Howard told authorities he was listening to

"2APACALYPSENOW" as he loaded his weapon, aimed it at the officer, and pulled the trigger.

Al Tanner, Howard's court-appointed attorney, said he intends to summon psychiatrists and sociologists to deliver expert opinions on whether violent entertainment can alter the behavior of impressionable young people. "In all my years of defending inner-city clients, I have never introduced music before as a mitigating circumstance in a murder case. But I do believe it applies in this case. Without the music riling him up, I do not think this incident would have occurred," Tanner said.

Time Warner is a major entertainment company which earlier had released Ice T's "Cop Killer" promoting the killing of policemen.

God's law says, "Thou shalt not kill," but by tolerating even a degree of this virulent philosophy, spewed at our children by America's dollar-lusting entertainment industry, the nation is saying, "Thou shalt kill if you wish."

Seventh Commandment: No Adultery

"Thou shalt not commit adultery."

It is a bit too easy to blame the entertainment industry for what is happening to fidelity in marriage in contemporary America. True, like in violation of the previous commandment, those who fuel their lust for power and wealth by selling our culture on the excitement to be found within sin are guilty. But, the statistics on divorce and those on infidelity within marriage tell the story that adultery is on its way to becoming the norm rather than the exception. Why? Because people will be people.

History, ancient and modern, shows that man — that is, men and women — when living in relative affluence and freedom, inevitably sink into sexual immorality. Sexual drive in man is a consuming fire that can only be controlled and contained on a consistent basis in one of two ways. One, by inordinately strong, personal character and moral resolve, possessed by very few; and two, through a regenerate mind which only the Holy Spirit can give. That happens when one accepts Christ and turns his life, soul, and body over to God, and His Spirit conforms His child to His Son's likeness and transforms that life into one of righteous behavior (see Rom. 12:1-2).

The entertainment industry is simply giving a degenerating

American culture what it wants — a godless feast of sensuality. All of society, particularly the children, are paying the high price of that adulterous orgy.

Eighth Commandment: Don't Steal

"Thou shalt not steal."

Stealing infects the human race in many forms. It is perhaps the most marked characteristic of fallen human nature. From the child who picks up a toy with the thought to steal it, to the most elaborate Brinks-type robbery, stealing has always been a pronounced and most grievous sin in America.

More and more, in our day, violence accompanies theft, to the extent it is made difficult in many cases for investigators to determine whether the victim is murdered as part of the robbery itself, or robbery was committed in order to cover up another motive for the murder.

Larceny is indeed in the hearts of many in America today. We've all heard or read the accounts of the Girl Scout leaders who abscond with the cookie-sale funds, embezzlements within business and major corporations, and ongoing thievery within governments — municipal, state, and national.

Taxation, even with representation — particularly the sort of representation we sometimes see taking place in the halls of Congress and the executive — can be tyranny. What about when those who are supposed to guard the public trust wantonly tax and spend on pork-barrel pet projects, or to appease one lobbyist or special interest group or another? It is stealing, plain and simple! Likewise, the usury taking place — interest rates far exceeding that needed for a reasonable margin of return — is nothing short of legalized theft.

The desire to take what does not belong to oneself is demonstrably, deeply ingrained within the dark side of the national character. An article in the May 3, 1993, issue of *U.S. News & World Report* by Lewis Lord, entitled "From Tourist to Victim," states:

> Suddenly travelers are seeing signs that their welfare is a matter of real concern. Following the highly publicized murder of a German tourist who got lost in Miami and was subsequently beaten and run over in front of her mother and two children, some rental-car outlets in southern Florida now hand out brochures advising drivers how to prevent a car-jacking. The American Automobile Association has notified the 22,000 U.S. hotels and motels it

rates that they will be dropped from AAA guides in 1995 if they don't provide deadbolt locks and peepholes. In May, more than 2,600 motels will start running safety tips on in-room television sets for the first time. Even campers in national parks are being warned about roving gangs of thieves.

Does this mean America is becoming a more dangerous place to vacation? In Florida, tourism officials say an out-of-stater's chance of being a crime victim is less than 1 in 1,000. But with the six tourists murdered in the state since last December, Miami has erected road signs to shunt tourists away from the most dangerous areas. Indications are that tourists have become preferred targets.

Con-artists prey upon good-hearted people by falsely soliciting funds while others lie about helping victims' families — as some did in the case of three little boys murdered in West Memphis in May 1993. Then there are the respected charitable organizations whose bureaucracies, we eventually learn, are spending the bulk of contributed moneys to support their own elaborate lifestyles. At the other end are the gangs and mobs who rob people of their dignity and their lives through drugs, prostitution, and other means. All reflect that the Unites States has become a society that defies God's commandment, "Thou shalt not steal."

Ninth Commandment: Don't Lie

"Thou shalt not bear false witness."
The apostle Paul wrote, under inspiration in 2 Timothy, about the perilous times that will come upon the end-time generation. One of the characteristics God saw fit to warn about was that there would be many ". . . false accusers . . ." (2 Tim. 3:3).

Fallen man is certainly sufficient within his own desperately wicked heart to find motive for "falsely accusing" others. But in America's dog-eat-dog system of climbing the ladder of materialism, the inclination to step on one's "competition" in the drive to win — even if that means telling lies about the competition — is rampant and expected.

Tenth Commandment: Don't Covet

"Thou shalt not covet . . ."
Which brings us to the central cause of false accusation. The

desire to have more, better, bigger, prettier things than one's neighbor. The feeling of power is derived from such heady, though woefully unfulfilling "status."

The recent tragedy in the figure skating world, in which Nancy Kerrigan was mercilessly throttled in the knee by those seeking to eliminate her from world-class competition points to coveting in its vilest forms.

Breaking the commandment, "Thou shalt not covet," is the manifestation of "the love of money," which Christ said is "the root of all evil." In this regard, our blessed nation has gone the way of Lucifer, who desired to have and to be more than even God who created him.

No Way Out?

As America sinks ever deeper into decay, liberty's torch is about to go beneath the quicksand of satanically-planned decadence. This magnificently endowed nation, in this writer's view, has been so favored by God's generosity primarily for three reasons:

1. To produce the godly people who have spread the gospel and who even now continue to shed abroad the message of light: the good news that Jesus Christ came to redeem lost mankind from sin;

2. To produce the technology that makes that mission possible through human agencies; and

3. To serve as God's chosen national sword with which to protect His beloved Israel during the crucial time of its regathering for human history's final act.

Is the U.S. indispensable to God in this regard? No.

God, more often than not, chooses to use human agents, including entire nations, to accomplish His purposes, rather than spectacular, supernatural demonstrations. This has been particularly true during this present dispensation. Make no mistake, God does not "need" America — America needs God. But He does love America, and, thankfully, continues to use this nation.

Why is America, so mightily used of God, not mentioned by name in His Holy Word? What is to be America's fate since it is not listed among end-time nations? Good questions, and perhaps questions to which only God himself has answers. However, there has been much conjecture on the subject by godly men who have intensively studied His prophetic Word.

Dr. Richard W. DeHaan, in his book *Israel and the Nations in Prophecy,* wrote the following:

> (The) revived Roman empire will be a Western power. At the time of its greatest extent, Rome covered Western Europe, including England, the Middle East, Egypt and North Africa. This gives us good reason to believe that the ten-kingdom alliance of the future will cover these geographical areas, and perhaps include other nations and territories. It will be worldwide in influence and power according to Revelation 13:1-10. We cannot deny the possibility that the United States, or other nations of the Western Hemisphere, may be part of this end-time empire. Some conclude that because the United States is not specifically named in the prophetic Scripture, it will be either completely destroyed, or a second-rate power when the final confederacy of nations is formed. But, this is not necessarily a correct deduction. In view of its alignment with the nations of Western Europe, it is quite possible, even probable, that the United States will play a significant role in the empire dominated by Anti-Christ.[5]

Others take a much more speculative approach to the question. S. Franklin Logsdon, in his book *Is the USA in Prophecy?* says the following, which he bases on a number of Scriptures found throughout the prophetic Word.

> If you ask, "Is the USA mentioned by name in prophecy?" the answer, of course, is "No." But if you ask, "Is the USA in the framework of prophecy?" the answer in an unqualified "Yes."
>
> Actually, it is unthinkable that the God who knows the end from the beginning would pinpoint such small nations as Libya, Egypt, Ethiopia, and Syria in the prophetic declaration and completely overlook the wealthiest and most powerful nation on the earth. Too long have we evaded the question. Too long have we summarily grouped our country with the so-called revived Roman Empire. Too long have we persisted in terming the USA in prophecy as one of the "lion's cubs," thus giving her but an inferential mention in the shadow of a diminishing Britain.[6]

David Allen Lewis, in his book *Prophecy 2000* presents yet another significant thought regarding America's place in biblical prophecy:

> The spread of the gospel to all nations in the end-times is a prophecy of major importance in Scripture. Jesus said "This gospel shall be preached in all the world for a witness to all nations, and then shall the end come" (Matt. 24:14). If one could locate a nation that God is using primarily in the fulfillment of this prophecy then we will have located a nation of destiny, fulfilling a major prophecy. The consequences of that prophecy's being fulfilled would be greater than that of the Gog and Magog prediction of Ezekiel 38 and 39.
>
> The atmosphere of religious freedom in this country, which has prevailed for two hundred years, contributes to the fulfillment of Jesus' prophecy. No other nation in history has ever seen two hundred continuous years of religious toleration.
>
> Since America, with the liberality of its government and churches has been the major instrument in the hands of God, fulfilling the prophecy of Matthew 24:14, it follows that the U.S.A. enjoys a most exalted position in the scheme of events that lead up to the end of the age.
>
> The story of God's dealing with America in past centuries is an exciting saga of modern history. Is it possible that there is a special divinely-appointed destiny for our nation? If this is found to be true, what challenge does this present for the Church today? What role should we play in fulfilling the prophecy of the last days?[7]

Thomas Jefferson, in his "Notes on Virginia," wrote, "Indeed I tremble for my country when I reflect that God is just."

We should be thankful to God that He is also merciful. Without His mercy, subject only to His justice, the planet itself would have long since ceased to exist. Looking back at how far America has strayed, knowing this physically strongest, most beautiful, most technologically advanced nation in the history of earth is not once mentioned by name in God's prophesies about the end-time world, it must be asked with concern: Is there no way out of the quagmire of sin in which we as a nation find ourselves?

Only one. It is based solely on God's mercy rather than on His justice. That one way to liberation from the sins that beset us as individuals — as Americans — is a person. His name is Jesus. He is the true light of the world, the One, true God who gives liberty, who alone has the power to make men, women, children — and nations — free indeed!

9

America Abandoned:

The Delta Factor at Work

Joseph J. Carr

Change: To make radically different; to transform; to give a different . . . course or direction to; to replace with another; to undergo modification; to put different clothes or covering on.

Change. It can be a wonderful thing; it can be a real blessing, an immense benefit. Change is progress. Change can be an opportunity to right wrongs or make things better. Change can also be an on-rushing locomotive or a berserk destroyer.

Scientists use the Greek letter "delta" to symbolically represent change; therefore, we shall call change the "Delta Factor."

The Delta Factor characterizes the nineteenth and twentieth centuries more than it characterized any previous period of history. Change is so great and comes so fast today that people born 50 or 60 years ago barely recognize the world they live in. In fact, some older people are hopelessly bewildered by the changes that have taken place. Even 40 year olds sense that something precious has slipped away, perhaps forever.

Change accelerates so fast today that one commentator identified a pathological condition resulting from change and named it "Future Shock." It is obvious that a major paradigm shift is underway in Western culture. The question is whether the change is painful or pleasant.

Knowledge has increased explosively over the past dozen or so decades; and that itself feeds change. The old Judeo-Christian morality passed away in some aspects and is severely altered in others. Today, what was once unthinkable is now commonplace; what was once obscene is now called decent; what today is viewed with revulsion, may tomorrow be customary. Even cultural roles are no longer so well defined as they once were.

As with Milton's *Paradise Lost* we have said: "Evil, be thou mine good."

As we plunge headlong into the third millennium after Christ, some people see mankind on the cusp between two great ages. Christian prophecy buffs, secular pundits, Futurists, New Age seers, and occultists of all stripes feel that a major turning point is in the wind. They sense that a significant alteration in our Western way of seeing things is in the offing. The expected epochal shift is viewed with excitement by some, and mounting dread by others (especially in the Church).

Most people outside of the Church see the turning points of history as merely a series of discrete quasi static steps in man's evolution. Humanists accept this gospel of evolution on little real evidence because it is more comfortable for them than wrestling with the God they say doesn't exist.

New Agers, on the other hand, accept evolution as the theory that explains the progress of the soul human from mineral, through animal to rediscovered divinity. Thus, for New Agers, evolution is a religious theory, as perhaps it is also for atheists.

The Quasi-Static Change

Scientists must often analyze physical systems that are not easily changed. In some systems, a large change of state is too complicated to analyze even with a computer — although tiny changes are handled easily. In other cases, the system is so unstable that any small change at all perturbs the system and provokes a radical, sometimes violent, response.

In order to cope with such systems, scientists invented an analytical method that serves as a metaphor for the Delta Factor in previous decades: quasi static change. Something "static" is unchanging, so by quasi static we mean something that is nearly unchanging. A quasi static change is nearly infinitesimal; it is too small to be of immediate consequence; it is a tiny, almost imperceptible step.

By making the changes small enough and waiting for the effects of the present change to die out before making another small change, the scientist can eventually effect a large total change without perturbing the system into a violent reaction. While the large all-at-once change results in a violent and often uncontrollable reaction, a large number of small quasi static changes summed together gently reaches the same goal unnoticed.

Quasi static change is easily assimilated without notice as society has a chance to think, reflect, and evaluate change . . . or even control it carefully. But when change comes too fast, then the system may go wild and respond in an unpredictable manner.

In other cases, the quasi static change is bad because people don't see it coming. It's like the old story about boiling frogs. If you throw a frog into boiling water, he will jump out immediately . . . and stay alive. But if you put him in room temperature water, and then slowly heat it up, the frog will not notice the change and will be boiled alive.

When someone wants to change, or destroy a society, the best way to accomplish it is by small, incremental steps: a little more media violence this year (more than last year, not as much as next year), a slight alteration in a definition, the slight easing of moral strictures, a little bit at a time.

The Neo-Nazi Plan for America

The Identity movement claims that the Battle of Armageddon described in Scripture will take place in the United States, and is a racial "Holy war" between the Aryan and non-Aryan races. They have an apocalyptic view of the near future and put their belief into practice by arming themselves and learning military skills in preparation for the coming war. Often masquerading as "survivalists," these groups have national gatherings in which weapons and military instruction are a prominent feature. According to one informant, "They got you outgunned by a long, long way."

The most chilling factor about the Neo-Nazi movement is its violent nature. At least some of these people teach that murder, under the right circumstances, is useful as a character-building exercise.

The Washington Post magazine quotes an Aryan Nations leader:

"Looking down the road, the Aryan movement is going to make the Third Reich look like a third-grade school picnic . . . we are just on the very outer edge of tremendous violence." The Third Reich destroyed most of Europe from the Atlantic Ocean to Moscow, from the Mediterranean to the North Cape of Norway . . . and murdered millions upon millions of people! And that was a "third-grade school picnic" compared with what the Neo-Nazis plan for America!

The Neo-Nazis have the firepower to carry out their violent threats, for firearms are seen in their midst almost everywhere. When Geraldo Rivera visited Neo-Nazi camps, he saw military-style semi-automatic assault rifles, along with large collections of regular rifles, shotguns, and pistols.

An illegal Identity arms cache found in the California desert was the largest ever discovered, and included both machine guns and explosives. One report claimed that the find was so extensive it was not possible to fully photograph its extent except from the air. Law enforcement officials have confiscated illegal fully automatic machine guns in Identity camps. At least one MAC-11 submachine gun was used in a political murder.

Alan Berg was a Jewish radio talk show host in Denver. His evening show brought the outspoken liberal Berg into regular conflict with the Aryan Nations and other Neo-Nazi groups. On June 18, 1984, they honored Berg's First Amendment rights by mowing him down in a torrent of .45 caliber MAC-11 bullets outside of his home.

The submachine gun was found on October 18, 1984, in the Sandpoint, Idaho, home of an Aryan Nations extremist following a shoot-out between the FBI and Gary Lee Yarbrough. Ballistics tests proved that the submachine gun was the one that killed Alan Berg. Also found in Yarbrough's home was a small arsenal of firearms, a disguise kit, and a supply of plastic explosives.

A friend of mine in Denver reports that the Denver Jewish community believes that *Christians* killed Berg! When two of four defendants were convicted in the Berg affair, it was not for murder, but rather for violating his civil rights. While murder is the ultimate civil rights violation, such a lightweight conviction sends an appalling message to the Jewish community.

Although described as "Right-Wing," the hate groups bear little resemblance to Conservatives, whom they despise along with Liberals, Jews, and Blacks (Satan is an equal opportunity bigot). Identity speakers describe both communism and capitalism as organs of

International Jewish Zionist control, and despise both with equal vigor.

These groups believe that the U.S. Government is controlled by the Jewish Zionists and call it the Zionist Occupational Government, or "ZOG." They want to take over the United States and institute a Fascist dictatorship. Democracy, they claim, is a joke because it allows people of all races and religions to participate in the political process. And they take action on their violent political beliefs. Like certain other cults, and even elements of the Christian Right, they teach that God is phasing out democracy.

On December 7, 1984, one man was killed (Robert Matthews) and four others arrested during a fiery gun battle on Whidbey Island in Puget Sound, north of Seattle, Washington. The men were members of a Neo-Nazi group called "The Order" and were wanted in a $3,600,000 armored truck robbery in California.

When FBI agents searched the remains of the house where the men were holed up, they found a "Declaration of War" against the United States dated November 23, 1984. It called for the execution of federal officials and beheading informants. The battle plan for the war, and the name of the group, were extracted from a novel titled *The Turner Diaries* by Dr. William Pierce. The novel was published by the National Alliance, an Arlington, Virginia, Neo-Nazi group that seems to have evolved out of the American Nazi Party of the late George Lincoln Rockwell.

The plot of *The Turner Diaries* calls for an armed rebellion of a National Socialist group called The Order. The rebellion, which supposedly starts in 1991, is funded by armed robberies, counterfeiting, and other crimes. The rebellion is finally successful after eight years of struggle, and includes murders of Jews and blacks, the bombing of FBI headquarters in Washington, DC, a suicidal nuclear terrorist attack on the Pentagon (in which Turner dies), and destruction of the Jewish press. Following the establishment of the National Socialist government, the United States mounts a nuclear war against the nation of Israel.

High-Tech Hatred

The Order of Robert Matthews, or its sympathizers, are suspected in two bank robberies, three murders, two building bombings, and two assaults on armored cars. They were stopped before they could implement their plan to disrupt the infrastructure of a major U.S. city. Some of them had apparently hoped to foment riots by interrupt-

216 • *The Triumphant Return of Christ*

ing the water supply to Los Angeles. A group of members from The Order were tried and convicted of various crimes in a celebrated trial in Seattle during 1986.

In the Arkansas camp of a related group, authorities found targets cut out in the shape of state police officers, anti-tank weapons, a supply of homemade plastic explosives called "elephant snot," and 30 gallons of cyanide poison. Unanswered is whether the cyanide was intended for a mass suicide ala Jim Jones' Peoples Temple or an attack on the water supply of a major city.

High-tech hatred is a modern wrinkle of the Neo-Nazi movement. Several personal computer bulletin boards are in operation bearing names such as the "Aryan Liberty Network" and the "Liberty Bell Network." These bulletin boards allow anyone with a compatible personal computer and modem to call in and receive the latest anti-Jewish diatribe. One bulletin board is operated by an immigrant German who was once a member of the Hitler Youth.

Several layers of security are used on the bulletin boards. While the general public can access the highest level offerings, only those users with the correct access codes can access the deeper levels.

One of the most ominous features of some bulletin boards are "Enemy Lists" of "race traitors" and people who oppose the movement. Although there is nothing necessarily illegal about posting enemy lists, they form a means for communicating with the violent faithful. These lists can be very intimidating.

After all, people who work against the movement might be chilled into silence if they find their name, address, telephone number, car description, and license tag number posted on the Neo-Nazi enemies list. Some "enemies" have been killed, assaulted, or threatened.

What should be done about the "Christian" Neo-Nazis? Kansas Attorney General Robert Stephan said in *Newsweek:* "History has shown that those who preach hate and violence don't survive well in the sunlight."

One way to let the sunshine in is to inform yourself about anti-Semitism and the claims of Identity; the truth will counteract Neo-Nazi lies about the Jews. Most ministries to Jewish people can supply information on anti-Jewish bigotry. Especially recommended is "Even Your Best Jewish Friends Won't Tell You," which appeared in the March 1985 issue of *The Chosen People* (published by the American Board of Missions to the Jews).

In 1930, a Jewish writer named Maurice Samuel wrote in his book *The Great Hatred:*

> It is of Christ that the Nazi fascists are afraid. It is in his omnipotence that they believe; it is him they are madly determined to obliterate. But the names of Christ and Christianity are too overwhelming and the habit of submission to them is too deeply ingrained after centuries and centuries of teaching. Therefore, they must make their assault on those who are responsible for the birth and spread of Christianity. They must spit on the Jews as the Christ killer, for they long to spit on the Jews as the Christ givers.

The Book of Revelation also shows us the origins of Jew-hatred (see Rev. 12:1-6). From the shadow of the Cross to the Battle of Armageddon, Jew-hatred is at its root an expression of Satan's hatred for our Lord Jesus Christ. The true basis of anti-Semitism is that Satan needs to eliminate the Jews in order to keep prophecy from coming true: no Jews, no fulfillment.

The Nazi/New Age Connection

When I was writing *The Twisted Cross* I had no idea that it would directly address two of the most critical turning point issues confronting the Church in the 1980s: the New Age movement and the Neo-Nazi "Christian Identity" movement.

The Twisted Cross exposes the occultic New Age religion of Adolf Hitler and his top Nazi cronies. One ranking SS general claimed that National Socialism (Nazism) was ". . . not like a religion, not similar to a religion . . . it is a religion with its own rites, rituals and sacraments." That religion made Hitler its Messiah, Heinrich Himmler the High Priest, and the officers of the SS its clergy.

The Nazi religion is based on the occultic ideas of theosophy. It is thus fair to say that Nazism and the New Age movement (which is also based on the same ideas) are doctrinally one and the same. The New Age movement is a loose worldwide coalition of groups that share a common occultic world view and common mystical experiences. The movement has religious, political, and cultural agendas that are at odds with Christian values.

Both Nazism and the New Age movement seek the evolutionary transformation of man into a higher form of being called Ubermensche (or "Superman") by the Nazis and Homo Noeticus or Homo Universalists by New Agers.

Oddly, some Christian churches, mostly on the ultra fringe, claim to foresee the same evolutionary leap to a type of ultra-Christian: the Manifest Sons of God (MSOG). This new man will supposedly possess great psychic powers over himself and the forces of nature. There is very little difference between MSOG, Ubermensch, Homo Universalists, and Homo Noeticus. Gentle New Agers and "Kingdom Now" Christians would do well to listen to Hitler concerning the New Man: "I have seen him . . . and he terrifies me!"

There is an ugly mood in the country today. Anti-Semitism — raw, vile Jew-hatred — is rapidly rising. If the hatred was limited to a few lunatics on the fringes of reality (as it was in the past), then they could be simply scorned and ignored. But the farm financial crisis that gripped the nation in the mid-1980s, especially in the Midwest heartland, allowed Neo-Nazi change agents to sucker decent, hardworking Christian folk into believing their hideous lies. They teach them that same old discredited "World Jewish Conspiracy" lie, and pretend that it is biblical doctrine. *It's sick.*

During his 1985 exposé, Geraldo Rivera said (referring to the Identity Churches): "If Adolf Hitler had a religion, then this one would be perfect for him." Well, Geraldo, Adolf Hitler did have a religion, but it wasn't any form of Christianity: it was New Age occultism.

A friend of mine once worked for a group that is now allied with Identity (he quit when he found out what they teach). He tells me that employees of that group have occultic outlooks, and one even practiced "astral projection" (a distinctly New Age concept)!

One Identity preacher claims that they have revived the old Albigensian heresy (i.e. Gnosticism), which is a precursor to the New Age movement. In addition, another Identity leader studied the *Rig-Veda* (Hindu scriptures) while serving as an army officer in India during World War II. This fact is made interesting because the New Age movement is intensely Hindu in outlook.

Another New Age connection is the fact that the books of Eustace Mullins are popular among Identity people. Constance Cumbey showed me a booklet listing Mullins as author. The imprimatur? The Aryan Nations group! One of Mullins' books contains distinct, unmistakable New Age statements.

Both the original Nazis and modern Neo-Nazis are New Age.

Both of these occultic movements are Luciferic at their base — they are not Christian in any sane sense of the word (even though both claim to be Christian).

Why should *you* be concerned over these movements? The reason is that the Church cannot afford to remain silent. Pastor Martin Neimoller was a leader in the German Christian resistance against Nazism. He once put this problem in proper perspective:

> First they came for the Jews, but I'm not Jewish, so I did not react; then they came for the Catholics, but I wasn't Catholic so I did not object; then they came for the workers, but I wasn't a worker so I did not stand up; then they came for the Protestant clergy . . . and it was too late for anybody to stand up.

When Christians are silent about evil, then they will eventually be swallowed by that evil. Pre-war German Christians learned that lesson the hard way and wept for their omission. We must speak out today, in our own time, whenever hatred rears it's ugly head, lest we also be found wanting. Or as Rev. Frank Eiklor put it: "Silence isn't always golden, sometimes it's just plain yellow."

When God is Outraged

In much of this chapter we have talked about change, and how it affected some societies in the recent past, and also about some of the ills in our own society: Neo-Nazism, occultism, and the like.

Changes have swept American society for the past several decades. Change has come so fast that many Christians are unable to assimilate it. In fact, they *cannot* assimilate it because of conflicts with sound biblical doctrine.

With the decline of a religious sense in society, attacks on the Church have come fast and furious. Some of them may have been deserved because many of us practice an arrogant form of separation that makes others see us as not righteous, but rather haughty and distant. But much of the criticism is not based on any of our shortcomings but on a desire of men and women to be free of God.

They threw God out of the public schools a generation ago, and now can only look perplexed at a rising generation of violent youth who are markedly amoral (which is far more dangerous than being simply immoral).

In Washington, DC, the murder rate topped 450 a year for

several years in a row, with mostly fourteen to thirty year olds committing the crimes. And it's not just drug dealers fighting over "turf" knocking each other off (a crime that some ill-advised conservative Christians actually say is just fine with them). Criminals spraying gunfire into a public swimming pool that is crowded with small children no longer seems so outrageous to a public numbed by TV violence that is unmodulated by any sense of godliness.

Society has lost the knowledge that God is outraged when innocent blood is shed.

Through novel and bizarre interpretations of the Separation of Church and State Doctrine, found in the U.S. Constitution, Liberals (how many people recall when "liberal" meant "open-minded?") are attempting to push Christians out of the public square altogether. Most will not admit it and will pretend they believe that all voices should be heard. But when the rubber meets the road, it is silencing of the voice of Christians they seek.

When a pro-life candidate speaks out against abortion, the Liberal crowd moans that the Christians are trying to "... impose their religious beliefs on others." Yep! That's right. But so what? All laws are an attempt to impose some group's will on other groups. And many of our most cherished laws are based firmly on principles taken directly from the Bible: Thou shalt not steal. Thou shalt not murder.

By its nature, a pluralistic republic like the United States has many competing groups. Each puts its agenda before the public and attempts to win votes and support for them. As long as Christians aren't trying to overthrow the government by force or fraud, then our "attempting to impose our religious beliefs on others" is merely a valid exercise of our fundamental constitutional rights. And society is free to either accept and adopt our views, or reject them and go spinning off into the wilderness they have crafted for themselves. But to claim that Christians should be banned, either explicitly or implicitly, from attempting to push for support of our agenda, denies us our fundamental rights as citizens.

The attack on Christian belief is nowhere more intense than on college campuses today. Now that an amoral generation of 1960s and 1970s vintage New Lefties are in power in academic institutions, the anti-democratic tendencies they showed then are made into social pressures and even law on the campuses of the 1990s. At many institutions — University of Wisconsin, Stanford University, University of Pennsylvania, for example — students are punished if they speak out incorrectly. Students know they must be politically correct or their academic careers will come to a quick end.

The First Amendment to the U.S. Constitution guarantees, among other things, the right to free speech and the right to practice religion free from government interference. The doctrine of separation of Church and state, not just prevents religions from imposing themselves on the unwilling, it also protects and shelters religions . . . or at least it's supposed to work that way.

Freedom of speech, however, is under attack in America; surprisingly, it's on the campuses of colleges and universities that the suppression of speech that's not "politically correct" is most at risk. Impeding religion has been sport for many years, but today it's mostly Christian and Conservative students who face growing persecution in the New Fascist Academy.

Suppressing Free Speech

The founding fathers knew the problems of suppressed speech all too well. From the time of the first American colonization, attempts were made to censor or suppress the speech of dissidents.

In New England during the 1600s, the Puritans (who themselves were exiled from theocratic England for their own attempts to speak their minds) routinely branded religious heretics on the face with the letter "H." Heresy is the uttering of opinions not favored by religious authorities, and, while the concept of heresy may be appropriate for members of specific religious groups, it has no use whatsoever in the secular public square.

There were several campaigns to root out heretics in colonial America, including one shameful incident where Quaker women were herded from town to town, naked from the waist up, to be flogged mercilessly by each town constable in turn. Only the intervention of the townspeople at one stop, after the women's backs were pulp, stopped the purge.

We all know about the Salem witch trials of 1691-1692, after which 31 male and female "witches" were hanged and one man was crushed under a load of rocks piled on his chest. This experience, along with their own experience with the British government of King George III (and other oppressive crowns of Europe), was what informed the authors of the Bill of Rights. For that reason they wanted their rights specifically enumerated in the U.S. Constitution.

Attempts to suppress free speech are found in modern times as well. It seems that many of us have forgotten the bitter lessons of the past and, as a result, may be doomed to relive them.

The early 1950s gave us the McCarthy purge of everyone that the senator from Wisconsin considered a Communist. Careers were ruined, some people went to prison, and the entire body politic was badly injured as people feared speaking out against the evils of Joe McCarthy and his band of unholy henchmen.

For over a century after the Civil War, there was systematic denial of freedoms for African-Americans, especially in the South. Those who dared speak out opened themselves to ostracism, community shunning, loss of jobs, violence, and even murder.

Joe McCarthy is dead, his movement is too; and in the South people can speak out against racism or anything else, for that matter. When attempts were made to suppress free speech in the old days, the local sheriffs were either part of the conspiracy or looked the other way; today they are more likely to arrest anyone violating your rights. Not universally, perhaps, but then again it's not 1960 either.

Whether it is McCarthyism, southern white racism, or some leftist form of suppression of speech, a common thread flows among them: It was the First Amendment to the U.S. Constitution, enforced by decisions of the U.S. Supreme Court, that forced change on the violators. Without free speech, the civil rights movement would probably have been beaten.

The horror of Martin Luther King's assassination by James Earl Ray is not just that a great man was slain, but *why* he was killed: for expressing contrary opinions; for thinking that was at odds with the majority; for exercising his own constitutional rights. In an environment where such outrages are tolerated, no one is free, and no one is safe thinking unpopular thoughts.

Suppression of free speech, however, is a common sin and is committed by some of our most respectable people, not just James Earl Ray and Joe McCarthy. Today one need not look to some poorly educated, heathen Ku Kluxer to find suppression of free speech; the local college dean will enthusiastically do the same job.

Where No One Is Free

More than 300 colleges and universities have adopted codes of conduct that ban certain types of speech. Banned from the former bastions of free speech are ". . . 'discriminatory' utterances based on race, color, creed, religion, national origin, age, marital status, handicap, or Vietnam-era status that has the purpose or effect of creating an intimidating, hostile, or offensive environment for academic pursuits, employment, housing, or participation in a university activity."

It is claimed that such codes are right because the *majority* of the university community approves of them. A junior high school civics teacher taught me that the beauty of the U.S. Constitution is that it allows majority rule while protecting the rights of minorities. That the majority of a community approves of oppression does not make it in any way right. Popularity does not validate a wrong position!

Under these anti-speech codes, a New England university expelled a sophomoric sophomore because he shouted a series of racial epithets on a campus street late at night. I might consider punishing him for disturbing the peace, but the liberal university administration, perhaps fearful of angering minority students, celebrated the young man's First Amendment rights by expelling him *because of the content of his speech.*

A young woman at Harvard University got into trouble — there was talk of expelling her, but it did not take place — for the crime of expressing her southern pride by flying a Confederate flag out her dormitory window. Minority students were offended by the flag and demanded that it be removed. She refused, and the fight was on. The young woman was terribly insensitive, but probably not any less sensitive than the protesters. But at Harvard, it seems that mere offense taken by a minority is considered just grounds for violating the constitutional rights of another student.

A minority student exercised her own free speech rights by flying a Nazi "blood flag" out her window. But, when Jewish students explained that the flag was deeply offensive to them, she had the decency to remove it. I wonder what would have happened if the minority students who objected to the Confederate flag had frankly discussed the issue with the young woman, rather than filing a loud, public protest? So much can be accomplished by calm, civil dialogue.

Perhaps the saddest aspect of the Confederate flag incident was the statement of a graduating, female African-American student who said she was going to law school, after which she would make a career out of legally suppressing speech she considered offensive. Hopefully, some constitutional law professor, who hasn't succumbed to the temptation to routinely violate the Constitution on campus, will teach her two truths about the First Amendment: *No one* has free speech if *anyone* is denied free speech, and there is no constitutional or natural right not to be offended.

An incident at the University of Pennsylvania in 1993 shows the utter stupidity of university administrators, not to mention a logical consequence of the argument from intimidation. A white student was disturbed by a group of female minority students who were loudly partying outside his dormitory room. He shouted at them, calling them "water buffaloes" in the process. They filed a charge of racist utterances against the man under the university's anti-free speech code. Even the university's community of African-American scholars couldn't find any racial connotation to the remark.

It was reported in *The Washington Post*[1] that the offending white student is orthodox Jewish [he was Israeli-born], and that he had used a rough English translation of the slang epithet *behema,* which means "thoughtless persons" or "inconsiderate fools."[2] According to a report on National Public Radio news, the man was told by the university that the charges would be dropped if he apologized and attended an exculpatory bit of brainwashing called "racial sensitivity classes."

The report said he was going to fight the charges. At a later time, the offended students dropped the charges, but not before making it clear that they still believed a violation had occurred.

In other times, these incidents would merit no attention from the authorities whatsoever; today they make headlines. Where is reason when ". . . a gnat landing on the shoulder" causes people to ". . . shoot from the hip."

At the same university a far more serious breech of other peoples' rights occurred when some students, identifying themselves as "The Black Community," confiscated about 14,000 copies of *The Daily Pennsylvanian,* claiming that articles in the newspaper violated the university's speech code on racial harassment. The administration failed to discipline the students, who should have at least been suspended for the rest of the semester, and perhaps expelled.

University president Sheldon Hackney, however, claimed that "two important university values, diversity and open expression, appear to be in conflict." What Hackney fails to understand, a failure that is astounding for a liberal university official, is that there can be no conflict in these values — for one is a desirable thing and the other an "inalienable right." That is, diversity is a secondary value, while free speech is a primary value on which secondary values depend.

Free expression knows no compromise and cannot be in conflict with any other right. Does Dr. Hackney want to fatally harm the diversity value? Then let him continue to squelch free expression, and he will get the oppressive police state that he so richly deserves . . .

indeed that he helped create.

Even his own law school faculty reportedly objected to Hackney's morally bankrupt position. Writing to Hackney, they asserted: "The important university values of diversity and open expression were not in conflict here. The offensive columns in no way prevented the university from carrying out its policy of diversity . . . . Removal of the newspapers struck at the heart of the most fundamental diversity which the University should foster— diversity of thought, views, and expression."

If You Can't Take the Heat . . .

That there is still suppression of speech in the USA, despite the First Amendment, is not surprising. It happens all the time, and we must be constantly on guard against it. That's why the Supreme Court docket has so many "First Amendment" cases so often.

The human condition is never so virtuous that we can live without the First Amendment. Indeed, the Founding Fathers knew that fact all too well. One of the reasons for writing a constitution in the first place was to guard against the very nature of sinful mankind; it was to be a principle-centered government of laws, not of majority whims. Only through principle-centered governance could the rights of minorities be protected.

That some students might be "psychically injured" is not a valid criterion for suppressing speech. A university is a place for adults. It is not only a place for adults but for clearly superior adults who possess the record of intellectual achievement required for admission. The university is not a place where students are sent to feel good, but rather, it is a place where one's most basic assumptions are challenged. After all, the unexamined opinion is not worth holding.

Christian students attend universities, and their faith is tested by agnostics and atheists aplenty. And that's all right, for if they are prepared for the experience by their parents, then that faith will be strengthened by the whetstone of having to defend it. Of course, there will be a few casualties, but that's the nature of warfare — spiritual or otherwise.

I once heard a caller to a radio talk show state that "African-American parents don't send their kids to universities to hear a lot of racists." I also hear many conservative Christians bleat that they don't send their kids to universities to hear a lot of atheist, Darwinist professors teach heresy.

The answer to both is the same: "Tough!"

The purpose of the university is not to make ideas safe for the students, but rather, the other way round: to make the student safe for ideas. If your kids' ideas are sound, then exposure to the rough and tumble atmosphere of a properly conducted university will only validate them . . . and if they cannot be validated, they don't deserve to be held.

If the youngster is so fragile, so inept, and so in need of strong, unexamined guidance as to need the protection of speech codes, then they should not be in the university. Students who belong in the university might be initially somewhat fragile, but in the process, through constant testing and retesting of ideas, they become a lot more robust. Those that are too subject to "psychic injury," whatever that is, should be encouraged not to come in the first place or to drop out if they can't stand the stress.

What is "Acceptable" Speech?

The principal problem with limiting speech that some groups find offensive is that "acceptable" speech becomes a matter of the sensitivities of whatever gang of thugs happens to be in power today. In the arena of public opinion, when principles are thrown out with the trash, it is the range of the moment fads of mushy thought of the public's worst elements that decides what speech is "in" and what is banned. As a result, all reason is abandoned.

Vox populi is a fickle and changing thing. When southern racists were the loudest criers on the public square, they suppressed the speech of African Americans and civil rights workers. But they claimed to represent the majority in their communities, so by the illogic of hate speech codes (like those of the University of Pennsylvania) it was their right to suppress others' speech.

Today, we live in a time when such racism is out of favor. But what happens when racists become more numerous? What happens when some other dirty, smelly bad guy gains the public favor? What happens? It's simple: right and wrong speech is determined by the heel of the jackboot and the muzzle of a gun.

It is distressing that America has fallen into such a state that we've forgotten the principles laid down by Thomas Jefferson and the other founding fathers. We don't trust the public, and we don't trust ourselves.

President Woodrow Wilson was once asked what he would do about those socialist agitators of his time who wanted to destroy the entire basis of American freedoms. Wilson's first impulse was to blurt out "Hire them a hall and let the good sense of the American people find them out."

These awful "hate speech" codes were not promulgated by the Aryan Nations or the Ku Klux Klan, nor were they taken from the Communist Party USA, the Soviet Union, or Nazi Germany; they are the law on campuses of our best, previously most liberal, colleges and universities! Traditionally, these institutions were the very center of free speech in our culture.

Developing new knowledge often requires questioning the received standard wisdom, defying convention, and pressing against the frontiers of thought in a way that outrages adherents to older ways of thinking. That leading edge thought is now in jeopardy.

If Heinrich Himmler and Lavrenti Beria wanted to concoct a scheme to kill off public debate in their police states, while seeming moral, they could not do better than to adopt the University of Pennsylvania anti-free speech code.

Finding our national political direction in any era requires a vigorous public debate of issues that are often "clashes of absolutes." Respect for the First Amendment keeps the debate civil and ensures that the rights of the minority are not violated. It also helps the correct opinion to bubble to the surface. But when "offensiveness" becomes grounds for the punishment of the utterer of offensive words, the debate is debased and all freedoms are quashed.

"When political utterance descends to such levels, fanatics enlist in the crusade, but sensible people tend to wash their hands of it."[3] When sensible people abandon the public square, thugs take over, and free speech, free thought, and freedom itself become crimes.

Free thought requires free speech; liberal discourse cannot take place without it. Those who would suppress others' freedom of speech would do well to consider that "[anyone] . . . who violates individual rights cannot claim, defend or uphold any rights whatsoever," including their own.

Let me repeat what I told a caller on a radio talk show in Bridgeport, Connecticut. She approved of my disapproval of New Age mysticism, and bragged that, as a Christian, she protested to a local shopping mall manager and got some New Agers banned from soliciting support on the mall sidewalks. Expecting support from a "kindred spirit," she was taken aback when I expressed disapproval of her actions, and suggested a better alternative was to set up her own table and solicit support for her own view.

228 • *The Triumphant Return of Christ*

No one is hurt by her expressing disapproval of the others' position; they both get to exercise their First Amendment rights. I told her: "Be cautious ma'am . . . . While you are busy fastening the lockplate on the door of their church, listen very carefully over your shoulder. That thin, distant whirring sound you hear might be someone else drilling the holes for the lockplate on the door of *your* church."

How to Subvert the Church

Elsewhere in this chapter I stated that Christians basically gave their culture away to secular forces. Much of what happens today — that which Christians bemoan — is rooted in our own lack of saltiness and our own extreme separation from society.

Os Guinness, writing in his book *The Gravedigger File,*[4] teaches that the destruction of the Western church will occur not from a frontal attack but from subversion from within. We fight a "war without frontiers," with the enemy worming in little by little.

In Guinness's book, he sets a "10-10-80 rule" for subversion of the church: 10 percent infiltrated as a counter-elite, working on 80 percent of the church who are passive and accepting, and then Satan can ignore the 10 percent of Christians who are active and aware.

Guinness might have his proportions wrong, but the scheme is viable . . . and may already be in execution.

Four factors — derived from Guinness — affect the viability of the modern American church: secularization, displacement, privatization, and the religious supermarket.

Secularization is the gradual loss of the Church's influence in successively more important, and wider ranging, spheres. At one time, Christianity was a comprehensive religion that could inform all manner of human activity. But, as the Church turned inward, it slowly abandoned first one sphere then another. Like peeling an onion, the religious covering of our society was stripped away.

Once the onion began to peel, the *displacement* factor set in. A secularized society, no longer concerned with the opinions of Christians, began to turn to other things to find meaning in their lives. "He who dies with the most toys, wins" was the pathetic sob of the Yuppie culture; although to many it was a sob that sounded like a boast.

Privatization is the notion, often aided and abetted by Christians, that religion is a private passion that must be kept to oneself. Richard John Neuhaus wrote of the loss of Christian input to public debate in his book *The Naked Public Square*. In our private piety we can be trusted by secular society to ". . . accept the place allotted to us."[5] When displacement and privatization went too far, it became apparent that Christians could safely be attacked with impunity in the public square.

Recall the flap that Vice President Dan Quayle got into when he criticized the TV show "Murphy Brown?" Quayle's speech actually had little to do with the TV show, it was a speech on family values, but the media ignored the content of the speech and attacked what amounted to an off-hand remark. It became a liberal media cause of national proportions.

In the April 1993 edition of *Atlantic* magazine, however, there was an article titled "Dan Quayle Was Right." The article reported that the sociology research was in, and it showed that children of single-parent families fare much worse than expected; that significant social ills resulted from the fact the mothers are no longer at home with their children. So why were the sociologists so surprised? To Christians it was apparent for decades.

The supermarket effect refers to the large variety of different sects and flavors that Christianity finds itself broken into. We cannot unite on every point because there are real doctrinal differences between denominations. But we can unite with most other groups on major points, and in our stand against the evils that we see.

Some Christians — suffering from the supermarket effect — flit and flirt with a variety of churches on a week-by-week basis. Never finding a fellowship that suits them, they will attend first one church and then another. Taking from each of them what they want, "getting fed" but never feeding, being ignited but never igniting, never being grounded in solid doctrine. There is a poor quality to such spirituality, and it is destructive to both the Church and its mission: the Great Commission.

The supermarket effect does not stop with the myriad of different churches and fellowships. Many Christians delve into a lot of different "doubtful things."

We eagerly adopt Carl Jung's occultic version of psychology and pretend it is "healing of memories." We adopt New Age occultism and pretend that it's a reawakening of [gnostic] gifts lost in the early years of the Church. And when television preachers — whose god must be a deadbeat given that he never seems to send them enough support — stray into heresy, they are not corrected by the Body. Indeed, when someone concerned with good doctrine raises an objection, the heretics lash out and snarl at the critic.

One need not look far to see heresy abounding on religious television. It seems good doctrine is not as exciting as the false teachings that yield religious experiences resembling those things forbidden in Deuteronomy.

Re-Infiltrating Our Culture

Another factor that causes the modern American church to lose some of its saltiness is the dismaying tendency to be all too fuzzy about where their Christian principles leave off and cultural principles begin.

We come to think that our customs and habits are somehow uniquely Christian just because we are Christians. After all, if we are Christians, then what we do and how we do it must be "the Christian way." Nothing makes us less relevant than this tendency! We not only condemn the practices of non-Christians (often in a manner that makes evangelism impossible) but those of other Christians as well.

English Christian journalist Dan Wooding told me that he was utterly surprised — no shocked — when he interviewed for a job in a well-known Christian organization in Europe. Many evangelical British Christians view consumption of alcohol in the same way as many American Christians, but on the continent Christians often partake of beer and wine.

By failing to allow for cultural differences, by refusing to grant credibility to the worship and life practices of others — as long as they don't violate a *clear,* non-debatable biblical doctrine — we give aid and comfort to the enemy.

Others of us abandon the faith by forming alliances with groups that are not only non-Christian but hostile to Christian values. To gain some temporary political advantage, some Christians allied themselves with Reverend Moon's people. Yes, we share some common goals, but by making the alliance on a political issue we seem to be telling the world that we are essentially the same as the Unification Church.

Many Christians believe that we are in the end times and may well be heading at breakneck speed toward turning point omega. We need to re-infiltrate culture and take back what we abandoned. Not in the heretical manner of the Reconstructionists — who claim that we must take over the earth for Christ — but rather to win souls from the jaws of hell.

10

The Russian Bear:

Out of the North

J. R. Church

At 5:00 o'clock that afternoon, I eagerly awaited my appointment with one of Israel's leading archaeologists. I met him at the Western Wall and was quickly escorted under Wilson's Arch, the ancient bridge that spans the Tyropeon Valley. I was there to take photographs of his excavations along the Western Wall of the Temple compound.

As we walked northward along the bedrock that supported the massive stone blocks dating back to the time of Herod the Great, we discussed Israel's burden with history. Signs of first-century conflict with the Romans were evident all around us. Broken boulders, burned stonework, and layers of debris reminded us of the suffering Israel had endured toward the close of the first century.

I was curious to learn his perspective about the continuing conflict between the Jews and Arabs since the birth of Israel in 1948. We discussed the 1967 Six-Day War and the Yom Kippur War of 1973. Our conversation soon got around to the prophets and their prediction that the chosen people would someday return to their promised land only to face renewed conflicts.

We discussed the Arab nations that opposed the formation of the state of Israel, and I asked him what he thought about a possible solution. His answer was a bit surprising. He said, "Our problem is not really with the Palestinians and Arabs. They are but pawns in the game. Our difficulty lies with the motivating force behind them namely, the Soviet Union. Our problem is not really with the Arabs, but with the Soviets." He told me that someday Israel must face the predicted "Battle of Gog and Magog."

Since that delightful evening in Old Jerusalem, I have watched the "evil empire" crumble. After 70 years, Soviet-styled communism failed to capture the enthusiasm of its people. There is no more Soviet Union. In its place are the several republics that once menaced the planet. But Israel still faces a continuing conflict with the Arabs. Was my friend wrong? Or better yet, how do we now interpret the prophet who wrote about a future conflict with Gog and Magog?

The questions are heard over and over again. Now that the Soviet Union is dissolved and Russia remains, can we really look forward to an era of peace? The Cold War seems to be over — is it, really? Will Russia become part of the free-market West? That is the dream of Boris Yeltsin.

Theologians are naturally perplexed about current events in Russia and its satellite republics. The popular media images of post-Soviet peace and the free-market revolution are at odds with our traditional prophetic view.

Ezekiel called for an invasion of re-gathered Israel by a northern enemy who gathers allies from the Middle East. This unholy consortium will enter the Holy Land with a vengeance. Many have said that this event can't be too far into the future. How then, do we reconcile these two seemingly contradictory points of view?

The Current Chaos

Let us begin by looking at current events in Moscow. Russia's economy has been totally destabilized. There is no organized flow of goods and services. Black market and free-lance bartering are the rule of the day. Runaway inflation has necessitated that large numbers of rubles be quickly printed and rushed into the marketplace. These scenes remind us of life in Germany between World Wars I and II. Between the wars, life was characterized by social instability of exactly the type we see in today's Russia. It set the stage for the rise of Hitler's Third Reich.

Put in plain language, people can take only so much economic battering before they welcome any leadership that can promise them food, clothing, shelter, and transportation. Today's Russia has been unable to provide these basic necessities.

In this setting, we find the embattled regime of President Boris Yeltsin struggling for its political life, as he clings to his program of radical economic reform. After a continuing series of failed programs, even his own vice president, Alexander Rutskoi, opposed his policies.

The Russian president is besieged on still another front, and this one is the most ominous. A man who was once a staunch supporter of Boris Yeltsin is now one of his most vigorous opponents. His name is Ruslan Khasbulatov, and he is chairman of the Supreme Soviet. A handsome, articulate man, he is said to have a deep desire for power and a shrewd political patience. Traveling about Russia, he proclaimed that Yeltsin was the man who ruined the country and that he can be the one who fixes it.

But there is a dark side to Khasbulatov whose sympathies lie with the traditional communist way of doing things. And his links to power are said to lie with the powerful hawks of the Russian military establishment.

Obviously aware of his background, a *Time* correspondent recently asked him about his own political aspirations. He inquired whether his rise to power might bring the danger of "a restoration to Communist power."

Khasbulatov's answer was a classic evasion: "This is a big bluff, a primitive myth created by Yeltsin and his entourage. Ever since Gorbachev's reforms, despite all the suffering, Russians realize there is no way back. You should see this political struggle from a different angle. It is the executive branch that is seeking to use neo-Bolshevik methods. Entire sections of the former Communist Party Central Committee simply drifted into the president's administration, together with their archives, safes, and even their telephones. Under the guise of working for a democratic president, they are simply restoring old party ways. They have no use for laws, the constitution, or democracy. This is where the real danger lies."

Though intended to assure the *Time* reporter that there was no danger of a Communist return to power, Khasbulatov actually revealed, by his statement, that Communists are still lurking in the wings.

Most probably, they are hard at work protecting their interests and waiting for the right moment to align themselves with the right leader. There is a very dark and opportunistic side to Russia that appears about ready to emerge.

What Is Really Going On?

In Western minds, there is a nagging question — what is the real Russia? We hear stories about the rapid spread of the gospel there; about the big-hearted hospitality of the common citizen. But, we also hear stories about the rampant corruption, the huge Black Market, and epidemic alcoholism. Then, we remember that the man on the street has very little to do with the direction taken by political leaders.

What is really going on behind the scenes?

A recent event may give us some insight in this area. During March 1993, Russian Foreign Minister Andrey Kosyrev spent about a week in Tehran. There, he conferred at length with Iran's President Rafsanjani. Reportedly, he returned from this meeting having made a 25-year mutual-defense pact with the Iranian government. Among other things, the two countries agreed to continue defense and technical cooperation.

It must be remembered that Iran is the world's chief exporter of state-sponsored terrorism. Groups like Hamas, the Muslim Brotherhood, the Popular Front for the Liberation of Palestine, Islamic Jihad, the Black Panthers, Unified Command, Fatah Hawks, and the PLO/Fatah organizations are all backed by Iran. In particular, the enormous Iranian-backed Hamas group gives support, aid, and comfort to all the above-mentioned lesser groups.

Kozyrev and his superiors are perfectly aware of Iran's evil aspirations. Yet, they agreed to mutually defend each other in the event of outside interference.

Russia's deal with Iran also comes on the heels of generous military support. Tehran has already purchased three kilo-class submarines from Russia, plus at least four nuclear warheads and their delivery systems.

From the *Jewish Press*, (February 7, 1992), we quote the opening paragraph of a front-page article: "Iran has recently purchased three atomic weapons, if the information contained in the usually reliable *London Sunday Times* and a French magazine can be believed. The purchase was made from a secret source in the former Soviet Union for nearly $150 million dollars. The British and French publications did not elaborate on what types of weapons were actually obtained."

Does it really matter what types of nuclear weapons they now hold? Regardless of the type, they are capable of committing nuclear blackmail against the Western world. As religious fanatics, they can justify virtually any action, however repugnant or immoral it might appear to other societies around the globe.

Another very reliable news source in the United Kingdom has issued a similar news release. This newsletter, in continuous publication since 1935, mentions what it calls, "the nuclear black market." It says, "The Iranian Government already bought two nuclear weapons on the Black Market [from the former USSR] for $80 million. It has also hired 50 former USSR nuclear technicians at wages of $2,700 per month."

In one sense, such deals stem from Russia's very practical need to keep peace in the five Central Asian Republics along its southern border. Russian leaders know that if it wanted to, Iran could raise a revolution among the 60 million Muslims who live in this region.

In another sense, however, Russia is neither practical nor noble. She has always supported the enemies of Israel. Syria, Jordan, Libya, Communist Ethiopia, and other similar Mideast powers have always depended upon Russia for military support. So, Russia's record is perfectly aligned with Iran's anti-Israel foreign policy.

Black Market Nuclear Weapons

It seems my Israeli friend was right. Russia has always supplied military equipment for Arab use against Israel. For example, in 1982, when Israel moved into Lebanon to rout the PLO, they uncovered an enormous hidden cache of Russian arms and war material. Clearly, the Russians were planning an invasion of some sort. Has their intent changed in the years since that event? Apparently not.

As reported in the *Intelligence Digest,* (April 2, 1993), "The Russian foreign ministry . . . believes that Russia must secure Iran's restraint in Central Asia by supporting Tehran's more-important ambitions elsewhere, notably, in the Persian Gulf and Red Sea regions."

According to this point of view, it would almost appear that Russia is being forced by geopolitics into a submissive support of Iran's aggressive foreign policy. But, the *Digest* also adds this note: "The main objective for Rafsanjani was to secure Russian acquiescence and cooperation in Iran's southerly ambitions. As this was also precisely the bargain Kozyrev wished to emerge with, there were no impediments to agreement. The only constraint on the Russian side was its need to keep one eye on Western opinion . . . ."

Russia knows what it is doing. It has agreed to cooperate with a government known for its expansionist policies. But, Iran is perhaps best known for its bellicose chants of "Death to America!" and "Death to the Zionist Conspiracy!" (its term for the modern State of Israel). Russia has placed their approval on such activities.

But, Iran is not the only Mideast country that has gone nuclear. There is a rapid spread of this technology among all the Arab states.

With the breakdown of the old Soviet Union, the fate of its approximately 27,000 warheads and their fissionable materials is now open to question. According to *Economist* magazine (March 14, 1992), the Russians have produced "100 to 150 tons of weapons-grade plutonium" and "500 to 700 tons of highly enriched uranium" over the last forty years. "Both," it says, "are valuable commodities. A small amount of uranium was discovered recently in the trunk of a car in Germany."

The message to small, but militant, countries around the world is loud and clear — why go to the trouble and expense of manufacturing your own nuclear materials, when they can be so easily obtained on the black market?

The top headline of the *Jewish Press* (February 14, 1992) screamed, "Syria Acquires Nuclear Bombs." The accompanying article (written by Arizona's Secretary of State, Richard Mahoney) opens, "By ignoring Syria's President Hafez Assad's deadly actions and treating him as an ally, President Bush is enabling Syria to acquire nuclear bombs. Assad is much smarter than Iraq's Saddam Hussein, and has concealed his securing a nuclear bomb in the shroud of Palestinian statehood."

He continues, "American intelligence has established that Soviet nuclear bomb technicians are quitting Russia and heading for more remunerative waters to peddle their wares. According to recent CIA testimony on Capitol Hill, Syria, after failing to purchase Soviet SS-23 intermediate-range ballistic missiles, has now acquired a possible nuclear-delivery system from North Korea. Syria has also tried to purchase 980 grams of enriched uranium as well as a nuclear research reactor from China."

This report is given credence by an event that occurred in the first week of March. As reported in the *New York Times* (March 8, 1992), "A North Korean freighter believed to be carrying Scud missiles to Iran and Syria is still well outside the area where American warships are prepared to intercept the vessel, and any confrontation over the shipment is not likely to occur for days, Administration officials said today." Following the publication of this report, the United States later decided not to stop the shipment.

In the second week of March, the ship docked at an Iranian port and its cargo was swiftly unloaded. Reports stated that the missiles were disseminated throughout Iran and Syria, where they were hidden in many different locations.

Expert opinion tells us that those missiles can accurately deliver nuclear warheads into Israel, with a warning time of only a few minutes, and perhaps as little as a few seconds.

Bombs for All?

The *Economist* also reported, "In 1984, China helped Iran build a nuclear-research center at Isfahan. A Chinese research reactor may follow." It adds, "There are persistent reports of Chinese and Pakistani experts setting up uranium-enriching centrifuges at Moallem Kalayeh, north of Tehran, although inspectors from the International Atomic Energy Agency found nothing there in February. Iran has signed the Nuclear Non-Proliferation Treaty: It hopes to buy — from India, China or both — 'a few' legitimate civil reactors soon."

Once again, it can be seen that the mere signing of a treaty has virtually no meaning, except as propaganda. In Iran, Syria and other Middle-Eastern countries, non-proliferation now means proliferation. The nuclear arms race that has captivated the world for the last 40 years has now shifted to a new arena.

The *Economist* adds another interesting note: "For Algeria, the Chinese are building a large research reactor at Ain Oussera. This looks fishy. The Algerians kept it secret until it was spotted by satellites." Under the title "Bombs for All"?, the editors of this prestigious magazine had the following to say: "The Soviet collapse has raised fears that would-be bomb makers, from Iran to North Korea, may get their hands on Soviet nuclear skills, weapons or materials. But, the really bad news is what Iraq had been up to under the noses of inspectors from the International Atomic Energy Agency. It shows that, against a determined cheat, existing safeguards are alarmingly inadequate."

No wonder the ancient prophets spoke in language that told of fire that would sweep in judgment across the land. Though the Middle East is the flashpoint, that fire seems destined to sweep around the world.

We don't know the full details yet, but stories now leaking out of the Middle East speak a spine-chilling truth. The world's most horrifying weapons are now in the hands of terrorists.

The Invasion of Syria?

Let's look at the events leading up to the predicted "Battle of Gog and Magog." According to Isaiah's view, Syria may play an important role in the conflict that leads to the invasion by Gog. Somehow, the Syrians will force a showdown with devastating results. During a war with Syria, Damascus — for the first time in its history — will be destroyed. The Bible speaks of this event: "Behold, Damascus is taken away from being a city, and it shall be a ruinous heap" (Isa. 17:1).

Such a destruction has not yet occurred in the history of Damascus, which is said to be the oldest continuously occupied city in the world. I feel that when Damascus is destroyed, Israel will occupy Lebanon and Syria — all the way to the Euphrates River. The borders between Israel, Lebanon, and Syria seem to be coming down in verse 3: "The fortress also shall cease from Ephraim..." (Isa. 17:3).

Some interpret this to mean that the Lebanese border will cease to exist and that Israel will occupy Lebanon and Syria. Isaiah continues: "... and the kingdom from Damascus, and the remnant of Syria; they shall be as the glory of the children of Israel, saith the LORD of hosts" (Isa. 17:3).

Ephraim's northern borders with Lebanon and Syria will be dissolved. Both countries will become part of a greater Israel — as God promised Abraham in Genesis 15:18.

But, this occupation will not be without a price. Just as Iraq was condemned for annexing Kuwait, the United Nations will condemn Israel for this acquisition. Instead of the United States leading the invasion force, as it did against Iraq, the Soviet Union will take the initiative and head up the armed forces against Israel. Such a scenario could result in the battle of Gog and Magog.

Instead of the Soviet Union sitting back and cooling its heels, as it did in the Iraq situation, we could see the Soviet Union play a dominant role and the United States sitting back. The Soviet invasion could come as a result of Israel's conflict with Syria. Isaiah describes the deployment of a massive invasion following the destruction of Damascus:

Woe to the multitude of many people, which make a

noise like the noise of the seas; and to the rushing of nations, that make a rushing like the rushing of mighty waters!

The nations shall rush like the rushing of many waters: but God shall rebuke them, and they shall flee far off, and shall be chased as the chaff of the mountains before the wind, and like a rolling thing before the whirlwind.

And behold at eventide trouble; and before the morning he is not. This is the portion of them that spoil us, and the lot of them that rob us (Isa. 17:12-14).

This could be a description of the Russian invasion. It corresponds quite nicely with Ezekiel 38. The term "spoil" is used by both prophets. Notice, the battle will begin about sundown, and by the next morning the mighty invading army will be devastated.

From the North

When the prophet wrote in Isaiah 14:31 that there would come from the north a smoke, he was referring to one of the great wars of the end time. I think the key to the prophecy is that word "north." And there are other prophetic Scriptures which also describe an invasion from the north.

And the word of the Lord came unto me the second time, saying, What seest thou? And I said, I see a seething pot; and the face thereof is toward the north.

Then the Lord said unto me, Out of the north an evil shall break forth upon all the inhabitants of the land (Jer. 1:13-14).

These verses seem to describe an end-time invasion of Israel. Again, Jeremiah 4:6 says:

Set up the standard toward Zion: retire, stay not: for I will bring evil from the north, and a great destruction.

Thus saith the Lord, Behold, a people cometh from the north country, and a great nation shall be raised from the sides of the earth. (Jer. 6:22).

Behold, the noise of the bruit [news] is come, and a great commotion out of the north country, to make the cities of Judah desolate . . . (Jer. 10:22).

Micah also wrote about the war: ". . . the day of thy watchman and thy visitation cometh, now shall be their perplexity" (Mic. 7:4).

The word "watchman" comes from a Hebrew word which some have translated "north." The Jerusalem Bible translates the verse this way: "Today will come their ordeal from the north, now is the time for their confusion."

Indeed, it will be an "ordeal" when the Russians come over the hill. The prophet Joel also described the invasion of a northern army when he wrote in Joel 2:20: "But I will remove far off from you the northern army, and will drive him into a land barren and desolate, with his face toward the east sea, and his hinder part toward the utmost sea, and his stink shall come up, and his ill savor shall come up, because he hath done great things."

Many Bible scholars believe this verse to be a description of the Battle of Gog and Magog. Zechariah seemed to be referring to the end time when he wrote in Zechariah 6:8: "Then cried he upon me, and spake unto me, saying, Behold, these that go toward the north country have quieted my spirit in the north country."

Finally, Daniel seems to link the Battle of Gog and Magog to events of the end time when he referred to the antichrist in Daniel 11:44-45: "But tidings out of the east and out of the north shall trouble him: therefore he shall go forth with great fury to destroy, and utterly to make away many. And he shall plant the tabernacles of his palace between the seas in the glorious holy mountain; yet he shall come to his end, and none shall help him."

"Tidings out of the north" may be a reference to the Russian invasion, and "tidings out of the east" may be a reference to the awesome Armageddon.

All of these verses appear to describe the wars of the Tribulation Period in general terms. Very few specifics are given. Therefore, we must leave the unfolding of the events in the hands of God. We can only speculate as to what will happen next, but I believe we can say with a fair degree of accuracy that the darkest hour of world history is upon us. The world is soon to see a Russian invasion of Israel and the unfolding of the last seven years of world history.

Thinking an Evil Thought

At this point, our thinking falls naturally to the dark phrase found in Ezekiel 38:10: ". . . thou shalt think an evil thought."

This statement refers to Gog, the one who leads an invading force into Israel. Many have wondered just what his thought might be. Will Russia take the opportunity to beef up her failed economy by rallying the patriotism of her people to make war? According to historians, wars have often been used to export unemployment and get a poor economy moving again.

The results from Gog's evil thought is voiced in verses 11 and 12: "And thou shalt say, I will go up to the land of unwalled villages; I will go to them that are at rest, that dwell safely, all of them dwelling without walls, and having neither bars nor gates. To take a spoil, and to take a prey; to turn thine hand upon the desolate places that are now inhabited, and upon the people that are gathered out of the nations, which have gotten cattle and goods, that dwell in the midst of the land."

There are probably hundreds of written commentaries that describe the conditions that will prevail when Gog invades from the north. Virtually everyone agrees that the land described in these two verses is Israel. Furthermore, it is an Israel at peace and at rest. Since walls, bars, and gates are a metaphor of strategic preparedness, Israel seems to have lowered its defenses at the time this prophecy comes to pass.

This could mean that some sort of peace treaty with the Arabs may finally be worked out. Currently, the so-called "Madrid Peace Process" is still the medium of peace talks. Its progress is quite variable — at some times seeming on the verge of some basic agreement — at others, dead in the water. Still, there is a drive to bring it to some sort of completion that is agreeable to the "Palestinian" contingent. Prophecy would seem to indicate that this, or a successor treaty, may finally be effected.

And yet, this does very little to define the "evil thought" that is mentioned in Ezekiel 38:10. Israel's simple lack of defensive preparedness would not, by itself, be a good reason for Russia to attack them. There must be other circumstances.

That brings us to verse 12. "To take a spoil, and to take a prey," simply means to seize spoils and plunder booty from Israelis who, according to this verse, acquired livestock and possessions. But, is this reason enough for Russia to attack a tiny country that is in reality only a sliver of land? Compared with the vastness of Russia, Israel is almost a geographic nonentity. The land of Israel is only about 225 miles in length, compared with Russia's giant 4,000-mile span! And at the moment, Israel has no precious resources developed.

The Navel of the Land

Some have mentioned the Dead Sea's potential as a resource for chemical compounds, including fertilizer products. But it is by no means an exclusive source. So, what would be Russia's motive for invasion? Could it be that there is another clue we haven't examined?

Indeed, there is. And it seems to relate to geopolitics. As we have noted, Israel seems to have little or no geographic importance. And yet, the concluding phrase of verse 12 seems to suggest an almost hidden quality that may make Israel an attractive target for invasion. Referring to the people of Israel, it reads, ". . . that dwell in the midst of the land."

What makes this phrase interesting is its reading in the original Hebrew language. Its literal translation is, ". . . dwelling upon the navel of the land." In fact, the word "land" could just as easily be translated "earth," as it is in Genesis 1:1. This is less a description of the land, itself, than a picture of the land's geographical and geopolitical position.

Just as the human navel is located at the center of the body, Israel could be said to lie at the "center" of the world. This was the ancient designation of the term "navel," when applied geographically. Several ancient countries, when at the peak of their glory, claimed to lie at the center of the world's most important region. Greece, Rome, Egypt, and others all claimed to be the "navel of the earth." In other words, they claimed geopolitical superiority.

Where could they have gotten that idea? Might they have usurped it from the Bible's statement that Israel is the true claimant to this position? This is most probably the case, since Satan always manages to counterfeit God's truth.

This may finally explain why Israel attracts Gog's evil attention. Strategically, Israel lies at the crossroads of Europe, Africa, and Asia. Furthermore, it effectively controls the eastern end of the Mediterranean Sea. Perhaps, when reduced to the simplest terms, Russia will become convinced that the only way to succeed on her own terms will be to capture the "high ground." By the definition found in Scripture, itself, that would be ". . . the navel of the earth." This may, at last, explain Gog's motive for invasion.

It has long been known that Russia has designs upon ruling the world. For the moment, those plans seem to have been thwarted. But the Bible says in no uncertain terms that Russia will ultimately make that final power play. No doubt, she will believe that there is a good chance of attaining world domination, to be administered along a Moscow/Middle-East axis. Viewed through Gog's evil eyes, there would also be the bonus of destroying Israel in the process of capturing the most important piece of real estate on planet earth.

Magog's Accomplices

For years, students of Bible prophecy have read Ezekiel 37-39 which talks about the re-gathering of Israel and its invasion by a northern army. In verses 5-6, he names Magog's accomplices: "Persia, Ethiopia, and Libya with them, all of them with shield and helmet; Gomer, and all his bands; the house of Togarmah of the north quarters, and all his bands: and many people with thee" (Ezek. 38:5-6).

Persia may be considered as modern Iran. Ethiopia's communist government has been overthrown, and political chaos abounds. Some 30,000 black Jews have fled the country since 1984. Libya and its ruler, Muammar Quaddafi, is also ripe for becoming a part of the invasion force.

For many years, theologians have considered Gomer to be Germany. With the fall of Communist East Germany's regime, however, students of Bible prophecy are perplexed as to how such an alliance could develop. Perhaps their military will be joined through the auspices of the United Nations, which appears to be taking on more and more global power since their successful enforcement of "International Law" in Operation Desert Storm, the stabilization of Somalia, and present efforts in the former Yugoslavia.

Togarmah has long been thought to be Turkey. This, too, presents a problem as far as present developments are concerned. Turkey is a Western Ally. However, there can be no mistake about the prophecy. We shall simply have to await the outcome. At present, anti-Israeli Hezbollah forces in southern Lebanon receive their war material from Iran by way of an over-land route through Turkey and Syria.

Turkey, another Moslem country, is clearly in the Arab camp. In verse 16, Ezekiel writes: "And thou shalt come up against my people of Israel, as a cloud to cover the land; it shall be in the latter days, and I will bring thee against my land, that the heathen may know me, when I shall be sanctified in thee, O Gog, before their eyes."

Ezekiel's prophecy concerns an event that is predicted to come to pass "in the latter days." This is a term used widely by the Old Testament prophets to refer to events of the end-time. When considering all of the other prophecies that were predicted for the "latter days," we are led to conclude that the prophets were discussing events that would occur toward the close of the sixth millennium and the introduction of the seventh millennium.

In Ezekiel 38:19 and 22, God says: "For in my jealousy and in the fire of my wrath have I spoken, Surely in that day there shall be a great shaking in the land of Israel; And I will plead against him with pestilence and with blood; and I will rain upon him, and upon his bands, and upon the many people that are with him, an overflowing rain, and great hailstones, fire, and brimstone."

God's wrath continues unabated into chapter 39. In verse 4 we see: "Thou shalt fall upon the mountains of Israel, thou, and all thy bands, and the people that is with thee: I will give thee unto the ravenous birds of every sort, and to the beasts of the field to be devoured."

God's supernatural wrath has never been seen more clearly in history than it will appear in the day Gog attacks Israel. The mighty army of Gog and Magog will be defeated by God. I think this will happen shortly after the destruction of Damascus. Presently, the Russians have a defense treaty with Syria. This could obligate them to come to Syria's defense against Israel. After Israel has occupied her promised territories in Lebanon and Syria, the tiny nation will face the allied powers of Russia, Iran, Ethiopia, Libya, and others. But God will intercede in a most spectacular way.

The Seven Year Clean-Up

There are various views about the timing of the battle of Gog and Magog. Some see it as part of the awesome Armageddon. Others have written that it may occur in the middle of the Tribulation Period. Let me suggest the possibility, however, that it could come near the start of the Tribulation Period.

Such a theory can be supported by a careful view of Ezekiel 39:9: "They that dwell in the cities of Israel shall go forth, and shall set on fire and burn the weapons, both the shields and the bucklers, the bows and the arrows, and the handstaves, and the spears, and they shall burn them with fire seven years."

Could these seven years represent the Tribulation Period? If the battle of Gog and Magog took place at the end of the Tribulation, then we would have seven years of clean-up moving into the Kingdom Age. If it takes place during the middle of the seven-year Tribulation Period, then the clean-up would overlap the Messianic Era by three and a half years.

Jewish theologians believe that the Battle of Gog and Magog and the Battle of Armageddon are one and the same battle. Many descriptions seem to link them together — with descriptions of the one being similar to the descriptions of the other.

For instance, Ezekiel 39:17 makes a reference to the birds who will come to eat the flesh of the slain on the battlefield. This same description is given of the Battle of Armageddon in Revelation 19:17. Is it the same scene, or is it different? In Ezekiel 38, no mention is made of 200 million soldiers from the kings of the East. Yet in Revelation 16, there is no mention of Meshech, Tubal Persia, Ethiopia, Libya, Gomer, or Togarmah.

It is possible that by the time we get to Ezekiel 39:17-20, the world will have concluded seven years of great devastation — at which time God will invite the birds of the air and the beasts of the field to eat the flesh of the slain.

> And, thou son of man, thus saith the Lord God; Speak unto every feathered fowl, and to every beast of the field, Assemble yourselves, and come; gather yourselves on every side to my sacrifice that I do sacrifice for you, even a great sacrifice upon the mountains of Israel, that ye may eat flesh, and drink blood.
>
> Ye shall eat the flesh of the mighty, and drink the blood of the princes of the earth, of rams, of lambs, and of goats, of bullocks, all of them fatlings of Bashan.
>
> And ye shall eat fat till ye be full, and drink blood till ye be drunken, of my sacrifice which I have sacrificed for you.
>
> Thus ye shall be filled at my table with horses and chariots, with mighty men, and with all men of war, saith the Lord God.

This description could be that of Armageddon, for in Ezekiel 39:21, God said: "And I will set my glory among the heathen, and all the heathen shall see my judgment that I have executed, and my hand that I have laid upon them."

God has promised in this verse that He will "set His glory among the nations." This could refer to the arrival of our Lord Jesus Christ.

Why Have the Jews Suffered?

In the following verses God laid out His reason for punishing the Jewish people down through the centuries:

> So the house of Israel shall know that I am the Lord

their God from that day and forward.

And the heathen Gentile nations shall know that the house of Israel went into captivity for their iniquity: because they trespassed against me, therefore hid I my face from them, and gave them into the hand of their enemies: so fell they all by the sword.

According to their uncleanness and according to their transgressions have I done unto them, and hid my face from them (Ezek. 39:22-24).

Why have the Israeli people suffered down through the centuries? At least partly because of their iniquity.

Why did the Babylonians destroy Solomon's Temple and the Romans destroy Herod's Temple? God says because the people of Israel trespassed against Him.

Why did the Romans empty the land of its people in the year A.D. 135 and scatter them throughout the nations of the world to wander for 1,813 years? Because they had sinned against God.

Why will they yet suffer the horrors of the Tribulation Period, including the Battle of Armageddon? "According to their uncleanness and according to their transgressions have I done unto them, and hid my face from them" (Ezek. 39:24).

These verses teach about the conclusion of those seven years and the establishment of God's promised kingdom. Therefore, it is my opinion that the Russian prince of Moscow and Tobolsk will invade Israel at or near the beginning of the Tribulation Period. The following seven years of God's judgment upon an unbelieving world will be concluded with the great Battle of Armageddon.

If the battle of Gog and Magog opens the Tribulation Period, then it may come to pass in the very near future. We have arrived at the last decade of the sixth millennium, which ends around the year 2000. According to some early theologians, the seventh millennium should be the great Sabbath rest — the millennial reign of Christ.

Now we have a very interesting scenario developing. We have a preliminary battle in which Israel's territory expands, the Arab threat is reduced, and a short time of peace ensues. Suddenly an invasion from the north is thwarted by God's supernatural intervention.

God Will Redeem Israel

Following the battle of Gog and Magog, God says:

And I will set my glory among the heathen Gentiles and all the heathen shall see my judgment that I have executed, and my hand that I have laid upon them.

So the house of Israel shall know that I am the LORD their God from that day and forward.

And the heathen shall know that the house of Israel went into captivity for their iniquity: because they trespassed against me, therefore hid I my face from them, and gave them into the hand of their enemies: so fell they all by the sword.

According to their uncleanness and according to their transgressions have I done unto them, and hid my face from them.

Therefore thus saith the Lord God; Now will I bring again the captivity of Jacob, and have mercy upon the whole house of Israel, and will be jealous for my holy name;

After that they have borne their shame, and all their trespasses whereby they have trespassed against me, when they dwelt safely in their land, and none made them afraid (Ezek. 39:21-26).

God will destroy the northern army. He will establish the tabernacle of David and place His stamp of approval upon the house of Israel. The whole world is going to know that God is there. In addition, He is going to pour out His Spirit upon them. In Ezekiel 39:29 He says: "Neither will I hide my face any more from them: for I have poured out my spirit upon the house of Israel, saith the Lord God."

That is going to be a fantastic day. In fact, the pouring out of the Spirit is a very special occasion. On the Day of Pentecost, following the crucifixion and resurrection, the Holy Spirit was poured out — like tongues of fire on each of them — and made the bodies of the believers to become the temples of God.

Now, God has spoken through Ezekiel and said that in the future, he is going to pour out his Spirit on Israel once again. There are other prophets who concur with that. Zechariah 12:10 makes a very similar statement.

And I will pour upon the house of David, and upon the inhabitants of Jerusalem, the spirit of grace and of supplications: and they shall look upon me whom they have pierced, and they shall mourn for him, as one mourneth for his only son, and shall be in bitterness for him, as one that is in bitterness for his firstborn.

Joel also mentions that in the last days, God will ". . . pour out my spirit upon all flesh; and your sons and your daughters shall prophesy, your old men shall dream dreams, your young men shall see visions" (Joel 2:28).

This prophecy of Joel was not only fulfilled in the New Testament account of Pentecost, which was the near fulfillment, but we have a far fulfillment that is yet to come to pass during the Tribulation Period.

Israel will finally realize that Jesus Christ really is both Lord and Messiah. What a glorious day that is going to be. Watch the events as they unfold. They're coming to pass more rapidly every day.

11

The Nation of Israel:
At Center Stage for
God's Finale!

J. R. Church

The return of the Jews to re-establish their national homeland is one of the most important fulfillments in all of Bible prophecy. Many of the Old Testament prophets wrote of this event. Among them was Jeremiah, who gave an unusual description of Israel's unique return: "Turn, O backsliding children, saith the Lord; for I am married unto you: and I will take you one of a city, and two of a family, and I will bring you to Zion" (Jer. 3:14).

Please note the detail "one of a city, and two of a family . . . ." This is exactly what happened in the late 1940s when the beleaguered Jewish people fled the ravages of war-torn Europe and Germany. Often times a Jewish immigrant would be heard to say something like this, "I am the only one in our family from Berlin who has survived. But I've just met one other member of the family who has also survived, my uncle from Hanover."

In each story the name of the town might differ; the country might be Poland or Austria, rather than Germany. Rather than an uncle it might be a married sister or a cousin or a nephew. But the essential feature of Jeremiah's prophecy remained the same, "one of a city, and two of a family."

Yes, the prophecy of Jeremiah has come to pass even in the smallest detail. After 1,813 years of wandering among the nations of the world, suffering severely in every generation, a remnant has returned. The Jew is back in his land.

The modern Zionist movement is the culmination of many attempts down through the centuries to restore the nation of Israel. In almost every century efforts were made to regather the people and restore the nation, but all failed until, in the providence of God, the prophecy was to be fulfilled.

Through the centuries, however, the Jews managed to maintain their identity as a people. They kept their faith in the book of the Law, in the writings of the rabbis, and in the observance of the Sabbath. Year after year, around the Passover table, they would declare, "Next year in Jerusalem!"

Throughout the long centuries the Jewish people suffered. There was the slavery of imperial Rome and the Crusades of religious Rome. In A.D. 1290, the Jews were expelled from England. For 300 years no Jews were allowed in the country.

When Shakespeare wrote his play, *The Merchant of Venice,* he wrote a portrait of the Jewish people and called him Shylock. The character projected a stereotype of a people who were thought to be treacherous and covetous, whose only profession was usury. This is the way the English felt about the Jews from the thirteenth to the sixteenth century.

It is said that the worst sufferings of the Jewish people were inflicted upon them by Christians. Christian anti-Semitism declared that the Jews were guilty of deicide — the murder of God. Many believed that the Jews were under a perpetual and irrevocable curse of God. False rumors followed the Jews wherever they went. It was generally believed that the Jews murdered Christian children in order to use their blood for secret ceremonies connected with the Passover.

When the Bubonic Plague swept across medieval Europe, the Jews were blamed. While a fifth of Europe's population died by the Black Plague, the Jews were not affected. Because of this, the Europeans accused the Jews of poisoning the water and bringing on the plague.

Little did they know that the Jews managed to escape the Bubonic Plague because they refused to live in the filthy, rat-infested environment of most Europeans. The Jewish people ate kosher foods and washed their hands before eating. They kept clean homes and clean bodies. No wonder they escaped the Bubonic Plague. They were declared guilty, however, by an ignorant and superstitious Europe.

The Dream Survives

Under twenty centuries of severe persecution, there was just one ray of light for dispersed Israel — Zion. It has been the dream of the Jew in every generation to return to Zion. From time to time a leader would arise and attempt to lead an expedition back to the Promised Land.

In 1525, David Reubeni appeared in western Europe and sought to raise an army to reconquer Palestine. He came from the east and announced that his brother was the ruler of a Jewish kingdom in the Middle East near the Promised Land. He even presented himself to the pope and, amazingly enough, the pope received him, endorsed him, and sent him off with a letter of recommendation to the king of Portugal, Charles V, who was emperor of the Holy Roman Empire.

The Jewish people throughout Europe rallied to David Reubeni and felt that the time had finally come to return home again. Unfortunately, when Reubeni finally reached Charles V, he was arrested and executed. The resulting fifteenth century inquisition in Spain and Portugal seemed to seal their fate. Jews were forced to convert to Catholicism or die. In many cases, if the church was not satisfied that their conversion was genuine, they died anyway.

Toward the end of the fifteenth century, the city of Jerusalem was almost desolate of inhabitants. Only 4,000 families lived in Jerusalem. Of these, only seventy families were Jewish, and they were "of the poorest class, lacking even the commonest necessities."

Such was the description of an early pilgrim on the plight of the Jews in Palestine. The desolation of the land had somehow come to stand for the miserable state of the Jewish people. Both were desolate; both were in hostile hands; both awaited God's redemption.

In the sixteenth century, the Jews again experienced a brief moment of hope. Joseph Nasi, a wealthy Portuguese Jew who had fled to Turkey, rose high in the favor of the sultan and received the title, Nasi — Duke of Naxos. He was given an island in the Aegean Sea and granted complete rights to the Tiberias section of northern Palestine.

Joseph Nasi planned to use his great wealth and influence to settle a large number of Jewish families around the Sea of Galilee, obtaining silk worms as a means of livelihood for his colony. Before the plan could be carried out, however, war broke out between Turkey and Venice. In the turmoil, Joseph Nasi fell from favor and lost his power.

Again, Jewish hopes were dashed. But with that failure in the sixteenth century, there arose another ray of hope — this time coming from England. With the translation of the Bible into English in the 1500s, there developed a renewed confidence in the authority of the Scriptures. The Christians in England began to understand the prophecies of a restored Israel.

Hopes Dashed

In 1589, Francis Kett expounded upon the theory of a regathered Israel. His theory was not well-received, however, and he was declared a heretic and burned at the stake. But the idea did not die with him. Other Elizabethan churchmen, including the Puritans, began to speak and write about the predicted Jewish homeland the restoration of Israel.

Most of those early theologians believed that the Jews would convert to Christianity, whereupon God would forgive them for their unbelief and restore them to their land. In 1621, Sir Henry Finch published a book entitled, *The Restoration of Jews,* in which he wrote that "all the Gentiles shall bring their glory into thy empire." Such a statement provoked immediate and violent opposition in both the church and state.

James I considered the book personal libel, and arrested the elderly Sir Henry and his publishers. Though they were held only a few weeks, it had a chilling effect upon the seventeenth century English theologians. Still, despite opposition and persecution, the idea had taken root and would continue to grow among the Puritans and others. Someday, they said, the Jews will re-establish the nation of Israel!

The Christian concept of a restored Jewish nation flourished in England between 1640 and 1666. It was believed that the regathering of the Jews to their homeland would usher in the Messianic Age.

There was a flurry of ideas. Among them was the belief that the English were members of the ten lost tribes of Israel. This gave rise to the theory called "British Israelism." The English were Anglo-Saxons, and the word Saxon was thought to be a derivative of the term "Isaac's sons." The Danish people were considered descendants of the tribe of Dan, and the city of Denmark was thought to be a derivative of "Dan's mark."

In 1666, a Jewish tradesman from Smyrna, named Sabbatai Zevi, gained widespread attention when he proclaimed himself the Messiah of the Jews. He announced that he would lead his people back to their homeland. Hopes revived. Some thought the time had come and that the Messiah had finally appeared.

Sabbatai Zevi traveled to Constantinople to see the Sultan but found he had taken on an impossible task. Instead of taking the Sultan's crown, he became the prisoner of the Turkish ruler. It is said that he was given the choice of converting to Islam or dying. This self-proclaimed Messiah of the Jews converted to Islam. Once again Jewish hopes were dashed.

Keeping the Hope Alive

Several books on the return of the Jews surfaced in those early years. One book was entitled *Nova Solyma,* written by Samuel Gott and published anonymously in 1648. It was a utopian novel about the return of the Jews to their homeland. Its author was said to have been influenced by John Milton, author of *Paradise Lost.* The book disappeared, however, and came to light again in 1902.

Another such book of the period was called *The Way of Light,* by Johann Amos Comenius, who foresaw a Messianic Age that would be preceded by the restoration of the Jews in their homeland. Its author was a Czechoslovakian living in England. His book, published in Latin in 1667, also dropped out of sight until it was rediscovered, translated into English, and printed in 1938. Both of these books, among others, were 300 years ahead of their time, for they espoused the idea of a regathered Israel.

The Puritans in the early 1600s adopted the idea that the Indians in the new world must be the ten lost tribes of Israel. Many were the strange and unusual theories that arose in the wake of the Protestant Reformation and the translation of the Bible into English. Not all theories were based upon an accurate interpretation of the Bible.

The most significant Jewish leader in the 1600s was Manasseh Ben Israel, rabbi of Amsterdam. His book, *The Hope of Israel,* linked the messianism of the British Puritans with the messianism of the Jews. In the book, he accepted the Puritan notion that the Indians of the New World made up the ten lost tribes of Israel. His studies in the book of Daniel, coupled with a prophecy from Deuteronomy that the Jews would be scattered from one end of the earth to the other, convinced him that those Indians must be Jews.

Furthermore, he believed that England must re-admit Jews within her borders. He worked together with British Christians to bring this about. Manasseh Ben Israel believed in the regathering of the chosen people, but many of the Jews during the seventeenth and eighteenth centuries did not agree.

The idea of a restored and regathered Israel was largely a Christian concept. It was the evangelical Christian community over the past 200 years that promoted the concept of a regathered Israel in their national homeland. In 1787, Joseph Priestly, a world-renowned naturalist, philosopher, and theologian, proposed that Jews acknowledge Jesus as their Messiah, come to the end of their sufferings, and be regathered into the Holy Land.

Why — the very idea! Suggesting that the Jews acknowledge Jesus as the Messiah! Such a thought was disgusting to the Jews in 1787. In fact, David Levi, the first Jew to translate the Pentateuch into English, responded to Joseph Priestly with anger and revulsion. Most of the devout Jews of his day were not anticipating either the coming of the Messiah or a return to their land.

In 1799, Napoleon Bonaparte invaded Palestine and was called upon by the British Christian Restoration movement to grant the Jews a homeland. They believed that the fall of the Turkish Ottoman Empire was inevitable and felt that the time had come for the regathering of Israel. Napoleon's victory was short-lived, however, and his retreat after only one month ended the hope of restoration. There were a lot of people during the nineteenth century who embraced the concept of a restored Jewish state. They were men like John Adams, Robert Browning, and Benjamin Disraeli.

One of the most colorful was Sir Lawrence Oliphant, a member of the British parliament. In 1878, he set out to secure the land of Gilead east of the Jordan River for the Jewish people. In 1880, he went to Constantinople to see the Sultan.

It is said that the land of Gilead (northern Jordan) was bought from the Turkish government for the purpose of resettling the area with Jewish immigrants. Though the land was bought and paid for by the Jews, the British occupied the land in 1918. Three years later, in 1922, Winston Churchill, British Secretary of the Colonies, partitioned the land of Palestine, created the Hashemite kingdom of Transjordan, and gave the land of Gilead to the Arabs.

Yes, the land of Gilead was bought and paid for by the Jews, but the Jews were never allowed to possess their territory. King Hussein of Jordan rules over Gilead today — refusing to recognize Jewish ownership of the territory.

Sir Oliphant moved to Haifa in the 1880s in order to assist Jewish immigrants returning to their homeland. He died there in 1888.

Fulfilling the Dream

The name of Theodor Herzl is forever inscribed in history as "the father of modern Zionism." He conducted the first World Zionist Congress in Basel, Switzerland, in 1897, and declared afterward what appears to be a prophetic statement: "At Basel I founded the Jewish state! If I said this out loud today I would be greeted by universal laughter. In five years perhaps, and certainly in fifty years, everyone will perceive it."

Seven years later, Theodor Herzl was dead. But exactly 50 years later, on November 29, 1947, the United Nations voted to establish a Jewish state in Palestine. Though it was not intended as a prophecy, the dream of Theodor Herzl came to pass.

Theodor Herzl was a Jew. Behind the scenes, however, a Christian clergyman, named William Hechler, worked to bring Herzl's dream to reality. From his study of Bible prophecy, Hechler became convinced that 1897 was the crucial year for the restoration of the Jewish state. When he read Theodor Herzl's book, *Der Judenstaat* (The Jewish State), Hechler went to Herzl and volunteered to help him bring the vision to reality.

Early in his career, William Hechler had served as a tutor to the children of Frederic, Grand Duke of Baden, who was the uncle of Kaiser Wilhelm. Using his biblical charts and diagrams, he persuaded the Grand Duke, and other members of the German royal family, that the Jewish state should be restored.

Theodor Herzl knew that the British Christian community believed in the prophetic regathering of Israel and would probably be his strongest ally. He was right. Evangelical Christianity has always stood by the side of the Jewish people.

The British clergyman, William Hechler, arranged a two-hour audience for Herzl with the Grand Duke Frederic, and in October 1898, also arranged a meeting with Kaiser Wilhelm. They met both in Constantinople and Jerusalem. The tireless efforts and prayers of William Hechler on behalf of Theodor Herzl should not be forgotten in history.

In 1902, the World Zionist Congress was offered the Sinai for settlement. The British had control of the land and offered to give it to the Jews. The plan collapsed, however, and in 1903, the African territory of Uganda was offered to the World Zionist Congress. With their letter offering Uganda as a place of refuge for the Jews, the British Foreign Office officially recognized the Zionist movement as a diplomatic entity in 1903.

Herzl was willing to accept the land in East Africa, but Hechler argued that accepting Uganda would destroy all hopes of resettlement in their true homeland of Palestine. By August 1904, Theodor Herzl was dead, and when the World Zionist Congress met again, it abandoned the Uganda plan.

Between 1904 and 1915, however, some 40,000 Jewish immigrants arrived in Palestine nearly doubling the Jewish population.

In 1917, General Edmund Allenby surrounded the city of Jerusalem and conquered the land of Palestine, carrying out the Balfour Declaration which stated, "His majesty's government views with favor the establishment in Palestine of a national homeland for the Jewish people . . . ."

The Balfour Declaration — issued on November 2, 1917 — did not create a Jewish state, but prepared the way for events that led to the establishment of the nation in 1948.

Please note: General Allenby was a Christian; William Hechler was a Christian; and the British Restoration movement was a Christian movement. Yes, over the past 500 years, with the development of the printing press and the translation of the Bible into English, there came a return (in Protestant Christianity) to a literal interpretation of the Bible and the eventual establishment of the Jewish state. Although the regathering of Israel is a Jewish movement, it has been encouraged and aided along the way by Bible believing Christians.

Birth Pangs of a Nation

The rebirth of the state of Israel is the most important fulfillment of Bible prophecy in this century!

Jeremiah predicted that the Exodus out of Egypt would pale into insignificance when compared with the final regathering of Israel:

> Therefore, behold, the days come, saith the Lord, that
> it shall no more be said, The Lord liveth, that brought up
> the children of Israel out of the land of Egypt;
> But, The Lord liveth, that brought up the children of
> Israel from the land of the north, and from all the lands

whither he had driven them: and I will bring them again into their land that I gave unto their fathers (Jer. 16:14-15).

This prediction is an absolutely amazing proclamation.

For more than 3,000 years, the Jewish people have celebrated their deliverance from Egypt with the observance of the great Passover. Year after year, around the Passover table, the Jews have commemorated those days when Moses led the Israeli Exodus out of Egypt.

But Jeremiah wrote that the day will come when this great Passover deliverance will pale into insignificance when compared with the second ingathering of the Jews from all lands — particularly from the land of the north, which includes Germany, Poland, and Russia. That is how much more important this second worldwide exodus will be when compared to that first exodus out of Egypt.

Little did they know how important were their plans — when Theodor Herzl convened the first World Zionist Congress in Basel, Switzerland, in 1897. Their efforts in the eyes of God would far exceed the original exodus!

Israel's rebirth was not an easy one, however; it was attended by war and heartache. The birth of Israel was bathed in blood, fulfilling the prophecies of the Bible which refers to the event as the "birth pangs of travail."

Jeremiah elaborated upon their suffering in his great prophecy and described the second exodus as being greater than the first. Then, in the next verse, he gave a vivid picture of the agents God will use to bring about this second deliverance of the Jewish people:

> Behold, I will send for many fishers, saith the Lord, and they shall fish them; and after will I send for many hunters, and they shall hunt them from every mountain, and from every hill, and out of the holes of the rocks (Jer. 16:16).

Please note the two kinds of people designated by the Lord who will be responsible for the regathering of Israel and for the re-establishment of the nation — the fishers and the hunters. A fisherman draws his prey toward him with bait, and a hunter drives his prey away from him by fear.

We Are the Fishers

In my opinion, the evangelical Christian community has fulfilled the prediction of the fishers. With the sixteenth century Reformation, the invention of the printing press, and the translation of the Bible into English, there came a return to the literal interpretation of the Bible. For the past 400 years, Christians have encouraged and aided the Jewish people to return to their homeland, believing that such a return must precede the Second Coming of Christ. Keep in mind — a fisherman draws his prey toward him with the bait, and a hunter drives his prey away from him by fear.

The fishers of Jeremiah could well have been the ones designated by Jesus as "fishers of men." Every attempt over the past 400 years to restore the nation of Israel has been promoted by Christians, sometimes behind the scenes, but they were there.

William Hechler, aide to Theodor Herzl, was a Christian. Lord Balfour was a Christian. General Edmund Allenby was a Christian. We are the fishers!

The Balfour Declaration did not create the Jewish state, but it prepared the way for one. Lord Balfour was a Christian who believed in the restoration of Israel. One month later, on December 10, 1917, the British army, under the leadership of General Allenby, took the city of Jerusalem. It is said that Allenby dismounted his horse and entered the city on foot, for he, being a Christian, felt that the only conqueror who had a right to ride into the city would be the Messiah himself, Jesus Christ.

So, Allenby walked through the gate into the city of Jerusalem on December 10, 1917, under the mandate of the Balfour Declaration. What a historic day! The evangelical Christians around the world rejoiced, and the Jewish people throughout the world also rejoiced. Hope was high for the regathering of Israel.

The rejoicing was short-lived, however, for the British government over the next few years ignored the Balfour Declaration.

Along with the fishers, however, God sent the hunters.

The Arab Movement

In 1920, the first High Commissioner was appointed. His name was Herbert Samuel, a Jew, who worked to improve conditions for the new settlers. He also established Hebrew as the third language of the country.

Almost from the beginning there were problems between the Arabs and the Jews. The policy and methods of the British government differed decisively from those of the Turks who had ruled the area for 400 years. At the same time, a large influx of Jewish immigrants from various backgrounds, cultures, and languages arrived in Palestine. The whole character of the country was undergoing a radical change, and the Arabs, who strongly resented all of this, began to organize anti-Jewish riots.

In 1919, the Zionist movement made an agreement with Emir Faisal, the leader of the Arab movement, and thought that they could live peaceably side by side. In 1921, however, Faisal's brother, Abdullah, moved into eastern Palestine with a band of guerrillas. At that time, Britain controlled Palestine, a large area of territory which covered not only modern-day Israel, but what became the country of Jordan as well. Because of the uprisings of Arabs against the Jews, the British tried to placate the Arabs by giving them four-fifths of the total territory.

In 1922, Winston Churchill (British Secretary of the Colonies) recognized Abdullah as the political leader of the Arabs and, with a stroke of his pen, partitioned Palestine, creating the Hashemite kingdom of Transjordan. The border was to be the Jordan River Valley from the Lake of Galilee in the north, through the Dead Sea, and south to the port of Eilat on the Gulf of Aqaba.

From the very beginning, Jews were denied access to the land east of the Jordan, while at the same time, the Arabs were allowed to immigrate west of the Jordan into Israeli territory.

Winston Churchill's concessions to the Arabs did not put an end to their opposition. The Arabs continued to riot against the Jews. In 1929, for instance, the Arabs rioted over the issue of Jews praying at the Wailing Wall, and then massacred seventy defenseless Jews in Hebron on the Sabbath.

The Desert Blooms

In spite of all these difficulties, Jewish development continued to flourish. In the mid-1920s, Jews from all over the world began to immigrate to Israel. They settled the towns and the cities — built factories, shops, hotels, and restaurants. Construction and road-building became major industries, and everywhere the Jewish people settled, the Arabs came to take advantage of the higher wages and living standards resulting from Jewish development.

Though no Jewish immigration was permitted to eastern Palestine — the land east of the Jordan River — no such restrictions were placed upon Arab immigration into the Jewish homeland. In fact, while the Jewish population rose by 375,000 between World War I and World War II, the non-Jewish population increased by 380,000.

It is interesting to note that the Arab increase was largest in the areas of intensive Jewish development and negligible where there was little Jewish influx.

During the early 1930s, some 164,000 Jews settled in Palestine. Many of the Arab landlords took advantage of the situation and sold their useless land to the Jews. Between 1933 and 1935, the Jews paid more than $20 million to Arab landowners. They bought swampy, rocky, and sandy soil. Then they drained the swamps, watered the deserts, and planted trees and crops. During those years, they developed an almost uncanny skill for making barren land produce abundant crops.

The world had scoffed, saying that the Jews didn't know anything about farming — only banking. Everywhere else in the world the Jews had made very poor farmers but excellent financiers. In Israel, however, the Jews have become the world's most proficient farmers, yet they cannot seem to control their own inflation.

The inflation rate for the past several years has been severe. The government even changed the currency from the Lira to the biblical Shekel. Still, inflation continued out of control.

No Help From the British

When World War II broke out in 1939, almost the entire Jewish population between the ages of eighteen and fifty volunteered to serve in the British army. By the end of the war, more than 26,000 Jews from Palestine were serving in the Jewish brigade. Most of the Arabs in Palestine, however, were either indifferent or pro-Nazi. In fact, in 1941 the Arab leadership in Jerusalem visited Germany to offer Arab assistance to the Nazis' so-called "final solution to the Jewish problem."

With the aid of other anti-Semites, the Nazis' became the most sadistic and calculated "hunters" of the Jewish people in modern times. The rest of the world, including Britain, closed their eyes and turned their heads to the Nazi atrocities.

In spite of Jewish support for Britain and Arab support for Germany, the British continued to restrain the Jews and appease the Arabs in Palestine. After World War II ended, tensions between the Arabs and the Jews continued to increase. The British would not allow a large influx of Jewish immigration from war-torn Europe. The Jews who escaped the concentration camps of Germany were placed in the concentration camps of the British.

The British occupiers of Israel's homeland continued to placate the Arabs and restrain the Jews. It was felt necessary, then, to drive out the British and assume control of their own destiny. Jewish underground organizations began to retaliate for what was considered to be both British and Arab discrimination.

On November 29, 1947, the United Nations voted to partition western Palestine into two separate states — one Jewish and one Arab. In 1922, the British had given four-fifths of the territory of Palestine to the Arabs — calling it Transjordan — but in 1947, the U.N. carved away again more than half of the Jewish homeland and gave it to the Arabs.

The U.N. moved the border from the Jordan River to the heart of Jerusalem. From that point on, the situation in Jerusalem degenerated rapidly into a state of undeclared war. Jews and Arabs were no longer willing to live side by side. The city was split up into a number of armed camps — some controlled by Jews and others by Arabs.

Officially the British were still responsible for the maintenance of law and order. Although the military forces at their disposal were more than sufficient to enable them to carry out their task effectively, they did not do this. Instead, they openly tolerated — at times even supported — the looting and murders carried out by armed bands of Arabs against the Jews. They also used their military superiority to prevent the Jews from acquiring the weapons they needed to defend themselves.

The Birth of Israel

On May 14, 1948, British forces finally withdrew from Palestine, and the state of Israel was officially proclaimed.

Within a week, however, all of the surrounding Arab nations declared war and set about to destroy the new nation. More than 40 million Arabs — with modern, well-equipped armies — declared war on a tiny newborn nation of less than 640,000 people, whose volunteer army had been assembled on a few days notice. The Jews had no heavy equipment — only an assortment of handguns and rifles.

Humanly speaking, it was impossible for Israel to survive. The proverbial birth pangs were so intense, it looked as if the baby would die. But slowly the tide of war turned against the Arabs. By the end of 1948, virtually all of the invading Arabs had been forced to withdraw.

The state of Israel had been established. It was a miracle, and the Jews survived. It was not easy, but the Israeli people managed to win against overwhelming odds — just as Isaiah said they would:

Who hath heard such a thing? who hath seen such things? Shall the earth be made to bring forth in one day? or shall a nation be born at once? for as soon as Zion travailed, she brought forth her children (Isa. 66:8).

That is exactly what happened on May 14, 1948. Israel was born as a complete nation with its own government, armed forces, and all necessary administrative functions. It is true that everything had been improvised hastily and on a small scale, yet all the necessary ingredients were there to make Israel a nation within its own borders, ". . . for as soon as Zion travailed, she brought forth her children."

Great Britain's Decline

It had been on November 2, 1917, that the British government issued the Balfour Declaration promising a homeland for the Jews. Thirty years later, on November 29, 1947, the British government placed the matter of Israel's future before the United Nations, resulting in another declaration — that being the establishment of the state of Israel. After all of that, the British government attempted to undermine the decision of the U.N. by resisting the establishment of Israel.

It was inconsistency and hypocrisy of the highest order. Such a conduct tarnished the reputation of Britain and proved to be the first stage of a prolonged national decline. The shift in British policy came at a crucial moment in the history of the Middle East without any official decision of the British Parliament and without the majority of the British people being aware of what was taking place.

Why did the British politicians change horses in the middle of the stream? Why did they turn against the Jews in favor of the Arabs? Well, it is said that there were two reasons. First of all, as early as 1939 it had become clear that the world would someday face an ever increasing dependence on oil. Even then a major supply of the world's oil was controlled by the Arab nations of the Middle East. Secondly, on the part of many there was an underlying sentiment of anti-Semitism, which colored British thinking.

Those in Britain who opposed the Jews overlooked one important fact — there is a moral and spiritual force at work in the destinies of nations. The responsibility of government goes beyond mere calculations of economic or military expediency. To sacrifice moral and spiritual principles on such an altar will never serve the best interests of any nation.

Before 1948, the sun "never set" upon the British Empire. That great nation was in control of colonies on every continent from Africa to the Far East. Since that time, however, the once great British empire has lost almost every colony and has faced the decline of her economy. Worse than that, the moral fiber of that once great nation has been on the slide ever since. And may I add, what happened to the British has also been happening to the United States.

America, Israel's only ally, has been wavering in recent years. Our politicians in Washington have attempted to placate the Arabs while restraining the Israeli government. Arab oil has been used to blackmail the United States over the past decade.

Oh, will we never learn? Someone has said that if there is anything we have learned from history, it is that we do not learn from history.

The Growth of Israel

The *rebirth* of the nation of Israel was a miracle. But that's not all. The *growth* of that tiny new nation has also been miraculous.

In 1948, there were only 640,000 Jews living in the land. Over the following ten years, however, they tripled their population with new immigrants — most of them refugees. They housed them, clothed them, and fed them. They taught them the Hebrew language, trained them, and placed them in jobs. At the same time, Israel built up its military to defend itself against the Arabs.

The pressures to which Israel has continuously been subjected are possibly without parallel in history: hostile neighbors, six wars, terrorism, inflation, media misrepresentation, economic boycott.

The tiny nation with a population of less than four million occupies an area of less than 8,000 square miles. In contrast, its hostile Arab neighbors number more than 150 million people living on five million square miles. The armies of the Arab League number nearly one million men, while Israel's army consists of 164,000.

In spite of tremendous odds, the nation of Israel has continued to grow and flourish. In the face of all their pressure, the Israelis plant and harvest; they build and manufacture.

Behind this lies one inescapable fact: Israel's survival is at stake. The very fact that Israel still lives today after all these years is a miracle without equal. Of course the key to understanding this miracle can be found in the prophecies of the Bible. The regathering of Israel is the central theme of biblical prophecy. Those 2,500 year-old prophecies are coming to pass before our very eyes. Isaiah was right!

Who hath heard such a thing? who hath seen such things? Shall the earth be made to bring forth in one day? or shall a nation be born at once? for as soon as Zion travailed, she brought forth her children (Isa. 66:8).

Whose Land Is It?

The restoration of Israel is one of the most controversial political issues of the century. Palestinians have claimed that the land is theirs and that the Jews have no right to even one square foot of it. They make these claims in spite of the fact that the area had been under the control of the Turkish government for some 400 years — not Palestinian control.

Just who deserves the land? Do the Jews? Do the Palestinians? Do Jews have a right to control the land in the so-called "occupied West Bank" areas?

Though the United Nations established Israel in 1948, most of the world no longer supports the concept of Jewish sovereignty and regret ever giving them any territory in the Middle East. The controversy rages today as much as it ever did. The children of Abraham are still fighting it out!

If the fate of the Israeli government were placed in the hands of any human court, the verdict would probably be disastrous. Time and time again, the United Nations has taken the side of the Arabs against Israel.

While dedicated Christians around the world are in favor of Israel's existence, their governments are not. The only political ally on the side of Israel is the United States — and many in Washington are wavering. In light of these developments, let us appeal to the court of heaven for the final verdict in the case.

There is one verse of Scripture that declares the absolute ownership of, not only the Middle East, but of the entire world: "The earth is the Lord's, and the fullness thereof; the world, and they that dwell therein" (Ps. 24:1).

Since God created the earth, the right to ownership is His. Whether man recognizes the existence of God or not is irrelevant for, in the final analysis, God will lay claim to His earth. He not only owns the world but also everybody in it.

Among the continents, however, there is one special area to which God lays a unique claim. It is the land of Israel. There are several places in the Bible where God calls the land, "My land."

For instance, in Ezekiel 38:16, God condemns the mighty Gog and Magog for the invasion of His land: "And thou shalt come up against my people of Israel, as a cloud to cover the land; it shall be in the latter days, and I will bring thee against my land."

Here, God emphatically calls the land of Israel His land. That claim is repeated in Joel:

> I will also gather all nations, and will bring them down into the valley of Jehoshaphat, and will plead with them there for my people and for my heritage Israel, whom they have scattered among the nations, and parted my land (Joel 3:2).

Both of these verses pronounce a judgment upon Gentile nations for their part in denying the Jews a right to live in *His* land. Notice that God calls Israel, "My people," and He calls their land, "My land." When Gentile nations challenge the integrity of the land and its people, God steps forward to proclaim His judgment upon them.

God is the absolute owner of the land and as such had every right to evict the Jewish people 20 centuries ago. But, He also has a right to bring them back in this century. God is Sovereign over the land.

The Three Covenants

Let us review Genesis 17 — the days of Abraham — and determine God's sovereign disposition over *His* land.

> And I will establish my covenant between me and thee and thy seed after thee in their generations for an everlasting covenant, to be a God unto thee, and to thy seed after thee.
>
> And I will give unto thee, and to thy seed after thee, the land wherein thou art a stranger, all the land of Canaan, for an everlasting possession; and I will be their God (Gen. 17:7-8).

There can be no doubt that such a covenant was declared and recorded 4,000 years ago. Ah, but the Arabs also claim to be descendants of Abraham. Does not the land then also belong to them? You may recall the Arabs are descendants of Ishmael, while the Jews are descendants of Abraham's other son, Isaac.

The controversy was settled in Genesis 26:3-4. It is there that God narrows down the covenant to exclude the children of Ishmael.

It was to Isaac that God said:

> Sojourn in this land, and I will be with thee, and will bless thee; for unto thee, and unto thy seed, I will give all these countries, and I will perform the oath which I sware unto Abraham thy father;
>
> And I will make thy seed to multiply as the stars of heaven, and will give unto thy seed all these countries; and in thy seed shall all the nations of the earth be blessed (Gen. 26:3-4).

God not only promised to Isaac the land called Israel, but He gave what the Scripture declares to be "all these countries." In fact, He used the term twice in His promise to Isaac.

But wait a minute. Isaac had two sons — both Jacob and Esau — and there is a good deal of evidence that the Palestinian people who live in the land today could be descendants of Esau. Do they not also have a claim to the land?

God said no. He narrowed the inheritance of the land to Jacob and his descendants:

> And God said unto him, I am God Almighty: be fruitful and multiply; a nation and a company of nations shall be of thee, and kings shall come out of thy loins;
>
> And the land which I gave Abraham and Isaac, to thee I will give it, and to thy seed after thee will I give the land (Gen. 35:11-12).

The proclamation is clear. God has promised the land to Jacob and his descendants — namely the twelve tribes of Israel.

When we consider these three covenants together, the line of descent through which the land is promised is evident. In each case, God narrowed His promise of the land — from Abraham, to Isaac, to Jacob, and then to his descendants after him.

In view of these covenants made by the God of heaven with the people of Israel, we must declare a verdict in favor of the Israeli nation. As a people of the Book, who claim to believe the Bible, we have no choice. We stand without reservation on the side of Israel.

Israel's Right to the Land

The Psalmist wrote: "He is the Lord our God: his judgments are in all the earth" (Ps. 105:7).

Do you believe this? Then read what the Psalmist wrote in the following verses:

> He hath remembered his covenant for ever, the word which he commanded to a thousand generations.
> Which covenant he made with Abraham, and his oath unto Isaac;
> And confirmed the same unto Jacob for a law, and to Israel for an everlasting covenant:
> Saying, Unto thee will I give the land of Canaan, the lot of your inheritance (Ps. 105:8-11).

The writer of this psalm emphasized two important points.

First, he left no doubt as to the line of descent through which the promise of the land is given. It is from Abraham, to Isaac, to Jacob, to Israel.

Secondly, the Psalmist sought to establish the sacred and unchanging nature of God's commitment to Abraham and his descendants. He first spoke of the covenant as being God's "Own covenant." He then called it "the word which He commanded." Next, the Psalmist refers to it as "His oath unto Isaac." Then, he labels it "a law," and finally "an everlasting covenant." That's a pretty powerful set of words! How can one be more emphatic than that?

Furthermore, He declared the covenant "unto a thousand generations." That would take at least 20,000 years. Yes, we must conclude the land of Israel has been given by God to the people of Israel — to the descendants of Jacob.

Psalm 105 declares the land to be forever Israel. However, we know that the people were evicted from their land by their Landlord, God, almost 2,000 years ago.

It is the prophetic Scripture to which we must look for the final disposition of the land — and the prophecies do not differ from the original covenant.

For instance, Jeremiah wrote:

> For, lo, the days come, saith the Lord, that I will bring again the captivity of my people Israel and Judah, saith the Lord: and I will cause them to return to the land that I gave to their fathers, and they shall possess it (Jer. 30:3).

There is only one area of land in all the earth that fits that description. It is the land of Israel. Notice, please, God spoke of the captivity of "My people Israel and Judah," and, further, He said they would return to the land "that I gave to their fathers." In fact, He said they would possess their land.

Then there was Ezekiel, who wrote:

> For I will take you from among the heathen, and gather you out of all countries, and will bring you into your own land (Ezek. 36:24).

This is clearly a prophecy concerning the last days of world history when the Jew will return to his land and the Messiah will come to establish a world kingdom. When God promised to bring Israel back to the land at the close of the age, He still called it "your own land." In God's sight, the ownership of the land has never changed and never will. He gave it to Abraham, to Isaac, to Jacob, and to his descendants — the people of Israel.

Even the prophet Amos concluded his book with a similar emphatic prediction:

> And I will plant them upon their land, and they shall no more be pulled up out of their land which I have given them, saith the Lord thy God (Amos 9:15).

Amos predicted that God will plant them upon "their land." It is obvious to all who believe the Bible that the hand of God can be seen in what must be considered as the incredible miracle of this century — the return of the Jew to His land.

These prophecies were given from 2,500 to 4,000 years ago and cannot be modified today by the United Nations, the PLO, the Arab nations, or even Russia. God has decreed that Israel is the land of the Jew.

These Scriptures are extremely emphatic. They don't simply imply the restoration of Israel, they declare it. Perhaps God, through His foresight, knew that such a move would be vigorously opposed by the Arab world. Therefore, He emphasized Israel's inalienable right to the land.

Had It Not Been For Israel

Humanly speaking, we owe all that we have and all that we are to Israel. If there had been no Israel, there would have been no patriarchs, no prophets, no apostles, no Bible, and no Saviour.

In John 4:22 Jesus, himself, summed up all of this in one simple statement. He said, ". . . for salvation is of the Jews."

Regardless of our nationality or background, we owe a spiritual debt to the Jewish people that can never be calculated. Unfortunately, historic Christianity has never recognized its debt to Israel. From at least the fourth century forward, the Christian church consistently treated the Jewish people with prejudice, contempt, injustice, and cruelty.

Most Christians today are almost totally ignorant of these historical facts. But it is true that Christian anti-Semitism was a warped form of theology held widely in the church for many centuries. Historic Christianity has believed that the Jewish people were responsible for the crucifixion of Christ and were thus guilty of the most terrible crime of all — the murder of God, himself. On the basis of this theology, many Christians felt that the way to show their loyalty to Christ was to express their hatred toward His murderers — that is, the Jewish people.

For instance, the fourth century theologian, John Chrisostom, described the Jewish people in his sermons as "lustful, rapacious, greedy, perfidious bandits . . . inveterate murderers, destroyers, men possessed by the devil . . . debauchery and drunkenness have given them the manners of the pig and the lusty goat. They know only one thing — to satisfy their gullets, get drunk, to kill and maim one another."

On another occasion, Chrisostom said, "I hate the synagogue precisely because it has the Law and the Prophets . . . . I hate the Jews also because they outrage the Law . . . ." The most tragic thing about this is not that a renowned Christian theologian could espouse such sentiments toward the Jewish people, but that he had a profound effect upon the attitude and theology of Christianity for many centuries to come.

During the Crusades of the eleventh century, the soldiers massacred entire Jewish communities — sparing no one. When they reached Jerusalem, they found an entire Jewish congregation gathered in a synagogue and proceeded to burn down the synagogue killing the people. All this was done in the name of Christ and in the sign of the cross.

Sad to say, not even the leaders of the Protestant Reformation were free from the guilt of anti-Jewish prejudice. When Martin Luther first published his teachings, he anticipated that the Jewish people would be convinced by them and would convert to Christianity. When this did not happen, Luther was disappointed and embittered.

On one occasion Luther wrote:

> The Jews deserve the most severe penalties. Their synagogues should be leveled, their homes destroyed, they should be exiled into tents like the Gypsies. Their religious writings should be taken from them. Their rabbis should be forbidden to continue teaching the law. All professions should be closed to them. Only the hardest, coarsest work should be permitted them. Rich Jews should have their fortunes confiscated, and the money used to support Jews who are willing to be converted. If all these measures are unsuccessful, the Christian princes should have the duty of driving the Jews from their lands as they would rabid dogs.[1]

During the 1930s, the Nazis of Hitler's Germany used such statements by Martin Luther to advocate their anti-Semitic policies. I guess we could say that the Nazis merely reaped the harvest that the Church had sown. No wonder the Jews have ill feelings toward historic Christianity.

It is time for us to denounce such anti-Semitism and to take our stand on the side of Israel in fulfillment of the central theme of biblical prophecy — the establishment of God's kingdom on earth.

Israel: The Central Theme

Geographically, the Bible is set in the land of Israel, and historically, its theme is the people of Israel. It is a Jewish Bible penned by Jewish men giving both the history and the future of those children of Abraham, Isaac, and Jacob.

For centuries Gentile Christianity has laid claim to the Book declaring that Israel has been dispossessed by God. Historic Christianity claims that the chosen people are no longer chosen and that God has instead turned His back forever on the children of Israel.

Though it is true that God has punished the Jewish people over the past 3,000 years for their unbelief, it is not true that God has cast away His people forever. The central theme of Bible prophecy is the restoration of the Israeli people — both to their land and to their God.

The first 11 chapters of Genesis serve as an introduction. They fill in the background and set the stage for all that is to follow. From that point forward, the Bible is essentially the history of Abraham and the nation that descended from him through Isaac and Jacob. The

Bible is basically the story of Israel embracing both the past and future.

But what about the New Testament? Isn't it distinctly Christian? It's a little difficult for Gentile Christianity to admit that even the New Testament is a Jewish book, yet it is true.

First of all, Jesus Christ, the most important person in the New Testament, was of Jewish descent, and He did not lose His Jewish identity after His death and resurrection. Fifty years after Calvary, Revelation 5:5 still referred to Jesus Christ, in heaven, as the "Lion of the tribe of Judah, the root of David." He is still identified with the family of David, the tribe of Judah, and the people of Israel. He is forever an Israelite.

Furthermore, well over 90 percent of the people portrayed in the New Testament are Israelites. The only exceptions would be a few Gentiles, such as the Magi from the East, or the Samaritan woman at Jacob's well, along with a sprinkling of Roman officials and military personnel. Essentially, the New Testament represents a record of Israelites and their faith in the Messiah.

The New Testament books were penned by Jews — with the one possible exception being Luke. The twelve Apostles were Jewish. Paul, who became the apostle to the Gentiles, was likewise a Jew. Most of the co-workers of these great men were also Jewish.

The writer of Hebrews tells us that the ultimate goal of all true believers is the "city which hath foundations whose Builder and Maker is God." In Revelation 21, the Holy City, New Jerusalem, is described for us. On its gates are inscribed the names of the twelve tribes of Israel. On its foundations are the names of the twelve Apostles of Jesus. Every name inscribed in the New Jerusalem is a Jewish name. I must say that no one with anti-Semitic prejudice could ever feel comfortable in the New Jerusalem.

Why, then, does it seem strange — in fact, almost unthinkable — to associate the Jewish people with the New Testament? The answer lies in what Christians perceive to be the judgment of God. Because the leadership of the nation had rejected Jesus Christ as Messiah, the people of Israel were separated from their land. At the same time, the early Jewish Christians were separated from their role as leaders in proclaiming the gospel and building the church.

This double break determined their role in history for the next eighteen centuries. They became a nation of exiles. Not only were they exiled from their land, but they were also exiled from the very religion of which they themselves were the founders. It seems as if God sacrificed the chosen people in order to bring the message of salvation to the great masses of Gentile nations around the world.

The Second Return of Israel

We are the benefactors of that great break in the continuum of history. Let us not forget, however, that God has not forever forsaken His people.

Just as Jesus rose again on the third day, in like manner, the resurrection of Israel has been promised in the prophecies of the Bible. Hosea wrote: "After two days will he revive us: in the third day he will raise us up, and we shall live in his sight" (Hos. 6:2).

The 1948 resurrection of the Israeli nation not only fulfills Hosea's prophecy but is the central theme of each prophet in the Old Testament.

For instance, Isaiah wrote concerning the regathering of Israel:

> And in that day there shall be a root of Jesse, which shall stand for an ensign of the people; to it shall the Gentiles seek: and his rest shall be glorious.
>
> And it shall come to pass in that day, that the Lord shall set his hand again the second time to recover the remnant of his people, which shall be left, from Assyria, and from Egypt, and from Pathros, and from Cush, and from Elam, and from Shinar, and from Hamath, and from the islands of the sea.
>
> And he shall set up an ensign for the nations, and shall assemble the outcasts of Israel, and gather together the dispersed of Judah from the four corners of the earth.
>
> The envy also of Ephraim shall depart, and the adversaries of Judah shall be cut off: Ephraim shall not envy Judah, and Judah shall not vex Ephraim.
>
> But they shall fly upon the shoulders of the Philistines toward the west; they shall spoil them of the east together: they shall lay their hand upon Edom and Moab: and the children of Ammon shall obey them (Isa. 11:10-14).

These five verses contain some astounding prophecies, most of which have already been fulfilled and others which are yet to be fulfilled — perhaps in the near future.

First of all, Isaiah wrote in verse 10 that the entire picture revolves around one person — the Root of Jesse. He will stand as an "ensign," or a banner, of the people, and to Him "shall the Gentiles seek."

Jesus Christ fulfilled the prophecy of the Root of Jesse. And when He was lifted up on Calvary's cross, He became a banner for all the Gentile nations. Since that day, Gentiles around the world have found, through Christ, the forgiveness of their sins. We have been drawn to the foot of Calvary, and there we have found salvation.

Then, wrote Isaiah, "His rest shall be glorious." Over the past 20 centuries Jesus Christ has been lifted up to the throne of God and has been seated at the right hand of the Father in heaven. He is presently awaiting the establishment of His earthly kingdom, which shall last for a thousand years. It will come to pass in the seventh millennium — the great Sabbath rest. Yes, His rest shall be glorious.

Isaiah tells of the redemption of Israel: "And it shall come to pass in that day, that the Lord shall set his hand again the second time to recover the remnant of his people . . ." (Isa. 11:11).

Isaiah wrote of a specified time, "in that day." How do we know we live in that day? Because of the following words: ". . . the Lord shall set his hand again the second time to recover the remnant of his people . . . ."

Isaiah wrote in the days before the Babylonian captivity, but he did not simply write that the Lord will set His hand to recover the remnant of His people. He went beyond that. He saw a second dispersion of the Jews from their land and wrote that "in that day the Lord shall set His hand AGAIN the SECOND time."

I believe we live in that day. The return of the Jew to his land in this century does not represent the first return or the third return. The rebirth of the nation of Israel in 1948 marked the second return of the Jews to their land. Isaiah, then, zeroes in on this generation in the giving of his great prophecy.

A Worldwide Return

In verse 11, Isaiah continues by giving the locations from which the Jews shall return: ". . . from Assyria, and from Egypt, and from Pathros, and from Cush, and from Elam, and from Shinar, and from Hamath, and from the islands of the sea" (Isa. 11:11).

In the first dispersion, the people were led into Babylonian captivity, and when they returned, they returned from Babylon. But in that day designated for the far future, the Israeli people will return from many lands: "And he shall set up an ensign for the [Gentile] nations, and shall assemble the outcasts of Israel, and gather together the dispersed of Judah from the four corners of the earth" (Isa. 11:12).

Isaiah indicated that the second dispersion of the Jews would be to all nations and that when they returned one day, they would return from the four corners of the earth.

Isaiah wrote in a day when the Israeli nation was divided. There was a split between the north and the south. Ephraim was the leading nation of the north, and Judah of the south. There was a continuing feud between the two factions. However, Isaiah wrote that in that day when the Lord reaches out His hand the second time to regather the people, there would be no division among the tribes: "The envy also of Ephraim shall depart, and the adversaries of Judah shall be cut off: Ephraim shall not envy Judah, and Judah shall not vex Ephraim" (Isa. 11:13).

How indicative of the Israeli nation today! It is no longer a nation divided against itself. Israel is one. Surely this is the generation which marks the fulfillment of Isaiah's great prophecy. We have reached that point in history. The Jew is back in his land and all the tribes are united.

The next prophecy is fascinating: "But they shall fly upon the shoulders of the Philistines toward the west . . ." (Isa. 11:14).

This appears to be indicative of the 1956, 1967, and 1973 Arab-Israeli Wars. What happens in the rest of the verse, however, is yet to be fulfilled. Isaiah wrote: ". . . they shall spoil them of the east together: they shall lay their hand upon Edom and Moab: and the children of Ammon shall obey them" (Isa. 11:14b).

According to this prophecy, Israel will obtain an understanding with the Hashemite kingdom of Jordan. King Hussein once declared that he would not negotiate with Israel over the future of the confiscated West Bank. One Jordanian politician was upset. He was in favor of negotiations and said, "If we do not negotiate with Israel today over the West Bank, we may eventually have to negotiate with Israel over the East Bank." According to Isaiah's prophecy, it will come to pass.

Precious in God's Sight

In Isaiah the prophet again took up the theme of Israel's restoration: "But now thus saith the Lord that created thee, O Jacob, and he that formed thee, O Israel, Fear not: for I have redeemed thee, I have called thee by thy name; thou art mine" (Isa. 43:1).

In the previous chapter, Isaiah wrote about the judgment of God upon Israel. But in this verse, he turns from judgment to mercy and begins the verse by saying, "But now . . . ."

Oh, what a promise! What a glorious promise! God hath not forever forsaken His chosen people!

Please note two things Isaiah wrote in this verse. First, the Lord "created" the nation and, secondly, He "formed" the nation. When He created the people of Israel, a flaw appeared. Like the potter who remade his broken vessel, the Lord is now in the process of restructuring the nation.

First, He created them — today, He is in the process of forming them:

> When thou passest through the waters, I will be with thee; and through the rivers, they shall not overflow thee: when thou walkest through the fire, thou shalt not be burned; neither shall the flame kindle upon thee (Isa. 43:2).

Again, we can see the accuracy of biblical prophecy. The vivid phrases of this verse depict the history of the Jewish people through a period of almost 2,000 years. They have, indeed, passed through the rivers and walked through the fire. There is only one explanation for their continued survival as a people. God has been with them:

> For I am the Lord thy God, the Holy One of Israel, thy Saviour: I gave Egypt for thy ransom, Ethiopia and Seba for thee.
> Since thou wast precious in my sight, thou hast been honorable, and I have loved thee: therefore will I give men for thee, and people for thy life (Isa. 43:3-4).

The great message, in these verses, is that God loves Israel with a supreme love. This is a revelation of tremendous importance. God places a special value on His chosen people and, though He permits them to pass through the fire, He has a great purpose in it. Isaiah gives us the reason why: "Behold, I have refined thee, but not with silver; I have chosen thee in the furnace of affliction" (Isa. 48:10).

Because He loved them, He tested them — just as Job was tested. In these verses, God declares that His love for Israel has also influenced His dealings with other nations.

Finally, a distinction is given between those who return from the "east and west" and those who return from the "north and south":

> Fear not: for I am with thee: I will bring thy seed from

the east, and gather thee from the west;

I will say to the north, Give up; and to the south, Keep not back: bring my sons from far, and my daughters from the ends of the earth;

Even every one that is called by my name: for I have created him for my glory, I have formed him; yea, I have made him (Isa. 43:5-7).

Like the promises of chapter 11, Isaiah repeated that Israel will be regathered from the four corners of the earth. Note the precision with which he gave the prophecy. He said, "I will bring thy seed from the east, and gather thee from the west."

The "east," I believe, primarily refers to Asia and the "west" must surely represent the great concentration of Jewish people in Europe, Africa, the United States, and South America. The verbs used here do not indicate any particular opposition to the Jewish people returning from either the east or the west. In fact — especially in regard to the west — there seems to be the suggestion of a reluctance on their part to leave.

When we come to the "north" and "south," however, we get a different picture: "I will say to the north, Give up; and to the south, Keep not back: bring my sons from far, and my daughters from the ends of the earth" (verse 6).

How indicative of the north! The cry still goes out today, "Give up! Give up [My people]!"

From the North and the South

The north must surely represent not only eastern Europe but Russia as well. The former Soviet Union had a history of being extremely unwilling to permit Jewish emigration to Israel. This makes the message to the north especially appropriate: "Give [them] up! Give up [My people; let them come home]."

Let us not forget the *Miami Herald* (1983) newspaper story that pointed out the fact that there had been a strange disappearance of more than 100,000 Jews from the Soviet Union over a previous 10-year period. Some 100,000 Jews had been arrested when they applied for permission to emigrate to Israel. No wonder Isaiah wrote that the divine message to the north would be, "Give up [My people; let them come home]."

After hearing about an American schoolgirl's well-publicized letter to then Soviet Premier, Yuri Andropov, which received an answer, a 12-year-old girl in the Soviet Union wrote him a letter of her own. The content of the letter, however, was somewhat different. Irina Tarnopolsky, of Kharkov, in the Ukraine, appealed to Andropov on behalf of her father, a Jewish scientist who had been imprisoned on a charge of slandering the Soviet state. His crime? Applying for permission to leave for Israel.

Irina wrote, "Not long ago I came to know that an American school girl, Samantha Smith, appealed to you in a letter, and you answered her. So I decided to write you a letter, too. My father, Yuri Tarnopolsky, is in prison now. He is accused of slandering the Soviet system, and soon he will be tried. But my papa is an honest man. He has never lied. He is under arrest only because we are Jewish and want to leave for Israel."

In October, 1983, Irina's father had begun a hunger strike to protest the plight of Jewish families who were denied permission to emigrate. They were referred to as refuseniks. He had been fired from his job shortly after his application was turned down. Later he wrote, "I am unable to forget that in modern history the Nazi barbarians refused to allow Jews to emigrate, persecuting them at the same time."

Slander, in the Soviet Union, was punishable by a sentence of three years in a labor camp or five years of internal exile. The Tarnopolsky family had had no contact with him since his arrest the previous March. And Irina received no reply from Andropov. Such was the plight of the Jews in the Soviet Union. Once again we see both the accuracy and the authority of the Scriptures.

Finally, Isaiah wrote of God's message to the south: "I will say to the . . . south, Keep not back: bring my sons from far, and my daughters from the ends of the earth" (Isa. 43:6).

There are two southern areas to which this prophecy relates. The first is the country of Yemen, where nearly 50,000 Jews lived in 1948. Yemen is a fanatically Moslem country, strongly opposed to the state of Israel.

Who would have believed that a country like that would have released almost its entire Jewish population shortly after Israel became a state in 1948. In fact, 43,000 Jews were airlifted out of Yemen into Israel in what appears to be yet another fulfillment of Bible prophecy: "Ye have seen what I did to the Egyptians, and how I bare thee on eagles' wings, and brought you unto myself" (Exod. 19:4).

The other southern country with a large Jewish population was Ethiopia. And since 1984, a continuing effort to rescue the Falashas paid off with the massive airlift in May, 1991. All Ethiopian Jews are now safe in Israel!

> I will say to the . . . south, Keep not back: bring my
> sons from far, and my daughters from the ends of the earth;
> Even every one that is called by my name: for I have
> created him for my glory, I have formed him; yea, I have
> made him (Isa. 43:6-7).

Indeed, the return of Israel is the prevailing theme of all the prophets. Without them, nothing else could come to pass!

God Has a Plan

Why should God be concerned with such a small land — 40 miles wide and 220 miles long?

First of all, He is a covenant-keeping God. When God promises something, He follows through with it. If God did not keep His covenant with Abraham, Isaac, and Jacob, how could we expect Him to keep any promises to us?

Secondly, that little spot on the globe happens to be the land-bridge spanning three continents — Europe, Asia, and Africa. It is a strategic location for political, as well as spiritual, control of the planet.

There is yet another reason, however. It was given by Moses: "When the Most High divided to the nations their inheritance, when he separated the sons of Adam, he set the bounds of the people according to the number of the children of Israel" (Deut. 32:8).

The Lord not only established the land of Israel for the Jew, but He has established the borders of every nation under the sun. He chose the amount of land for each nation according to the population that nation will eventually attain. It is also true of Israel. God has given His Chosen People just enough land to take care of Israel's intended ultimate population.

The apostle Paul said basically the same thing when he spoke to the men of Athens: "And hath made of one blood all nations of men for to dwell on all the face of the earth, and hath determined the times before appointed, and the bounds of their habitation" (Acts 17:26).

God has not only determined where the nations shall dwell, but also when they shall dwell there. It all revolves around God's dealings with Israel.

God has a plan. It not only involves the restoration of the Jews to the land of Israel, it involves every nation in the world. When Christ returns, His kingdom will be a world kingdom. In fact, when Messiah comes, He will judge the nations upon one basic criterion — how they treated God's chosen people, the Jews. This is the basic teaching throughout the Bible. It is the central theme of the prophetic Scriptures and, therefore, has a very practical application for the citizens of every nation in the world.

We cannot afford to stand aside and say that Israel's fate does not concern us. We cannot take a neutral stand on the issue because the well-being of every nation is at stake. Until Israel enters into its full inheritance, the other nations of the world can never enjoy the blessings that God has in store for them.

One day God will bring an eternal peace to the nations of the world. He will solve the problems of famine, hunger, and poverty. He will eradicate all disease and death. He will create utopia. There will be no more war and bloodshed. But that world cannot come and Messiah cannot make His appearance until the Jew is back in his land.

To be sure, the restoration of Israel has been — and will continue to be — accompanied by great turmoil and strife. Many peoples and nations will suffer. But that too, is in the plan of God. Sin must be judged and the sinner must be weeded out before God can restore paradise.

Section III

The Curtain Draws Closed

12

The New World Order at Last:

A Time to Tremble

Phil Arms

TRIBULATION. This seven-year period climaxing the end of world history has struck fear in the hearts of many. Others, however, have considered the horrifying description of this time a hoax perpetrated by biblically illiterate fundamentalists.

The sheer magnitude of the predicted horrors, calamity, and disasters described defy the imagination; hence, many have considered them illustrative in nature or relegated them to a time long past. However, it is well to note that history has not been without its great disasters, some seemingly of biblical proportions. These include:

Epidemics:

1. During 1340-1350, over 25,000,000 people in Asia and Europe died of the Black Death.

2. In 1545, typhus killed 250,000 in Cuba alone.

3. In 1560, over 3,000,000 died of smallpox in Brazil.

4. In 1680, diphtheria killed 8,000 in Naples, Italy.

5. In 1792, nearly 1,000,000 in Egypt perished by the Black Death.

6. In 1802, yellow fever killed 30,000 of Napoleon's soldiers in Santa Domingo.

7. In 1827, Europe lost 900,000 due to cholera.

8. In 1851, tuberculosis killed 51,000 in England.

9. In 1863, 30,000 died of scarlet fever in England.

10. In 1918, some 30,000,000 perished during a worldwide epidemic of influenza.

Volcanic Action:

In 1902, Mt. Pelee erupted in the West Indies, killing over 30,000 people.

Earthquakes:

On January 24, 1556, some 830,000 died in China after a massive earthquake.

On September 30, 1993, an earthquake struck southern India and resulted in 30,000 deaths.

Fires:

On December 30, 1903, the most tragic fire in United States history killed 600 people who had packed the Iroquois Theater in Chicago, Illinois.

Tornadoes:

On March 18, 1925, nearly 700 people living in Illinois, Indiana, and Missouri lost their lives in a tornado.

Famines:

In 1877, nearly 1,000,000 people starved to death in Northern China alone.

Floods:

In 1887, China lost 900,000 due to one mighty flood.

Landslides:

On December 16, 1891, 200,000 died in China because of a landslide.

Cyclones:

On November 12, 1970, over 500,000 fell victim to killer water storms in East Pakistan.[1]

The point of all the above gruesome statistics is this: Catastrophe has been man's constant companion throughout recorded history. According to the Bible, however, there is coming a calamity unlike any this weary world has ever seen.

Although this future period will be of relatively short duration, it will nevertheless see the destruction of more of this earth's population than did all the previously quoted years combined. In fact, nearly one billion people will be struck down during the beginning of this terrible coming disaster.

Bringing Man to the End of Himself

The Scriptures clearly define this tribulation period as one designed to allow Satan — and man without God — willful reign without constraints so all humanity may witness the inevitable, inescapable results of the Devil's diabolic conspiracy against righteousness.

The blood-chilling events that take place in a rapid fire succession bring what is left of a world gone mad to desperation. In their last gasp for survival, humanity will reach out for social, economic, and political salvation. But alas, they will not reach out to Jehovah God. Their desperate cry for redemption will be heard by one prepared "for such an hour as this."

A series of events will set the stage for one man to step forward and be crowned King of the world. What kind of despair could cause nations to give up their sovereignty, their patriotic allegiances, and their individual destiny into the hands of one man?

The Word of God, as we have already seen, outlines the conditions that will bring humanity to their knees.

The catastrophes and simultaneous collapse of the economies of every nation on earth will be followed quickly by a nuclear exchange that begins with an invasion of Israel by Russia (spoken of so clearly in Ezekiel, Chapters 38 and 39). As a result, a breakdown of law and order in every civilized nation will characterize this most likely series of events.

In keeping with the biblically prophesied scenario, these events could leave a world population subjected to diseases, starvation, anarchy, and absolute despair. The nations, their leaders as well as the people will, at such a time, be on their knees begging for someone, anyone, to do something to bring order, sanity, and a semblance of authority out of the ashes of the earthly hell man will have created.

A sovereign God allows man to come to the end of himself and permits man, in his willful rebellion, to create such despair. It is only in man's despair that he will reach out to God.

In that coming tribulation period , however, we see a world full of people who refuse to turn to God. Second Thessalonians 2:11 tells us, "And for this cause God shall send them strong delusion, that they should believe [the] lie." The lie mankind will believe in their darkest hour is that man without God can bring life and light back to a world on the brink of its own destruction. Here is man, again seduced by Satan and willing to work in concert with unbridled evil.

God in His sovereignty allows it thus to prove again the depth of deception contained in the satanic claim.

In Isaiah 14 we see a picture of Satan's desire to be God. He has attempted to convince man from the beginning that he, not the Lord Jesus Christ, should rule the universe. Humanity will witness the satanic attempt to prove his deity, and they will suffer for their tolerance.

Additionally, this time frame is set aside to deal with the nation of Israel who, for over 2,000 years, has not known her God. John 1:11 tells us, "He (Jesus) came unto His own, and His own received Him not." And yet, as Paul clearly states in Romans 11:2: "God hath not cast away . . . ." the Jewish people and nation.

To the contrary, God, in this Tribulation period, will be purging Israel and calling out His people: "And I will cause you to pass under the rod, and I will bring you into the bond of the covenant. And I will purge out from among you the rebels . . ." (Ezek. 20:37-38).

Zechariah joins his voice to reiterate God's desire during this period to draw to himself the true Jew, who is a "Jew both inwardly and outwardly."

> And it shall come to pass that in all the land, saith the Lord, two parts in it shall be cut off and die; but the third shall be left in it. And I will bring the third part through the fire, and will refine them as silver is refined, and will [test] them as gold is [tested]; they shall call on my name, and I will hear them. I will say, It is my people; and they shall say, The Lord is my God (Zech. 13:8-9).

Clearly God will use these seven years to sift Israel and draw them to their true Saviour. "And he shall sit like a refiner and purifier of silver; and he shall purify the sons of Levi, and purge them like gold and silver, that they may offer unto the Lord an offering in righteousness" (Mal. 3:3).

In the midst of hell vomiting out its rage on earth and humanity, God will be doing a redemptive work.

But Satan will also be building his kingdom.

The Mother/Baby Cult

In Revelation 17, John the Revelator, speaks prophetically of a coming world church. He identifies her as "mystery Babylon" and tells us she will be a ruthless, bloody, unholy, God-hating "whore." Identified as a false church, she is the antithesis of the real Church, the bride of Christ — she is the wife of Satan.

In addition to providing an outlet for man's religious drive during the Tribulation, she will work in harmony with Satan's evil political machinery to "sanctify" the manipulation of human affairs. Her leadership will stand shoulder-to-shoulder with the Antichrist and supply the "spiritual energy" to fulfill his task.

This church is not going to be new on the scene. Her presence was felt long ago. In fact, many scholars believe Satan's church began in Genesis 11, as the Tower of Babel was under construction. Satan worship experienced its first revival since Eve accepted the invitation to come to a satanic altar. In fact, geographically, the Plain of Shinar, where the Tower of Babel was being constructed, was probably close to the border of Eden.

Readers of Genesis 10 remember the story of Noah's evil grandson Nimrod who began construction on the tower. Tradition as well as history report that Nimrod eventually married a very vile and wicked woman named Semerimus.

It is said that this evil woman gave birth to a son, naming him Tammuz. Claiming he was the fulfillment of God's prophecy, Semerimus heralded this son as the promised Saviour. People of that early era were fully aware of God's promise to send a Messiah and Saviour.

She then started a religion that obligated everyone to worship her, as the high priestess, and her son as divine. This mother-baby cult was later popularized in a multitude of religions that spread around the world.

Soon it reached to Phoenicia under the name of Ashteroth and Tammuz. Then it extended to Pergamos. You remember John's remark to the church at Pergamos, "I know thy works, and where thou dwellest, even where Satan's seat is" (Rev. 2:13).

Later it reached to Egypt and was known as Isis and Horus; to Greece where it was Aphrodite and Eros; and finally to Rome where the divine couple was known as Venus and Cupid.

Of this Dr. J. Dwight Pentecost writes:

Several years ago I visited an archeological museum in Mexico City. A recent find had just been put on display which Mexican archaeologists had authenticated as belonging to the period about 200 years before Christ. The object was the center of religious worship among some of the early Indians in Mexico. To my amazement it was an image of a mother with a child in her arms. This Babylonian religion spread abroad to become the religion of the world.[2]

Interestingly the teaching of Semerimus was that she, who later adopted the name "Queen of Heaven" was the way to reach God himself. It was taught that as "Queen of Heaven" she would, through administering such sacraments as sprinkling holy water, etc., grant salvation.

Additionally, Tammuz, the son, was believed to have been killed by a bear while hunting one day. However, it was said, he was resurrected some forty days later. To commemorate this resurrection, the temple virgins were caused to fast for forty days at a certain time every year. After the fast, a great feast, then called Ishtar, was instituted. Colored eggs were exchanged as a symbol of fertility and resurrection. A great number of traditions were started at this time.

God, however, intervened in the matter and around 2000 B.C. called Abraham out of this area. Sometime later, around the ninth century B.C., Israel returned to this satanic form of worship. This time it was under the title of Baal.

Jeremiah preached against this paganism, as did Ezekiel, warning of God's displeasure. "The children gathered wood, and the fathers kindled the fire, and the women kneaded their dough, to make cakes to the queen of heaven, and to pour out drink offerings unto her . . ." (Jer. 7:18; 44:25).

Ezekiel, in Chapter 8:14, reports, "Then he brought me to the door of the gate of the Lord's house, which was toward the north; and, behold, there sat a woman weeping for Tammuz."

Two thousand years later, by the time Christ had arrived, this false religion held such power in Rome that the Caesars were not only crowned Emperors of Rome, but were also known as Pontifex Maximus or "High Priest." And high priest of what? High priest of that satanic church that originated in Babylon.

Here it gets even more appalling as Satan moves his false religion into the very church of God.

In A.D. 306, the Roman Emperor Constantine was on the verge of being overthrown by a powerful enemy. Knowing he needed a miracle to mobilize, enthuse, and empower his army, Constantine reported he had seen a heavenly vision the afternoon before a great battle. It was, he said, a vision of a giant blue flag with a red cross emblazoned on it. Simultaneously, he had heard a voice say, "In this sign, conquer."

His army was quickly forced to march into a nearby river, where he declared them all to be "baptized Christians." He then ordered the sign of the cross to be painted on all weapons to act as an inspiration. At that point, Christianity became the state religion of Rome.

With this transition, the Roman priest of Tammuz made a dazzling maneuver. Instead of causing a religious revolution against Constantine, they found it very easy to create a hybrid religion by bringing in and promoting such traditions as the Madonna-child worship concept, trans-substantiation, and the use of holy water sacraments.

Satan had his angle. After three centuries of attempting to destroy the bride of Christ, he quit fighting it from outside and decided to join it, creating havoc within.

Today, this wicked false religious system is much alive. During the Tribulation, the church that ultimately evolves from it will have no hindrance, no resistance, and no rival. She will have at long last come into her own and will wreak her full fury on humanity. And alas, she will be aided and abetted by a man infused with the rage of hell itself.

Queen Nefertiti's Baby

Other than Jesus Christ, no man has been born with more personal power and ability than this supernatural, demonically ener-gized man who will rise to take control of the world. Many books, movies, and much copy has been devoted to describing this "man of sin."

I am convinced he is alive today, and awaiting his moment to step center-stage and fulfill his destiny.

The most famous prophecy outside Scripture concerning the Antichrist is found in a book by the famous clairvoyant and astrologer, Jeane Dixon. She describes a revelation in *My Life and Prophecies,* and states that this Antichrist was born February 5, 1962. Do bear in mind, this author considers Jeane Dixon a false prophet, and yet Satan, I'm convinced, does have the ability to empower his ministers, to a limited degree, with enough prescience to lend them some credibility that they may more easily deceive.

She writes:

> I gazed out my window and, although the sun was still hiding, what I saw was almost beyond description.
>
> The bare-limbed trees of the city had given way to an endless desert scene, broiled by a relentless sun. Glowing like an enormous ball of fire, the sun had cracked the horizon, emitting brilliant rays of scintillating light which seemed to attract the earth like a magic wand.
>
> The sun's rays parted, facilitating the appearance of an Egyptian Pharaoh and his queen. I immediately recognized her as Queen Nefertiti; the man with her I took to be her husband, reported by history to be Ikhnaton, the so-called "heretic" pharaoh. Holding hands as lovers do, they emerged from the brilliant rays, majestic in their bearing; Ikhnaton's royal headdress was a sign of his power under the sun . . . not of power under the Son.
>
> My eyes were drawn to Nefertiti and the child she tenderly cradled in her other arm. It was a newborn babe, wrapped in soiled, ragged swaddling clothes. He was in stark contrast to the magnificently arrayed royal couple.
>
> Not a sound broke the unearthly silence as they issued forth with the child. I then became aware of a multitude of people that appeared between the child and me. It seemed as though the entire world was watching the royal couple present the baby. Watching the baby over their heads, I witnessed Nefertiti hand the child to the people. Instantly rays of sunlight burst forth from the little boy, carefully blending themselves with the brilliance of the sun, blotting out everything but him.
>
> Ikhnaton disappeared from the scene. Nefertiti remained. I observed her walking away from the child and the people, into the past, into the secret past of the ancients. Thirsty and tired, she rested beside a water jug, and just as she cupped her hands to drink, a sudden thrust of a dagger in her back ended her life. Her death scream, piercing and mournful, faded out with her.
>
> My eyes once again focused on the baby. By now he had grown to manhood, and a small cross which had formed above his head enlarged and expanded until it

covered the earth in all directions. Simultaneously, suffering people of all races knelt in worshipful adoration, lifting their arms and offering their hearts to the man. For a fleeting moment I felt as though I were one of them, but the channel that emanated from him was not that of the Holy Trinity. I knew within my heart that this revelation was to signify the beginning of wisdom, but whose wisdom and for whom? An overpowering feeling of love surrounded me, but the look I had seen in the man when he was still a babe — a look of serene wisdom and knowledge — made me sense that here was something God allowed me to see without my becoming a part of it.

I also sensed that I was once again safe within the protective arms of my Creator.

I glanced at my bedside clock. It was still early — 7:17 a.m.

What does this revelation signify? I am convinced that this revelation indicates a child, born somewhere in the Middle East shortly after 7:00 a.m. on February 5, 1962 — possibly a direct descendant of the royal line of Pharaoh Ikhnaton and Queen Nefertiti — will revolutionize the world. There is no doubt that he will fuse multitudes into one all-embracing doctrine. He will form a new "Christianity," based on his "almighty power," but leading man in a direction far removed from the teachings and life of Christ, the Son.[3]

Whether Jeane Dixon is correct or not, I assure you the Scriptures detailing this incredibly wicked and powerful man are correct.

A Man for Desperate Times

According to 2 Thessalonians 2:3, his rise to power will be a diabolical conspiracy engineered by Satan himself.

Let no man deceive you by any means; for that day shall not come, except there come the falling away first, and that man of sin be revealed, the son of perdition . . . . Even him whose coming is after the working of Satan with all power and signs and lying wonders, and with all deceivableness of unrighteousness in them that perish, because they received not the love of the truth, that they might be saved, and for this cause God shall send them strong delusion, that they should believe the lie, that they all might be judged who believed not the truth, but had pleasure in unrighteousness (2 Thess 2:3, 9-12).

Revelation 13:2 also emphasizes the origin of this Antichrist's ability to move so quickly into a place of world leadership. "And the beast which I saw was like a leopard, and his feet were like the feet of a bear, and his mouth like the mouth of a lion; and the dragon gave him his power, and his throne, and great authority."

Lest one think Satan is so all powerful that he may "have his way" as it were, please bear in mind that Satan does nothing without God's permission. God is in control. Second Thessalonians 2:6-7 assures us that God has absolute power and is allowing events to unfold on His divine time table.

God revealed to the prophet Daniel in chapters 7-9, as well as to the apostle John in Revelation 12, 13, and 17, the scenario that unfolds, leading to the Antichrist's reign of terror. Through the formation of a 10-nation organization led by 10 dictators in a confederation of power, he steps onto the scene, after which he will defeat three of these dictators (Dan. 7:8, 24).

This revived Roman Empire will be the last of the seven Gentile world powers to harass the nation of Israel.

The political maneuvering, accompanied by the cooperation of a false religious system and the supernatural personality, charm, and intellect, will thrust this fascinating man into a position of absolute power. It is interesting to note that out of 91 references in the New Testament using the words "deceive and go astray" that 22 of them are in passages dealing with the Antichrist.

One said, "nature abhors a vacuum." I add, so too does society when it comes to leaders.

Man is desperate, even under the best of conditions, for someone to lead him, set the pace, and raise a standard. Conditions in the world will soon be so chaotic, so confused, and so disrupted that man's desperation and fear will drive him to accept any ray of hope that promises to bring resolution and stability back to his life.

At that time, all national infra-structures for commerce, economy, communications, law and order, as well as all travel will be disrupted. With no means of protection for body and soul, normally afforded by civilized societies, with little availability of food, water and shelter, man will be, in most cases, reduced to an animalistic existence of the survival of the fittest. He will be begging for someone, anyone, to put his life back together.

The picture in Scripture of the Tribulation is not a pretty one. Imagine nuclear holocaust with its accompanying destruction of civilizations, its radioactive fallout, its invisible death, leukemia, cancer, and diseases. Picture the starving masses that produce roving hordes bent on rape and pillage. Envision the loss of contact with all outside avenues of communication, no police, no corner grocery, no sewage, no clean water, no medical facility, no meat, no vegetables, and nothing but death, dying, destruction, and contamination. Worst of all, consider a world with no kind and caring people to help, to love, to lift, to bind a wound to be found anywhere . . . no light . . . no hope.

Anyone left alive in such a nightmare-world would welcome a promise by anyone to put food, shelter, security, and sanity back into his or her life.

And so it will be.

The Nations in Place

The unprecedented rise to power of this new world leader is marked by 1) the desperation of a world tottering out of control and pleading for answers, and 2) by a remarkable and never before witnessed diplomatic talent to bring resolve and solution to otherwise unimaginable and incurable problems.

It seems certain, because of the lack of references to the United States of America in prophecy, that, nationally, our nation will not play a major role in the last seven years of world history. If I may offer an observation as to why I believe America is so conspicuously absent in these prophecies: it could be for one of two reasons.

First, because America will be among the most devastated of the nations in a cataclysmic economic collapse — which I firmly believe is coming. She will likely become, at best, a third-world power, impotent in her ability to have significant effect on international matters. Her preoccupation, if she is at all viable, will most likely be with that of survival.

Secondly, I suspect that the invasion by Russia and her allies into Israel, spoken of in Ezekiel 38-39, will be accompanied by a nuclear strike upon the United States. It will be difficult for such an alliance to successfully invade Israel unless she first deals with Israel's allies. In spite of all the rhetoric about Russia's demise as a world power, she presently has over 30,000 nuclear warheads still aimed at the United States. Add to that the instability of Russia's government at the

294 • *The Triumphant Return of Christ*

moment, along with that nation's wrecked economy, and one can easily surmise how volatile things are in Russia.

It is probable that the USA will be a "non-factor" because of one or both of the above mentioned reasons. Hence the focus of this New World Order and its leadership will be on Europe and, more specifically, the ten nation confederacy spoken of by Daniel and John in Revelation 13. He referred to them in verse 12 as "Ten horns which . . . are . . . ten kings . . ." and verse 13 continues saying, "These have one mind and shall give their power and strength unto the beast."

Apparently, after bringing law and order back to nations in chaotic disarray and insuring their social, economic, and political well-being, this "Antichrist" will turn his attention to the consolidation of world power.

Ezekiel 38-39 indicate that after the failed Russian invasion of Israel, he will move rapidly to overcome opposition posed by three of the ten kings of his European Confederation and then quickly gain control over much of the Middle East. At long last the world has a man who seems to be able to bring real, lasting peace to the world's powder keg known as the Middle East.

He will surely move swiftly, convincing Israel that he is able to secure her borders and guarantee her safety if she will enter into a covenant or treaty with him. This treaty will allow the State of Israel to do two things every Jew has always dreamed of doing. Every Israeli longs to live at peace in secured borders within their own beloved Israel and to rebuild their sacred temple on the Temple Mount, which has been "off limits" to them for hundreds of years.

Again, this man of miracles will perform the unimaginable. He will bring the world back from the brink of annihilation and will no doubt grant the nations their greatest hopes and aspirations.

But alas, as they say, "If it sounds too good to be true, it probably is."

The miracle worker, the world's greatest politician, economist, diplomat and thinker will begin to show his true colors.

With his universal power almost consolidated, he begins to attack and destroy every semblance of authority that gave him assistance in promotion to his position as King of the world. He turns against the false religious system that facilitated his rise to power. Revelation 17:16 describes her total destruction by the Antichrist and his powerful political machine of the ten kings.

As he sets himself up as God and demands the worship of the

world, he mocks the living God and challenges the most high. "... and he shall speak great words against the most high and shall wear out the saints of the most high ..." (Dan. 7:25). Yes, according to Scripture, some will resist his tyranny, even turning to the Lord Jesus Christ, but it will be at the cost of their lives. Most of those who receive Christ during this seven-year period will be martyred.

The horrors of the beast's abominable tyranny can only be imagined through the brief prophetic glances into the future allowed by God's Word.

I Am God! Worship Me!

In 1964, William Hull wrote a novel, *Israel, Key to Prophecy,* in which he painted details as they might be when this satanically-energized, worship-hungry madman fully grips the reins of the earth. He writes insightfully about the work and personality of the Antichrist. I think you will agree that his insights, written over 30 years ago, were quite extraordinary:

> The United Nations Organization had ceased to exist as such. There is now one world leader and a super world cabinet. This council had been formed to take over all activities of the former U.N.O. with this difference: it had force to back up its decisions. All authority was now in the hands of the president and he delegated this as he wished to his council. The council consisted of seven ecclesiastical leaders and ten secular leaders. The seven were former cardinals of Rome. The office of Pope no longer existed, all the former power and authority of this position now rested in the president. He was infallible both in religious and secular affairs. The seven cardinals had complete control over all religious matters in every country and all religions had been unified. The only exceptions to this were the Jewish and Moslem religions. Members of these two religions were permitted to observe their form of worship, with certain reservations, but could not receive converts.
>
> The ten secular leaders were individually dictators in their respective countries, subject always to instructions from the president. They had control over all affairs of state in all countries. The combined council, with the president at its head, ruled the world. The president had for many

years been a popular TV figure. His appearances had been watched with interest and admiration, not only by Roman Catholics but also by Protestants. His smooth, glib speech, his bright piercing eyes, had all combined to win him a great following of admirers.

Religious worship was on an entirely new basis. Except for Jews and Moslems there was only the one religion in the world. Everyone was compelled to attend at least one service each week. The Bible was not used, nor were people permitted to have copies of this book in their homes. In place of it a new "Bible," based on philosophy, and setting forth the perfect way of life for each day, had been published. It contained in addition a catechism to be used for moral and religious instruction, a statement of doctrine and faith, information on a practical application of the suggested principles for everyday living and a long dissertation by the president setting forth the superiority and advantages of the new religion, as contrasted with the former religions of superstition and tradition.

Many were surprised when it was announced that Judaism would be permitted to continue and that Jews could worship their God in their own way. The reason for this favor was not evident. The ruling had come directly from the president himself, overriding the advice of his religious council. For some reason the world ruler seemed to desire to cultivate Jewish goodwill and friendship.

Shortly after assuming office the president called the leaders of Israel — the Chief Rabbis of Jerusalem, the Prime Minister, the Minister of Foreign Affairs and the Minister of Finance — to a conference in Washington. The matters discussed were not made public but it was learned that a secret agreement had been entered into between the World Authority and the Government and Rabbinate of Israel. Rumor was that Israel had signed a seven year contract. This was to guarantee Israel sufficient funds to restore her land to its original condition of productivity, both agriculturally and commercially. Much more than this, however, was the rumor (as yet only spoken in a whisper among the Jews), that the Temple Area was to be given to Israel and funds furnished to build a magnificent temple outshining any previous temple or any building in the world. What Israel was to give in return for all this was not yet clear. What had Israel to offer for such munificence?

As the months went by Jerusalem became aware of activity on the former Temple Area. Solomon's Temple had stood there thousands of years ago, but since the destruction of Herod's Temple in A.D. 70 by the Romans under Titus, no Jewish building had occupied this site. Since the occupation of Jerusalem by the Moslems in A.D. 637 the former Temple Area had been considered a "Holy Place." Next to Mecca and Medina, Jerusalem was the third most holy site in the world to Mohammedans. However, the activity observed was not that of Moslems. Only Jews were seen now on this site, where formerly they had been forbidden and where it had meant instant death for any Jews to enter.

Then the story broke. It was a seven-day wonder and papers all over the world revealed details of the secret agreement made between the president and the Jews. The Temple Area was to be made available for the worship of Jehovah. Moslem leaders had been secretly informed by personal representatives of the world ruler. There had been no public outcry, for the Moslems had been told that for them it was a case of give up the Haram Esh-Sherif or Islam would cease as a permitted religion. There was no doubt that the leader was able to enforce such an ultimatum and to eliminate this religion from the face of the earth. It was clear that the president was favoring the Jews and seemingly could not do enough for them. Yet why this should be was still a mystery to the world, and to the Jews. What had the Jews to offer to pay for all these favors and help?

Some years were to pass before the Temple would be completely finished and shine in all its glory. This, however, would not hinder the restoration of worship at an early date. Work was ordered so that the central part of the Temple could be rushed to a degree of completion which would enable services to be held and the priests to officiate. The great altar and the laver also were to be erected at once. The choosing of the High Priest was to be made an event of outstanding importance in the history of Israel.

With the appointment of the high priest the whole setup of government was changed and put on a theocratic basis. The High Priest was supreme and in a short time had organized both the secular ruling authority and the priesthood.

The last Jewish sacrifice had been made three weeks before the Temple had been destroyed in A.D. 70. Jerusalem had been besieged at the time by the Romans and finally all the sacrificial animals had been slain and no further living animals were available. The priests had carried on the Temple worship without sacrifices for another three weeks. Then, on the ninth of Av, the inner walls of the city fell; the Temple was desecrated and destroyed and there had been neither temple nor sacrifice since that day nearly two thousand years ago.

It was decided that the daily sacrifices must be renewed at the earliest possible moment.

As the day for the renewal of Temple service and sacrifices drew near, people poured into Jerusalem from all parts of the world. The president was unable to attend but a vast television screen had been prepared on the front of the Temple building, and with the development of world television relay in recent years, his image, as he spoke in Washington, would appear on the screen. This new development was called Rayscreen. The relay was produced by reflecting rays back and forth from earth stations to satellites suspended five hundred miles above the earth. In this way the above could be encircled in any direction. Hundreds of thousands of people would face the screen in Jerusalem and see the World Leader and hear him speak.

The day dawned bright and clear. Hours before, people had begun to assemble in the Temple courtyard. At dawn the first sacrificial lamb was led out to the altar. The knife of the priest flashed, smoke began to rise from under the altar and the sacrifice was consumed in the flames. Suddenly the sky darkened, a most unusual phenomenon at that time of year. Lightning flashed from one end of the heavens to the other, accompanied by peal after peal of deafening thunder. Then came a downpour of rain which threatened to wash away sacrifice, altar, priests and the great concourse of people. The storm was over in ten minutes but the sky remained dark and the sun did not appear again that day. People asked one another, "What did this portend? Was God displeased?"

At seven in the morning (midnight in Washington) the face of the president appeared on the great screen. A smile lighted up his face, but his words were like steel bullets pouring forth from the many loud-speakers.

"High Priest, leaders and citizens of Israel, visitors in Jerusalem," he orated. "On this day which is outstanding in the history of Israel, I offer my congratulations to a nation revived, restored and rebuilt in its land after an absence of nineteen hundred years. It has been my pleasure to help restore both your land and your Temple.

"On this occasion of the restoration of your Temple worship it is well to remember that this site was chosen by your God as His dwelling place on earth. Here you worshiped and sacrificed to your God. Here your God put His name and accepted your worship. Here I have permitted and enabled you to rebuild your Temple and to worship. I have kept my word. I have fulfilled my covenant. I will continue to be your protector and herewith command you to worship in this Temple. I have spoken."

The cheers which followed the brief and abrupt speech of the president were given dutifully, in view of the presence of many high representatives of the president and hundreds of secret police ever ready to report any lack of enthusiasm for the World Leader. However, most of those present sincerely rejoiced, believing that the God of Israel would be pleased with the renewal of Israel's sacrifices on the Temple altar, and would henceforth smile on their nation.

In spite of the beauty and richness of the great buildings there was one thing lacking. Israel sensed this lack and wondered — there was no glory cloud, no feeling of God in their midst. Where was God? Was their return to Temple worship and sacrifices not pleasing to Him? "Oh God of Abraham, Isaac and Jacob, bless Your people and Your Temple. We have wandered nineteen hundred years.

We are weary and tired of our wandering and would solace our souls once more in Your presence. Return, Oh God, and bless Your people Israel! Speak again, and Your servants will hear and answer."

Three and one-half years had passed since the renewal of Temple worship. Israel, by now, was accustomed to the form of worship. The smoke and fire of the altar, the bleating and bellowing of the sacrifice animals and the daily ministration of the priests had become almost commonplace to the Jews. For the last few months, however, there had been some strange foreign activity in the Temple courtyard which no one seemed to be able to explain.

It had started shortly after the receipt of a note which came from the president. The note had informed the High Priest that certain construction work would be undertaken in a small area of the Temple courtyard. The work was to be done by workmen sent from America, who would require no assistance from the Jews but must be permitted to work unhindered. Work would be suspended on Saturdays and Sundays.

The workmen arrived and began to construct a tall wooden structure, one hundred feet square and a hundred fifty feet high. All material had been brought on their ship and moved to the site in closed trucks of great size. All the workers were close-mouthed and kept entirely to themselves. They never entered into conversation with any of the Jews, and from the beginning the construction work had been guarded night and day by a large force of World Police, changed and replaced every three days. None were permitted to approach the hastily built building. Some, however, had said that they had heard the sound of hammers on stone coming from within the building.

Eventually it became evident that a new stage had been reached in the work. The rough covering forming the building was now being dismantled board by board. Within could be seen a small building or covered object. When all the wooden framework was removed there remained what appeared as a steel frame of four uprights encircled by iron loops. The actual frame could only be conjectured at, for it was covered and almost concealed by a rich tapestry covering. Not the slightest hint was offered as to what was inside this queer tent-like structure.

Jerusalem, Tel Aviv and other cities and villages were enjoying the end of their Sabbath. As usual the main streets of the cities were thronged with strolling couples and groups of Jews dressed in their Sabbath clothes and filling both sidewalks and roadways and making it almost impossible for cars to push their way through. They were gay, happy throngs, all well-clothed and prosperous looking.

Not only prosperity but peace had finally come and it seemed as though the "controversy of Zion" was ended. Sabbath was surely a time when all Israel could show its enjoyment of its new freedom and liberty. The future outlook was bright, even beyond the dreams of the early Zionist "dreamers." This night was much as other end-of-Sabbath nights, until a trumpet suddenly sounded through the streets. The blast had come from the loudspeakers put up at the strategic points in all cities, villages and kibbutzim throughout the country. It indicated a special message to be issued from World Headquarters in Washington. First the message would be given in English, immediately followed by a Hebrew translation.

The laughing, moving throngs became tense, rigid, as words began to pour forth. All gathered as close as possible to the many speakers and hung on every word.

The message stated that next Sabbath, at twelve noon, an event of outstanding importance would take place in the Temple Area in Jerusalem. The president himself was flying to Israel to take part and to make a personal announcement at that time. All Jews that could be accommodated in Jerusalem were to proceed there immediately for this event. The message was repeated every hour through the night and next day, so that none could be ignorant of its content. It brought amazement and wonderment in Israel and was a headline story in the world press. What could it be? What could be so important to bring the great World Leader to Jerusalem? Not only Jerusalem, but throughout the world people discussed the announcement and what it presaged.

Exactly on the dot of twelve a tremendous blast from one hundred trumpets heralded the arrival of the president. As he slowly proceeded along the carpeted way every eye was upon him. At least two million people watched him reach the steps and ascend to the platform. On the platform a large golden throne had been placed and the president, the ruler of the world, seated himself. Following the president, at a distance of fifty paces, the seven cardinals had come in, two by two, with the seventh bringing up the rear. They too presented a dazzling sight, with pure white robes almost hidden under crimson dyed capes of beautiful marten fur. On their heads were golden framed headpieces covered with Russian sable dyed crimson to match their capes. They too ascended the platform and took their seats in a semicircle facing, and at the foot of, the throne.

Then came a brilliant array of ecclesiastics and representatives of all nations. The head of this column stopped at the foot of the steps to the platform and remained standing facing the president, while the long column of dignitaries closed ranks until they too presented a great mass of faces as they stood on the carpeted pathway between the two ranks of Bodyguard troops.

Thus was arrayed the greatest pageant the world had ever witnessed. There was an element of mystery to it all, for only a few knew what was to follow. The plans and preparations had been executed with such secrecy that not a whisper had reached the ears of any except those involved in the work. Now the stage was prepared. The setting was magnificent, with the great Temple building, its golden roof shining in the bright sun, as a background, and the vast concourse of people crowding almost every inch of space in the courtyard, on the walls and buildings and on the Mount of Olives. The bright colored robes of the chief participants and leaders were as brilliant jewels in a massive setting. Dominating all was the beautifully tapestried tower, before which the president sat on this throne. The covering of the tower was woven in brilliant colors forming most extraordinary patterns. Four scenes were depicted on this tapestry. One was of fiery red serpents crawling out of a pit. The second was a beast of most unusual ferociousness, its right paw lying heavily on a prostrate human form. The third depicted a huge golden image of a man, the face vaguely familiar to those able to see it from their positions, and the fourth showed the figure six, appearing three times, each figure entwined with the other, giving the appearance of a chain hanging down the tapestry. The figures were in gold on purple.

Rising slowly, as every eye watched and every tongue was stilled, the president stood to his feet. His raised hand may have been a gesture of salutation or a demand for silence. If the latter, it was unnecessary, for the air seemed hushed and still awaiting the revelation to come.

"My people," the leader began, "this day is unique in the history of man. You are gathered before me in this city of Jerusalem or you view me on your Rayscreens. You are gathered at my command. I speak to all people but my remarks apply specifically to those of the Jewish religion.

"It was on this site, at the command of your God, that your father King David prepared for the erection of your first Temple. This Temple was erected by King Solomon and in it you worshiped your God, Jehovah. You believed that your God dwelt in this Temple and your Bible claims that he supernaturally revealed His presence at the time of its dedication.

"And now, after nineteen hundred years, I have graciously permitted you to once more worship your God in this newly erected Temple which I enabled you to build. I have restrained all opposition, and have restored to you opportunity for worship as it existed when your fathers dwelt in this land and possessed all authority.

"For three and a half years you have worshiped your God according to your ancient rites and laws. Now the time has come for you to be enlightened and you will know why I have sponsored the reorganization of your Temple worship and sacrifices. Give honor to whom honor is due. In years gone by your God was not able to maintain His residence in the Temple nor to protect it from destruction by His enemies. Your God could not protect you as you were forced to flee from your land and to serve nineteen hundred years in bondage. Your God could not enable you to build your Temple again, BUT I DID!

"Let all the world behold!"

At this cry the great tapestries covering the high tower slowly parted at the front and gathered together at the back of the metal frame. Then was disclosed to all eyes a huge stone image one hundred feet high. It was an image of the president, a perfect likeness, standing with arms folded and a sardonic smile on the face. Suddenly, while the people gazed with mingled feelings of awe, fear and admiration, the image began to speak.

"Men and women of the earth: For millenniums of time, since you first lived on this earth, you have worshiped gods. In your ignorance you have worshiped gods many, or god singular, yet you have not known me.

"Today, I have chosen to reveal myself. This day is the most important in all the history of man. This day I am opening your eyes and permitting you to see and to acclaim the true God. I AM GOD! WORSHIP ME I AM THE CREATOR I MADE HEAVEN, I MADE EARTH. THERE IS NO GOD BESIDE ME. SEE MY POWER!"

Suddenly the sky was rent, a great pillar of fire flashed down and rested upon the dome of the Temple. The earth trembled and rocked.

Then the image continued to speak:

"Henceforth you will worship me as God. You will bow down to me. You will be marked with my mark and everyone who fails to bow to me and to receive my mark will be ostracized from society. You will not be able to purchase the necessities of life, you will not be able to sell your time or produce. You will die the death which I have ordained.

"Israel — I am your true God. You have ignorantly worshiped your false God — Jehovah — but now I have opened your eyes. For this purpose I enabled you to erect your Temple and to restore worship as in the days of your fathers. NOW I COMMAND YOU TO WORSHIP ME — I AM GOD, WORSHIP ME!"

His closing words ended on such a high pitch as to be almost a screech.[4]

And so we have it as God has revealed the matter.

God indeed is gracious. Gracious enough to allow us to look ever so briefly into the future. Though it is an appalling, frightening, and chilling look into things to come, for the believer it is not a time of fear nor alarm. We have a "blessed hope," an assurance of deliverance. These matters should motivate, stimulate, and provoke us to holiness, to action, and to prayer.

As evil reigns and the satanic plot that began to unfold in Genesis 3 in the Garden of Eden continues to move toward its full manifestation of the embodiment of wickedness, we know there is more to the story. It's His story, and He will not allow it to end until the earth is restored to its former glory and the true King of kings sits on His throne, high and lifted up.

Even so, come Lord Jesus.

13

Israel and the Coming Millennium:

A Time to Rejoice

John Wesley White

When the dust of war had settled, Desert Storm had resolved nothing in the eyes of the Israelis or the Islamics. Postwar peace talks accomplished little.

Billy Graham, who supported President Bush in his efforts to bring justice to the Middle East, said, "It seems that everything we do in the Middle East doesn't work out." In the final analysis, the Middle East situation will not be resolved until Armageddon.

Jesus said that when Israel returns to her ancient homeland and is reestablished as a nation, this will be the beginning of the final conflict. "Know that it is near, even at the doors" (Matt. 24:33). He spoke through the parable of the fig tree: "When his branch is yet tender, and putteth forth leaves, ye know that summer is nigh" (Matt. 24:32).

Jesus' announcement in verse 34, however, is the one that

carries with it such crucial import for our times: "This generation shall not pass, till all these things be fulfilled."

The word "generation" is interpreted by some people to mean "nation." Jesus was saying that restored Israel — as a nation — shall not pass away until these prophecies have been accomplished. Link this to the Psalmist's statement, "When the Lord shall build up Zion, he shall appear in his glory," and "This shall be written for the last generation" (Ps. 102:16,18, as translated from the original languages).

Israel alone — its history, its modern renewal as a nation, and many other facets — brims over with fulfillment of end-time prophecies. Many such events have transpired in our lifetimes. Many are going on now. Taken together, they give us a better view of God's history clock, which is ticking ever closer to midnight.

A Restored Israel

New Testament commentators are generally in agreement that Jesus' use of the fig tree refers to Israel as a people, a nation under God (Luke 13:1-10).

Early in the Crucifixion week, Jesus and His disciples noted a solitary fig tree that was flush with leaves but barren of figs. Jesus, having the day before wept over Jerusalem for its rejection of His messiahship and alerting the people that judgment was impending because of their spiritual barrenness, cursed the tree (Matt. 21:19), and it withered.

Jesus later used the tree in a parable:

> Behold the fig tree, and all the trees; when they now shoot forth, ye see and know of your own selves that summer is now nigh at hand. So likewise ye, when ye see these things come to pass, know ye that the kingdom of God is nigh at hand (Luke 21:29-31).

Jesus was saying that the fig tree shooting forth new leaves is a picture of a restored Israel in the era when "the times of the Gentiles be fulfilled" (Luke 21:24).

The reference to "all the trees" could well refer to the proliferation of new nations that sprang into existence in the wake of World War II, joining in the formation of the United Nations. These in turn are being joined by the many new nations of the 1990s, such as Estonia, Latvia, and Lithuania. But amidst "all the trees" there was to be a special tree, Israel. So Jesus assured His disciples that before He came back to the earth amid the carnage of Armageddon, Israel would have returned to her homeland and become a nation again.

God's fulfillment of His promise to restore the Jews to their ancient homeland has its roots in His promise to Abraham four thousand years ago:

> Now the Lord had said unto Abram, Get thee out of
> thy country, and from thy kindred, and from thy father's
> house, unto a land that I will shew thee: and I will make of
> thee a great nation, and I will bless thee . . . and I will bless
> them that bless thee (Gen. 12:1-3).

It is significant to notice that God specified the boundaries of the Promised Land (Gen. 15:18), and it included Lebanon. It's also important to note that God insisted the land would belong to Abraham's seed as "an everlasting possession" (Gen. 17:8).

Even when a minority of the Jews, comprised of their political and religious leaders, conspired with the Romans to crucify Jesus, even when the church was opened to the Gentiles — this did not entail God's abandonment of the Jewish people as His chosen nation.

Paul dealt with this theme in Romans 9-11. He asked, "Hath God cast away his people [Israel]? God forbid. . . . God hath not cast away his people which he foreknew" (Matt. 12:37; Rom. 11:1-2. See also: Mark 12:37; Matt. 26:5; Mark 11:18; and Acts 4:25-28).

Yet, they would be set aside while Christ called out a people for His name — the Church. Paul said "that blindness in part is happened to Israel, until the fullness of the Gentiles be come in." It should be noted that while partial blindness is upon Israel, the Gentiles are in total darkness until they accept Christ (2 Cor. 4:4).

And so, all Israel shall be saved: as it is written, "There shall come out of Zion the Deliverer, and shall turn away ungodliness from Jacob: for this is my covenant unto them" (Rom. 11:26-27). This refers to the coming again of Christ as Israel's Messiah at the time of Armageddon. "A nation," prophesied Isaiah shall "be born at once . . . as soon as Zion [travaileth]" (Isa. 66:8). As Israel corporately receives her Messiah, all her surviving people will experience spiritual rebirth.

Roses in the Desert

So, where is Israel's return to its ancient land prophesied in the

Bible? The Scriptures are so many that they could fill a small book.

Isaiah 11:11-12 states, "It shall come to pass in that day, that the Lord shall set his hand again the second time to recover the remnant of his people." (The first time, of course, was when they were brought home from Babylonian captivity during the sixth century B.C.)

And from where would the Lord bring Israel? From many lands, including "the islands of the sea" (Isa. 11:11) and "the four corners of the earth" (Isa. 11:12). Not until modern times could the Jewish people have been found in "the four corners of the earth," meaning all over the globe.

U.S. General S.L.A. Marshall was an astute observer of modern Israel from early in this century until the nation's repossession of Jerusalem in the 1967 war. He was convinced there was only one word to describe their restoration to their ancient homeland and their reoccupation of Jerusalem, against all human odds: miracle.

The late Charles Malik, a Harvard University scholar and a Lebanese statesman who served as the first president of the United Nations, said that to ignore the prophetic word concerning the restoration of Israel to its homeland and instead to ascribe it to a mere humanistic "politico-economic struggle, is to have no sense whatsoever of the holy and ultimate in history."

This miraculous side to the restoration of Israel — indeed, to the very survival of the Jews as a distinct religious/ethnic people over the centuries — is even more remarkable when you consider the persecution they have endured.

When Jesus was on earth, Israel had been occupied for six centuries (from 586 B.C.). Our Lord predicted that within a generation of His crucifixion the land would be overrun by Gentiles in an en masse massacre, and not one stone of the then-resplendent temple would remain upon another.

In A.D. 68, 20,000 Jews were killed by the Romans in Caesarea; and in A.D. 70, Jerusalem was conquered and the temple completely demolished. More than 100,000 bodies of Jews were thrown over the wall of the city, having for the most part been crucified. Another 100,000 Jews were sold at auction to slave traders from near and far. An estimated one million Jews were murdered during this period.

Under Emperor Hadrian (A.D. 117-138), the Romans destroyed another 985 towns and killed 580,000 men (in what by then had been renamed Palestine). Jews were banished from Jerusalem, a policy that succeeding Roman emperors pursued relentlessly.

During the second to the sixth centuries, Palestine was occupied, desolated, and decimated by the Romans. Then, for 1,000 years, the land was overrun by Islam. From the sixteenth century to 1917, it was in the hands of the Turks, at which time it became a British Mandate.

True Evangelical Christians and Orthodox Jews throughout the centuries never doubted that Palestine would be reoccupied by a restored Israel. Both communities clung to such clear passages as Ezekiel 36:24, "For I will take you from among the heathen, and gather you out of all countries, and will bring you into your own land."

Amos prophesied:

> And I will bring again the captivity of my people of Israel, and they shall also make gardens, and eat the fruit of them. And I will plant them upon their land, and they shall no more be pulled up out of their land which I have given them, saith the Lord thy God (Amos 9:14-15).

The promise of fruitful gardens brings to mind Jerusalem Mayor Teddy Kollek's observations as to how modern Israel carved its fruit orchards and flower gardens out of a 2,000-year-old wilderness. And even though the Jewish population has escalated to five million, 80 percent of their fruit is in excess of their domestic needs. Israel is only one of six countries that grows more food than its people consume, and is, therefore, a net exporter of food.

In another amazing fulfillment to prophecy, Kollek noted, "Our second biggest export is roses." Isaiah prophesied, "The desert shall . . . blossom as the rose. It shall blossom abundantly" (Isa. 35:1-2).

Furthermore, the restoration would mean to "strengthen . . . weak hands, and confirm the feeble knees," and God's reward would be that "the parched ground shall become a pool, and the thirsty land springs of water" (Isa. 35:3,7). This vividly expresses the impressive irrigation systems of modern Israel — implemented by faith and hard work.

The Twentieth Century Miracle

How did all this come about in the twentieth century? A combination of Orthodox Jews and Evangelical Christians believed in claiming the promises of God that Israel would become a restored nation, with Jerusalem as its capital. When these two communities combined in faith, God performed miracles — some of them judgments — without which modern Israel simply would not exist.

British scholar Ian MacPherson points out that it was an evangelical Christian Jew, William Heckler, who wooed and won to Zionism professor Theodor Herzl, a Jew from Budapest, in the late nineteenth century. Herzl in turn won to Zionism scientist Chaim Weizmann, the first president of Israel, and Weizmann recruited David Ben-Gurion, the first prime minister of Israel.

Herzl, in 1897, masterminded the first Zionist Congress, held in Basel, Switzerland, where it was resolved "to create for the Jewish people a home in Palestine secured by public law." At this time, there were only 50,000 Jews in Palestine among a total population of 625,000.

By December 11, 1917, when British General Edmund Henry Allenby walked reverently into Jerusalem (he refused to ride, as Christ had done) and declared Palestine a British mandate, free from the Turks, there were 100,000 Jews, as compared to 700,000 non-Jews.

As a child, Allenby had adopted the daily prayer, "Lord, forget not Thine ancient people. Hasten the day when they shall be restored to Thy favor and to their land."

On the evening of December 10, Allenby felt a deep leading to pray and search the Scriptures — and he did so throughout the night. He was led to Isaiah 31:5, "As birds flying, so will the Lord of hosts defend Jerusalem; defending also he will deliver it; and passing over he will preserve it." So, on the morning of December 11, moving his army in from Egypt, he issued strict orders to his British air force to fly low and in waves over Jerusalem — without firing a single shot — to invoke the Turks to surrender. The Turks retreated without any resistance.

Complementing this amazing conquest of Jerusalem by Allenby was the Zionist factor which, in cooperation with Bible-believing statesmen, produced the crucial Balfour Declaration of 1917 in Great Britain. It declared, "His Majesty's Government views with favour the establishment in Palestine of a national home for the Jewish people, and will use their best endeavours to facilitate the achievement of this object."

The prime mover by then was an Orthodox Jew, Weizmann. He had succeeded Herzl as head of the Zionist movement and had worked for a dozen years to influence Lord Balfour, Lloyd George, Winston Churchill, and indirectly, even President Woodrow Wilson, all of whom were sympathetic, being familiar with the biblical promises relating to a restored Israel in their ancient homeland.

Joint efforts of Evangelical Christians and Orthodox Jews have surfaced in other areas. The Oscar-winning film *Chariots of Fire* was such a project. Other Christian-Jewish film productions would include Billy Graham films *The Hiding Place* and *His Land.*

Also, as reported in *Time,* there is the annual International Christian Celebration during the Feast of Tabernacles (Succoth), which brings Christians and Jews together to Jerusalem. *Time* reported that these conferences represent "tens of millions of Evangelicals around the world" who believe that the Messiah is coming to the world to install universal peace and prosperity, initially appearing at Jerusalem. These conferences draw up to 3,000 delegates from some 35 countries. They include parades, cook-outs, and musical services.

A Painful Turning Point

One glaring episode in the Jews' modern history is the Holocaust.

Did God have to permit this tragedy? Hebrew scholar Arthur W. Kac points out that previous to the Balfour Declaration in 1917, the vast majority of Jews lived in Europe and that this was still true up to World War II. Some had adopted a secular, humanist outlook and were deeply attached to the countries of their adoption, which had been their domicile for 1,000 years or more.

Kac points out that the Holocaust and the establishment of the state of Israel in 1948, with the huge exodus of the surviving Jews from European and Arab nations, marked the end of the great dispersion — the longest era in Jewish history. History knows of no other instance of a people which, while separated from the country of its national origin for some 19 centuries, not only retained its ethnic and theological identity, but also, at the end of those two millennia, returned from far and near to its ancient homeland.

Kac, along with many others, insists that Ezekiel 20:32-37 encompasses the dispersion and the Holocaust that precipitated their return. In this passage, God warns Israel that just when their dispersed people think they are a permanently settled and integrated part of the Gentile community, saying, "We will be as the heathen," things would really begin to happen.

> As I live, saith the Lord God, surely with a mighty
> hand, and with a stretched out arm, and with fury poured
> out . . . I will bring you out from the people, and will gather

you out of the countries wherein ye are scattered, with a mighty hand, and with a stretched out arm, and with fury poured out. And I will bring you into the wilderness of the people . . . . and I will cause you to pass under the rod, and I will bring you into the bond of the covenant (Ezek. 20:33-37).

That "bond of the covenant" took place when Jehovah covenanted with Abraham. It was affirmed in this century when Israel became a sovereign, unoccupied nation for the first time in 2,500 years.

Even then, but for the grace and sovereignty of God, the plan for the nation would have aborted.

Britain turned the Palestine matter over to the newly formed United Nations. Turmoil ensued. On November 29, 1947, the General Assembly of the United Nations passed a resolution stating, "The Mandate for Palestine shall terminate . . . not later than August 1, 1948. Independent Arab and Jewish States, and the specific international regime for the City of Jerusalem . . . shall come into existence."

This almost didn't happen. A fierce war between the Arabs and the Jews broke out, in which the Israelis were out-numbered fifty-three to one and were under-equipped. Nevertheless, they prevailed sufficiently to proclaim themselves a nation on May 14, 1948, with Chaim Weizmann as president and David Ben-Gurion as prime minister.

U.S. President Harry Truman recognized the new state, and the Soviet Union followed suit. Truman, in fact, was the strongest Gentile supporter for Israeli statehood, according to Henry Kissinger and other observers.

Truman's efforts for the Jews may have helped him more than he would ever realize. Later in 1948, Truman had to campaign for a second term as president. In the greatest upset in American history, he was voted in ahead of a heavily favored Thomas Dewey. This was inarguably a vindication of God's ancient promise to Abraham, "I will make of thee a great nation" and "I will bless them that bless thee, and curse him that curseth thee" (Gen. 12:2-3)

On a broader scale, one of North America's keys to peace and prosperity has been God's favor resulting from magnanimous treatment of the Jewish people. Thomas Jefferson insisted that the new republic receive with open arms Jewish people into all walks of life to which they might aspire.

Before his death, Woodrow Wilson was a strong supporter of

Israel's right to evolve into a sovereign nation. This has been true of all American presidents in the latter half of the twentieth century. It was President George Bush, who in September 1991 placed before the United Nations the imperative that the 1975 resolution, which had connected Zionism with racism, be rescinded.

The restoration of Israeli statehood has indeed been a remarkable fulfillment of prophecy. Israel's troubles, as well as its prophetic roles in end-time events, were only just beginning on May 14, 1948.

Crowded, Hated, Scrutinized

More than half of U.S. foreign aid goes to a tiny country on the other side of the globe. It is not some impoverished African land nor some Third World island nation that gets watered by this stream of $20 million a day. No, this aid goes to Israel. In Israel's military alone, *U.S. News & World Report* reckons that Americans have invested $20 billion.

Why does this tiny sliver of real estate carry such clout with the United States? Why do its events make headlines so frequently? Why does it aggravate so many nations? As we will see, these seeming inconsistencies also line up with God's revealed plan for Israel and the role it plays in the end times.

Israel is extremely hard-pressed for space now that a million Jews from the Soviet Union are pouring in. This makes Israel that much more determined to continue settling the West Bank, much to the irritation of not only its enemies but even its friends, such as the United States. That is why in September 1991, Yitzhak Shamir finally avowed before the world that no one, but no one, would stop Israel from settling the "homecoming" Soviet Jews in the West Bank, which he refers to unabashedly as the "Greater Israel."

Of course, Israeli leadership knows how much it can get away with and still keep from alienating those who matter. As writer William F. Buckley pointed out, "It is unquestionably the case that Israel's political influence is out of proportion to Israel's strategic importance to the U.S."

Pat Buchanan, the newspaper columnist who's regularly seen on CNN, greatly angered worldwide Jewry by saying there were only two groups that beat the war drums for Desert Storm: "the Israeli Defense Ministry and its amen corner in the United States."

It is said that Israel receives at least a hundred times as many headlines in North America as any other comparably populated country on earth. One possible reason is that the media of both the

United States and Canada in particular, and much of the Western world in general, are masterminded by Jewish interests. It is estimated that 70 percent of the upper echelons of the media are Jews. Even the Jews coming out of the Soviet Union to Israel are, on average, in terms of education, a part of the upper 7 percent of the population. Gorbachev noted this in October 1991 and lamented the brain drain.

Jewish penetration of media, commerce, and other strongholds worldwide is but one more infuriating aspect for those given to hating the Jews. According to the *New York Daily News*, "Anti-Semitic vandalism, assaults, and harassments increased sharply in the United States last year. The Anti-Defamation League of B'nai B'rith reports . . . anti-Semitic incidents were up 250 percent."

This itself is the beginning of the fulfillment of Jesus' prophecy that prior to His coming, Jews would be "hated of all nations." (Matt. 24:9). The last vote on an Israeli issue in the U.N. General Assembly that I noted was 127-2 against Israel, something too typical to attract much notice.

Expecting Messiah

Another crucial passage is Zechariah 12:3, "In that day will I make Jerusalem a burdensome stone for all people: all that burden themselves with it shall be cut in pieces, though all the people of the earth be gathered together against it."

David Shipler writes in *The New York Times* of this burden: "Israelis increasingly are feeling the terrible 'burden of their modern nation.' "

Back to Zechariah: "I will make Jerusalem a cup of trembling unto all the people round about, when they shall be in the siege . . . against Jerusalem" (Zech. 12:2).

James Reston of *The New York Times* wrote that we have come today to look upon "Jerusalem, of all places, [as] not a symbol of spiritual reconciliation, but of division, hostility and potential war."

When we refer to Jerusalem, we're on the most volatile subject in both the Jewish and Arab worlds. We must keep in mind here that Jesus promised — in the times leading up to Armageddon — that Jerusalem would be compassed about with "armies," and that Jerusalem would be "trodden down of the Gentiles, until the times of the Gentiles be fulfilled" (Luke 21:24).

Jerusalem probably has not seen the last of outside armies. *World Press Digest* made the crucial point that "the Arab Muslim countries regard the Israeli occupation of Jerusalem and the West

Bank . . . as a more heinous and long-standing aggression than the Soviet threats."

This is by no means to say that the Russians are to be shrugged off. It's well known that the huge paw of the Russian Bear is hanging over the Middle East ready at any time to strike. Their descent on Israel, however, will be triggered by the Islamic factor: the "hooks" in the jaws of the Russians (Ezek. 38:3-4), spurred on constantly by the fact that entering the 1990s, 37 percent of the Soviet army was already Muslim.

The Muslims will never rest until the Soviets invade Israel. It is very significant indeed that the five former Soviet republics who refused to join their new "Union" of September 1991 are non-Muslim republics. Of the ten who joined, six have majority Islamic populations. This is a crucial point to understanding what's currently happening in the former Soviet Union.

Throughout the history of the restored nation of Israel, every Israeli prime minister has reiterated that the real enemy they fear in the Middle East was and is that former bloc, now the Soviet Union. The future will most certainly show that those fears have been warranted.

Is it any wonder that — in addition to the enormous weaponry Israel is "given" by the United States and others, including Western Europe — she is currently spending $6 billion annually on her military? At the age of 18, young men and women must enter the army for three years and thereafter serve every twelfth month. Virtually every Israeli over 18 is a trained soldier. One in four of Israel's labor force works in defense-related jobs. This is the military effort Israel feels is necessary, claiming that the Arab states surrounding it actually have one million more men under arms than all the NATO countries combined.

Will Israel's defenses be enough? Not on their own! A poll indicates that 40 percent of Israelis are fed up with the war syndrome and, were the right strong man to come along, would give him a close look.

"Democracy isn't perfect and dictatorship isn't all bad," said Yossi Sarid, member of the Knesset, adding, "They say dictatorship has its advantages. It solves economic problems. It weakens inflation, puts the trade unions in their place . . . why not try it?"

Concluded James Reston in a *New York Times* assessment of Israel's dilemma in the Middle East, "Perhaps then, if we listen attentively, we shall hear . . . the gentle stirring of life and hope. Some will say that this hope lies in a nation; others in a man."

A man? Exactly! Israel is yearning for the coming of the Messiah.

As Israel adjusted to its shock in the autumn of 1990 over Saddam Hussein's actions, the media carried articles on the hoped-for imminent arrival of the Messiah in Israel. For example, *The Grand Forks Herald* (North Dakota) of September 9, 1990, quoted fundamentalist Rabbi Mendel Fogelman, "What is going on in Iraq is definitely a sign of the imminent arrival of the Messiah. When? Maybe before you get this story written."

Of the 17 million Jews worldwide, each who is true to his faith prays every morning, "I believe with complete faith in the coming of the Messiah; even though He tarry, yet I will wait for Him every coming day."

Israel's primary worry as a nation is security. This will be the open door for the Antichrist when he signs a peace pact with Israel immediately after the rapture of the Church. Israelis' euphoria will be enormous. But, they'll be betrayed.

Seven years later the real Redeemer will come to Zion to introduce a worldwide kingdom of peace and prosperity. Jerusalem will be the capital, and Jesus Christ the King will reign from His throne in Jerusalem for 1,000 years. Certain key events, with specific locales in Israel, must first take place.

Laying a Cornerstone

A century ago the Hebrew language was as dead as Moses. Then, Eliezer Ben Yehuda took on the impossible: to revive the language from the grave and to convince an entire group of people to learn it and use it as their native tongue.

To this cause he became a fanatic. He succeeded.

Today, Orthodox Jews are more strict about Hebrew in Israel than any Francophile ever has been about French in Quebec.

Such is clearly a fulfillment of prophecy: "For then will I turn to the people a pure language, that they may all call upon the name of the Lord, to serve him with one consent" (Zeph. 3:9). And with the Hebrew Old Testament an intellectual focal point of Israelis today, the world is reading again and again of their dreams and visions of the coming Messiah.

Yet there is a second, and much more complicated, indicator of end times that involves Hebrew culture. In fact, Armageddon will pivot on this one issue: the Temple Mount.

When Jesus prophesied, "Ye therefore shall see the abomination of desolation, spoken of by Daniel the prophet, Stand in the holy place (whoso readeth, let him understand)" (Matt. 24:15), He was speaking of a temple in Jerusalem during the Great Tribulation.

Paul elaborated that the Antichrist would surely come, "That man of sin [shall] be revealed, the son of perdition; who opposeth and exalteth himself above all that is called God, or that is worshipped; so that he as God sitteth in the temple of God, shewing himself that he is God" (2 Thess. 2:3-4).

Christianity Today quoted Sheik Saa al-Dinal-Alami, Islam's Supreme Muslim Council head, as saying that Muslims are prepared to die to keep Jews from praying on the Temple Mount. Meanwhile, a group of prominent Orthodox rabbis have issued a call for the construction of a temple on the Temple Mount.

Will the millennial temple be built before, during, or after the Great Tribulation? That is a moot question. There certainly will be a temple in use during the Tribulation, and certainly Christ will have the most glorious temple of all during His millennial reign.

In the 1980s, the Israeli prime minister dedicated what Reuters News Agency called "the world's most beautiful synagogue, a soaring $14.5 million building in the heart of Jerusalem. The Jerusalem Grand Synagogue . . . took 10 years to build . . . . Some 1,700 oak seats encircle the marble ceremonial area." Many Orthodox Jews, as well as studious Evangelicals, avow this will be Israel's temple of the Tribulation. However, it will not qualify as the millennial temple.

On the other hand, there are those who believe the Tribulation-era temple must be exactly in the place where currently the most sensitive building on earth stands — the Dome of the Rock. The Mosque of Omar (another name for the Dome of the Rock) was built first in the seventh century around the protrusion of bedrock where the prophet Mohammed, according to Muslim tradition, ascended to heaven on his horse. It is Islam's third holiest shrine.

One Easter Sunday in the early 1980s, Alan Harry Goodman, age 37, an American-born Israeli soldier with an automatic rifle, shot his way into the Dome of the Rock, killing two and wounding nine. In Goodman's possession was literature from the Kach movement of extremely Orthodox Jews, led by the late ultra-nationalist Rabbi Meir Kahane.

A *New York Times* article noted that this movement contended uncompromisingly that Bible prophecy promises that the adjacent mosques of Omar and Al Aksa must be replaced with a new temple because this is "the site of the original Jewish temple built by Solomon, and of the second temple which was destroyed by the Romans in A.D. 70."

In the mid-eighties, 20 men were accused of illegal possession of huge arms caches with the intention of blowing up the Dome of the Rock Mosque in Jerusalem. They believed, according to their interpretation of Scripture, that the mosque is an abomination and that its destruction would prepare the way for the Messiah.

In October 1990, there was the slaughter on the Temple Mount of 21 Palestinians by the Israeli police. The incident was triggered by a group of zealous Zionists endeavoring to lay a cornerstone for the third temple.

Messianic Jews in the Last Days

When the Church has been raptured to heaven, there will be 144,000 Jewish evangelists during the Great Tribulation, going forth preaching the gospel to the whole world amidst horrific holocaust and persecution (Rev. 7:4). It will be they in particular who will be "hated of all men" for Jesus' name sake (Luke 21:17).

Billy Graham's longtime associate, Roy Gustafson, who has been to Israel more than 130 times, notes that the million Jews returning to Israel from the former Soviet Union during the 1990s have among them an astonishingly high percentage of born-again Christians. Many are outspoken in their testimony that Jesus is their Messiah and personal Saviour.

Sid Roth, a Hebrew Christian with a worldwide radio ministry, has computed that for the first time in 1,900 years of Church history there is a larger percentage of Jews per capita being born again in today's world than Gentiles. So, joyfully he reaffirms Paul, "I am not ashamed of the gospel . . . for it is the power of God unto salvation to every one that believeth; to the Jew first, and also to the Greek" (Rom. 1:16).

We should expect that Jews in unprecedented numbers will continue to become Christians. Many will become martyrs, while other millions will make their way toward Jerusalem to await the coming Man on the white horse prophesied in Revelation 19.

A Time of Peace

President Bush, in his State of the Union address of January 29, 1991, described the coming New World Order as one where "diverse nations are drawn together in a common cause to achieve peace." On March 5, amid the euphoria of an astounding triumph, the president exclaimed again before an ecstatic Congress that, yes, there's "a New World Order coming into view, a world in which there is a very real prospect of a New World Order."

When the war was a month past, however, Bush conceded, "The victory over Iraq was not waged as 'a war to end all wars.' Even the New World Order cannot guarantee an era of perpetual peace."

How right he was! As the war broke out, *The Los Angeles Times* on January 18, 1991, commented that during our lifetime we've lived through 500 wars. And at "any given time there are 25 border conflicts and usually 35 insurgencies." It predicted accurately, "There will be as many divisions and as much tension in the Mideast after we get out as there was before we went in. One of the most cherished illusions is that the United States can bring an end to the Arab-Israeli conflict."

As we will see, many people have sensed an era of peace, a secular version of the Millennium, as being just around the corner. But the grim reality is that there is no reasonable hope of worldwide peace — if for no other reason than the fact that there is no rational expectation for an end to the Arab-Israeli conflict prior to Armageddon.

There is coming a true Millennium, a period of 1,000 years, in which Christ will reign in peace and prosperity.

President Reagan boldly affirmed before the United Nations Second Special Session on Disarmament, "The Bible tells us there will be a time for peace." He was right. The millennial reign of the Messiah over the world is inevitable because God keeps His promises.

"Ring out the thousand wars of old. Ring in the thousand years of peace." By engaging this quote from Alfred Lord Tennyson's "In Memoriam," Senator Ted Kennedy brought to a tumultuous climax the 1980 Democratic Party national convention. It was eloquent rhetoric, but man is incapable of ringing this bell.

Adolf Hitler's grandiose notion of nazism was to aggrandize his imperialist regime into the entire earth. It would then last a thousand years. It didn't happen.

Time has cited Mao Tse-t'ung's "global export of revolution" to dominate the world of the future for a thousand years. Mao Tse-t'ung is dead, and so is his dream.

The former Soviet communism, too, was to be the inevitable wave of the future, burying democracy and capitalism in history's trash can. The Soviet Union has instead unraveled.

All these have proved to be pipe dreams. In perhaps the last great quest for a man-made Millennium, the Antichrist will speak of worldwide peace. For a brief period, it will look as if the world finally will be consolidated under one dictator. It won't happen. As we have seen, the Antichrist's ascendancy will collapse in chaos after 42 months (Rev. 13:5).

Jonathan Schell's "Bible" of the secular humanists, *The Fate of the Earth,* envisages, according to *Time,* a day when "existing institutions must give way to some sort of transcendent sovereignty and security, presumably by a government that embraces all mankind, in fact 'world government.' "

That will happen, but only when Jesus Christ comes again! Only Christ can free humankind from terror, establish justice, and effect peace. That new era will be the Millennium.

King of the World

Our Lord's prophetic words in Matthew 24 describe the Great Tribulation, which sinks man into a cataclysmic carnage, and the period to follow. For there will be persecution such as the world has never before seen in all its history — and will never see again. In fact, unless those days are shortened, all mankind will perish. But they will be shortened for the sake of God's chosen people:

> For as the lightning flashes across the sky from east to west, so shall my coming be, when I, the Messiah, return .... And the nations of the world will see me arrive in the clouds of heaven, with power and great glory. And I shall send forth my angels with the sound of a mighty trumpet blast, and they shall gather my chosen ones from the farthest ends of the earth and heaven (Matt. 24:27,30-31;TLB).

Matthew 25 picks up the action:

> When I, the Messiah, shall come in my glory, and all the angels with me, then I shall sit upon my throne of glory. And all the nations shall be gathered before me. And I will separate the people [or nations] as a shepherd separates the sheep from the goats, and place the sheep at my right hand, and the goats at my left. Then I, the King, shall say to those at my right, "Come, blessed of my Father, into the King-

dom prepared for you from the founding of the world. For I was hungry and you fed me; I was thirsty and you gave me water; I was a stranger and you invited me into your homes; naked and you clothed me; sick and in prison, and you visited me" (Matt. 25:31-36;TLB).

First of all, note that it is the nations (verse 32) that Christ — now crowned King of the world — judges. Which nations? Those that survive Armageddon. Their leaders have all come (Rev. 16:14).

It will be history's foremost summit; only it will be summoned in a valley newly created by the all-time blockbuster earthquake. Zechariah says that the nations will stand before Him whose "feet will stand upon the Mount of Olives, to the east of Jerusalem, and the Mount of Olives will split apart, making a very wide valley running from east to west, for half the mountain will move toward the north and half toward the south" (Zech. 14:4;TLB).

This happens just prior to when "the Lord shall be King over all the earth. In that day there shall be one Lord — his name alone will be worshipped" (Zech. 14:9;TLB).

There the judgment of the nations will take place. It will be based on how the nations have treated those of Israel who have received Christ as their Messiah, along with those redeemed and discipled by the 144,000 Jewish evangelists during the Great Tribulation.

Two-thirds of all the nation of Israel will be cut off and die, but a third will be left in the land. I will bring the third that remain through the fire and make them pure, as gold and silver are refined and purified by fire. They will call upon my name and I will hear them; I will say, "These are my people," and they will say, "The Lord is our God" (Zech. 13:8-9;TLB).

The "fire" refers to the Tribulation and the holocausts, including Armageddon. The hammer of history will have come down on the anvil at Armageddon. The crushing of the nations, at the beckoning of Christ, will determine who goes to hell and who goes into the millennial kingdom.

These will be joined at Christ's installation of the Millennium by the newly resurrected tribulation saints (a sizable percentage of whom will be martyrs), along with the Old Testament believers up to the time of the Church, who also will be resurrected at this time. The total

Church will also consist of those saints who come with Christ in His second coming.

There is no scriptural basis that any of these groups will receive glorified bodies at this point. Rather, they will be resurrected as Old Testament believers were on the occasion of Christ's resurrection. They will, however, live a thousand years because Satan and the Adamic curse on nature will be removed.

In Revelation 20, John foresaw what would happen when Christ came back to earth and defeated the Antichrist at Armageddon.

> Then I saw an angel come down from heaven with the key to the bottomless pit and a heavy chain in his hand. He seized the Dragon — that old Serpent, the devil, Satan — and bound him in chains for 1,000 years, and threw him into the bottomless pit, which he then shut and locked, so that he could not fool the nations . . . .
>
> Then I saw thrones, and sitting on them were those who had been given the right to judge. [Author's note: These will be members of the Church, who are in their glorified bodies.] And I saw the souls of those who had been beheaded for their testimony about Jesus, for proclaiming the Word of God, and who had not worshipped the Creature or his statue, nor accepted his mark on their foreheads or their hands. They had come to life again and now they reigned with Christ for a thousand years.
>
> This is the first resurrection. (The rest of the dead did not come back to life until the thousand years had ended.) Blessed and holy are those who share in the first resurrection. For them the second death holds no terrors, for they will be priests of God and of Christ, and shall reign with him a thousand years" (Rev. 20:1-6;TLB).

The first resurrection refers to a "who" rather than a "when," that is, those who are Christ's — from whatever era — are assumed to be included in His first resurrection. Those who are not Christ's will be resurrected to the great white throne judgment and sentenced to their eternal destiny (see Rev. 20:11-15).

For those of us who anticipate reigning as His bride and presiding with Christ for a thousand years over this earth, it could all begin as soon as seven years from now.

A True Millennium

Considering its importance, the Millennium is certainly one of the least written-about and unpublicized of themes. Instead, man invents plans for a utopia.

Since Adam and Eve were ejected from the Garden of Eden, prophets, poets, musicians, political philosophers, theologians, and artists have dreamed of an eventual golden age when — under the benevolent reign of an all-seeing, all-knowing, all-powerful ruler — one could live in harmony with his maker, family, and society. Such dream schemes have proved to be just that — dream schemes.

Yet, man keeps dreaming.

On September 27, 1991, eight scientists (four single women and four single men) locked themselves into a glassed-in, geodesic biosphere 30 miles north of Tucson, Arizona, for two years. The purpose was to experience what Texas billionaire Edward Bass, its financier, called the Garden of Eden restored.

The steel and glass compound housed 3,800 varieties of plants and animals. It was designed to provide the perfect environment for humans, surrounded as they were with biomaterial such as pot-bellied pigs, Tilapia fish, and Pygmy goats (for milk). Staples included papayas and all kinds of vegetables. Contact with the outside world was limited to videocassette recorders, telephone, and computer communications.

The experiment proved interesting, but it's certainly not a microcosm for a peaceful world. Its results and successive experiments will not serve as blue prints for a true Millennium because they still depend on man. Besides, God has a totally different plan.

The only accurate plan for a Millennium is found in the Bible. God's Word assures us that a golden age lies just beyond Armageddon — an age of unprecedented peace and prosperity. This idyllic age will not be a democracy, a monarchy, or a socialist state. It will be a theocracy. Christ will be Lord and King over all the earth. What the Antichrist will have failed to do with militaristic might and computer surveillance, Jesus Christ will do by His omniscience, omnipotence, and omnipresence.

Isaiah prophesied:

> The government shall be upon his shoulder. These will be his royal titles: "Wonderful," "Counselor," "The Mighty God," "The Everlasting Father," "The Prince of Peace."

His ever-expanding, peaceful government will never end. He will rule with perfect fairness and justice from the throne of his father David. He will bring true justice and peace to all the nations of the world. This is going to happen because the Lord of heaven's armies has dedicated himself to do it! (Isa. 9:6-7;TLB).

At this time the angel's prophecy to Mary will be fulfilled: "And the Lord God shall give him the throne of his ancestor David. And he shall reign over Israel forever; his Kingdom shall never end" (Luke 1:32-33;TLB).

Israel, a tiny land, will be enlarged from the Nile to the Euphrates, with the future regathering of Israel being vastly expanded over what we've seen during the last 100 years.

Today, four and a half million of the world's 17 million Jews are in Israel.

And what of the ten tribes? God knows who and where they are and just how He will arouse them to return. In the Millennium, Israel will be divided according to the ancient twelve tribes. (Ezek. 47-48 gives the precise divisions.)

All nations and peoples will worship King Jesus, God's anointed One (Ps. 2:2). No longer will people take pilgrimages to Washington, Rome, Moscow, or Mecca.

In the end, those who survive the plague will go up to Jerusalem each year to worship the King, the Lord of Hosts, to celebrate a time of thanksgiving. And any nation anywhere in all the world that refuses to come to Jerusalem to worship the King, the Lord of Hosts, will have no rain (Zech. 14:16-17;TLB).

And who will rule over the flourishing twelve regions of Israel? Jesus replied, "When I, the Messiah, shall sit upon my glorious throne in the Kingdom, you my disciples shall certainly sit on twelve thrones judging the twelve tribes of Israel" (Matt. 19:28;TLB).

When Christ comes again to set up His thousand-year reign, His capital will be Jerusalem. With supra-metropolitan Jerusalem as the capital, and a vastly expanded Israel as the center of the earth, the Millennium will be resplendent. The world will flourish amid the worship and service of Christ the King, as the Abrahamic covenant will be fully realized.

The worldwide dominion of our Lord will include the multitudinous tongues of the Gentile nations (Amos 9:12; Mic. 7:16-17; Zech. 14:16-19; Isa. 66:18).

There will be a total transformation of the geopolitical configuration, as prophesied in Isaiah:

> In that day the Lord will make himself known to the Egyptians. Yes, they will know the Lord and give their sacrifices and offerings to him . . . . In that day Egypt and Iraq will be connected by a highway, and the Egyptians and the Iraqi will move freely back and forth between their lands, and they shall worship the same God. And Israel will be their ally; the three will be together, and Israel will be a blessing to them. For the Lord will bless Egypt and Iraq because of their friendship with Israel. He will say, "Blessed be Egypt, my people; blessed be Iraq, the land I have made; blessed be Israel, my inheritance!" (Isa. 19:21,23-25;TLB).

Yes, even Egypt and Iraq! Only a miracle could bring about such a change, and that's exactly what the world has in store.

The Perfect Paradise

On a statue across from the United Nations headquarters is the inscription: "They shall beat their swords into plowshares." That really will happen — in the Millennium, when the Lord will rule the whole world from Jerusalem! Micah says:

> He will issue his laws and announce his decrees from there. He will arbitrate among the nations, and dictate to strong nations far away. They will beat their swords into plowshares and their spears into pruning hooks; nations shall no longer fight each other, for all war will end. There will be universal peace, and all the military academies and training camps will be closed down. Everyone will live quietly in his own home in peace and prosperity, for there will be nothing to fear. The Lord himself has promised this (Mic. 4:2-4;TLB).

Peter urged us to "love the brotherhood" (1 Pet. 2:17). The trouble with our world today is that we have more hoods than brothers — brothers meaning those who've been born again into God's kingdom. One day the true brotherhood of God will prevail. It will happen when Christ comes again to establish His kingdom. And so transformed will the world be that even the beasts will be tamed:

> In that day the wolf and the lamb will lie down together, and the leopard and goats will be at peace. Calves and fat cattle will be safe among lions, and a little child shall lead them all. The cows will graze among bears; cubs and calves will lie down together, and lions will eat grass like the cows. Babies will crawl safely among poisonous snakes, and a little child who puts his hand in a nest of deadly adders will pull it out unharmed. Nothing will hurt or destroy in all my holy mountain, for as the waters fill the sea, so shall the earth be full of the knowledge of the Lord (Isa. 11:6-9;TLB).

Christ will remove all sickness, deformities, and handicaps. There will be no blindness, deafness, or dumbness; no need for eyeglasses, hearing aids, speech therapy, wheelchairs, or crutches (Isa. 29:18; 33:24; 35:3-6; Jer. 30:17; Ezek. 34:16).

Age as we know it will be altered. "The streets will be filled with boys and girls at play" while with the world in a state of "peace and prosperity" there "will once again be aged men and women" (Zech. 8:4;TLB). Like Adam and Methuselah, perhaps the aged will live up to a thousand years old.

And how will the earth support such a flourishing, proliferating population? The Lord will remove the ancient curse upon agriculture (Gen. 3:18). Even "the wilderness and desert will rejoice in those days; the desert will blossom with flowers. Yes, there will be an abundance of flowers and singing and joy! The deserts will become as green as the Lebanon mountains, as lovely as Mount Carmel's pastures and Sharon's meadows; for the Lord will display his glory there, the excellency of our God" (Isa. 35:1-2;TLB).

There will be no need for psychiatrists or "uppers" to lift people from depression. But of this present age Paul wrote, "Even we [as] Christians, although we have the Holy Spirit within us as a foretaste of future glory, also groan to be released from pain and suffering" (Rom. 8:23;TLB).

> For all creation is waiting patiently and hopefully for that future day when God will resurrect his children. For on that day thorns and thistles, sin, death, and decay — the

things that overcame the world against its will at God's command — will all disappear, and the world around us will share in the glorious freedom from sin which God's children enjoy. For we know that even the things of nature, like animals and plants, suffer in sickness and death as they await this great event (Rom. 8:19-22;TLB).

For all of history man has yearned for such an era of perfect peace and prosperity. The wonderful assurance of God's Word is that it's coming.

14

Predicting Christ's Return:

The Dangers of Date-Setting

David Allen Lewis

Bang-Ik Ha and his misguided Korean followers spent vast sums of money in 1992, announcing to the world that Jesus would rapture the Church on October 28, exactly at midnight. Large advertisements appeared in *USA Today* and other publications, telling that Jesus would come during the Feast of Trumpets and their *fyugo* (rapture) to heaven would take place.

A South African newspaper carried a Reuters report telling of adverse reaction in Korea: "Parent groups demand that the government act quickly for fear of mass suicides across the country if the predictions prove wrong." A Mr. Lee was quoted; "In outrage and despair, these believers, especially the young ones feeling betrayed, are very likely to end their lives blaming themselves."

The Reuters report added that South Korean prosecutors were probing complaints from parents alleging that these sects were abducting their children. When the whole thing failed on October 28, 1992, some of the preachers were attacked and even severely beaten by their enraged followers. There were reports of a few suicides. It was a tragedy.

In the nineteenth century, Rev. M. Baxter, an Anglican clergyman in England, identified Louis Napoleon as the Antichrist and predicted the battle of Armageddon for 1868. I have his rare, little, fragile pamphlet that speaks to me these words across the years, "Take warning! Learn not to repeat the errors of the past."

In the last century, Sir Robert Anderson, a fine scholar and great eschatologist, lamented, "And so in recent years, one date after another has been confidently named for the supreme crisis; but still the world goes on. A.D. 581 was one of the first years fixed for the event." Anderson was referring to the church father, Hippolytus, who said the end would come in the year 500.

Date setting is the curse of the Bible prophecy message and may prove to be more destructive than all external enemies put together. It is horrible to contemplate that a powerful biblical message may be eclipsed by the radical actions of the "friends of the message," but we sadly warn that this is what may happen.

Date-setting is not new. From the time of the early church until now, there have been thousands of date-setting, date-suggesting, and date-hinting schemes. All wrong. Now, there are books and pamphlets circulating *proving* that Jesus will come in every year from now until the year 2001.

I firmly believe Jesus is coming back. Over 300 Bible prophecies pointed to the first coming of Jesus. They were all fulfilled. The New Testament has 257 references to the future, literal return of Jesus to this planet. They, too, will be fulfilled. No one can destroy the plan of God, but a lot is being done to erode people's confidence in Bible prophecy.

Our Saviour clearly warned: "But of that day and hour knoweth no man, no, not the angels of heaven, but my Father only" (Matt. 24:36). In spite of that plain statement, schemes for dating the Rapture, the beginning of the Millennium, or the end of the world are recycled over and over.

Who Knows and Who Doesn't

On one hand, it can be demonstrated that God gave Israel timetables, but none were given for the Church. The Church is the hidden mystery that lies between week 69 and week 70 of Daniel's 70-

week vision (Dan. 9:24-27).[1] [See Sir Robert Anderson, *The Coming Prince*. Also, cross reference: 1 Peter 1:10-12; 1 Cor. 2:7; Rom. 16:25; Eph. 1:9-10; Eph. 3:1-11; Eph. 5:32; Eph. 6:18; Col. 1:26-27; Col. 2:2; Col. 4:3; and 1 Peter 1:10-12.]

God can set dates, for He is the planner and fulfiller of all future events. He knows everything about the future and when each event will take place. The date of the Rapture is fixed. It is marked on the divine calendar.

If God truly knows the date (He does), then it is fixed and cannot be changed. If it could be changed, then He does not know the date. If He does not know the date, then we have to redefine God and we may as well throw the Bible out the window. Either God is God and is omniscient, or He isn't. Jesus simply forbade us to attempt figuring it out. There is good reason for this.

While Jesus knew it would be over 1,900 years until He would return to earth, He wanted the Church of all ages to live in the light of that hope, and with a healthy anticipation of His coming. Those who die in the faith are not disappointed. They are in the presence of the Lord and will participate in the first resurrection at the time of the Rapture (1 Thess. 4:13-18).

People saved during the early part of the Tribulation will have opportunity to study the Scriptures, hear the teaching of the 144,000 (Rev. 7) and *exactly calculate the day Jesus will set foot on the Mount of Olives*. For, from the time of the abomination of the future temple by the Antichrist (Matt. 24:15-22; Mark 13:14; 2 Thess. 2:3-4; Dan. 9:24-27; 11:31; and 12:11), it will be exactly 1,260 days until Jesus fulfills Zechariah 14:4 when He sets foot on the Mount of Olives on the East of Jerusalem.

The timing of the rapture of the Church, however, is deliberately hidden and forbidden. To pry into this matter is open rebellion against God. It is defiant disobedience.

To prove this, one often hears the Words of Jesus quoted: "But of that day and hour knoweth no man, no, not the angels of heaven, but my Father only" (Matt. 24:36). In verse 42, the Lord exhorts, "Watch therefore: for ye know not what hour your Lord doth come." And in verse 44 He says, "Therefore be ye also ready: for in such an hour as ye think not the Son of man cometh."

Time to Watch and Pray

The date setters are quick to point out that Jesus merely indicated that we could not know the day nor the hour, that He did not rule out knowing the week, month, or year.

In Mark's Gospel, however, we find the one Scripture that is the date setter's downfall. After repeating the idea stated in Matthew 24:36, Jesus expands the forbidden territory of date-setting the Rapture: "Take ye heed, watch and pray: for ye know not when the time is" (Mark 13:33).

You know not when the time is! And, friend, a day is time, a month is time, a week is time, a year is time, and, *You know not when the time is.* This one statement settles it once and for all.

All date-setting displays disregard and disrespect for the Words of Jesus. We are commanded to live in anticipation. We are to "take heed," so don't ignore the message. To do so makes you as guilty as the date setter. We are to "watch and pray" (Mark 13:33).

> For the Son of man is as a man taking a far journey, who left his house, and gave authority to his servants, and to every man his work, and commanded the porter to watch. Watch ye therefore: for ye know not when the master of the house cometh, at even, or at midnight, or at the cock-crowing, or in the morning: Lest coming suddenly he find you sleeping. And what I say unto you I say unto all, Watch (Mark 13:34-37).

Do not ignore, nor fantasize, but take heed, watch, and pray. These are commands for all Christians of all time.

How could a Christian living in A.D. 1257 "watch" without the benefit of the date setters? The same as sane, well-informed Christians today watch for His coming while faithfully laboring day by day until He comes back again. Let not our keen daily hope for the Rapture be dulled with useless and disappointing date-setting schemes. Jesus may come today!

When is Jesus coming back? When is the world coming to an end? Too many people think they have this figured out and are recklessly setting dates, publishing erroneous books and pamphlets, and distorting the meaning and purpose of Bible prophecy.

The Purpose of Prophecy

If prophecy is not given for the purpose of figuring out the date of the Second Coming, then what is its purpose?

This subject has been exhaustively treated by great expositors of the Word such as John Walvoord, J. Dwight Pentecost, Stanley

Horton, Donald Barnhouse, and a host of others. It will not be necessary for me to treat this question in great depth since so much written material is available.

As H. L. Wilmington points out in his book, *Manuscript,* that prophecy proves the Bible is accurate. Hundreds of details of the prophetic word have already been fulfilled. This historic witness demonstrates the reliability of God's Word and the surety of the completion of His declared plans.

Prophecy proves that our existence is not meaningless. The existentialist philosopher may say, "The universe is a red-mawed beast grinding up the flesh of man and beast only to spew them out into an abyss of nothingness." The believer in Jesus says, "My life has purpose. It therefore has value and dignity. I will stand one day before the King of the universe for an evaluation of my life and performance. What I invest in this life accrues interest for eternity. We are saved by faith, but we will be rewarded for good works."

Bible prophecy promotes missions. Not knowing the time of the end, we are spurred on to greater effort in winning a lost world to Christ. In the church I attend, Evangelist Lowell Lundstrom stirred us with a powerful end-times message — challenging us to feed the hungry, visit those in prison, minister to the sick, share the gospel in deed as well as in word. Evangelical pre-millennialists have stood at the forefront of world missions outreach. We are not escapists, and our record of Bible based activism proves it.

We believe in studying the plan of God so we can intelligently implement His purpose on earth in our time. We do not labor to change the will of God, nor to thwart the will of God, but to cooperate with the revealed will of God. We are the first to shout from the housetops, "Faith without works is dead."

Prophecy is a call to spiritual warfare against the dark powers. *Prophecy is a call to intercessory prayer.*

Above all, *prophecy glorifies Jesus and directs worship to God* (Rev. 19:10).

Prophecy gives us hope for the future. Paul writes that we are "Looking for that blessed hope, and the glorious appearing of the great God and our Saviour Jesus Christ." Note that the Apostle prefaces this Word with an exhortation that we should live a sober, righteous, and godly lifestyle, "in this present world." He continues after the blessed hope passage to urge us on to a life manifesting a zeal for good works. (Titus 2:11-15).

Maybe Today!

All date-setting schemes, historically, have proven to be false prophecy, and have always brought disgrace upon not only the perpetrators but upon the Evangelical churches. By quoting biblical "proof" texts, date setters achieve an aura of authority that is impressive in the eyes of their misinformed or gullible followers.

We believe that the coming of Jesus is potentially imminent. Only God knows the exact time of the return of our Lord. But, He knows. To God, the idea of imminence is irrelevant.

To us humans, however, not knowing the time of the return, makes imminence meaningful and a stimulus to holy living as we await the return of Jesus. Not knowing the time of His return, we are mandated to work to improve the quality of life, wage war against evil, and carry out the Great Commission as if He were not even coming in our lifetime.

Jesus may come today!

Date-setting destroys the possible imminence of Christ's return. If I know Christ will return on September 25, then I do not have to look for Him today. It is the date setter, not the continual anticipator who will be caught off guard. Further, it is the unfaithful servant who says, "My Lord delayeth His coming."

Date setters, on the other hand, are saying, "Jesus will delay until the date I have calculated." (See Matt. 24:42-51.)

I must believe that Jesus could come today, and I must work each day, knowing that I may finish out my natural life before He returns. The correct understanding of pre-millennialism never promotes escapism or irresponsibility.

Polishing Brass and Planting Trees

Back in the 1920s, a cliché became popular in fundamentalist circles. Believing that the world is beyond hope and that we should only live for the Second Coming, many said, "There's no use polishing brass on a sinking ship."

Well, we may just have to live a while longer on this sinking ship, which has been sinking since the fall of Adam in the Garden of Eden. Thank God, there have been a few responsible people who have been "polishing brass," working to improve the quality of life in the present season.

When I was a teenager, I heard about the threat of blister rust to the white pine trees in Montana. My buddy, John Heier, and I hitchhiked out to Troy, Montana, to join hands with the forestry service and spend the summer fighting blister rust. Our team saved thousands of trees.

Each year, I plant trees with my own hands. We have pledged to plant 10,000 trees near the Sea of Galilee at our Christians United for Israel forest. So far, my friends and I have planted over 5,000 trees there.

You can complain about the environmental movement being dominated by New Agers all you want. I will simply ask, "Why did they get the chance to do so? Why were you not out there doing what God has ordered us to do — to care for the planetary home He has given us?"

Bible prophecy, properly understood, makes us the most responsible citizens possible both for this world and for the world to come.

When we speak out against escapism and date-setting, we are not undertaking a mere intellectual exercise. This dating game is dangerous. Let's take another brief look at the checkered history of the bewildering world of the date setters.

Of Trumpets and White Horses

Augustine suggested that the world would probably end in A.D. 1000. From about 950 to 1000, wealthy landowners all over Europe were encouraged to deed their holdings to the church for pardon for their sins.

Sir Robert Anderson wrote in *The Coming Prince,* "All Europe rang with it in the days of Pope Gregory the Great. And at the end of the tenth century, the apprehension of it amounted to a general panic. It was then frequently preached on, and by breathless crowds listened to; the subject of every man's thoughts, every one's conversation."

Anderson cites Mosheim:

> Under this impression, multitudes innumerable, having given their property to monasteries or churches, traveled to Palestine, where they expected Christ to descend to judgment. Others bound themselves by solemn oaths to be serfs to churches or to priests, in hopes of a milder sentence on them as being servants of Christ's servants. In many places buildings were let go to decay, as that of which there would be no need in the future. And on occasions of eclipses of sun or moon, the people fled in multitudes for

refuge to the caverns and the rocks.[2]

Further documents relating to that period of history speak of mass hysteria, pandemonium, then white-hot anger against the Church when the prophesies of the end of the world in the year 1000 failed.

Can you imagine what it will be like in 1999? Are you prepared for these kinds of events should Jesus not come before A.D. 2000?

Unfortunately, date setters throughout history have continued to wreak havoc in the lives of their deluded followers.

In 1832, William Miller first preached: "And so brethren, it has been revealed to me that the world is coming to an end. Repent, repent, I say for you have but 11 years to be washed clean in the blood of the Lamb. In mighty fire and terror the world will end in 1843."

As 1843 approached, anticipation turned into a kind of madness. People abandoned homes, farms, material possessions, and even children to gather in homes, praying as they waited for the last trumpet.

In Westford, Massachusetts, about 500 people gathered wearing white robes to wait for the Coming. When the midnight hour of December 31, 1842, arrived, an old town drunk, known as "Crazy Amos," blew a trumpet outside the fine old mansion where the people were gathered. Pandemonium broke loose, and several were seriously injured in the stampede. Outside they found not Jesus, but a bleary-eyed, laughing, old drunkard.

Historians record a darker side of the debacle. Following disappointment upon disappointment and a continual readjusting for the dates, some lost their minds. The asylum at Worcester, Massachusetts, became so overcrowded that a large hall had to be appropriated to house the deranged.

In New Hampshire, New York, Vermont, Maine, and parts of Pennsylvania, the lunacy rate is said to have increased 300 percent in 1843-44 as a result of the date-setting.

Usually rational people went everywhere in flowing white robes, ready for ascension. Historians claim that suicide became common in the face of disappointment. I do not know that it was common, but evidently for some it was the way out of tragic disappointment.

When it was all over, the disillusioned faithful went back to try to pick up the pieces of the lives they had abandoned. Many became atheists.

Early in the last century, Dr. R. C. Shimeall wrote a book

predicting that the Millennium would come in 1868. In that same century, a converted Jew, Joseph Worlf, began prophesying that Jesus would come to the Mount of Olives in 1847.

Lady Hester Stanhope converted to his doctrine, moved to Palestine, and established residence on the Mount of Olives. She kept two, beautiful, white horses in a stable there. One was for Jesus to ride through the Golden Gate. Presumably the other was for her to accompany Him.

The Doomsday Effect

In 1918, H. C. Williams wrote a volume titled *The Revelation of Jesus Christ*. In it he said: "A.D. 1914 is the time limit set in the Scriptures for the concurrence of the war: that the war broke out and continues in all details as described by the prophets is a complete fulfillment of the prophetic record."

In the same book, Williams predicted that 1934 would mark the downfall of the Gentile nations, and in 1972, the Millennium would begin.

In 1975, a widely circulated book proclaimed that the Rapture probably would take place on September 5 or 6, 1975.

Following the interpretations of this man, others began to preach the September 1975, date. One pastor even borrowed large sums of money, which he had no way of paying back, to invest in missions. In a sermon, he explained that he had nothing to worry about since Jesus was sure to come back on September 5, 1975.

This is the stuff of which spiritual tragedies are made, for on September 7, the bubble burst. Only eternity will reveal the tragedies created by those playing the dating game.

Newsweek (September 16, 1974), carried an article entitled, "The Doomsday Effect." It is said that in 1982, all nine planets of our solar system would be in conjunction — that is, in a straight line in relation to the sun and all on one side of the sun. The combined gravitational pull could cause great storms on the sun. These storms could alter wind directions on earth, and this in turn could slow the speed of earth's rotation and trigger the worst earthquakes the world has ever known. I wrote several articles refuting the idea. I commented on it over TV and on our monthly cassette service, "Audio Prophecy Digest."

A number of nationally known Bible teachers had used this as a basis for suggesting that the world would be in the Tribulation by 1982, but I could not accept their predictions.

1982 came, the planets lined up, and life went on. It seems our conservative approach turned out to be right.

In September of 1988, I sat in the office of a pastor in Toronto, Ontario, Canada, who sorrowfully told me of the impact that the book, *88 Reasons Why Christ Will Return in 1988*, by Edgar Whisenant had on some of his congregation. He spoke of a couple in their mid-thirties who had disposed of their home, business, boat, and automobile, and had invested heavily in those who were "getting the last ditch message out."

"That couple is now penniless," the pastor told me, "and they are sitting in a hotel room charged to a credit card they will no longer be able to pay. They are sure that Jesus will come in September, and that they will not have to face the responsibility."

What a tragedy. What a poor witness for the Lord and His church.

I do not doubt that Whisenant's abortive effort to calculate the date(s) of the Rapture was the most widely heralded date-setting scheme since William Miller's 1843 attempt or the Jehovah's Witnesses' failed prophecy of the second coming in 1914.

In 1988, I met a man who had given a large sum of money to promote the distribution of Whisenant's book, *88 Reasons Why Christ Will Return in 1988*. It is very complicated, as most date-setting schemes are. I read it and could not understand it. I asked him if he understood the book.

The brother replied, "No, I don't understand it, but I believe every word of it!"

His reply astounded me.

Special Revelations?

Most date setter's books are intimidating. Some claim to have a special key, "revealed to them by God." Or, they have spent the last 20 years figuring out the numerology of the Scriptures. Some of these books are very nicely printed, some use scholarly language, and all offer very complicated reasons for the author's conclusion.

In addition, these authors make a claim to exclusivity. Only he or she has figured out the true date. The competition is fierce. One of my colleagues humorously suggested that soon, would-be date setters will have to do a computer search for a date that isn't already taken.

Contradictions are rife. The date setters cannot all be right. The fact is they are all wrong. Even if someone gets it right, he is still wrong to do it (Mark 13:33). You don't even have to read the books and pamphlets to figure that out. If they set a date, they are wrong.

If books and papers of this nature are thrust upon you, you should gently rebuke the purveyors of these errors. We cannot tolerate silence in this matter nor allow a readjustment of their calendar of miscalculation when their schemes fail.

Even though the books by Rapture date setters contain some truth, they are tainted with rebellion and must be avoided. Don't join them in their delusion. Keep yourself free from the degrading bondage and confusion engendered by date setters and the false teaching that *always* accompanies their theories.

Those involved in publishing date-setting literature must repent to the Lord and before the Church. They must repudiate their errors. They must put forth as much published material explaining why they were wrong as they did in promoting their errors.

Don't let anyone brainwash you or put you on a guilt trip. Just accept Jesus' words in Mark 13:33: "Take ye heed, watch and pray: for ye know not when the time is."

Live your life in the light of the blessed hope of His coming. Perhaps it will be today! Work and witness with well laid plans for a long time ahead. You will be ready for His coming, for you will be living in obedience, useful endeavor, and hopeful anticipation.

Which Generation?

Certain forms of date-setting are based on an interpretation of Jesus' words in Matthew 24:34: "Verily I say unto you, This generation shall not pass, till all these things be fulfilled."

They say a generation is 40 years. Israel (the fig tree referred to in Matt. 24:32) became a nation in 1948. So, 1948 + 40 = 1988. But, it didn't work did it? Will we ever learn from hundreds of past errors of this nature?

Now, a favorite formula is to start with 1967, year of the capture of Jerusalem, and add 40 years or whatever they think constitutes the length of a generation. There are several flaws in this superficial reasoning.

First, the generation concept is not that firmly fixed in Scripture. The word generation is not a technical nor scientific term. I am not sure that Exodus with the 40-year generation, nor the Book of Job with the 35-year generation, nor the statement that the days of man are "three score and ten" — indicating a 70-year generation — are to be taken as precisely describing a generation. The date setters choose whichever one fits their scheme.

Secondly, why select 1948 for the year when the "fig tree" (Israel) put forth its leaves? Why not the return of the Jews in the 1880s? Why not the founding of Zionism by Theodore Herzl in Basel, Switzerland, in 1897? Why not the founding of Tel Aviv, the first all-Jewish city in modern times, established in 1909?

A likely year would be 1917 due to two major events: General Allenby's liberation of Jerusalem and Arthur James Balfour's famous declaration that "His Majesty's government view [sic] with favor the establishment in Palestine of a national home for the Jewish people, and will use their best endeavors to facilitate the achievement of the object, it being clearly understood that nothing shall be done which may prejudice the civil and religious rights of existing non-Jewish communities in Palestine, or the rights and political status enjoyed by Jews in any other country." Many felt that surely this must be the budding of the fig tree (Matt. 24:32).

Various date setters chose one or another of those dates as a beginning point for their calculations. All wrong! Wrong! Wrong!

The capture of old Jerusalem by the Israelis in 1967 is considered as a date-setting possibility by many, because of the reference to Jerusalem being trodden down until the times of the Gentiles being over (Luke 21:24). They think that the times of the Gentiles are now ended. This could not be right since Revelation 11:2 indicates that one more time, after the Temple is rebuilt, Jerusalem will *again* be trodden of the Gentiles for 42 months.

No, the times of the Gentiles do not end until the "Rock cut out without hands" smites the image of Gentile world rule on the feet (Dan. 2). That takes place at the end of the seven years of tribulation, at the Battle of Armageddon.

May we suggest that it was not our Lord's intention in the Olivet Discourse (Matt. 24, 25) to provide a means of fixing the time of His return since He immediately says this would be an impossibility (Mark 13:33).

Thirdly, the word translated "generation" in Greek is "genea" and does not necessarily mean a literal generation. W. E. Vine gives one possible translation of genea as "a race of people." (See *Vine's Expository Dictionary of New Testament Words*. Look under the entries: generation, kind, age, and all relevant cross references.)

There are scholars who agree on that translation. If that is correct, then Jesus is simply declaring the indestructibility of the Jewish people. This would be allowable in the context of Matthew 24.

He is simply saying that this nation, or race, the fig tree people, Israel will not be destroyed, all these things will be fulfilled.

How About 1994?

Date setters in the Church who claim biblical authority can potentially play havoc with the credibility of the Second Coming message in the minds of millions. Not only the prophecy message will be hurt, there will be a general, negative fallout affecting the entire realm of evangelicalism. When people are disappointed with date-setting failures, they are tempted to "throw out the baby with the bath water."

Their downfall is in not being able to distinguish between the valid message of Christ's coming and the perversion as it is perpetrated by false shepherds, opportunists, and the sincerely deluded. We understand that many date setters are sincere, dedicated Christians who love Jesus and long for His coming. But they are wrong, and once enlightened as to the error of their ways, they need to repent and repudiate their teaching.

It looks like 1994 could be the year of the next great date-setting upset. Harold Camping's book, *1994?*, is preparing the way.

Camping is founder and owner of the Family Radio Network of 50 radio stations. Some say he is heard daily by more Christians than any other man. At present, his voice is the predominant radio voice in Russia, Nigeria, and some other countries in Africa. He has been viewed as a model of stability and Evangelical reliability for many years.

Harold Camping asserts the following:

1. The coming of Christ and the end of the world will take place between September 15 and September 27, 1994.

2. The church age ended on the Feast of Pentecost in the spring of 1988. On May 22, 1988, the loosing of Satan took place and the Tribulation began. The Tribulation is only six years in length.

3. God no longer approves of the Church but will allow the devil to destroy it.

4. God is no longer using the Church or speaking to us through our pastors. "True believers" will get out of the Church.

5. God will destroy the Church by allowing the devil to motivate the Pentecostal manifestation of speaking in tongues. Camping claims that speaking in tongues is the forbidden fruit of the last days, and Satan will bring about a fall just as he did with Adam and Eve and the forbidden fruit in Genesis.

344 • *The Triumphant Return of Christ*

True believers who do not leave the churches voluntarily will be "killed" by Satan. This does not mean that they will be put to death, but that they will be driven out of the church by those who remain in the church. While Camping condemns dreams, visions, and revelations in the churches, nevertheless, on page 322 of his book, *1994?*, he says, ". . . many new truths will be revealed to believers very near the end of time."

6. No one can be saved after September 6, 1994.

What will that do to missions giving if Camping gains influence over any more of our people? We know from reports of some Evangelical pastors that many Christians are faithfully supporting Family Radio and have done so for many years.

The book *1994?* is being sold not only over the airwaves and in religious bookstores, but also by Waldenbooks, B. Dalton, etc. The publisher is reluctant to give out numbers of copies sold, but Rev. Scott Temple, an Assembly of God pastor in New Jersey, found out that several editions have been printed in a short period of time. I do not know what Camping's motivation is, and I suppose he is very sincere, but he is wrong, and will do a lot of damage.[3]

An Eastern U.S. book publisher told me, "If you want to write a bestseller in the field of prophecy, name the Antichrist and set a date." There is something sinister behind that suggestion!

A.D. 2000 — Start the Millennium?

A periodical out of Florida calculated that the Rapture would take place soon, and that the Millennium would begin by 1979. Other dates being set are: 1993, 1994, 1995, 1996, 1997, 1998, 1999, and 2000.

The year 2000! It has a magnetic appeal! I recently heard a minister declare: "A day is as a thousand years and a thousand years as a day with the Lord. There were seven days of creation. It has now been six 'days' or 6,000 years from creation (or will be about A.D. 2000, according to Usher's chronology). That leaves one day of a thousand years — the Millennium, so, the end has to come by the year 2000."

Modern date setters are getting ready to rerun a tragedy of the magnitude of those in the past — or worse. As world crises mount, people will find the date setters' schemes alluring as a form of spiritual and psychological escapism.

Let us consider a possibility. If Jesus doesn't come in the 1990s, the date setters will have a heyday as the year 2000 approaches. It will be like a fever. It will sell pamphlets and books by the millions. But, if Jesus does not come back by the year 2001, it is hard to imagine any credibility being left for the Bible prophecy message.

Remember this vicious world will not differentiate between the David Koreshes, the date setters, and the Evangelical Bible churches in general. In your own vested interest, you had better get into the subject of Bible prophecy. You had better start refuting the date setters. There is still time for a rescue program if we start now.

From My Perspective

I know the dangers of date-setting first hand because I saw it in action and experienced the tragic effects it can have on the ministry of a church. Permit me to share a bit of my own experience and observations.

I accepted Christ as my Saviour in an Assembly of God church when I was 10 years old. When a German preacher, Hans Bretschneider, spoke in our little town, I sat nightly on the front row to drink in his every word. Hans had a lot to say about prophecy, the coming of Jesus, and even said that the Jews would one day return to Palestine and establish a new-old nation. That was in 1943.

Five years later, on May 14, 1948, I listened to the news over WNAX radio station and heard the announcement that President Harry S. Truman was the first head of a nation to recognize the newly born state of Israel. I knew it was happening.

A call of God had been on my life from the time I was 11, and now it was strongly reinforced as I came to an inner knowledge that the destiny of my life was somehow linked with the Jewish people. How I thank God for evangelist Bretschneider and his faithfulness to the Word of God. I never forgot how he used biblical prophecy to predict a coming event — without setting a date.

I also never forgot another evangelist who came to preach in my home church when I was a young lad, living in Britton, South Dakota. He announced that on a certain night, he would prove that Benito Mussolini, the Fascist dictator of Italy, was the Antichrist. The next morning, however, the newspapers announced the death of Mussolini, *the day he was to preach the sermon in the evening service.* What an embarrassment!

Growing up in the church, I heard some date-setting and naming of the Antichrist. I noted that these systems always failed and disillusioned people.

It was popular during the Second World War to say that Hitler was the Antichrist. When the war was over, and all the guessing was proven wrong, and all the dates set failed, the best way to empty the church was to announce a prophecy conference. People were fed up with fanaticism.

What should I do about the calling in my life if no one was interested in prophecy anymore? This was a big question for a teenager.

Pastor Silas D. Rexroat counseled me at length, and encouraged me to attend Central Bible Institute and Seminary (now Central Bible College) and prepare for the ministry. While in CBIS, I listened to some of the greatest Bible teachers of that time. Men like Stanley Horton, E.S. Williams, Donald Johns, J. Robert Ashcroft, Frank M. Boyd, O. Cope Budge, and others faithfully declared the Word with anointing and power. In those days, there was no lack of teaching in the field of eschatology.

After graduation, I started my preaching career as an evangelist in June, 1954. Ramona and I were married in December of that same year and held our first meeting together in Ishpeming, Michigan, for a Rev. Hodges.

My mentors of that time were two pastors, Rev. A. E. Peterson and Rev. C. G. Tiahart. I was preaching on Bible prophecy a good share of the time. God was good, and many people came to Christ. But I soon discovered that because of the prophetic debacles during the Second World War, not every church was open to our ministry.

Times were tough for us. It was difficult to find churches interested in hearing teaching on Bible prophecy, so we took any opportunity that presented itself. Because finances were very meager, we were often discouraged.

Restoring the Nobility of the Message

Two years went by. We had good meetings, and finally Ramona and I and our little Becky settled into a parish ministry for six years in West Virginia, where I was the pastor of the Old Pond Pentecostal Church of Hopeville Gap in Cabins, West Virginia. That is where Sandy was born.

Later, we pastored Trinity Assembly in Fairmont, West Virginia. When we launched out into traveling evangelistic ministry the second time in 1962, we traveled as a family, home schooling our daughters through high school.

While our family was holding a revival service for a church in Manchester, Connecticut, where Rev. Ken Gustafson was the pastor, an incident occurred that caused me to question my calling.

Ken had invited a singing quartet of four lads who were traveling for the summer between Bible college semesters. They furnished the special music for the meetings, and I remember that they were very good. When they told me about the fabulous bookings they were having in big churches, I couldn't help but envy their success and popularity.

After an evening service one night, the lads took me aside and had a heart-to-heart talk with me. One of them said, "David, we like you a lot. You have a nice little family. Your preaching is good. But, if you don't stop emphasizing this Bible prophecy stuff, nobody is going to want you. You need to start preaching a straight salvation message."

Already battling discouragement, I now began to question my calling. Maybe I should give up teaching about Bible prophecy. Maybe I had missed God somewhere along the line.

But, my sweet wife and little girls prayed with me, and we continued.

Not long after that incident I was in Detroit visiting with a Mr. Timco who had started a restaurant featuring Christian singers and entertainers. It was called the Crossroads. He asked me to take a position as the manager and host of the club. Again, I came close to abandoning my preaching and prophecy teaching ministry. But, we kept on.

As the years went by, things changed, and people forgot the disappointments of the Second World War prophecies. Eventually we received more invitations than we could accept. Things have gone well, and the ministry has grown and prospered.

Still, those early years of rejection of God's prophetic Word hurt not only our ministry but the Church in general. That is why I am so concerned about what I see happening in this last decade of the twentieth century.

If Jesus does not come back by the year 2000, it will be the same old story. My friends, Hal Lindsey, Grant Jeffrey, Tim LaHaye, Peter LaLonde, John Wesley White, and other colleagues, may have to consider a readjustment of emphasis! Who will want to listen to us? It is not that the message of the Second Coming is flawed, but that its credibility could almost be destroyed by professed friends of the message — the date setters.

What should the Church do in these crucial times?

The answer for pastors and religious leaders is not to be faint hearted and ignore the subject of eschatology altogether. The answer is not to bow before the onslaught of the dominionists and their ilk. The answer is to preach and teach our message in a responsible fashion, striving to restore the nobility of the message of our Lord's return.

Is the controversy surrounding Bible prophecy the reason why our Bible colleges and seminaries have all but abandoned the field of eschatology? That is not the answer we need for these momentous times. No, but the truth is the answer.

What Should We Be Preaching?

The writer of the epistle to the Hebrews speaks of the triumph of the kingdom of Christ Jesus (Heb. 10:12-13), of fearful coming judgment (Heb. 10:27), and of the return of our Lord Jesus; "For ye have need of patience, that, after ye have done the will of God, ye might receive the promise. For yet a little while, and he that shall come will come, and will not tarry" (Heb. 10:36-37).

He will not tarry!

A lay person recently corrected me on my use of the common terminology, "If the Lord tarries."

That person was right. He will not tarry, and when the set date arrives, He will come. He will come as foreordained by God Almighty on the day fixed in the divine mind, whether the Church has fulfilled its tasks or not, whether ready or not. All the accounts will be settled at the Judgment Seat of Christ (see Rom. 14:10, 1 Cor. 3:9-15, and 2 Cor. 5:10).

Between these prophecies in Hebrews 10, there is a sober exhortation:

> And let us consider one another to provoke unto love and to good works: Not forsaking the assembling of ourselves together, as the manner of some is; but exhorting one another: and so much the more, as ye see the day [of Christ's return] approaching (Heb. 10:24-25).

There is no biblical reason for the kind of abuse that prophecy is being subjected to, principally at the hands of those involved in attempting to set a date for the rapture of the Church and the second coming of Jesus Christ. There is abundant reason for teaching prophecy and end-times truth in a responsible manner, as it appears in the

Bible, without fantasies, fables, and fakery.

We are now at the point in Church history that, if reliable people do not wake up and rescue the Bible prophecy message from the hands of fanatics, we will see this entire area of theology self-destruct before our eyes. This will have a serious and detrimental effect on the Church. It could even be a principle cause of the "great apostasy" of the end times. It could be a prime mover in effecting social and governmental persecution of the Evangelical church. We could see a serious waning of the influence of biblical Christianity as a result of the misguided efforts of date setters.

We must come to grips with the question: "Does the pre-millennial understanding of Bible prophecy have a legitimacy apart from date-setting?" Some think not. It is my conviction that it does.

While most Bible colleges, seminaries, and some pastors of local churches ignore this subject because of its controversial nature, a small cadre of our colleagues are trying to rescue the message, fully realizing that no one can stop the plan of God from being fulfilled, but knowing that the credibility of the message can be destroyed in people's minds. That could be a great hindrance to the winning of the lost to Christ.

Pastor, understand that we do not wish to be exclusive nor to be viewed as the all time great experts in the field of eschatology. On the contrary, we wish to enlist you in our cause and will do everything we can to strengthen your hands in this end of the age of harvest time.

True and False Prophets

The authors of this book, and others, are the theological guerrilla fighters standing, against all odds, to confront the radical date setters, the dominionist, and Kingdom Now skeptics — a veritable host of formidable enemies arrayed against the message of pre-millennialism.

We believe in a literal Millennium — the future, visible mani-festation of the kingdom of God right here on earth. Before the new heavens and new earth and the eternal state are ushered in, there will be a 1,000 year reign of Messiah Jesus Christ on earth. We challenge the Church to restudy the prophets. Reconsider that over a third of the Bible is cast in the mold of prophecy. It is not a subject to be ignored.

Some who identify themselves as prophets today, however, are scorning the message of Bible prophecy relating to future events. The pattern for prophets is set in the Scripture.

Daniel studied Jeremiah's writings, and the prophets were familiar with the written works that preceded their own proclamations. Jesus, the greatest prophet, demonstrated His knowledge of Torah and the prophets by frequently quoting from them.

Any modern prophet who is ignorant of the Bible prophets is not to be heard nor heeded. They are unworthy of the office they claim. Furthermore, any modern prophet who goes so far as to make fun of Bible prophecy (as so many do) is a false prophet.

There are true prophets in the world today like Janabeth Lachenmacher and David Wilkerson. Billy Graham is another. Through the years I have noted several people fulfilling the prophetic role in the Church. These make no claim to a prophetic office. They simply declare what the Lord gives them, and furthermore, they are knowledgeable and respectful of the Bible prophecy message.

People who attend a seminar and become card-carrying prophets are not like the prophets in the Bible. Those true prophets, with the possible exception of Ezekiel, tried to avoid the office. They felt it was an undesirable burden to be a prophet of the Lord.

Calling for a Boycott

The guru David Koresh episode is bad news for the entire Evangelical church. Koresh gained his great authority over his cult members by constantly quoting the Book of Revelation. Of course he twisted the meaning of the Scripture, but he nevertheless used it to his own ends.

It is not just the members of the secular media who lump legitimate pre-millennial prophecy teachers with the date setters. If we have to take blows from our co-religionists how shall we fare with the hostile humanist world?

Well-known dominionist Gary DeMar commented critically on my book, *Prophecy 2000*.[4] He implied that I am in league with the date setters. His assessment of my book is a total error. It is apparent he doesn't even know what the book is about. His unscholarly approach shows that he never read the book he criticizes. (The alternate is to think that he deliberately distorted my views.)

Under his chapter title, "The Dating Game" (lifted? from my *Smashing the Gates of Hell*,[5]) he includes me in a litany of criticism against a number of date setters and some whom he *accuses* of being date setters. DeMar wrote, "David Allen Lewis came out with *Prophecy 2000 — Rushing to Armageddon*. The first chapter begins: '2000! It is like magic. You see it everywhere, like a universal logo.'"[6]

That's all, folks. And with this, DeMar tars me with same brush he uses on a host of date setters. A lot of DeMar's criticism of the date setter is justified, but his uneducated response illustrates the lumping together factor. He totally ignores the fact that I am the person who has for years been circulating a "Manifesto Against Date-setting."

And, did he read on the back cover of *Prophecy 2000* where it says, "This is the book that can help you chart your course in the 1990s! Do troubled waters lie ahead? What will your world be like by the year 2000 *if Jesus has not come by then?*"

Did Gary DeMar read my chapter headed "Setting the Date for Christ's Return?" Could he have overlooked the fact that in the first paragraph of that chapter I condemned all date-setting schemes as false prophecy?

Given his close association with dominionist Gary North, it is understandable that DeMar attacks me in this manner. After all, it is Gary North (co-author with DeMar on some books) who has said that he wants to go down in history as the man who destroyed the message of pre-millennialism.

If we get this kind of treatment from conservative Christians like DeMar and North, what will the out-and-out humanist world do to us in the wake of the greatest religious disaster of this century, if Jesus does not come back by A.D. 2000? This by no means implies that the dominionists are right, but they will laugh in our faces if we allow our own prophetic message to be ruined and disgraced by the date setters.

Ignoring this problem will not make it go away. Only by preaching the true and dignified message of the Lord's return and by strongly denouncing date-setting can we hope to maintain confidence in the Bible message of Jesus' return.

Pastors, evangelists, teachers — please do not neglect the prophecy message because it is too complicated, or because it has been abused by fanatics. Preach the Word. Only truth, strongly declared, overcomes error. I suggest that every pastor furthermore question any prophetic speaker, in depth, to determine his or her attitude on date-setting — before allowing them in your pulpit.

Yes, I am calling for an all out boycott against date-setting! The message of prophecy is too important to let it be ruined by fanatics, deceivers, and even sincerely deluded people.

I hope Jesus comes back before A.D. 2000. I am ready for Him to come right now. But if we are still here in A.D. 2001, the Bible prophecy message will be just as valid as it is today.

The question is, will anyone be listening?

On the Edge of Eternity

A friend once asked the great evangelist Dwight L. Moody, "Mr. Moody, if you knew Jesus was coming back at six o'clock this evening, what would you do today?"

I am sure the questioner was surprised at Moody's answer for he said, "If I knew Jesus was coming back this evening at six o'clock, this afternoon I would plant apple trees."

This is a beautiful answer.

If you knew Jesus was coming back tonight, what would you do today? If there is something you would feel compelled to rush out and do, then you had better do it, for Jesus might come back tonight! On the other hand, if you are daily living your life in His will, then you would not have to change one thing you are planning to do!

God designed His revelation to us so that we are always living on the edge of eternity, and yet always planning for our future here in this life.

Suppose He had revealed the very date of the Rapture of the Church 1,900 years ago? I doubt if the Church would even be in existence now. It is good to live in anticipation and make your five-year and 25-year plans. If the Lord comes before you complete your venture, so be it. We won't mind the interruption in the least!

The moment you set a date for the Coming, you upset this divine balance, and you create havoc and distrust in the body of Christ. I tell you, date-setting is a sin and should be denounced from every pulpit as such.

Pastors, if you ignore the subject of prophecy or accept some of the modern reinterpretations of prophecy, you have solved nothing. Only by diligent study of and declaration of the Word of God in this realm will you bring real hope and good works with stability to your flock. Ignore prophecy, and the fanatics and distorters will have a field day.

Nature abhors a vacuum. If you create a spiritual vacuum by ignoring the prophetic Word, false teachers will supply something to fill that void. Watch out, pastor, they are coming for you and your congregation. They have already infiltrated. You will ignore this warning to your own peril.

Jesus said:

> Watch therefore; for ye know not what hour your lord
> doth come . . . . Therefore be ye also ready: for in such an

hour as ye think not the Son of man cometh. Who then is that faithful and wise servant, whom his lord hath made ruler over his household, to give them meat in due season? Blessed (happy) is that servant, whom his lord when he cometh shall find so doing (Matt. 24:42-46).

I believe the coming of Jesus is potentially imminent. He could come back today. But He may not. It serves us well to be prepared for either eventuality.

I have believed that fact since I was 10 years old. If you had asked me then if I thought I would live to be a man in the late summertime of life (not autumn yet), I would have said it was highly unlikely. After all, I heard the pastor and the evangelists say that "Jesus is coming soon." But what is soon to a little 10-year-old boy isn't soon to an adult.

The word soon is relative and can mean a lot of things. So, along with "tarry," I have thrown out the word "soon." On the other hand, *He may well come back today.* If not, I shall live in anticipation of His coming while doing the work of the Kingdom.

I will continue to proclaim His coming as potentially imminent. But soon? I am not sure how you define the word soon, and the closer one gets to defining the word, the closer one is to being a date setter. I can only say I believe we are living in the final era of the day of grace, the Church Age.

It is better to live as if Jesus were coming today and yet prepare for the future as if He were not coming for a long time. Then you are ready for time and eternity.

15

When the King Comes!

God's Final Plan for Mankind

Dave Breese

A stunning event is coming for our world!

It is the event that will settle every argument, right every wrong, resolve every contradiction in the lives of us all. It is the event that will show everything for what it truly is. In fact, that event is really the consummation of human history in the way that it is lived now.

What is this stupendous event? It is the coming of the great King.

It is probable that most people on our troubled planet share the view that life just goes on and on, and that it has no real purpose. Consequently, most invent small, intermediate purposes like "bowling tonight," "working tomorrow," "planning the weekend," and the like.

Along with vacations and holidays, the months and the years slip by almost unnoticed. Along the way, perhaps after the majority years of life have been lived, they think for a brief moment about a possible goal in life. Usually soon, however, the thought is brushed aside in favor of a new and more trivial pursuit.

There are few greater mistakes that a person can make in life than to so insult one's mind by thinking not at all about larger things than this moment, this passing comfort. How foolish to never ask, "What kind of a world is this? Why am I here? What are the final appointments which I must keep?" To leave these questions unanswered is irresponsible to the point of near insanity. Especially is this true when the answers are available and important. They are, in fact, matters of life and death.

For a driver not to look at the road ahead is to inevitably misinterpret reality. Such neglect of examination of the future could result in a fiery crash and a very painful death. Not to look at the road ahead can be disastrous also for you and me, for we are drivers, too. We steer our car down the hill or up the street. Just so, we steer our lives. We must! But why? Where?

To answer this, we must face the fact that this world is not what most people think it is. It is not merely a foggy planet moving through undetermined space. It is not even a benign little democracy in a political sense. No, indeed! It is an important part of a great kingdom!

The King of the Universe

Yes, the universe is a great kingdom of which the earth is a most vital province. It is a kingdom ruled by a great and majestic King.

The King is infinite in His wisdom and His power. He is awesome beyond anyone's ability to describe Him, and He is able to do anything. He, in fact, made the universe in the first place and everything that is in it. He also made you and me, and He keeps us alive each moment along with sustaining our ability to think, to move, to be.

Having created us, He has also honored us by bestowing upon us a wonderful degree of a thing called "autonomy." We are, within certain limitations, free. That means free to choose, free to be lazy or industrious, free to love or hate. We are even free to help other people or to harm them. We are free even to kill other people, as is so common in our present time.

But, the thing to remember is that all of our acts and attitudes will one day be judged. They will be evaluated as to being true or false against a perfect standard which the King has set up.

Yes, the King of the universe will one day bring into judgment every person, every lesser kingdom, every thought that has coursed through the minds of men in all of time. Whether we like it or whether we do not, no matter, for there is no escape.

People may ridicule such an idea — and they do — but nothing will take away from the fact that each person who lives will one day give an account of himself to God. There is inevitably coming a day of judgment, reward, punishment, congratulations for all who will have lived. There is a day called "that day" toward which the lives of us all and the life of the universe is heading.

Who is this mighty King who commands such authority, and who has told us of a day in which in power and glory He will return to judge the world?

Who is this King? His name is Jesus Christ!

He is coming one day to set up His kingdom in this world. So powerful and total will be that Kingdom that everyone who lives on earth will be required to come before His throne and do obeisance to the great King.

Who then is this Jesus Christ, this head of that government which presides above the universe? In the Word of God, the apostle Paul, writing to Timothy, said, "Now unto the King eternal, immortal, invisible, the only wise God, be honor and glory forever and ever. Amen" (1 Tim. 1:17).

Here, the apostle Paul, speaking about Jesus Christ, reminded us of the awesome nature of the King of the universe. He is the one to whom the apostle Paul also referred, saying:

> Who is the image of the invisible God, the first-born of all creation; for by him were all things created, that are in heaven, and that are in earth, visible and invisible, whether they be thrones, or dominions, or principalities, or powers — all things were created by him, and for him; And he is before all things, and by him all things consist (Col. 1:15-17).

So, we have presented to us in the Bible one of the basic facts of life. That fact is that we human beings live in a Kingdom and Jesus Christ, the second person of the Trinity, is the King of that Kingdom.

Questions in Need of Answers

When we know this, we sense that there emerges out of this knowledge a question that some find difficult to answer. That question amounts to, "If the universe is a kingdom controlled and managed by Jesus Christ, why is it that so often things seem to be out of control in the world in the midst of which we live?"

This question is one of the common ones of life. Who has not at one time or another asked, "If there is a God, why . . .?" That question can be finished with the description of one of a thousand different problems, concerns, and heartaches that every living individual faces in life.

When we look at those places of cruelty or squalor in the world, we wonder. When we see wars, famines, carnage of many kinds, we are tempted to allow our minds to drop into confusion about the question of whether or not someone is in charge. "If there is a King, why is it that so many times things seem to be so dangerously random? In fact, if there is a benign master of the universe, why do we have such awful things as suffering and death?"

There is no doubt that when anyone asserts that we live in the midst of a well-managed Kingdom, he must then defend his assertion against those who see anarchy everywhere. Is there an answer to all of this?

There must be and, in fact, there is.

The explanation of the seeming anomaly between the conditions of earth and the implied perfection of a heavenly kingdom that rules over all is found in a marvelous set of treatises whereby these things are explained to us. That marvelous set of letters, historical records, poetry and prose has now been assembled into one book. That book is the Bible.

The Bible explains the important facts of life and eternity, and that same kind of an explanation comes from no other source whatsoever. Philosophers, scientists, scholars of all sorts have examined the degree of reality of which they are aware (and no one is aware of it all), and they come up with meager explanations, which are little more than words upon words.

The mind of man has severe limitations and cannot give us the final answers to things. These must come from the mind of God, and happily, we have the mind of God presented to us in the pages of Holy Scripture.

Why Is the World the Way It Is?

What does God say about the reason that the world is what it is?

First of all, God tells us that the world, the universe and all else that He does, was created in perfection. In its original state, all of natural reality round about us was cooperative, harmonious — it was perfect.

But now, as we see distressing exceptions to that perfection, we can be forgiven for asking the questions, "What happened? Why did the world become the place that it is today? If there is a God, why are there such things as slums and graveyards?"

The King also gives us the answer to those questions.

The Bible records the fact that the Lord of the universe made man in His own image. Originally, man was very much like God and his very thoughts were similar to the thoughts of God. Man could name the beasts of the field and the flowers and trees of original earth, evidencing thereby his astonishing intelligence. In the beginning, there was no such thing as sin and degradation.

That changed, however, when man chose (as he was permitted to do) to disobey God rather than to follow the divine instructions that he was clearly given by God. The Lord God spoke to the original man and the original woman, Adam and Eve, and told them of the blessings and the single prohibition that they would face.

The single prohibition was that they must not eat of a certain tree. God said, "But of the tree of the knowledge of good and evil, thou shalt not eat of it; for in the day that thou eatest thereof thou shalt surely die" (Gen. 2:17). Just a few verses later, we have the account of what happened in response to that prohibition. Being free to choose, what did they do?

> And when the woman saw that the tree was good for food, and that it was pleasant to the eyes, and a tree to be desired to make one wise, she took of the fruit thereof, and did eat, and gave also unto her husband with her; and he did eat (Gen. 3:6).

From that moment on, Adam and Eve moved from a state of spiritual life into a state of spiritual death. Spiritual death refers to a condition whereby the spirit of man is separated from God. Spiritual death does not mean that the body or the spirit cease to exist, to be alive in an animated sense. It, rather, means that sin has come between the person and God.

The New Testament comments on this saying, "Wherefore, as by one man sin entered into the world, and death by sin, and so death passed upon all men, for all have sinned" (Rom. 5:12).

In this verse of Scripture, we have the explanation of sin that contains all others. Why murder? Why rape? Why lies? Why wars? Why suffering? The answer to these and every other question about iniquity that begins with the word "why" is contained in this single verse of Scripture. Sin has entered into the world and death by sin. There you have it!

Man, by his own choice, is a sinner and that's the reason for the problems of the world. Yes, this planet, this province of the Kingdom, is in a state of rebellion against the King.

Where is the World Headed?

It is customary for the sophisticates of this world to speak about "critical issues" and they name them as being economic, social, military, cultural, demographic, and so forth, *ad infinitum*. In response, schools are built, clinics are constructed, hospitals are erected, counseling is initiated, and a thousand other activities and entities are produced by the people of our time in order to, as they would say it, "solve the problems of the world."

A thousand subjects are now studied in the realm of academia and all of them are presented in the hope that they will produce "some kind of improvement" in the lives of students and, through them, an improvement in the social structure.

The problem with all this is that very few of the planners of our world have read that great analysis of history and its problems, the Book of Romans. They do not have the slightest idea of the meaning of the Scripture which says, "sin hath reigned unto death" (Rom. 5:21).

The majority of the intellectuals of our time think that they can rewrite the Scripture that says, "For the wages of sin is death, but the gift of God is eternal life through Jesus Christ, our Lord" (Rom. 6:23).

Because of lack of this knowledge on the part of the people of the world, the problem of sin and its consequences continues. The increasingly corrupt culture in the midst of which we live resembles less and less anything that would be built by a gracious, loving King who rules benevolently over all.

This condition, that of a deteriorating world, is with us because of the progressive nature of the sin that already pervades this world of ours.

The rebellion continues.

Consequently, not surprisingly, we have the condition that will prevail at the time of the end carefully delineated to us in the Word of God. The Scripture says, "But evil men and seducers shall become worse and worse, deceiving, and being deceived" (2 Tim. 3:13). Therefore, Paul also says in this passage, "This know, also, that in the last days perilous times shall come" (2 Tim. 3:1).

We can, therefore, be sure that the Bible does not promise a continually improving condition in this war zone called "the world."

Rather, it is just the opposite. The world will see progressive deterioration until the end of a period of time that is literally named in Scripture. It is called the "Great Tribulation."

The King is Coming!

Speaking about those last days, our Lord Jesus says:

> For then shall be great tribulation, such as was not since the beginning of the world to this time, no, nor ever shall be. And except those days should be shortened, there should no flesh be saved; but for the elect's sake those days shall be shortened (Matt. 24:21-22).

Here, in the words of Christ, we have two promises. One is that the world will suffer through a fearful decline, and secondly, that those days of the Tribulation will be shortened by divine intervention.

What is that divine intervention? It is the return of Jesus Christ, the King, to this world.

Yes, the King is going to come to this world again! Jesus Christ announced His return as He spoke about those days, addressing the believers who listened at the time of His earthly ministry. He said:

> Immediately after the tribulation of those days shall the sun be darkened, and the moon shall not give its light, and the stars shall fall from heaven, and the powers of the heavens shall be shaken. And then shall appear the sign of the Son of Man in heaven; and then shall all the tribes of the earth mourn, and they shall see the Son of Man coming in the clouds of heaven with power and great glory (Matt. 24:29-30).

Christ later said:

> When the Son of Man shall come in his glory, and the holy angels with him, then shall he sit upon the throne of his glory. And before him shall be gathered all the nations (Matt. 25:31-32).

In addressing the high priest in the Gospel of Mark, Christ said in response to the question, "Art thou the Christ, the Son of the Blessed?" (Mark 14:61), "I am; and ye shall see the Son of Man sitting on the right hand of power, and coming in the clouds of heaven" (Mark 14:62).

Christ addressed this same subject of His coming in the Gospel of Luke saying:

> And then shall they see the Son of Man coming in a cloud, with power and great glory. And when these things begin to come to pass, then look up, and lift up your heads; for your redemption draweth nigh (Luke 21:27-28).

Further attesting to the day of His glory, Jesus said, "Hereafter shall the Son of Man sit on the right hand of the power of God" (Luke 22:69).

In the Gospel of John, Christ spoke with great assurance to His disciples, saying, "If I go and prepare a place for you, I will come again, and receive you unto myself, that where I am, there may ye be also" (John 14:3).

Such an announcement by our Lord certainly cancels the liberal, unscholarly nonsense that Christ was merely a great teacher. Anyone who announces that He will return from heaven and judge all nations and all people — this person is saying what only God can say. His announcement of His glorious return is another of His claims to deity.

The Invasion From Heaven

In each one of the Gospel accounts of His life, death, and resurrection, Christ announced that He would return.

The same announcement was made on His behalf in the Book of Acts on the occasion of the address of the men standing by after His resurrection. They said, "Ye men of Galilee, why stand ye gazing up into heaven? This same Jesus, who is taken up from you into heaven, shall so come in like manner as ye have seen him go into heaven" (Acts 1:11).

From this point in the life of the early church, the New Testament continues and again and again refers to that glorious event, the return of the King.

No one can profess to be familiar with the New Testament Scriptures who denies that the Bible teaches that Christ is coming again in power and great glory. Even the practices of the Christians in the New Testament were done in the light of the return of Jesus Christ.

For instance, concerning the communion service, the Bible says, "For as often as ye eat this bread, and drink this cup, ye do show the Lord's death till he come" (1 Cor. 11:26). In the light of passages such as this, one marvels at the fact that many Christians have listened to preaching in a given church or denomination for years without hearing a single reference to the return to earth of Jesus Christ, our Lord and King.

The promise of the return of Christ is what lends substance, hope, motivation toward purity, and many other things that are called upon to be evident in the lives of Christians.

This is especially true when we remember that one of the final great pictures of the New Testament is the picture of the King returning. One should oft take the time to read the following verses so as to print upon his mind the glorious denouement of history:

> And I saw heaven opened and, behold, a white horse; and he that sat upon him was called Faithful and True, and in righteousness he doth judge and make war. His eyes were like a flame of fire, and on his head were many crowns; and he had a name written, that no man knew, but he himself. And He was clothed with a vesture dipped in blood; and his name is called The Word of God. And the armies that were in heaven followed him upon white horses, clothed in fine linen, white and clean. And out of his mouth goeth a sharp rod of iron; and he treadeth the winepress of the fierceness and wrath of Almighty God. And he hath on his vesture and on his thigh a name written, "KING OF KINGS, AND LORD OF LORDS" (Rev. 19:11-16).

Here, we have a stunning picture of a mighty invasion from heaven, the movement of an army that will be the greatest in history to accomplish the most profound result imaginable.

This army will depose the Antichrist and establish the kingdom of the Lord Jesus in this world for a thousand, blessed and unforgettable years. This is the overwhelming event described by John when he says, "Behold he cometh with clouds and every eye shall see him and they also who pierced him; and all kindreds of the earth shall wail because of him. Even so, Amen" (Rev. 1:7).

We, therefore, see that it is clearly taught in Scripture that Jesus Christ is coming again with power and great glory. In this coming, He is called "King of kings and Lord of lords," which is His proper title. On that occasion, every eye shall see Him — even those who murdered Him on the occasion of His first coming.

Every person who has lived in the history of the world will be overwhelmingly aware at that time that Jesus Christ is Lord and King. Would that they could discover that fact when it matters so much in these days before His coming!

How Did the World Get in Such a Mess?

The fact that the culture of our time is already in an advanced state of deterioration causes us to ask the question, "Why? How did all of this come to pass?"

As we have already established, the answer to the cause for cultural deterioration in a Gentile world is the same. It is sin. In fact, it is new and creative sin.

It began the day Eve, and then Adam, reached out a hand trembling with heinous anticipation, and took of that deadly, forbidden fruit. They ate, and "therefore by one man sin entered into the world and death by sin" (Rom. 5:12). The awful consequences are quite apparent in history, and they multiply before us today.

So important is the question as to the beginning and the growth of evil, that the Scripture is careful to present to us the, as it were, "blow-by-blow account" as to how it has come to pass. Speaking about the explanation for the deterioration of the morals of humanity, the Word of God says:

> Because that which may be known of God is manifest in them; for God hath shown it unto them. For the invisible things of him from the creation of the world are clearly seen, being understood by the things that are made, even his eternal power and Godhead, so that they are without excuse (Rom 1:19).

Having presented the beginning of this grim subject of global iniquity, the Word continues, saying:

> Because, when they knew God, they glorified him not as God, neither were thankful, but became vain in their imaginations, and their foolish heart was darkened. Professing themselves to be wise, they became fools, and changed the glory of the incorruptible God into an image made like corruptible man, and birds, and four-footed beasts, and creeping things (Rom. 1:21-23).

Here is presented to us with clarity the progressive downward stages of Gentile world unbelief and rejection of God. There was a time when the whole world of people knew about God. However, in that they refused to glorify Him as God, they opened the door to pathetic, progressive corruption that has grown into the vast degeneracy we now see.

Every reader of these words should realize that what has happened in the world also happens in the lives of individuals. Sin is progressive! Once it gets a foothold, it keeps on working like a moral cancer until it consumes, as a deadly parasite, the body to which it is attached.

This awful activity called "sin" has certainly attached itself to the body, the mind, the spirit of every individual within society who has not made Jesus Christ Lord of his or her life. The corporate impact is that sin works broadly in society itself.

Seeing Man Through God's Eyes

Seeing this and remembering that God is perfectly righteous and perfectly holy, we are not surprised at the result of this rejection by the Lord of the Gentile world. This result is described to us in Scripture:

> Wherefore, God also gave them up to uncleanness through the lusts of their own hearts, to dishonor their own bodies between themselves, who exchanged the truth of God for a lie, and worshipped and served the creature more than the Creator, who is blessed forever. Amen (Rom. 1:24-25).

The following verses, then, should be read with tears but also with intelligence. Do we not see before us a perfect description of the degenerate condition of our present society?

> For this cause God gave them up unto vile affections; for even their women did exchange the natural use for that which is against nature; and likewise also the men, leaving the natural use of the woman, burned in their lust one toward another, men with men working that which is unseemly, and receiving in themselves that recompense of their error which was fitting (Rom. 1:26-27).

This is then followed by the ultimate result of the fearful cancer of sin. Despite all of the sociological analyses, the present condition of man is described in the Word of God, saying, "And even as they did not like to retain God in their knowledge, God gave them over to a reprobate mind, to do those things which are not seemly" (Rom. 1:28).

It seems that this would be enough! Nevertheless, the Word of God continues with a description of humanity.

We live in a time in which the human prognosticators would tell us of the infinite perfectibility of man, his bright possibilities, and the like. In this, they do not pay careful attention either to the real situation in humanity or to the Word of God. The Bible says:

> Being filled with all unrighteousness, fornication, wickedness, covetousness, maliciousness; full of envy, murder, strife, deceit, malignity; whisperers, backbiters, haters of God, insolent, proud, boasters, inventors of evil things, disobedient to parents; without understanding, covenant breakers, without natural affection, implacable, unmerciful; who, knowing the judgment of God, that they who commit such things are worthy of death, not only do the same but have pleasure in them that do them (Rom. 1:29-32).

Upon reading this analysis of humanity as given to us in the Word of God, we should certainly be left very thoughtful. The condition of man as seen from the divine point of view is nothing like the propaganda we hear in this wicked promotional world of ours. Men and women are presented as bright, beautiful, well-dressed, filled with happiness, and various other similar pictures. These descriptions are simply not true.

Many a handsome man or beautiful lady are propped up for the photographers as a model of one thing or another. We all know that many of these individuals then return to an apartment filled with sadness and regret. All too often a full bottle of aspirin is the finish of a given day.

The heart of man is desperately wicked, that's what the Bible says. The sooner we recognize that, the better and the more truthful will be our outlook on life!

God's Amazing Offer

Upon noticing the biblical description of Gentile humanity, we certainly might be expected to say, "Well, all that these people deserve is to be tortured and sent to hell!" We might even say in a moment of candor, that they all should be killed and that would be the end of it. We would be right in concluding that man is unworthy of anything.

At this point, we can stop to rejoice that the end of the story of Gentile humanity is not simply that it is wicked beyond repair.

There is another chapter to that story, and that chapter is the announcement that "Christ died for our sins according to the Scriptures; and that he was buried, and that he rose again the third day according to the Scriptures" (1 Cor. 15:3-4).

In summarizing the condition of man, the Scripture says correctly and frighteningly, "All have sinned and come short of the glory of God" (Rom. 3:23). If this is all that we knew about humanity, we would drop into despair and endless death.

Happily, however, the Word of God further announces that we can be "justified freely by his grace through the redemption that is in Christ Jesus" (Rom. 3:24).

Therein lies a story that is wonderful indeed. It is the incredible but marvelous account that God has taken the initiative to do something for us. Yes, indeed, He has not now required that we find Him, but He has come all the way from the heights of heaven to our low estate to do something for us that we could not do ourselves.

There is no doubt whatsoever as to the fatal wickedness of man. There is, however, the happy announcement that the story of man moves from there, not to nothingness, but to chapter two. The initiative of God in love and tender care has been visited upon an errant humanity, and that initiative is the basis of a wonderful story. He has found us!

Let us, however, refrain from jumping ahead for just a moment, and mention the final outcome of the wickedness of the Gentile world. God has made a marvelous offer to every person on earth, Jew and Gentile, with which we shall familiarize ourselves in just a moment.

However, if mankind does not accept that amazing offer, there shall come to pass for wicked humanity an awful set of circumstances which the Scripture describes in very careful but frightening fashion. The Word says:

> And I saw a great white throne, and him that sat on it, from whose face the earth and the heaven fled away, and there was found no place for them. And I saw the dead, small and great, stand before God, and the books were opened; and another book was opened, which is the Book of Life. And the dead were judged out of those things which were written in the books, according to their works. And the sea gave up the dead that were in it, and death and

hell delivered up the dead that were in them; and they were judged every man according to their works. And death and hell were cast into the lake of fire. This is the second death. And whosoever was not found written in the Book of Life was cast into the lake of fire (Rev. 20:11-15).

Here is the final, frightening description of the ultimate end of wickedness and wicked men. They are cast into the lake of fire.

One Final Rebellion

By the time of this event, the Gentile world will have been given many chances to receive Christ and receive the gospel.

As we have seen, the Gentile world will, before the end, organize itself against God to the place where it marches in the attempted military conquest of the nation of Israel and the city of Jerusalem.

The Psalmist describes this spectacular event saying, "Why do the nations rage and the people imagine a vain thing? The kings of the earth set themselves, and the rulers take counsel together, against the Lord, and against his anointed, saying, Let us break their bands asunder, and cast away their cords from us" (Ps. 2:1-3).

This is the event that will produce the utterly spectacular response from God. As the nations gather against Jerusalem, Christ will come in that great and final battle called Armageddon.

The result of that battle will be an awareness by every person on the face of the earth as to the power and the reality of God. The armies of the nations will be defeated, turned into carnage and blood by the sword of the Lord and weapons wielded by the members of the army that returns with Him.

Who but an idiot could look upon this scene, or participate in it, without realizing that God is God. Many, however, will not make this realization and will further compound their judgment.

Judgment will be further compounded by the fact that millions of Gentiles will actually live in the world in the days of the earthly reign of Christ. He will be publicly visible to them, and they will not be able to doubt His existence or his kingship. Despite that undeniable evidence, many, actually millions, will not in fact believe. Even they will be given an opportunity to participate in one final rebellion against God. The Scripture, speaking about the time following the millennial reign of Christ, says:

And when the thousand years were ended, Satan

shall be loosed out of his prison, and shall go out to deceive
the nations which are in the four quarters of the earth, Gog
and Magog, to gather them together to battle; the number
of whom is as the sand of the sea. And they went up on the
breadth of the earth, and compassed the camp of the saints
about, and the beloved city; and fire came down from God
out of heaven, and devoured them (Rev. 20:7-9).

How astonishing that many will be alive in the days of the
millennial reign of Christ, and yet be faithless, unbelieving, still
characterized by the spirit of rebellion.

This picture which we are given in the Word of God as to that
final rebellion against the Lord is a most fascinating one. It gives us
the last picture of a corporate activity by the nations of the world on
earth — a final war against God and His saints.

In their vicious resentment of Jesus Christ and His lordship over
their lives, the nations and the individuals within them will attempt
one last desperate rebellion against God. At this point, we see an
impatient Lord no longer dealing in forbearance with the nations.
Rather, the outcome is simple and final — He sends down fire from
heaven to consume them. So it is that godless Gentile power is finally
and completely consumed in the fire of divine judgment.

The individuals of these nations in eternity will then, as we have
seen, stand before the Great White Throne Judgment of God. There,
at that time, will be totally convincing evidence that they did not
believe, and were not saved.

God's program with the Gentiles will reach into those last
moments of history, and that program will end with fire from heaven.
Knowing this, we must mount a greater than ever program of evangelism among the Gentiles — before the King returns.

What Is the Church?

Happily, we are told in Scripture that there is a third group of
people with whom God is dealing in history. In the Scripture, this most
interesting multitude is called, "the Church of God."

In the Church, we have an entity that is separate in the divine
program from the nation of Israel and also from the Gentile world. It
is of the greatest importance to each of us that we understand the
distinctive program God has for the Church, which is in contrast to His
intention for the nation of Israel and certainly, as we have seen, to His
plan for the Gentile world.

When we think of it — which thinking is not sufficiently done by many — we soon must conclude that the Church is a somewhat mysterious entity. It cannot be defined along the same human lines as Israel can be defined or as the Gentile world can be denoted.

A Jew is normally defined as a person who is not a Gentile. A Gentile or a member of the nations of the world is normally defined as any person who is on earth who is not a Jew. However, the Church cannot be so easily defined. Therefore, when we consider God's program with the Church, we must first ask and correctly answer some basic questions about this most interesting entity.

What, first of all, is the Church? Most will quickly agree that the standard ways in which the word "church" is used in our parlance are not correct definitions of the Church as such. The church is many times defined as a building and, of course, the church is not a building. It is many times defined as the people who are members of a given organization that calls itself by the name "church." All will quickly agree, however, that obviously many churches have members in them who are not Christians. Nor, can the church be defined as a denomination or any kind of an organization. One smiles at a denomination that calls itself a "church."

What then is the Church? It is given a name in Scripture that must be the true definition of the Church. The Scripture declares that God, "Hath put all things under his feet, and gave him to be the head over all things to the Church, which is his body, the fullness of him that filleth all in all" (Eph. 1:22-23).

This Scripture, therefore, in most basic fashion defines the Church not as an organization, but as an organism. It is a living thing. It is "the Body of Christ." Admittedly, it is difficult to define what that means exactly, because we cannot conceive of a living body that consists of individual and separate members. Here then the Scripture is asking for the use of our "sanctified imagination" as well as our faith.

We are to see ourselves as linked "physically" to Jesus Christ (members of His body) and to one another. We are to see the Church as something like a living, human body but functioning in a way that cannot be seen as can a physical person.

The Church: On a Heavenly Mission

We then ask the question, "How does the Church differ from the nation of Israel?" Quite obviously, we remind ourselves that the nation of Israel is a race of people as against being primarily a spiritual fellowship. The purpose of the nation of Israel was to reveal the reality of God to people who would look on that nation, and therefore, be induced by what they see to become Kingdom believers. That is, to be participants in the Theocratic Kingdom of Israel.

A lost person in the Old Testament could be defined as being a part of a group that were "aliens from the commonwealth of Israel, and strangers from the covenants of promise, having no hope, and without God in the world" (Eph. 2:12).

Now, this period of time in which we live is called in Scripture "the dispensation of the grace of God" (Eph. 3:2). In this dispensation of the grace of God, the Church is called "the mystery of Christ which in other ages was not made known unto the sons of men, as it is now revealed unto the holy apostles and prophets by the Spirit" (Eph. 3:4-5).

So profound is the spiritual nature of the Church that the apostle Paul declares that his mission is "to make all men see what is the fellowship of the mystery, which from the beginning of the ages hath been hidden in God, who created all things by Jesus Christ" (Eph. 3:9).

What then is the purpose of the Church? Again, we have the clear teaching of Scripture, which says, "To the intent that now, unto the principalities and power in heavenly places, might be known by the Church the manifold wisdom of God" (Eph. 3:10).

We may well then state that the Jews were God's earthly people with an earthly mission, whereas the Church is God's heavenly people with a heavenly mission. Concerning the Church and its members, the Scripture speaks about that purpose by declaring that we are ". . . called with a holy calling, not according to our works, but according to his own purpose and grace, which was given us in Christ Jesus before the world began" (2 Tim. 1:9).

We are to bring to the world "the hope of eternal life, which God, who cannot lie, promised before the world began" (Titus 1:2). We note with interest that the New Testament is filled with references about eternal life in heaven for Christians. In the Old Testament, however, there are very few verses that speak to the Jews about life in heaven which is to come.

By Grace Alone

What then is the distinctive message of the Church?

The breathtaking communication we have to bring to the world is the announcement that a person goes to heaven as a result of faith alone in Jesus Christ. We share in the joy of announcing "For by grace are ye saved through faith; and that not of yourselves, it is the gift of God — not of works, lest any man should boast" (Eph. 2:8-9).

We are here to proclaim the astonishing announcement brought to the world by our Lord and Saviour Jesus Christ who said:

> For God so loved the world, that he gave his only begotten Son, that whosoever believeth in him should not perish, but have everlasting life (John 3:16).

By contrast, the message brought to the world by the nation of Israel concerned the kingdom of God. It was the earnest call that people become members of that Kingdom by faith in God and by trusting in the efficacy of an animal sacrifice placed on the altar at the temple. That exact message, strongly preached but largely ignored in the Old Testament, was the same message brought to the world in the days of the earthly ministry of Christ.

As we have seen, John the Baptist announced, "Repent; for the kingdom of heaven is at hand" (Matt. 3:2). That same message was presented by Jesus Christ with the same words "Repent; for the kingdom of heaven is at hand" (Matt. 4:17).

We must, therefore, remind ourselves that the earthly message brought by John, by Jesus Christ and His disciples, is not what we call "the gospel of the grace of God." We know this because of a most telling account brought to us in the experience of the apostle Paul.

In Acts 19 Paul met with "certain disciples" who knew only the baptism of John the Baptist, the gospel of the Kingdom. They were asked then, "Believing, did you receive the Holy Spirit?"

Their answer was, "We have not so much as heard whether there is any Holy Spirit" (Acts 19:2). We have then, a description of the message believed by these disciples:

> Then said Paul, John verily baptized with the baptism of repentance, saying unto the people that they should believe on him who should come after him, that is, on Christ Jesus (Acts 19:4).

Based on this testimony, the people believed in Jesus Christ, were baptized in His name, and received the Holy Spirit. This reception of the Holy Spirit is presented to us as clear evidence that these people now properly believed in Jesus Christ as is required in this dispensation of grace.

The message, then, of the Church is the gospel of the grace of

God, which has only been available in its clear presentation of Calvary since the finished work of Christ on the cross. This, as we have seen, differs from the message Israel had presented to the world.

That message, "the kingdom of heaven is at hand," will be preached with great power in the world once again. That will be during the days of the Tribulation when tens of thousands of Jewish witnesses will press upon the world with a vengeance the earnest message that the King is about to return and people should believe in Him.

The Universe — Our Inheritance

This brings us to this interesting question: What will conclude the earthly mission of the Church?

The Church is called upon to labor in the world in this day of grace in order to bring to people the gospel which prepares them for heaven. It is to announce that by faith in Jesus Christ we have everlasting life and become members of His body.

There is coming a day, however, when the mission of the Church will be complete. It will be completed by a most remarkable event that will make a stunning impression upon the world and be the deliverance of the Church from the world, which by that time will have grown incurably wicked. This event we have come to call "the Rapture of the Church."

The apostle Paul presents the account of this marvelous event in answer to a question by the Thessalonian Christians as to how the dead shared in the return of the Lord. Paul's answer is quite instructive:

> But I would not have you to be ignorant, brethren, concerning them who are asleep, that ye sorrow not, even as others who have no hope. For if we believe that Jesus died and rose again, even so them also who sleep in Jesus will God bring with him. For this we say unto you by the word of the Lord, that we who are alive and remain unto the coming of the Lord shall not precede them who are asleep. For the Lord himself shall descend from heaven with a shout, with the voice of the archangel, and with the trump of God; and the dead in Christ shall rise first; Then we who are alive and remain shall be caught up together with them in the clouds, to meet the Lord in the air; and so shall we ever be with the Lord. Wherefore, comfort one another with these words (1 Thess. 4:13-18).

The conclusion of the mission of the Church in the world will come with the catching up of believers to be with Jesus Christ in heaven. From that event onward, we shall ever be with the Lord.

Paul expands on this somewhat by making a most remarkable announcement to the Christians at Corinth. Surely they were astonished to hear Paul say,

> Behold, I show you a mystery: We shall not all sleep, but we shall all be changed, in a moment, in the twinkling of an eye, at the last trump; for the trumpet shall sound, and the dead shall be raised incorruptible, and we shall be changed (1 Cor. 15:51-52).

The Rapture then will take the Body of Christ, all believers in the world, home to their true dwelling place, that is, heaven. At this point, it is helpful to remember that Daniel's seventieth week (Dan. 9:24-25) will begin.

The seventieth week of Daniel is called in the Scripture, "Jacob's trouble" (Jer. 30:7). During this seven-year period, Israel will endure its final cycle of discipline from the Lord. Out of the days of those persecutions, Israel will be saved. Having come to the Lord, Israel will then become a dynamic witness for the gospel of the Kingdom, preaching this message that "the kingdom of heaven is at hand," to the ends of the earth.

What is the eternal destiny of the Church by comparison to Israel? As we have said, the Church is the body of Christ. It is about the Church that the Lord makes the announcement that everything in the universe will ultimately belong to us. The Bible speaks to Christians saying:

> For all things are yours, whether Paul, or Apollos, or Cephas, or the world, or life, or death, or things present, or things to come; all are yours and ye are Christ's, and Christ is God's (1 Cor. 3:21-23).

In the same sense, the apostle Paul gives us the promise that contains all others: "He that spared not His own Son, but delivered him up for us all, how shall he not with him also freely give us all things?" (Rom. 8:32). It is clear then that the Church, as a joint heir with Jesus Christ, shares in the inheritance, which is the universe.

By contrast, Israel is given this world. The Scripture says, "For the promise that he should be the heir of the world was not to Abraham, or to his seed, through the law, but through the righteousness of faith" (Rom. 4:13).

By contrast to the destiny of the Church, the Scripture says that the throne of David will be set up in this world and will be the inheritance of Israel for ever. Again notice, "And the nations shall know that I, the Lord, do sanctify Israel, when my sanctuary shall be in the midst of them for evermore" (Ezek. 37:28).

Let us continue to rejoice therefore in that the members of the Body of Christ are creatures of a heavenly, eternal destiny. They will be the inheritors of the universe and will move into a future that is magnificent beyond description. In fact, the Scripture says that one of the reasons for our salvation is "That in the ages to come he might show the exceeding riches of his grace in his kindness toward us through Christ Jesus" (Eph. 2:7).

Certainly, every Christian, when he reads these things, says with the apostle Paul:

> Oh, the depth of the riches both of the wisdom and knowledge of God! How unsearchable are his judgments, and his ways past finding out! For who hath known the mind of the Lord? Or who hath been his counselor: Or who hath first given to him, and it shall be recompensed unto him again? For of him, and through him, and to him are all things: to whom be glory forever. Amen (Rom. 11:33-36).

What a glorious, unspeakably wonderful future we are presented in Scripture as the destiny of the Christian! In our wildest imagination, we would be unable to conceive of the glories that are set before us.

An Open Invitation to All

Sensing that astonishing future, we do well to ask the very specific question, "How do I become a member of the Body of Christ?"

One of the marvelous things about this is that Jesus Christ, himself, invites every person on the face of the earth to fully and freely receive the gift of God, which is everlasting life. There's nothing for which we may pay; nothing that we can do. It is only possible for us to receive that heavenly hope as an absolutely free gift.

"What, then, must I do to be saved?" The answer is clearly and simply given to us in Scripture, "Believe on the Lord Jesus Christ, and you will be saved" (Acts 16:31).

To believe means to hold as true the fact that Jesus Christ is the Son of the living and true God, and that on the cross of Calvary, He died for our sins. When I believe this and truly trust Him as my personal Saviour from sin, I am given the gift of God — which is everlasting life.

We are quite aware that some accuse God of partiality, being willing to save certain people, but not others. But alas, the Scripture says that God is "not willing that any should perish but that all should come to repentance" (2 Pet. 3:9). In fact, going further than that, the Scripture says:

> And the times of this ignorance God overlooked, but now commandeth all men everywhere to repent, because he hath appointed a day, in which he will judge the world in righteousness by that man whom he hath ordained; concerning which he hath given assurance unto all men, in that he hath raised him from the dead (Acts 17:30-31).

We can therefore see that an open invitation has been extended to all mankind. In fact, all men are also commanded by God to believe the gospel and come to Jesus Christ. There is, therefore, no excuse for any person on earth not being a Christian. We are also constrained to remember that by this statement, the responsibility to tell all men everywhere the gospel of Jesus Christ is upon us.

We must think also of a final question, namely: What are the requirements to be taken home to heaven to be with Jesus Christ?

The only requirement given in the Word of God is that we be "brethren." This, of course, means that we are members of the family of God, having received Christ as personal Saviour. Therefore, the requirement to be a part of the Rapture of the Church is simply that I know Christ as personal Saviour.

The idea of some kind of a "partial Rapture" is unknown in Scripture. The simple requirement to be in that great number taken home to be with Jesus Christ is the same requirement as for salvation itself. That is, faith in Jesus Christ.

Remember again that just as surely as we are here today, so surely Jesus Christ will come again. An earnest invitation is therefore extended to all from the Lord himself. We are invited by the Lord to believe the gospel and to then look forward with that bright expectation of the return of Christ. For those of us who are Christians, He will come for us, for His own.

To every non-Christian, however, there remains no sacrifice for sin if we pass by Jesus Christ. There remains only a fearful looking for of judgment and fiery indignation.

The choice, therefore, is up to us. We can receive Jesus Christ, today, as our Saviour, and meet Him in that day as our friend. Conversely, the person who neglects or refuses the gospel will not thereby avoid seeing Jesus Christ. Rather, he will meet Him then as the inexorable judge of the universe.

The invitation is always open to salvation, but the time is now! Every person on earth is enjoined, invited to receive Christ, and warned to make that decision for Him before He comes again.

Finale

Where Will You Spend Eternity?

William T. James

The Second Advent of Jesus Christ approaches.

His coming again to earth, however, is preceded by at least seven years of God's judgment and wrath being poured upon this Christ-rejecting world. How very near then we must be to His return in the atmosphere above the planet. For born-again believers (of the Church Age, dead and alive) God tells us in 1 Thessalonians 5:9 and many other Scriptures that there is nothing to fear. We are not to be subjected to the unimaginable terrors that will take place during the time of His righteous vengeance.

How very crucial, then, is the way in which you and I answer the question the Lord Jesus asks each and every human being who has the facility to consider the question and to answer. It is the same question He put to His disciple, Peter: "Who do you say that I am?"

The answer each person gives to this most profound of all questions determines whether he or she spends eternity in the glorious place where God dwells, called heaven, or in the place of perpetual torment with Satan and the angels who followed him in his rebellion against the Most High. God's Word calls this place "hell."

Our Only Hope

How can we say with such confidence that Christ's return appears imminent?

As always, the true child of God (that is, the person who has accepted Jesus Christ and Him alone as God's great grace gift for forgiveness of sin that separates him or her from God the Father) must predicate all such confidence not on personal opinion but upon God's Word, the Holy Bible.

God's Word tells Christians, time and time again, to be watchful for Christ's return and to be aware of the events surrounding their daily lives. As a matter of fact, the Scripture tells us that the reason Christians are to be aware of those circumstances and events is not for the exciting atmospherics they engender or foreknowledge they provide, but because they give confidence of the hope that is in the believer.

These events point to Jesus, Who is coming to take them home to heaven with Him. Also, this hope, this knowledge should inspire Christians to be conducting their lives "... in all holy conversation and godliness" (2 Pet. 3:11).

The apostle Paul, under divine inspiration of the Holy Spirit, wrote concerning this knowledge, this HOPE Christians have in the Lord Jesus Christ. In addition, the Apostle notes the responsibility each Chrstian has to be expectantly watching for His return.

Paul's God-ordained Words herein contain searingly prophetic significance for this momentous period of history of which we are privileged to be a part:

> But of the times and the seasons, Brethren, ye have no need that I write unto you. For yourselves know perfectly that the day of the Lord so cometh as a thief in the night. For when they shall say Peace and safety; then sudden destruction cometh upon them as travail upon a woman with child; and they shall not escape. But ye, Brethren, are not in darkness, that that day should overtake you as a thief. Ye are all the children of light, not of the night, nor of darkness. Therefore let us not sleep, as do others; but let us watch and be sober .... But let us who are of the day, be sober, putting on the breastplate of love; and for an helmet, the hope of salvation. For God hath not appointed us to wrath, but to obtain salvation by our Lord Jesus Christ .... Wherefore

comfort yourselves together, and edify one another . . . (1 Thess. 5: 1-11).

God, through Paul's pen, is telling the unique end-time generation of believers — those who will be instantaneously translated into the glorious presence of Jesus in the air — that it is not necessary that they know the exact hour, day, month, or whatever. The important thing for us to know is that the believer who is watching will not be caught by surprise when the Rapture occurs. And this, the Scriptures tell time after time, is exactly the expectant attitude the believer is to live within at all times.

At the same time, Christians must be "sober-minded," or seriously carrying out Christ's great commission to them while they go about the business of life on earth. Does this mean long faces and somberness? Of course not. One can be serious about his or her mission and yet be joyous in spirit and demeanor.

As a matter of fact, an important part of living the kind of life God wants us to live, His Word tells us, is being "joyful in the Lord." How can a lost, dying world of people see the marvelous light of Jesus, who is in each believer, when the Christian wears a veil of depression and gloom?

Does being joyful mean we will never be emotionally tested as Christians? Will we always be on the proverbial mountain top? Of course not. But, we must consistently strive to let Jesus live His life in and through our lives. If we submit to Him as we should, dying daily to self, as Paul wrote, the valleys will be fewer and more shallow between the heights to which God wants us to climb through obedience to Him.

Peace in the Holy Land?

The cover of the September 13, 1993, issue of *U.S. News & World Report* reads in letters that cover almost the entire front of the magazine: "PEACE IN THE HOLY LAND?"

Israel did the unthinkable on that very day, signing a "Mutual Recognition Pact" with a terrorist-enemy vowed to push them into the Mediterranean Sea. Yitzhak Rabin agreed to give up hard-won land — land God gave Mr. Rabin and his people — for the promise of being allowed to live in peace and safety.

Rather than depending upon Jehovah, the God of Israel, to assure the nation's security, Israel's deluded leaders have chosen wrongly — as did the Israelite leadership of old on innumerable occasions. Rather than depending on God for their people's safety, they have chosen Yasir Arafat, whose record of hate-filled rhetoric and vile acts rank with those of Syria's Assad and Iraq's Saddam Hussein.

The world as a whole cries for "peace and safety." The focal point of that cry — which is destined to become an even greater as time progresses — is that tiny land called Israel. Even more specifically, the real bone of contention, for not only the Holy Land but for the world at large, is being defined more sharply by the hour.

Less than one day before what the ebullient world press reported as a giant step toward a lasting peace took place, two contradictory statements were made. Arafat was overheard saying that soon the PLO flag would fly over Jerusalem, while Rabin was saying Jerusalem was the capital of Israel — forever! Such understanding among "former" antagonists is hardly the stuff of which lasting peace is made.

God put the facts of the matter precisely with regard to Israel, the world as a whole, and the so-called "peace process" as the time of the Messiah's coming nears:

> Behold, I will make Jerusalem a cup of trembling unto all the people round about . . . and in that day will I make Jerusalem a burdensome stone for all people: all that burden themselves with it shall be cut in pieces, though . . . gathered together against it (Zech. 12:2-3).

Although this prophecy relates primarily to the very end of the age, during the height of Armageddon itself, we see its early beginnings today. Regathered Israel's recent reliance on any other than God for their "peace and safety" indicates that such an unholy covenant will be offered and accepted at some point very soon. It will be the covenant with "death and hell" — with the Antichrist of the revived Roman Empire.

Cut in Pieces

We are watching nations literally gather "round about" this minuscule sliver of land, whose center is none other than the "apple of God's eye," Jerusalem! It is plain what is in store for any nation that "burdens" itself with the matter of God's regathered people. That nation or those nations are in grave danger.

Noted author Hal Lindsey, during his September 11, 1993, radio program "Week In Review," said regarding a report he had received from an unnamed source who assessed the Israeli-PLO signing:

> . . . They are making Jericho a free city, controlled completely by the PLO. They talk about this as the first stage. This is clearly designed to go on and create a Palestinian state in the West Bank and in Gaza. And, also it is designed to eventuate Syrian control of the Golan Heights. So in effect this is the nightmare that I used to hear about from the Israeli military planners when they said that when this happens Israel will no longer be able to defend itself with conventional weapons. As a matter of fact, the only thing they could do would be to fire off nuclear weapons and hope that the destruction of the capital cities of the people attacking them would stop them (somewhat).
>
> (A primary intelligence source) . . . says two reasons why Israel (signed the letter of intent with Arafat and the PLO) — and by the way, a great deal of Israel is not in agreement with this — is because of war weariness. There is hardly a family in Israel that hasn't been touched by tragedy of losing at least one member of the family in the constant war that's gone on since 1948. And, we can understand that.
>
> The second (reason for signing) is American pressure. And since the United States is the only ally that has been able to be counted upon by Israel, supplying them with things needed to survive in the wars they've had, if the United States withdraws that support, they know that they would have nothing . . . .

Lindsey then gave a frighteningly ominous reason for this pressure being brought to bear upon Israel:

> . . . the most important reason is that (the American leadership) wants to end this criticism (disfavor in the eyes of Arab nations and the world community at large) because they feel it's necessary for Washington's goal of a U.N. policed New World Order. So what's really behind American pressure on Israel is that they don't want anything to stop the going ahead of a U.N. police force that establishes a New World Order.

By giving up land for a tentative peace arrangement with a small segment of the Arab world — and a most questionable segment at that, from the standpoint of trustworthiness — Israel has dealt away buffer territory in the event of a future conflict with its neighbors. Israel must, from this point forward, depend upon outside military force to assure its territorial integrity and national security.

Very soon, the only option left to them might well be the use of their nuclear weaponry. The only outside force upon which they now rely is the U.S. But — to repeat — Scripture prophesies that there will come a time when Israel will covenant with the king of the fourth world-empire — the Antichrist.

Hal Lindsey and other prophetic scholars are of the strong opinion that this could be the beginning of the pseudo-peace process that will lead to that signing of what God calls the "covenant with death and hell."

The warning again reverberates in the attuned ear. "All that burden themselves with it (Israel/Jerusalem) shall be cut in pieces."

What's Wrong With Peace?

All major industrialized nations, the United States presently chief among them, have determined to "burden" themselves with the tiny nation of Israel. It has been so since the Middle East became the world's greatest producer of oil needed to fuel those nations' machinery — thus energizing and sustaining their economies.

Jerusalem is at the heart of the ancient struggle where hatred divides Arab and Jew in that city God calls "the apple of My eye." Unarguably, Jerusalem is the "burdensome stone" God said He would cause it to be, the "cup of trembling" it would become as the end of the age nears.

The volatility of the region known as the "Holy Land," even disregarding the oil, assures that all nations must, for geopolitical stability's sake, be "gathered round about," pressuring those nations of the region — particularly Israel — to come to the peace table set for them by the world powers that be.

At present, America has been selected by these powers to be the instrument through which the pressure is directly exerted. It is not an enviable position in which to be from a biblical standpoint. More to the point, it is a precarious position in which America finds itself, from the standpoint of God's prophetic Word.

You no doubt noted the familiar words of the late Beatle songwriter, John Lennon, as they were proclaimed by an uncharacteristically dapper Yasir Arafat — looking much like Lennon's one time colleague Ringo Starr, but with burnoose and beard. The "former" PLO terrorist told Israel, and the rest of the world, in that September 13, 1993, White House Rose Garden ceremony that it is time to "give peace a chance."

What in the world could be wrong with giving peace a chance in regard to Israel and the Palestinians? After all, God's Word tells us to "pray for the peace of Jerusalem."

That same Holy Word also says "The heart (the human being in his fallen state) is deceitful above all things, and desperately wicked." Human beings, spiritually separated from their Creator will continue to "Cry peace, peace, when there is no peace," because "there is no peace to the wicked, saith the LORD."

Manmade peace pacts, thus, have never lasted. Such attempts to "give peace a chance" dot the historical record of man on planet earth. It hasn't worked because it is not true peace.

Finding True Peace

What is true peace? God's Word defines it as "the peace that surpasses all understanding (of human wisdom apart from God's Spirit within people who need His peace.)"

To answer this question, we start and end with the same profound question posed earlier when Jesus asked Peter — and each of us — "Who do you say that I am?"

The peace that surpasses "human" understanding, the peace we must pray will come upon Jerusalem, the Middle East, the world, is the same peace each human being must accept in his or her own mind and heart before "war within our own members" (war within ourselves) can be abolished forever. That peace can, does, and will come only from Jesus Christ, the Saviour, the Lord, the Prince of Peace who makes all things righteous in God the Father's holy eyes. There can be no peace apart from righteousness, you see.

Dramatic evidence points to the reality that Christ's second advent is very near indeed. At that universe-shaking time, all peoples of all nations who have opposed the peace Jesus now offers, preferring instead the wickedness that wars within themselves, will be "cut in pieces."

The questions posed here are inseparable — the question Jesus asks: "Who do you say that I am?" and the question: "Where will you spend eternity?" Only you can answer.

Even so, come Lord Jesus!

Endnotes

Chapter 1

[1]*American Prophets and Preachers* (Oklahoma City, OK: Southwest Radio Publications, 1988), p. 13.
[2]Ibid.
[3]John Eidsmoe, *Faith of Our Founding Fathers* (Oklahoma City, OK: Southwest Radio Church, 1988).
[4]*Annals of America*, (Encyclopedia Britannica, 1976), 1790, vol. 3, p. 434.
[5]Eidsmoe, *Faith of Our Founding Fathers.*
[6]Ibid.
[7]Ibid.

Chapter 2

[1]Ken Ham, *The Lie: Evolution* (Colorado Springs, CO:Master Books, 1992), p. 124-126.
[2]*Science,* Volume 214, November 6, 1981.

Chapter 3

[1]Charles Darwin, *The Voyage of the Beagle* (New York, NY: New American Library, 1972). First published in 1839; known also as *Journal of Researches into the Geology and Natural History of the Various Countries Visited by H.M.S.* Beagle, *1832-1836,* vii.
[2]Ibid.
[3]Philip Foner, *Karl Marx Remembered* (San Francisco, CA: Synthesis, 1983).
[4]Aleksandr Solzhenitsyn, "Men Have Forgotten God," *National Review,* July 22, 1983, p. 872.
[5]Paul Johnson, *Modern Times* (New York, NY: Harper & Row, 1983), p. 4.
[6]Ibid.
[7]Ibid., p. 5.
[8]Gerard Lauzun, *Sigmund Freud: The Man and His Theories* (Greenwich, CT: Fawcett, 1962), p. 27.
[9]Ibid., p. 38.
[10]Ibid., p. 776.
[11]Dave Breese, *Seven Men Who Rule the World from the Grave* (Chicago, IL: Moody Press, 1990).

Chapter 4

[1]John Naisbitt, *Megatrends, Ten New Directions Transforming Our Lives* (New York, NY: Warner Books, 1982).
[2]Michael Scott Horton, *The Agony of Deceit* (Chicago, IL: Moody Press, 1992), quoted from correspondence on file with Christians United for Reformation (CURE), August 25, 1982.
[3]Horton, *Agony of Deceit,* quoting from a tape of a Kenneth Copeland crusade, July 19, 1987, on file with CURE.
[4]*Satan Unmasked,* Earl Paulk (Atlanta, GA: K. Dimension Publishers, 1984), p. 97.

[5] Nevill Drury, *Dictionary of Mysticism and the Occult* (San Francisco, CA: Harper/Row, 1985).

[6] Naisbitt, *Megatrends.*

[7] Ted Schultz, Ed., *Fringes of Reason: Whole Earth Catalog* (New York, NY: Harmony Books, 1989).

[8] Ben Byrd, *One Pastor's Journey.*

[9] Marilyn Ferguson, *The Aquarian Conspiracy* (Los Angeles, CA: J.P. Tarcher, 1980).

[10] George Trevelyan, *A Vision of the Aquarian Age* (Walpole, NH: Stillpoint, 1984).

[11] Albert Gore, *Earth in the Balance* (Boston, MA: Houghton-Mifflin Co., 1992).

[12] Swami Vivekananda.

[13] *Zolar's Encyclopedia of Ancient and Forbidden Knowledge* (New York, NY: Arco Publications, 1984).

[14] Byrd, *One Pastor's Journey.*

[15] David and Lucy Pond, *The Metaphysical Handbook* (Port Ludlow, WA: The Reflecting Pond Publications, 1984).

[16] Horton, *The Agony of Deceit.*

[17] Ibid.

[18] Leonard Orr and Sondra Ray, *Rebirthing in the New Age* (Millbrae, CA: Celestial Arts, 1977).

[19] Byrd, *One Pastor's Journey.*

[20] Ibid.

[21] Shakti Gawain.

[22] Marcus Allen, *Tantra for the West* (Mill Valley, CA: Whatever Publications, 1981).

[23] Gawain.

If you need any further information on the above footnotes for chapter 4, please contact: John Barela, Today, the Bible, and You, (918) 234-0462.

Chapter 5

[1] James W. Michaels, "One Size Fits All," *National Review,* June 21, 1993, p. 25.

[2] Daniel W. Seligman, "PC Comes to the Newsroom," *National Review,* June 21, 1993, p. 28.

[3] L. Brent Bozell III, "Smooth Talk by Media Twists Truth," *Insight,* August 23, 1993, p. 33-35.

[4] Ibid.

[5] L. Brent Bozell III, "Label-less Media Shade Policy Issues," *Insight,* September 27, 1993, p. 33.

[6] Ibid., p. 34.

[7] Michael Fumento, "Media, AIDS, and Truth," *National Review,* June 21, 1993, p. 45-47.

[8] D.A. Miller, "AIDS: The Plague of Deception," Stealing the Mind of America Conference; Vail, Colorado, speech, 1993.

[9] Ibid.

¹⁰Ibid.
¹¹Ibid.

Chapter 6
¹H. Peter Metzger, "The Coercive Utopians." Presented at the National Meeting of the American College of Nuclear Medicine, April 28, 1978 (updated June, 1979), Public Service Co. of Colorado; Denver, Colorado, p. 14.
²Larry Abraham, "Wipeout . . . the Ultimate Plan for Absolute Financial Power," *Insider Report*, 1990.
³Rael Jean and Erich Isaac, "The Coercive Utopian," p. 9-10.
⁴Larry Abraham, *Call it Conspiracy* (W.A., 1988), p. 12-13.
⁵Texe Marrs, *Flashpoint*, "Bill Clinton and the Bilderberger Conspiracy," September 1992.
⁶Larry Abraham, "Wipeout . . . the Use of Contrived Crisis," *Insider Report*, 1990, p. 8-9.

Chapter 7
¹*Time Magazine*, January 12, 1959, p. 23.
²Merry and Serge Bromberger, *Jean Monnet and the United States of Europe* (New York, NY: Coward-McCann, Inc., 1969), translated by Blaine P. Halperin.
³Ibid., p. 11.
⁴Ibid., p. 104.
⁵Ibid., p. 118.
⁶*Time Magazine*, July 20, 1992, p. 70.
⁷*Time Magazine*, July 20, 1992, p. 71.

Chapter 8
¹*Annals of America*, vol. 3, p. 489.
²Eidsmoe, *Faith of Our Founding Fathers*.
³Ibid.
⁴*Annals of America*, 2nd edition, 1, p. 21-22.
⁵Richard W. DeHaan, *Israel and the Nations in Prophecy* (Grand Rapids, MI: Zondervan, 1967), p. 38.
⁶S. Franklin Logsdon, *Is the U.S.A. in Prophecy?* (Grand Rapids, MI: Zondervan), p. 11,13.
⁷David Allen Lewis, *Prophecy 2000* (Green Forest, AR: New Leaf Press, 1990), p. 105-106.

Chapter 9
¹Dale Russakoff and Mary Jordan, "At Penn, the Word Divides as Easily as the Sword," *The Washington Post*, May 15, 1993, p. A1.
²Bonnie Angelo, "The Next Lani Guinier?" *Time*, June 14, 1993, p.29.
³Robert Hughes, *Culture of Complaint: The Fraying of America* (New York, NY: Oxford Univ. Press, 1993).
⁴Os Guinness, *The Gravedigger File* (Downers Grove, IL: Inter-Varsity Press, 1983).

[5]Richard John Neuhaus, *The Naked Public Square: Religion and Democracy in America* (Grand Rapids, MI: Wm. B. Eerdmans Pub. Co., 1985).

Chapter 11
[1]Martin Luther, *Concerning the Jews and Their Lies,* a pamphlet published by Martin Luther in 1543.

Chapter 12
[1]H.L. Willmington, *The King is Coming* (Wheaton, IL: Tyndale House Publ.), p. 57-58.
[2]Dr. J. Dwight Pentecost, *Prophecy for Today* (Grand Rapids, MI: Discovery House Publ., 1989), p. 133.
[3]Jeane Dixon, *My Life and Prophecies* (William Morrow & Company).
[4]William Hull, *Israel, Key to Prophecy* (Grand Rapids, MI: Zondervan Publ. House, 1964), p. 51-63, 67-71. Our thanks to Morris Cerullo World Evangelism of San Diego, California, for allowing the use of this excerpt.

Chapter 14
[1]Sir Robert Anderson, *The Coming Prince* (Grand Rapids, MI: Kregel), Fourteenth Edition, p. 4.
[2]Ibid.
[3]Harold Camping, *1994?* (New York, NY: Vantage Press, 1992).
[4]David Allen Lewis, *Prophecy 2000* (Green Forest, AR: New Leaf Press, 1990).
[5]David Allen Lewis, *Smashing the Gates of Hell* (Green Forest, AR: New Leaf Press, 1987).
[6]Gary DeMar, *Last Days Madness* (Brentwood, TN: Wolgemuth and Hyatt, 1991), p. 17.

William T. James

William T. James, "Terry" as he is addressed by those who know him, prefers to be thought of as an intensely interested observer of historical and contemporary human affairs, always attempting to analyze that conduct and those issues and events in the light of God's Holy Word, the Bible. He is frequently interviewed in broadcasts throughout the nation.

James authored, compiled, and extensively edited his book, *Storming Toward Armageddon: Essays In Apocalypse,* a series of in-depth essays by well-known prophecy scholars, writers, and broadcasters.

As public relations director for several companies, he has written and edited all forms of business communications, both in print and electronic media. Prior to that he worked as creative director for advertising agencies and did extensive political and corporate speech writing as well as formulated position papers on various issues for the clients he served. In addition to writing, he worked closely with clients and broadcast media in putting together and conducting press conferences and other forums.

He and his wife, Margaret, have two sons, Terry, Jr., currently a pre-med student, and Nathan, a tenth grade student.

His overriding desire for this book, as it was for *Storming Toward Armageddon: Essays In Apocalypse,* is that Jesus Christ be magnified before the world so that all people might be drawn to the Saviour, that the lost might be redeemed, and that the child of God might be persuaded to faithfully work to sow the gospel message while expectantly watching for the soon return of their Lord.

Phil Arms

Phil Arms is a nationally known evangelist from Houston, Texas, where he recently started the Houston Church and Worship Center, one of the fastest growing churches in America.

As founder and president of Phil Arms Ministries, he conducts city-wide and area-wide crusades, which are recorded for broadcast over his national television and radio programs.

His reputation as a young, dynamic minister with ability to communicate the truths of God as they relate to God's Word generated many invitations to speak from churches and interested groups around the nation. The ministry continues to expand on a nationwide basis.

Phil Arms' television program is now broadcast weekly, and his radio program can be heard daily in most major cities across America. Additionally, he often appears as a guest on both Christian and secular talk shows across the nation, addressing a wide spectrum of topics.

Phil Arms has authored two books on success in life for the Christian, *Wet Flies Can't Fly or (The Keys to the Victorious Christian Life)* and *The Winner in You.*

He and his wife, Suzanne, an accomplished author, recording artist, and speaker in her own right, have two daughters, Britanny, twelve, and Lindsey, eight, and a son, Phillip William, two years old.

The stated goal of Phil Arms Ministries is to reach vast cross sections of the American population with a clarion call to return to the moral and spiritual principles that made this nation great.

Converted as a young man who had grown up going to church regularly but who had rebelliously gone in a direction opposite to God's way, Phil Arms is known for his straight-forward, no-nonsense approach to presenting the uncompromising message of the marvelous, saving gospel of Jesus Christ.

J.R. Church

J.R. Church is widely recognized as among the foremost prophecy teachers in America. He has authored numerous books on the subject, among them, *Hidden Prophecies in the Song of Moses, Hidden Prophecies in the Psalms,* and *Guardians of the Grail,* which tells of European political intrigue and the move toward a New World Order. His books have sold hundreds of thousands of copies worldwide, having been translated into a number of languages.

In 1964, he organized a church in Lubbock, Texas, where he pastored for over 17 years, building a large bus ministry and a Christian school. He moved, in 1979, to Oklahoma City and over the years has developed the ministry, Prophecy in the News.

The ministry publishes a monthly newspaper on prophetic research entitled *Prophecy in the News* and presents a syndicated television broadcast by the same name, which airs on stations across the country and by satellite network to the entire western hemisphere.

Converted at age seven, he set out with one main goal in life — to win people to Jesus Christ. He and his wife, Linda, have been married 35 years. They have two children, a daughter, Teri, and a son, Jerry, Jr.

J.R. Church is in wide demand as a speaker and lecturer on matters pertaining to biblical prophecy, appearing at national and international prophecy conferences and seminars. In addition, he is often seen and heard on various television and radio shows throughout the nation.

His latest books include *They Pierced the Veil,* a commentary on the 12 minor prophets, and *The Mystery of the Menorah.*

John Barela

John Barela is busily in-
volved in one of the most active
Bible-centered ministries in
America today. As founder and
president of Today, the Bible,
and You Ministry, his efforts are
directed toward disseminating the
gospel of Jesus Christ on a daily
basis through radio and television programming, originating
from the Tulsa, Oklahoma, area.
Also, the ministry's newspaper,
Frontpage, provides valuable, in-
depth insights into issues as analyzed in light of prophecy.

He has pastored churches
in Nevada, Wyoming, and Oklahoma, where he currently serves as
pastor for Christ Community Church.

John Barela is at the center of a dynamic higher Christian
education movement both in his home area of Tulsa and abroad. He
is president of Tyndale Bible Institute, which offers an extension
program for Bible study, including the establishment of the Bible
Institute of St. Petersburg in St. Petersberg, Russia. This exciting, vital
program has more than 400 students enrolled at present.

John, who received his theological training at BIOLA (Bible
Institute of Los Angeles), has authored a number of books that have
generated considerable interest. His most recent books are *The
Coming Holocaust in the Middle East, Desert Storm, Phase 2,* and *The
New Covenant of Bill Clinton and Al Gore.*

He is a well-known national and international conference and
seminar speaker, focusing on Russia, Israel, Korea, South and Central
America, and Africa. Additionally, he is frequently sought out for
radio, television, and print media interviews on matters of biblical
importance, particularly as they pertain to God's prophetic Word.

He is past vice president of Independent Fundamentalist Churches
of America.

John and his wife, Sharon, have three children, Scott, John, and
Coral. They have nine grandchildren.

David Allen Lewis

David Allen Lewis is a clergyman, author, lecturer, researcher, publisher, and is active in national and international circles in promoting the welfare of the Church, of Israel, and the Jewish people. His ordination has been with the Assemblies of God for over 35 years.

Dr. Lewis speaks at churches, conferences, minister's seminars, colleges, camp meetings, district events, etc. In addition to short-term seminars and spiritual life emphasis in Bible colleges, he has taught short courses in eschatology and apocalyptic literature in both secular and theological colleges.

Having traveled to the Middle East over 50 times, he has visited and done research in Israel, Egypt, Turkey, Syria, Lebanon, Jordan, and Cyprus. He has also ministered in Hong Kong, Kowloon, Barbados, Virgin Islands, Iceland, Mexico, Canada, and has traveled to mainland China and many European countries.

David Lewis has conferred on numerous occasions with heads of state including Prime Ministers Begin, Peres, and Shamir of Israel, as well as members of Israel's Parliament, Mayor Teddy Kolleck of Jerusalem, Moderate Palestinian Arab leaders, various U.S. senators, congressmen, and has met with former President Reagan.

He was invited and appeared as a witness on the Middle East before the Senate Foreign Relations Committee in Washington, DC.

He has strong contacts with religious leaders in a broad spectrum of churches, with many Jewish religious and political leaders, and in diverse disciplines of the scientific communities.

Books by Lewis include *Prophecy 2000, Smashing the Gates of Hell, Magog 1982 Canceled, Dark Angels of Light, Coming Antichrist,* and *Holy Spirit World Liberation.*

Ray M. Brubaker

For many who comprise the cable television audience across America, "God's News Behind the News" and the name Ray Brubaker are synonymous. As director, Mr. Brubaker's on-the-air reports and fascinating interviews, as well as those conducted by his colleagues on "God's News," bring biblically prophetic insights into the issues and events that shape our times.

Mr. Brubaker was introduced into the broadcast arena during one tense moment of a program for the Moody Bible Institute in Chicago, which had no announcer at the mike at air time. A student at that time, Mr. Brubaker was employed as a "studio assistant," setting up studios, turning pages for musicians, assisting with the sound effects, and related duties.

Aware of the split-second timing essential in broadcasting, and with no announcer in sight, Ray grabbed the script, signaled for the mike, and introduced the broadcast on the air.

That was the beginning of an announcing career that in six months found Mr. Brubaker with his own newscast and soon becoming the director of the news department.

"God's News Behind the News" was one of several news features originated back in 1946. The television version is now carried on four satellite networks as well as on select stations across America.

With news clips and film footage, along with the powerful application from the Word of God, Ray continues in his unflinching, dedicated drive to let the world know that "Jesus is coming soon," and they must be ready.

David Breese

David Breese is an internationally-known author, lecturer, radio broadcaster, and Christian minister. He ministers in church and area-wide evangelistic crusades, leadership conferences, student gatherings, and related preaching missions.

He is president of Christian Destiny, Inc., of Hillsboro, Kansas, a national organization committed to the advancement of Christianity through evangelistic crusades, literature distribution, university gatherings, and the use of radio and television.

Dr. Breese is active in a ministry to college and university students, speaking to them from a background of theology and philosophy. He graduated from Judson College and Northern Seminary and has taught philosophy, apologetics, and Church history. He is frequently involved in lectures, debates, and rap sessions on university campuses.

Breese travels more than 100,000 miles a year and has spoken to crowds across North America, Europe, Asia, the Caribbean, and Latin America. His lectures and debates at universities in the United States and overseas center on the confrontation of Christianity and modern thought.

Breese is also the author of a number of books, including *Discover Your Destiny, His Infernal Majesty, Know the Marks of Cults, Living for Eternity,* and the latest, *Seven Men Who Rule from the Grave.* His books, booklets, and magazine articles have enjoyed wide readership across the world. He also publishes *Destiny Newsletter,* a widely-circulated periodical presenting the Christian view of current events.

John Wesley White

As an associate evangelist in the Billy Graham Evangelistic Association, Dr. John Wesley White is one of the special team of men selected by Dr. Billy Graham to assist him in the worldwide work of evangelism. These hand-picked evangelists assist Dr. Graham in the major crusades around the world. Along with responsibilities in the crusade services, Dr. White addresses the School of Evangelism, speaks at universities, civic clubs, professional sports team chapels, churches, and prisons during a crusade period.

In addition to these responsibilities, Dr. White holds area-wide, as well as occasional single-church evangelistic crusades, speaks at conventions and special meetings, and presents the gospel on radio and television.

John Wesley White, a native of Saskatchewan, Canada, has a B.A. degree from Wheaton College, Wheaton, Illinois and a Ph.D in the Origins and Development of the Modern Ecumenical movement from Oxford University, Oxford England. Additionally, he did extensive research work in Europe at Queens University, Belfast, Ireland, and Trinity College (Dublin University) in the field of ecclesiastical history.

Dr. White initially became interested in the work of Billy Graham in November, 1949, when he first heard him in Chicago, after which time he had a growing fascination with the work. Dr. Graham asked him to become associate evangelist in June 1961.

In recent years, he has been the speaker on "Agape" and "Join the Family" television programs. He currently is the speaker on "The White Paper," a news/prophecy television program seen coast to coast in Canada and the United States. In addition, he has authored 20 books.

Over the years, Dr. White has maintained a great interest in and commitment to higher education in Canada, most recently serving 16 years as chancellor of Richmond College in Toronto. He believes scripturally-based presentation of the gospel of Jesus Christ, set in the current events of the times in which we live, is the only solution to the problems our world faces today.

During his first European tour, he met Kathleen Calderwood in Belfast, Ireland. They were married in 1952 and are the parents of four sons. Dr. and Mrs. White reside in Ontario, Canada.